Praise for THE PE

"When haughty _   _erything about
China, set out for the Middle Kingdom during the Opium Wars as an employee of
the British Horticultural Society and under the pretext of collecting flowers, he didn't
anticipate that a formidable slip of a girl-warrior, Jadelin of the powerful House of
Poe, would capture his closed heart.

Presuming himself immune to the power of love, Fortune pursues a secret mission
that will, if successful, enable Britain to steal the secrets of China's coveted teas that
had enabled its economy to prosper and dominate the tea industry. The deeper Fortune
ventures into the forbidden inland mountains, the more he is seduced by the country he
scorns until he, too, dresses and acts like the Chinese and speaks their language. He
pursues Jadelin, oblivious of her deadly skills to protect her 5,000 year-old culture,
and befriends her brother, unaware that he will prove to be both his savior and enemy.

The Chinese have a saying, "You don't know where you're going if you don't
know where you've been." The Perfect Tea Thief takes the reader back to the source of
the tensions today between China and the West in a fast-paced and captivating read
based on the real life and letters of Robert Fortune."

--Barbara Bundy, PhD
Founding Executive Director Emerita, University of San Francisco
Center for Asia Pacific Studies

THE *Perfect* TEA THIEF

Also by Pam Chun

The Money Dragon
When Strange Gods Call
The Seagull's Gardener

Sept 2014

THE *Perfect* TEA THIEF

Aloha,

Pam Chun

A Novel

PAM CHUN

Cover Design by Laura Shinn Designs

ISBN 13: 978-1500164300
ISBN-10: 1500164305
Library of Congress Control Number: 2014910798
CreateSpace Independent Publishing Platform
North Charleston, South Carolina

Dedicated to my fellow adventurers and world explorers,
Fred J. Joyce III and Erzsebet and Ryan C. Leong

Table of Contents

Prologue

LONDON

On the tree-lined Kensington street, a figure ducked under the fog-shrouded sign which read, 'Chinese Antiques, Robert Fortune, Proprietor,' and jiggled the brass doorknob, an ornate lion's head. Locked. A powerful twist and the lock surrendered.

"Sing Wa!" Low and throaty, the voice called like a seductive South China breeze towards the back of the antique shop where towering Ming vases glowed in the gloom. The air smelled of old lacquer and older porcelain, of carved figurines oiled by decades of collectors' caresses.

From his desk in the back of his store, the wispy-haired Scot, once a towering wild-haired blond with muttonchops, craned his scrawny neck through the darkness and leapt to his feet. The paper-thin skin of his knuckles gripped the back of his chair. "Who are you?" he demanded.

"Sing Wa, remember me?" The frock-coated figure stepped into the circle of light, lifted a top hat, and released a black queue that uncoiled like a thick snake. Although dressed in the style of a British gentleman, the scent of sandalwood, of China, emanated from the folds of finely woven wool.

"I haven't heard that name in years," the antique dealer rasped. Long ago, he had lived that life in a different place. Now he recognized the strong dark eyes, arched eyebrows, and brow. He stumbled backwards in his chair. "What do you want?" His voice, once commanding, warbled from perpetually downcast lips.

"I want you! Disguised as Sing Wa, cloaked in the language you were forbidden to speak, you stole into the forbidden valleys where our greatest treasure grew. You betrayed us, Robert Fortune!"

The intruder's arms slung back with the grace of the Asian crane and struck.

The old man tried to scream as he crumpled backwards but no sounds came. His bowels emptied onto his precious Tianjian carpet. No! He tried to raise his hands, to plead that he was not responsible for the result of time and politics. He had scoured China for the most exquisite azaleas, peonies, and hundreds of trees and flowers in colors from brilliant reds to pale yellow, which were the pride of Kew Gardens, the Royal Horticultural Society, and dozens of private collections of the British gentry and nobility.

Too late. His attacker's leap exploded rare Ming vases. A fist shattered his lacquered desk and tea chests. Antique porcelains spilled onto the fine carpets and hardwood floor. Crushed underfoot in a layer of tinkling glittery shards, buried by the contents of shelves and cabinets, all tumbled in an unrecognizable heap of destruction. Dozens of tea caddies spilt open, releasing the luxurious jasmine pearls, swallow tongue greens, crinkled oolongs, and compressed blacks. China's greatest treasure would never touch his lips again.

From the splintered shards of the merchant's desk the intruder plucked the crystal snuff bottle that Mei had given the Scot when it was still warm with the heat of her body. "Buddhists believe in the sanctity of all life, so I cannot kill you. But you will find it harder and harder to get your breath. As your head screams for air, devils will come for the Christian soul you claimed made you superior to us heathens. As your pain grows second by second, think of the thousands of Chinese who died slowly in the turmoil and destruction you caused. You will lose control of your functions. You will suffer.

"Before I leave England, I will tell a constable you need help. If he doesn't arrive in time, he will think you've had a heart attack and flailed in despair. The natural death of a shriveled old man. The best of your collection, like China, is destroyed. I leave you to contemplate how you misused our friendship and stole China's treasures for England's glory. Farewell, Sing Wa."

Once, his attacker's dark eyes had haunted his dreams. That velvet voice had twined around his heart. He gasped now, his breaths short and painful. Silence engulfed him. Fortune struggled alone, more frightened than he had ever been in China where he had been stripped naked by brigands, chased by pirates, and tossed by waves higher than the moon.

He felt the night turn chilly, like the depths of hell when he had knelt in China's monsoon sea. "No," he screamed. He felt the waves sweep over the bulwark once again and tumble him into the abyss of his memories.

Part One: 1843-1845

One

ROBERT FORTUNE

*L*egends course through the kingdom about the first non-Chinese they had ever seen whose skin shone so white they called him *gweilo*, white devil. They say a monstrous fish, bigger around than he was tall, flew up from the China Seas and landed on his lap in a shower of glass. Others saw him race from the hills of Chapoo to the sea stark naked, chased by a horde of villagers waving his shredded clothes. Many curse that the monsoon storms should have swallowed him; his devious mission destroyed life for the tea farmers in the remote inland mountains where the air is clean and sweet. In the guise of a plant collector he stole China's most precious secret and emptied their treasuries. Although lost in time, the legends about him are true.

∾

*T*he sea swiped the deck of the timbered schooner with cold, frothy claws, but the crew clung fast. The sails, as salted and baked by the South China Sea as the men, snapped when the monsoon wind changed with the strong northerly current through the Formosa Channel. Captain Landers and his helmsman tightened their grip on the wheel and aimed for the wave's smooth face. They had sailed in seas worse than this.

Below deck, the fair-haired Scot braced his body. Land was where he belonged, not here, not tossed by blue-black waves. He heard the crew's shouts accompanied by the crash of splintered wood. He hunkered down and hoped his plants were safe and dry. They nestled in rich loam on the poop deck, encased within glass cases placed closest to the sun and furthest from the sea. "Damn you, Robert Fortune," Landers had cursed whenever he bruised his shins against the expanse of glass and wood. But the Scot had pulled his wool coat tight and scowled whenever the captain complained. Those cases contained the entire sum of his work in China and he had paid for their passage. He cursed when the cabin door flew open.

"Checking the barometer," Landers barked. Rain and seawater poured off him with every step. He planted his hands against the wall and leaned his nose against the instrument's face.

Just then the ship heeled and tossed both men across the cabin. The skylight above exploded in a firework of brilliant slivers. Silvery fish swam through the shower of shards. The sea poured in, one cold wave after the other. Fortune gasped for air as he slid across the floor and slammed from one side of the cabin to the other. He grabbed for purchase but his fingers failed to make contact. A fish as long as his own six-foot height attacked the Scot with powerful slaps as they struggled in a slippery knot of fins and limbs.

Landers cursed. What a waste of fish flesh. It could have fed his entire Lascar crew.

For three days Fortune hunkered in his sea-tossed cabin. On the fourth, he clamped on his smoked lens glasses and stumbled out.

"My plants," he howled. He collapsed to his knees amidst the wreckage of seasoned wood and glass sealed against the elements with caulk, aired daily on sunny days, and sealed shut when the sun dipped towards the horizon. He had hovered over them, shaded them when the sun got too strong, and clucked approvingly when the condensation collected in even drops. He had watched each leaf to be sure the humidity remained constant, ever vigilant against root rot, fungus, and insects. "I hate this place, these people, these primitive conditions," he howled. He couldn't wait to sail back to England, back to its horticultural gardens among familiar flowers and plants. Back to logical Britain, where people ate with knives and forks and spoke English.

When he found Landers standing amidst a salt-soaked deck covered with coiled lines and splintered wreckage, he shook a shriveled green stalk in his face. "All my plants are destroyed!" He had hiked miles through hostile countryside and braved the stares of the shopkeepers from Hong Kong to Amoy to collect these camellias and azaleas, so unusual in color and shape from anything found in Britain. He had personally planted each with a slight depression to catch the condensation that dripped onto the hand-mixed loam.

"You're lucky to be alive," Landers spat. His calculation that in three days the monsoon winds had pushed them south of their starting point threw him into a foul mood. He was more concerned with the weather bulwarks that had splintered and crumpled inwards which fortunately, had held. Otherwise the long boat, which had been swept to leeward from where it had been secured in the middle of the ship, would have knocked his crew overboard. They were worth a hundred times more than any plant.

That night Landers guided the schooner into the shipyard at Chimoo. At first light, shipwrights swarmed the schooner, scrubbing, sawing, and grinding. Sail makers hoisted the shredded sails off while food and supplies were loaded aboard.

Captain Landers peered up from where he was working alongside his crew and caught the Scot staring at the little villages surrounding the bay. Without his plants to fuss over, Fortune scuffled around the deck looking for something to do. "Stay aboard, mate. If you thought Hong Kong was a nasty place, Chimoo's bandits will strip you naked." Landers' hair hung lank to his shoulders. His one green eye, the other was sunken and stitched closed, stared through the Scot as if he knew what he was thinking. "I'll have my man boil water so you can wash." He jerked his head towards his own laundry flapping off the bow. "You can pay my man to wash your clothes, too."

The Scot shook his head. He had bathed last week in Amoy. "I need to stretch." He flung an arm in the direction of the villagers in the marketplace and dock. "Besides, I'm bigger than any of those miserable creatures."

The captain harrumphed at his prejudice. "Take a couple of my men. They're armed."

"I can take care of myself," Fortune countered. Enthused with a purpose, he grabbed his walking stick. He summoned his translator.

"No, no," Bing complained as Fortune strapped his wooden collection box to his back. "Mr. Fortune, I'm not a servant. I translate, not carry."

"You do as I say if you want your cash." Fortune dragged him down the gangplank and towards the pointed towers with the corners of each floor's roof curved up towards the sun.

"Pagodas," puffed Bing.

Fortune intended to explore each one. He gasped delightedly and dashed to each green bush, inspecting their leaves, excavating many with the trowel he carried in his coat pocket.

The villagers stared at the first non-Chinese to wander their lands. Tall, with pale blond hair, he clomped about in heavy leather shoes, a coat down to his knees, and a curious wool cap. At first they thought he was playing a game. They yelled and pointed out plants he could dig up. Fortune dug. The crowd was delighted. They pointed. He followed. The game changed quickly. Hands slipped into his pockets, grabbed his hat, the silk scarf he wound around his neck, and his jacket. They grabbed Bing's collection box, scattered his plants, and tore off his clothes. Now he regretted turning down Landers' offer for armed men. The horde of locals had grown so large he could not see his man. "Help!" he shouted. But the crowd had accosted Bing as well, tearing the shoes from his feet. They raced towards Chimoo Bay. By the time the two reached the mud flats both Bing and Fortune had been stripped naked.

Up on the poop deck, Landers aimed his spyglass at the unusually large mob running over the barren hills towards the water pursuing two nudes, one tall and white and the other stocky and brown. He shouted for his men to row the longboat for all they were worth. One of his crew leapt off when they reached the mudflats and ran a half-mile towards Fortune. As soon as he was close enough, Fortune leapt on the wiry Lascar's back. The Lascar dug his heels in and, with Bing close on his heels, leapt into the longboat, which immediately headed towards the schooner.

∾

*J*ohn Poe fastened the silk covered buttons of one of his simple mandarin robes, dark blue edged with green, before heading to Landers' cabin. Even though the Captain cared only that a man was honest, he wanted to appear worthy on his first solo voyage.

"John, my young friend," Landers greeted him when he entered his cabin for dinner. The Captain's one green eye crinkled. He had watched the son of his old friend Mandarin Poe grow to a young man of sixteen.

"Your seamanship bested the monsoon." John bowed to his protector.

"My Lascars are born to the sea. They read each wind and wave as if it were their mother tongue." Landers' smile beamed warm and expansive as he thought of his crew.

"Your passenger survived," laughed John. He had observed the naked men racing from the throngs as he lay in the shade of a sail on a hammock strung between two masts, out of the way of the sailors and boat wrights. The Westerner and his servant had hiked over the scrublands beyond Chimoo village, a town of hardworking craftsmen who specialized in boat building and sail making. He should have expected that people would be curious about seeing a non-Chinese for the first time. Many generations would pass on the tale of how the naked White Devil raced across the sands on the back of a seaman.

"Dratted Scot. Stubborn and self-important. The sea did me a favor by clearing out his plants, although he tried to get himself killed on land."

"Ah, the plant boxes." John Poe had inspected them a few times while Fortune was below deck. "His specimens are common to the area. Curious, these British."

"Weird, he is," growled Landers. "There's a difference between him and British men like me." He pounded his fist to his chest. "He's from Scotland, a wild and chilly place that borders our north. It's so damn inhospitable the Roman Empire built a tall stone wall to keep them out." The Scot entered at that moment to the captain's mischievous chortle. "Robert Fortune," introduced Landers. "John Poe, Sixth Son of a Shanghai mandarin."

Fortune gruffly offered a hand to shake. Poe bowed instead.

John appraised from the Westerner's awkward jerk and surprised look that he hadn't known there was another paying passenger aboard. At least he smelled better now, like the soap Landers bought in the markets in Canton, a scent that reminded him of a clean rock. The Scot wore heavy trousers and a shirt in a style similar to the garments that had been torn off.

The men took their seats around the Captain's table that had been cleared of charts and instruments. The Cantonese chef brought in a tureen of rice, platters of fish layered with green onions, and chicken with slivered ginger and vegetables. Landers grunted his approval. They had been unable to eat during the tumultuous storm. This was a feast worth waiting for.

Fortune looked disdainfully at the chopsticks by his bowl. "I need a fork, Landers."

The captain squinted at him with his one eye. "Won't find any here." He picked up a pair of bamboo chopsticks the chef had plopped on the table alongside the bowls of food and filled a rough stoneware bowl with rice. He slid off a layer of fish and plucked a juicy slice of chicken and vegetables.

Fortune stared. "That's barbaric, Landers. Have you abandoned the civilized manners of your country?"

"Mr. Fortune," John Poe said in a low, measured voice. "While in China, you must use chopsticks. You will find them versatile and convenient." He produced his own pair from a silk holder within the folds of his robe. He watched Fortune pick up a pair of chopsticks in his fist and stab at the food. "Here," John held out his hand and demonstrated. Fortune would get hungry enough to learn. Everyone eventually did.

Two

THE ESTATE OF MANDARIN POE

SHANGHAI

*J*adelin leapt over the moon-arched bridge and joined the warriors who burst into her garden. The night clanged with swords, staffs, and spears as they paired off among the artfully pruned trees and ancient limestone rocks. She flew a flying kick at the chest of a giant twice her height. He chuckled and smote his sword. She leapt his swing and twirled with a backward kick. His challenge spurred her defiance, a challenge she met. Strength was no promise of victory, knowledge no guarantee of success. The flat of her opponent's sword tumbled her backwards onto the pebbled pavement. Grunting, she rolled to her feet.

Mei had been reading in the quiet of her study when she heard the shouts emanating from her usually serene, classical Chinese garden. Recognizing the voices, she walked to the overhanging window to watch the siblings pair off in her courtyard. How could Jadelin think she could defeat her brothers she laughed, and shook her head to see how the three eldest had paired off against the three youngest. She changed into her black fighting silks of a master and slipped into the fray to teach the older ones a lesson.

She flew between one of the dueling pairs and beat back the larger of the two with feints of a thick stave until he was pinned. Then she accosted the next pair. She feigned weariness, then claimed victory with potentially fatal thrusts.

But the sudden entrance of the black-clad warrior distracted Jadelin. "Pay attention," barked her opponent, the largest and fiercest of the warriors, who turned her weakness into his advantage. She ducked his glinting spear but lost ground, stepping backwards stone by stone over the lily pond until she landed with a splash.

Flush with two victories, Mei challenged Jadelin's opponent whose long sword sported ribbons of victory attesting to his prowess. The courtyard rang with their blows, spear against stave, in this contest of strategy and precision.

"Yield," Jadelin's former rival growled. His voice commanded surrender. Based on experience, a spar with this black-clad interloper, his father's Third Wife, could last for hours without exhausting her repertoire of deadly moves.

"No! You surrender, Benjamin," Mei ordered. He leapt up and over a moon bridge. She pursued him, front flipped onto the path beyond, and checked the thrust of his spear with her stave.

His voice was both gruff and bold. "Never! But I don't want to tire you, Auntie."

His next move could have knocked her to her knees but she flew to the side with the grace of a gazelle. "You must be feeling your age. Your quiet wife is sapping your ch'i," she teased.

Benjamin laughed and bowed. "We'll call it a tie." He reached down and effortlessly lifted Jadelin from the middle of the lily pond onto the garden path. "Any hurts, little sister? Any pains? Good. You'll live to fight me again." He and his brothers, in the blue silks of Grand Master Ping, whipped off the hoods they had worn for protection.

Mei turned to the three largest men. "Wasn't that an unfair practice? You sons of First Wife are much larger than your siblings." Now she pulled back her hood, shook out her thick glossy hair, and frowned at her daughter's boldness. Sparring with the men!

"The only way to perfect one's technique is to practice with a superior artist." Benjamin flashed a wide smile. "We work ten hour days and never have time to practice. First brother Adam is out of shape because he's the Emperor's Official Watcher of the Imperial Water Bowl."

"How exciting to live with the Emperor in the Forbidden City," Jadelin mused, untying her hair so it fell to her waist. Her eldest brother's rare visits were always triumphant occasions, filled with the pomp of the Imperial Court, banquets, and streams of official visitors. She smiled shyly up at him as she squeezed the water out of her clothes. He had passed the Civil Service Exams in Peking and been appointed to his exalted post at the capital before she was born. Everything about him, from his ornately embroidered robes to his tales of the Forbidden City, suggested glamour and intrigue. He looked even more imposing than during his last visit. So when her brothers entered her mother's garden with the intention of making their eldest sibling sweat, she had seized this chance to prove she was their equal; she could fight like a man.

A wrinkle creased Adam's brow as he unfastened his queue from where he had wound it atop his head. His voice, deep and strong, betrayed a slight Peking accent. "No, my family lives outside the palace walls," he answered. "Eunuchs are the only males, besides the Emperor and his sons, permitted to live within the walls of the Forbidden City." He glared at Benjamin and shook his head. "As you can see by how hard my brothers are laughing, Benjamin is joking about my title. The Emperor relies on thousands of advisors like me with duties too intricate to explain and titles as long as a Peking winter." His dark eyes lingered on Mei. He frowned when she looked down and away.

Trying to hide her heavy breathing, Jadelin inspected what she knew would be a nasty bruise on her shoulder. She was fifteen, on the cusp of womanhood with innocence as fragile as a rose petal, but she preferred combat and the freedom of trousers.

Adam tilted Jadelin's face up with one hand and brushed back the dripping strands curling on cheeks still plump with youth. He saw Mei's brown eyes reflected in those of her daughter. As she grew up and lost her adolescent softness, she would grow into her mother's grace. "I have a daughter your age," he said softly. "It's true, all the rumors I've heard. You're a treasure, like your mother."

This time, Mei met his lingering gaze.

"Adam!" Mandarin Poe's buoyant stride charged the air in the court-yard with his energy. "When I came back from my meeting with the Governor of Shanghai, my warehouse guards said my sons had left with their eldest brother. I imagined my sons building their solidarity and sharing brotherly time together. And this is how I find you," he chuck-led. "Still fighting." He raised an eyebrow at his daughter, who stood at attention, dripping wet. But he said nothing to cause her embarrassment.

All eyes quickly turned when Mandarin Poe approached, his silk gown flowing from powerful shoulders. A charismatic statesman in dark blue with a visage honorable men would immediately character-ize as noble and trustworthy, he owned one of the largest tea hongs in Shanghai. His eldest sons, known to their Western business contacts by their English names as Adam, Benjamin, and Daniel, resembled their mother, Mandarin Poe's First Wife, a towering northern woman with husky shoulders and breasts like sun-ripened melons. Her loyalty and generous heart were dependable pillars. Edward and Paul, sons of his musically gifted Second Wife, were slight in build. Jadelin and her broth-er John, his only son not present, were slender and tall like their mother, Third Wife Mei.

"Father," Adam bowed, "As soon as I arrived in Shanghai, Benjamin advised you were meeting with the Taoutae, the governor. When I came home, my brothers and sister suggested a friendly challenge. I disap-pointed them all."

"Why didn't you send word to prepare for your arrival?" Mandarin Poe looked about for his eldest son's entourage, the dozens of Imperial guards who protected Adam wherever he traveled, and the many assis-tants and servants who required beds and food.

"I came on urgent business, alone. Our governor's son, a ranking mandarin with access to the Imperial naval ships, arranged passage on one of his swiftest boats with a seasoned crew of forty." For twenty days they had rowed nonstop from Peking, changing crews through the night. Vessels in the Grand Canal quickly cleared a passage for the sleek Imperial junk heralded by thundering drums, blazing lanterns, and Imperial banners flying from the topmast. Adam lowered his voice and his troubled eyes searched his father's. "I rushed home to warn you the Emperor's men are scouring the land for the most beautiful young girls. Our sister Jadelin is on their list."

Jadelin shivered with a sudden chill, wrapped her arms tightly around herself, and stepped closer to her mother.

"Again!" Mandarin Poe thundered.

Mei gasped and met her husband's eyes. She herself was only fifteen when she was brought to his household. At forty, Mandarin Poe was consumed by his business; he had no wish for a Third Wife. But the Emperor's army had come to Mei's father's house in Soochow for his only daughter, chosen to be one of 10,000 concubines to pleasure the Emperor and produce an heir for the Son of Heaven. Her father refused to allow the daughter he had educated and trained to the same proficiency as his nine sons to waste her life in the Forbidden City. So he hastened Mei to Shanghai to his talented student, Mandarin Poe.

But another had not been so lucky. Years ago, before Mandarin Poe had grown politically powerful, the Emperor had claimed his first daughter, only twelve then, whose skin was as white as the full moon. Every month she sent plaintive letters to her father, bemoaning the Forbidden City's cruel gossip and the futility of her idle life in her palace prison. The older women poked at her bun-round cheeks and cackled that whoever the Emperor chose for the night would be strip-searched by his advisors, wrapped naked in silk, and carried to the imperial bedchamber. She feared the day the Emperor would choose her. She pleaded to her family to bring her home. On her thirteenth birthday, she leapt off a tower to her death.

Mandarin Poe squared his jaw. "Benjamin, prepare our fastest junk. You sail as soon as the night wraps us in its cloak."

Mei gestured to her daughter. "Come, Jadelin, practice is over."

Her daughter sensed a change in the air, a chill wind. So, like the keen-eyed hawk that can hear a mouse breathing in its den while soaring fifty feet above, Jadelin tuned her ears to the men's conversation as she turned to follow her mother, leaving only droplets trailing behind her.

∾

A servant in dark blue brought fine cotton towels and scented water for the men to clean their faces and hands. Another set out teacups, a pewter tea canister, and boiling water. And when they were refreshed, Mandarin Poe motioned his sons to join him on the porcelain stools set under a flowering peach tree. He studied their faces and tried to think how each would cope in China's new political and economic climate.

Even after the Celestial Empire pleaded directly to Queen Victoria for help to stop British ships from shipping opium to China, British gunboats had crumbled China's armies and navy. From 1838 to 1842 the Opium War brought death and merciless ruin. Thousands of Chinese had died defending their villages and forts against the militarily superior British. The Chinese with arrows and swords couldn't defend themselves against British warships blocking their harbors and Western firepower blasting their coast. Despite China's centuries old ban against the drug, England won the right to continue to flood China with over 20,000 cases of opium a year. To further cripple the Celestial Empire, China had to pay six million dollars for the illegal opium they had destroyed, plus twelve million dollars for expenses the British had incurred in bringing China to its knees.

No one compensated the Chinese for tens of thousands of dead, the destroyed villages, and bombed coastal fortifications.

"Thank you, Adam, for leaving your family in Peking and risking your life to save your sister." The Mandarin's voice was sure and decisive. "Alas, I have more bad news, my sons. The Taoutae and high Mandarins met Captain Balfour, who represents Victoria, Queen of Great Britain and Ireland. Balfour said he desires peace, as we all do. But he commands all Chinese move from our waterfront sites so the English can build their homes and warehouses. We protested. Our businesses and homes have been established for generations. How could we move our families, homes, gardens, and ancestral graves? The Taoutae offered the English vast tracts of uninhabited land that surround Shanghai. Captain Balfour laid out the map he had already drawn. He pointed out where he wished to build his house, where the British should live, and where they wished to position British businesses on the Huangpu River's waterfront. His gunboats are anchored in the river."

Mandarin Poe had left with a feeling of invasion and loss. So when he saw his sons, daughter, and wife practicing the martial arts in the ancient tradition, hope filled his heart. The future of Shanghai, indeed of China, was in the hands of these young warriors.

∾

As she listened to the men, Jadelin folded the few things she needed into a small bundle. The Emperor's army would come for her tomorrow, Adam said. She whispered farewell to the rosewood bed curtained with bright embroidered silk where childhood dreams had bloomed and ran her fingers along the top of her desk and chair, both well-worn by generations of young women practicing their calligraphy. She had no toys. She shared her brothers' books. She closed the sliding door to her chambers and hurried to her mother's room. She drew back, her bundle clasped to her chest, when her mother's maid swept past her and whispered, "Madame, the First Son wishes to see you."

"Mei," Adam called from outside the silk-draped entrance of her private chambers.

Mandarin Poe's Third Wife quickly shut the lacquered trunk set upon a low table and whirled to face him when he entered. "Adam." Her voice caressed his name. She scanned the corridor behind him. He was alone. She cocked her ear to catch the high-pitched trill of Second Wife's harp, distant and sad. She came from a weak family with expensive tastes, a plethora of daughters, and no sons. In the morning, her exquisitely clear songs drifted into all the open gardens and courtyards and everyone knew her mood for the day: sunny, sullen, plaintive, or pouting. Although she was without any original thoughts, her fair face and soul-touching singing made up for her lack of education. Today, her song yearned for the days when her beauty had drawn admirers from as far as Peking. Despite the herbal potions and creams of hummingbird eggs and white peony petals, new wrinkles creased the corners of her eyes and the edges of her pouty lips. When Second Wife married Mandarin Poe thirty years ago, she had ordered a hundred mirrors mounted throughout her rooms so she could confirm her grace and beauty every minute she was awake. Now they were reminders of her mortality.

Even further away, First Mother's wing of the estate was absolutely silent. The undisputed matriarch of the Poe clan sat as still as a spider when embroidering her silk shoes and dainty things. At sixty-five, her moon-face was unadorned by makeup, her robust shoulders still hefty, and her spirit calmed by daily prayers at the family's private altar to Kwan Yin, the Goddess of Love and Mercy. She knew all and heard all. She feared nothing and no one. She had done her duty for the Poe dynasty—three strong and accomplished sons. She preferred to spend her time embroidering, playing mah-jongg, and ruling the lives of the other wives and children with calm power.

"My father left with Benjamin to load the ship," Adam assured Mei. He searched her face and smiled when her eyes meet his.

"Ah," she folded her hands in front of her. A quick meditative touch of fingertips to palm centered her thoughts. Fresh from his bath, in mandarin robes of the finest court silks with the embroidered medallion of his office upon his chest, she saw how impressive Adam, in his prime at forty-three, must look among the powerful and wealthy in the Forbidden City. "You risk death to return to Shanghai if the Emperor discovers your true purpose," she said in a gentle voice. "I thank you." She shivered to think of the consequences: his wife and children would be publically beheaded in front of him before he, too, were stripped of rank and executed. The Emperor was mercilessly brutal.

He lowered his voice. "Your daughter is the one in danger."

"No matter what excuses you may have given to the court, the Emperor's spies know all." Her voice trembled with anxiety for his safety. She lowered her eyes so he wouldn't see the tears that came unbidden at the thought.

"They know only my official mission, to meet with the Taoutae of Shanghai to protest Britain's request for extraterritoriality. The Emperor's spies are lazy. I am a small fish in their gigantic sea."

Mei met his eyes. "The British! Your father says that if Chinese laws to protect the order of society do not apply equally to the British, as they request, they will take advantage of their power. Shanghai will not be safe. They kill hundreds of Chinese in retaliation for slights, but are immune from Chinese law. Now bands of British can murder and rob us with impunity. Adam, I worry about the future of our family and of China."

"Let me do the worrying." He took her hands in his. "You know my other true purpose."

"No, you must never think of me." She pulled her hands back and clasped them at her waist. She pressed her thumb to her wrist to steady her pulse.

"You entered my heart the moment I met you. I thought you were an angel when you came down the steps to the dock in Soochow behind your father and brothers to meet us. The day you stepped within our walls in Shanghai, Mei, I thought you had come to be my wife, that our parents had betrothed us to each other. You could have been mine. How wide-eyed and innocent you looked. A shy blossom in a strange city."

"We were too young. Your father, not you, had the power to deflect the Emperor." She tenderly returned his gaze, touched that he dared to speak of their youth. She remembered how terrified she was when her sedan chair, held aloft by four porters, entered the great gates of the Poe compound. When she peeked through the curtains, the first person she saw was Adam, then a handsome young man, tall and broad-shouldered with a look of anticipation. She and her brothers had spent hundreds of hours practicing with the Poe brothers at Grand Master Ping's in Soochow. They had chased each other around the Great Hall with staffs and swords and bare hands. They had shared each other's tears and laughter, pains and bruises. They had studied, groaned, and suffered together. Adam had not yet developed his serious demeanor, then. They had become friends, hoping for more.

"I'm glad he succeeded." He lifted her chin to his face. "You are a blossom at the pinnacle of splendor."

"I'm past my prime, a mother of two grown children." Embarrassed by his direct gaze, she looked down and smoothed her pink gown embroidered with dainty peonies along the collar. She was glad she had changed out of the figure-hugging fighting silks.

"You will always be my ideal of beauty, Mei. Not one of the ten thousand women in the Forbidden City adorned in jades and silks from the Imperial workshops can compare. I willingly risk my life for you and your children." He spied the trunk behind her. "You've packed?"

"Yes." She looked down at her small trunk.

"And Jadelin?"

"She's ready." Mei sensed her daughter's presence just beyond the threshold, waiting for Adam to depart, not wishing to alarm either of them.

"I wish you both speed and darkness."

Mei reached out and clasped his hands. They were as comfortingly warm and callused as she remembered. "Thank you for saving Jadelin and in doing so, saving my heart. I couldn't live if anything happened to her. Do your mission quickly and return to Peking, to your family."

He bowed so close to her face, the sweet scent of her breath was his. "You will always be my dearest friend. I wish no harm to ever touch you or your children."

She returned his bow. As he turned and walked out to the courtyard she whispered, "Goodbye, my young love." When his broad shoulders disappeared beyond the silks, a tear rolled down her cheek.

"Mama." Jadelin was disguised for her escape in the simple indigo blue trousers and tunic of a boy.

Mei knew she had seen and heard. Her daughter had inherited her extraordinary hearing. She knelt down. "That was long ago, Jadelin. Your grandfather sent me to your father because only Mandarin Poe possessed the power to shield me. Now we must protect you."

Her daughter held her mother's face between her hands and kissed her cheeks. "I know," she assured her. But she was afraid. She was a fugitive, her future unknown.

"It was not meant to be," Mei repeated for the millionth time as she rang her bell for her maid, Big Amah.

Before night obscured the sky, Mei, Benjamin, and Jadelin disappeared across the waters of the Yangtze River.

∽

$\mathcal{M}$andarin Poe looked out over the fertile plains below. From the corner tower of his estate, the farmers appeared as mere dots in the distance and the rivers that fed their thirsty farms rippled like silver ribbons. He clasped his hands behind him already missing his youngest wife Mei and her daughter Jadelin. They were the lively sparks that balanced the formal propriety of his life. He shook his head and put his hand on his broad chest as he surveyed his domain. Life would go on for him as it did for those farmers, for this was China, a civilization proud of its five thousand year history. He was at the height of his powers with three wives and six sons, commanding a tea empire stretching thousands of miles inland, where the most premium teas were grown. His eldest son honored his clan with a position with the Emperor of China and his youngest was a scholar of the aesthetic arts. He whirled at the approach of steps.

"Baba," Adam Poe's voice was low and solemn. "I've come to say farewell. Twenty coolies arrived with a shipment of late harvest tea so my brothers had to return to the warehouse." He stood a head taller than his father with the heft and brawn of his mother, First Mother. Adam's coal black hair was swept in a distinguished topknot for travel.

Poe placed a muscled hand on his eldest son's shoulder. His emotion resonated in his deep voice. "You know we worry about you and your family. So rarely do we hear from you."

"The roads from Peking are too long and far."

"Your timing is fortuitous, for I have news from your younger brother of another kind of threat."

"John? Where is he now?" Adam smiled. Mei's only son had the best qualities of his mother.

"The British are ravenous for our teas, so we sent him to Hong Kong to meet with potential contacts. He is the most fluent in English."

"Like his mother," agreed Adam.

"Your brother warns that one of the barbarian adventurers is headed our way." The Mandarin handed the rice paper scroll to his eldest son. "Find a way to tell the Emperor he must alert his armies and navies for another attack. The Opium War cost China thousands of lives, ravaged our coasts, and put English gunboats in our harbors. These foreigners move with impunity within our lands, knowing they cannot be held to China's laws or tried in Chinese courts."

Adam looked into his father's eyes and received his silent message. He must find a way for the Emperor to learn about the adventurer without being the one who bears bad news, which was always political suicide. He unrolled the scroll and read.

To Mandarin Poe, Shanghai
From your Sixth Son, John Poe
Honorable Father,

I trust this letter finds you and my brothers healthy.

I am humbled by your generosity to let me pursue my interests in the gardens of China.

Captain Landers is known as a scandalous rogue, but he's the best captain on the China Seas. He can read the wind, seas, and stars better with his one green eye than other captains with two. I heard he talks to the sea demons and that his lover is the siren of Chimoo Bay, a sea creature with a nymphomaniac's appetite. It must be she who kept our schooner steady through the violent monsoon and brought us to Chimoo.

A British plant hunter named Robert Fortune boarded at Hong Kong. When the monsoon shattered our bulwarks in the Formosa Strait and the sea poured in, a monstrous fish landed in his lap while he cowered below in the captain's cabin. Landers himself would have eaten it raw--I've seen him rip the flesh from a freshly hooked sea bass clutched in his hairy hands; it was frightening to see the pleasure it gave him, as if he were delighting in an orgy of the Thousand Pleasures with his lips.

The Westerner was concerned only with his glass plant boxes tied to the deck. Curiously, after the storm I saw him fall to his knees, pick up a sea-soaked azalea from one of his boxes, and hold it to his cheek. Then he flung the plant and shards of glass into the sea, howling as if he himself had become a sea demon. When the monsoon passed, Landers put into Chimoo to do repairs. The Captain warned Fortune that it was safer to stay aboard than to wander the town, which has been taken over by the British and opium dealers. It is my observation that Westerners feel invincible, especially since the Treaty of Nanking awards them immunity from Chinese laws.

In the late afternoon I observed Fortune running naked across the sandy marsh chased by the ruffians who attacked and stripped him. Our crew rowed across the bay to rescue him. Chased by hundreds of villagers waving long guns and bamboo poles, the barbarian leapt onto the back of our boatman and rode him the half-mile sprint to our long boat.

The white man is awkward and graceless, without honor, dignity, or face. His translator Bing is an honest man from Macao, with a wife and five children, trying to earn a living in a country wracked by droughts, floods, and earthquakes. It is against the law for Westerners to speak Chinese, so it behooves Fortune to establish a trusting relationship with his translator if he is to survive in China. It was wise of the Emperor to confine trade with the Westerners to only five ports so they can't contaminate our country with their ill manners. Fortune writes copious reports to England in duplicate, which he hands to his translator to post. Bing promised to pass one of each letter to me. I enclose the first.

Fortune and Bing are headed to Ningpo, then to Shanghai.

I look forward to my visit to the garden grottos of Dr. Chang in Ningpo.
John Poe

Three

DR. CHANG'S GROTTO GARDENS

NINGPO

"Is this the home of Dr. Chang?" demanded Robert Fortune. The glowering guard scrutinized the pale eyed Westerner, his blond hair, bushy mutton chops, heavy long coat, and well-patched umbrella. The Scot turned to his translator, "Bing, tell him I sailed from Canton with John Poe, a friend of Dr. Chang."

Bing apologized for the foreign devil's appearance and manners. He explained that Mandarin Poe's son had told the *bak gwei* that he would be allowed to see Dr. Chang's gardens. Were the honorable Dr. Chang and John Poe available to receive this unworthy guest?

The crag-faced sentry unbolted the iron gates with a tremendous clang and led Fortune and Bing down a corridor through a flower-filled courtyard, where green and red flower tiles embedded in the walls sparkled in the sun. He gestured for them to enter the main reception hall which opened to the courtyard through wide sliding doors. Inside, the air was cool and thick, hushed by plush Tianjian carpets, and bathed by the sounds of a waterfall, perhaps many.

Minutes later, John Poe entered in a robe of midnight blue with a bandolier of jade beads to welcome Robert Fortune and his translator

Bing to the famed gardens of Dr. Chang of Ningpo. "Mr. Fortune, notice that besides plants, Dr. Chang appreciates other expressions of Chinese culture." The sixteen-year old picked up a bowl intricately painted with a profusion of flowers and held it up to the sunlight; light streamed through the porcelain so it glowed in his hand. "These egg-shell-thin porcelains were made during the reign of Emperor Ch'ien Lung over a hundred years ago." Fortune watched, enthralled. John Poe then walked to one of the high-backed chairs and ran his hands along the rail. "These chairs and tables, of a graceful and light design, are of huanghuangli, a tropical hardwood prized for decades by the Imperial workshops."

Jadelin parted the silk curtain of the adjourning room to spy on her brother and his guest. She noted how the fine blond hairs that covered the back of the Scot's large hands when he stroked the smooth wood caught the light. Were they soft as silk or stiff as dog hair? His fingers were chapped, his fingernails torn straight across without thought or care. If he dared to reach for the eggshell porcelain her brother had held out, it would shatter.

John bowed when Dr. Chang entered flanked by an entourage of the Mandarins of Ningpo in resplendent robes. The doctor nodded as John made the introductions and translations in the local dialect.

Fortune bowed nervously. "Dr. Chang, the British in Chusan extolled the beauty of your gardens. I'm honored to be your guest." He held out the pot he had tucked under his arm as if its leaves were of gold. "I apologize that this rose is not in bloom right now, but next summer it will be covered with fragrant red blossoms which are a favorite of our Queen Victoria." Bing translated his effusive greetings for their host.

Dr. Chang gestured his guests to sit in one of the high-backed carved chairs designated for visitors. Two girls in silk trousers and tunics embroidered with birds entered bearing trays of teacups and pastries. The solemn one, alabaster-skinned with doe-like eyes, poured tea for all while the other, black hair pulled back from a flawless pale complexion, accepted the plant from Fortune and handed it to the doctor. They swooped among the guests with tea and sweets. The tallest held a porcelain cup up to Fortune so he could smell the aroma of chrysan-themums and admire its delicate color accented by the pure white of the cup.

When Dr. Chang asked for his impression of China, Fortune, through Bing as translator, described his awe of the remarkable cormorants that fished for their masters and the beauty of the Chusan Islands, which reminded him of his Scottish Highlands. "In my travels near Amoy and Foochow, I have visited many temples and pagodas, always in the most auspicious locations with views of mountains and valleys and blessed by swift waterfalls. It seems to me that the monks there spend most of their time cultivating the tea shrubs that surround their temples."

The Mandarins narrowed their eyes and clenched their fists. Their Emperor had specifically ruled that all tea-growing lands involved in tea and its processing were off-limits. The British had signed that treaty, yet this foreigner defied it.

Dr. Chang hid his dismay by sweeping a long-fingered hand towards the sunlight and green shadows viewed through the ornamented fret-work. "Monks grow tea because it stimulates their mind and aids their meditation. But I'm curious what you think of my humble gardens. Our friend," he acknowledged John Poe with a respectful nod, "a connois-seur of garden design, tells me that you came to China specifically to see our exquisite flowers."

Robert Fortune wheeled to take another look at John, whom he had dismissed as just another Chinese peasant and certainly not as an expert.

"It was he who suggested I allow you to see my gardens." The girls rushed forward as he got to his feet. "My daughters, I'm not in my dot-age yet." He waved them back and turned to Fortune. "My wife and I adopted eighteen girls. As I approach my eightieth birthday they smoth-er me with attention."

Fortune flushed when Bing translated the doctor's remarks. "I thought they were your concubines." He had shrunk at their approach and eyed them with disdain.

Dr. Chang had noticed. "You British like to sensationalize our cus-toms as exotic and titillating." He solemnly sipped his tea and studied the red-faced Scot with piercing eyes. "Our five sons brought us so much joy we wished to spread our happiness." At first, he encouraged his patients to keep their girls until he saw that many drowned the infants in the river like unwanted kittens. So he placed the babies with families for whom any child was a blessing. A few, whether it was their sunny disposition or smile, he carried home. Some lived with his cook to learn culinary skills, and those who loved the outdoors were taught to garden. They married into good families. "They are treasures. How many children do you have?"

"None." Fortune squirmed. In all his wanderings and writings, the taciturn Scot discussed only his plants, the Horticultural Society, and the East India Company.

Chang seared him with a gaze. For the Chinese, ancestral history and family gave each person their identity in the social hierarchy. This pitiful barbarian was alone, rootless as a pebble. "Then come, let me show you the wonders of my gardens."

He led them through naturalistic rock formations that opened into spectacular courtyards, past Chinese bronze pots dating back a thousand years to the Zhou Dynasty, towering Ming vases with the girth of a warrior, and porcelain bowls from the finest Jingdezhen kilns. They admired views from latticed windows and artfully framed passageways: an exquisite flowering azalea on a hill of moss-covered rocks, a pine bent over a pond glittering with goldfish, and miniature fruit trees laden with normal-sized fruit.

"Notice how the branches of the tree echo the curve of the rocks. A Chinese garden needs water to bring it alive, just as it needs bees, birds, and butterflies." Water snaked through the convoluted openings of an especially tall limestone rock pitted with crags, then tumbled into a pond edged by slate. Sun glittered on the flickering tails of gold and silver goldfish.

While Bing translated for Chang and Fortune, the mandarins peppered John about this Scot, the first Westerner they were appalled to see up close. They viewed Fortune as the physical manifestation of all the horrific tales they had heard about the barbaric English.

John caught the glisten of silk when two women stepped from the shadows into the grotto where the air was heavy with the scent of jasmine. The ladies floated on the path on the far side of the fishpond, their hair curled in elegant sweeps that accentuated their height, fair skin, and almond eyes. Mei regally lifted her head when she saw the men. Her son suppressed his smile as he followed the steps set in moss around the pool. "Father did not tell me you were coming to Ningpo." He bowed. "I would have come for you."

"Your second brother was sailing from Shanghai. Since your sister and I longed for your company, your father suggested that you accompany us to Soochow." She had reasoned with her husband that the Emperor's spies were everywhere and this was the last time she could be with her son since she and daughter would be sequestered for many months. Mandarin Poe never let his wives and daughter leave the city unless he accompanied them himself. But Third Wife Mei, the daughter of a Grand Master, pushed the boundaries of his rules. Accompanied by his trusted sons, both trained in the martial arts, they would be as safe as if he guarded them himself.

Dr. Chang slipped from his guests to join them. "Welcome, my two beauties from Shanghai." He motioned them to a set of stone benches placed under the willow where one could see the sweep of the courtyard without being seen by others. "You've arrived just in time to see a Westerner who has journeyed from afar to collect China's flowers and plants."

Mei held out a long-fingered hand to shield her face. "A barbarian in your house?"

John's eyebrows arched in surprise. "You didn't tell me my mother and sister were here, Dr. Chang."

"They wanted to surprise you." The doctor's queue bobbed and swung with his laughter. "Don't you want to meet the barbarian from England?" he asked the ladies.

"No, I do not wish to meet the *gweilo*." When the men entered the courtyard, Mei had turned away from the sight of the foreigner's bushy hair and unruly muttonchops as pale as sun-washed straw. The severe cut of his clothes matched the dour set of his mouth. She recalled the terror when a double column of British ships towing men-of-war steamed up the Huangpu two years ago to anchor in Shanghai. The unarmed Chinese fled from the hundreds of armed soldiers. The British set up headquarters in the Yu Gardens, a classical Chinese garden that had taken twenty years to create over four hundred years ago. In five days marked by looting, rape, and murder, the British army demolished the exquisitely carved garden pavilions for firewood. No, they were barbarians in deed and looks.

"I do," Jadelin whispered to her brother.

"Absolutely not," he retorted.

"You sailed up from Hong Kong with this *gweilo*, a red haired devil, a white ghost." she pouted. "Why can't I meet him?"

"Because you are too young to be exposed to a barbarous Westerner. Baba would not approve."

"I am fifteen, old enough to be married." She could and would wear him down with arguments.

When the mandarins moved on to the next garden, John raised his hands in defeat. "All right," he conceded. "Don't tell anyone."

Mei opened her mouth to protest. Dr. Chang held up a wizened hand. "She's curious, that's all. He will not harm your daughter. And you are going far away for a long time. We can watch and hear every word from here."

The bells stitched to the hem of Jadelin's skirt tinkled as she followed her brother along the garden path to where Fortune stood alone. Her legs were not as long as his, and her little shoes, only three inches in length, stumbled on the uneven stones.

"Mr. Fortune," John said when they faced the astonished Scot, "my sister wishes to meet you." In Chinese he said, "Jadelin, this is Robert Fortune, the red-haired devil I met sailing through the monsoon with Captain Landers. I attest that he's proof that Western barbarians are uncouth and without manners. He's from England, the country that waged war on China, murdered thousands, demanded we open five ports to trade, and flooded our country with opium."

His sister tipped her face up and examined the tall Scot. "John, his eyes are as pale as the washed sky in winter. It's as if I'm looking right through his head to the sky. Is there nothing in there?"

John turned to Fortune, who looked bemused by the girl who inspected him as if he were a camel for sale. "My sister wanted to see if your skin was really as white as a *bak gwei*, a white ghost. My father would not approve."

Jadelin stared at the hand the Scot held out as if it were a day-old fish. He did smell like one. "Are you truly a barbarian?" she enunciated carefully in English. "Why are you in China?"

"I warn you, Fortune, we have the same English tutor," cautioned John. "So be careful what you say. She has perfect recall."

Fortune cleared his throat yet his voice came out rough, his cadence as uneven as a gravel road. "I came as the official plant collector for The Royal Horticultural Society to collect China's flowers for England."

"Why collect China's flowers? Don't you have any in your own country? Why do you want to steal ours? And what is wrong with your English?" To Jadelin's ears, his words rolled together like close-set waves onto shore.

"I'm from Scotland." He stared, entranced. She reminded him of a wee bird. And her soft voice had a bell like clarity. He wondered what country her English tutor had come from.

"Ah, Scotland. It must be a dialect of English." She pondered this new information and tipped her head in thought. "Your country must be like China where every town speaks a different dialect." She stared at his round pale eyes. "If my father agrees, I would like to speak more with you to improve my 'ear.'"

He inhaled her perfume, as fine as liquid silk. Chinoiserie was the rage in Victorian England and collectors went mad for Chinese porcelains and scrolls and Oriental decor. Now he was actually meeting a bonnie Chinese beauty, graceful and slight, as lovely as if she had stepped from a painted scroll.

Jadelin gestured toward an approaching figure and exclaimed, "And now you will meet my older brother." She smiled with genuine affection.

At six-feet-six, Benjamin resembled a human tidal wave with the broad beefy shoulders of his mother. He had dark eyes, a swarthy complexion, and thick bushy brows that stretched across his brow like a fuzzy caterpillar that curled up at each end. His nose was broad, his lips thick and full, and his ears were cauliflowered from too many hand-to-hand combats. Not only was Benjamin Poe number two in command of the family business, he was in charge of the thousands of cases of tea that were transported in and out of the hong. Unlike John's elegant bias-edged gowns, he wore thick silk that could withstand his energetic work.

"John," Benjamin greeted him in Chinese, "your mother and sister are as bull-headed as you are. In Shanghai they barely escaped the clutches of the Emperor, yet they insisted I stop at Dr. Chang's because you were here. I promised to take all of you to Soochow. We sail tonight." He put his hands on his hips and inspected the Scot with a scrutinizing glare. "And what is this thing?" he thundered.

"The barbarian Robert Fortune I wrote you about."

"The one the villagers stripped naked and chased across the sand?" Benjamin's eyebrows bounced when he broke into a hearty laugh, which revealed white, strong teeth.

Although Fortune didn't understand a word, he backed away and his face blanched as pale as hulled rice.

John chuckled. "Yes, dear Benjamin. Your mother, wife, and sons are well?"

Benjamin's broad smile was as wide as his bulk. "My three sons are half as tall as myself, excelling in their study of the Analects of Confucius. One day, one or all of them may enter the Emperor's service in Peking like our First Brother Adam," he said proudly. He shook his head and frowned at his little sister. "Our father treats her like one of his sons. She dresses like a boy and continues her kung fu with the men. She attends classes with their tutors in Chinese and English. A waste of an education."

"Someday I may have to defend you, Second brother," she quipped.

"It's a good thing she's as pretty as the fairies of the East Mountain," grumbled Benjamin. "It will be easier to arrange a marriage with a hapless dolt."

"Humph," she flushed.

Benjamin took his leave after advising Third Wife Mei that they would leave when the night was cloaked by stars.

Jadelin slipped her hand into John's. "Promise you will tell me everything that the barbarian does. His oddity intrigues me."

"Forget the barbarian, little sister. You watch out for the Emperor's men."

In the excitement of seeing her brothers and meeting her first barbarian, Jadelin had forgotten that she herself was in danger.

∾

*S*oft-footed servants clad in black silk bore quails braised with mushrooms, crisp-skinned roasted ducks, slow-simmered stuffed tea chicken, poached fish so fresh their tails still wiggled, and shrimps in lobster sauce, all on platters of hand-painted porcelain. The servers' queues whipped with precision as they removed half-eaten courses and replaced them with new delicacies while the mandarins, in silks and jade bandoliers, with special feathers or jades atop their hats to denote their rank, complimented, compared, and savored. Candle-lit lanterns glowed throughout the dining room.

Before dinner, Fortune and Bing had argued over money, as usual. Fortune had objected to the cost of the junk to Shanghai that Bing had hired; he wanted to travel cheaply but he also wanted to get to Shanghai as quickly as possible. He accused Bing of not bargaining the wily boatmen down even more.

"I quit." Bing threw up his hands. His brain was worn out by Fortune's haggling, the way the barbarian accused the Chinese of squeezing every last cash from the bargain. He recounted the indignities he suffered, from lugging plant boxes on Fortune's forays as if he were a common coolie, to being attacked and stripped naked in Chimoo when they hunted plants where everyone warned them not to go.

"How dare you," Fortune scowled, insulted that any Chinese would walk away from his money. Then he remembered that England was opening the port of Shanghai. He was sure a British ship would take him to Shanghai, for free. He counted out, to the cash, the smallest unit of Chinese money, Bing's wages to that minute. He refused to pay Bing's passage home to Macao. He could work his way back. Without a civil farewell, he stomped to dinner alone. Now he craved the potent Chinese rice wine to dull his argument with Bing. If he got too drunk to walk home, he would ask Dr. Chang to send him home in a chair.

Throughout the evening the mandarins asked the Scot many questions while John translated. They asked, "We heard how the British slaughter Indian maharajahs and loot their palaces. Your soldiers tear the jewels off the bodies of the princes and enslave their princesses. Is that the way your country treats its colonies?"

"The British are munificent rulers," Fortune sputtered. "The wealth and power of the British Empire benefits her colonies. There may have been violence in the past, but we strive to improve the lives of our subjects with cheaper products we produce with superior Western technology." He described their cotton mills, iron foundries, steam ships, coal mines, and innovative machine tools. He didn't mention that British factories using cotton grown in Egypt put the traditionally cotton-growing regions of India out of business. Nor was it necessary to tell them that the British found that growing opium in India reduced the trade deficit so their money-losing colony now produced a handsome profit.

One of the mandarins asked Fortune his opinion of China. The Scot put down his chopsticks and admitted that China was like nothing he had expected. His job was to collect seeds and plants of the finest specimens so the Royal Horticultural Society could cultivate them. "When the people of England see for themselves the variety of flowers and trees that grow here, they will see why China is called the Flowery Land."

Mandarin Tai, a thin scowling man who believed that there was nothing outside of China of any worth, tapped his fingertips together. "And our ladies are our most elegant blossoms."

Fortune blurted, "Their bound feet are barbaric." Their three-inch Lotus feet clad in embroidered slippers, smaller than his fist, had repulsed him. He had expected to see the well-born ladies hobbled in this fashion, but was appalled by how the hard-working street vendors and rough-clad servants tottered awkwardly on their stubs.

Insulted, the mandarins' eyes narrowed. One hissed, "You are the barbarian, you *bak gwei*, white-skinned ghost." Although John refused to translate, Fortune got their gist.

Dr. Chang cleared his throat and calmed his guests with soothing hushes. He turned to Fortune. "A woman whose feet have been properly bound sways gracefully as the bamboo. Her dainty feet show she can bear great pain and suffering to bring respect and honor to herself and her family. She displays her creativity in the Lotus Blossom slippers she embroiders."

"But why?" blustered Fortune.

"It's an ancient custom which, like most things in China, is rooted in history." Chang placed his chopsticks on its jade holder and leaned back. His fingertips tapped gently as he thought back to the tale he had told each of his daughters when their turn came. "One legend recounts that foot binding began when Li Yu ruled one of the Ten Kingdoms a thousand years ago. It was a glorious period, the flowering of art and culture. Prince Li Yu's favorite concubine danced on a golden platform shaped like a lotus. Lithe and creative, she wore silk socks wound with silk bands that fluttered with each step, so enticing and graceful. All the other ladies in the palace followed her example and bound their feet with silk."

"But not all women in China bind their feet," John Poe interjected. "The Manchus of the Ch'ing Dynasty, who now sit on China's throne, outlawed foot binding hundreds of years ago when they came into power. Tradition in China does not die easily."

Fortune remembered how Jadelin swayed through the gardens and how her gown rippled on the stone pathways. He had seen the tips of her tiny slippers nudge the hem of her skirt stitched with tiny bells. It appeared that she possessed the perfect three-inch Lotus Blossoms, the result of a lifetime of tortuous foot binding.

One of the mandarins, a tall man with streaks of white through his hair and skin the color of burnished almonds, leaned forward, his voice low and intense. "Those little shoes are very useful during foreplay." He laughed at Fortune's flustered coughs and the sweat that beaded at his hairline.

The men strolled through the gardens after dinner. Moonlight transformed the flowers--white, pink, and yellow during the day--to silver. Flickering stone lanterns created miniature worlds under dwarfed trees. They listened to the water tap tapping on stone and to leaves rustling in the wind.

"Ah, that scent." Dr. Chang led his guests to a green-leafed shrub covered with small white flowers. "My Arabian jasmine releases its sweetness only at night." He bent down to a thick bouquet of white petals that curved inward like tiny fists. On the spot, Mandarin Tai composed a poem extolling the moment. The men, inspired by their host's excellent wine, strove to outdo each other with spontaneous verse.

Fortune didn't understand their Chinese poems, and in the pale glow of the moon he couldn't examine any plants. How could he leave without offending the mandarins any more than he already had? "Dr. Chang," he bowed to his host, "thank you for your hospitality. Your gardens rival the finest in England." He bowed his goodbyes to him and the others. "I'm wanting to leave. Will you have a servant show me the way out?" Emboldened by wine, he turned to John. "May I say farewell to your sister?"

∾

*T*he women had thrown open the doors of Treasures of the Night, a sumptuous pavilion decorated with ancient bronzes and translucent porcelains. Lit by dozens of thick ivory candles clustered on every surface, the room glowed as if lit by pearls. Dressed in silks and sparkling hair ornaments, the women played music and sang.

During Jadelin's solo on a slender bamboo flute, Dr. Chang's servant sidled up to Mei. After a quick exchange, Mei shook her head. She gestured for her daughter to stay with Dr. Chang's daughters.

Jadelin nodded. But as soon as her mother left, she slipped her feet from under the fur blankets and ran in the opposite direction. Heralded by the tinkling bells on her hem, she raced down curtained corridors. She ducked into the grotto gardens when she saw the men's lanterns and followed in the dark. She stumbled over an artfully placed rock, untangled her feet from the folds of her robe, and continued, more cautiously now. She stopped when she saw Fortune's tall shape, then shadowed him in a parallel path, stealing looks through the window fretwork. When he arrived in the entry hall, he looked around as if he expected someone. She tiptoed up to the window. She spied his wispy blond hair and muttonchops, his eyes as pale as water, and his long lanky body buttoned up in a long wool coat.

Big Amah swayed down the long corridor to the first reception hall near the front entry where two guards stood, weapons at their side. Her broad shoulders brushed the sides of the arched doorways and the silk fringes of the wall hangings whooshed as she passed leaving a scent of lilac. Her wide face and height obscured all the lights that glowed in the hallway behind her as she approached the foreigner waiting in the foyer between the door guards. She fixed her almond eyes on him. "*Bak gwei*," she bellowed. White Ghost. She commanded him to step forward.

He eyed her clutched fists and mighty shoulders. Instead, he took a step back.

Big Amah eyed him up and down. "Humph," she grunted. She stepped aside to reveal Mei, elegant in a green silk gown embroidered with pink peonies, her face composed and serene.

This woman in golden hues that shimmered in candlelight was probably Jadelin's emissary, Fortune thought. He pointed towards the front gates. "I'll be saying good-bye." He pantomimed elaborately that he was sailing away. He gestured around him. "China is very nice."

Mei frowned at his sign language and choppy speech. She watched his elaborate gestures, his confusion at whether she understood. And after a long silence, she bowed her head in acknowledgement. She had refused to meet him earlier. Upon reflection, she decided it was better to inspect her country's enemy up close, to probe for his weaknesses. "Mr. Fortune, are you trying to tell us you are leaving for the evening or that you are leaving Ningpo?" she asked in clear, unaccented English.

With almond eyes that imparted an aura of wisdom and mystery, she appraised his shock, his jaw dropping in disbelief. "My father was so happy with nine sons to carry on his name that he found it easier to treat his only daughter like one of his sons so I, too, learned English." She fixed him with a defiant look. "Which is especially useful with so many foreigners in our country."

Fortune fingered the buttons on his coat and stammered, "I wanted to say good-bye to John's sister before I left for Shanghai."

She lifted her chin, appalled at his presumption. "Goodbye, Mr. Fortune. May you have a speedy voyage." She nodded dismissively and turned. Big Amah hulked forward and followed Mei down the long corridor where laughter rang like bells in the night.

John slipped from a shadowed corridor that glowed with thousands of candles and echoed masculine laugher. If he had seen Fortune's exchange with his mother, he didn't acknowledge it. He nodded to the two guards when he arrived. As they slid open the locks on the front gate, he turned to Fortune. "I am leaving Ningpo. Without me or Bing to translate, you are on your own."

"Are you going to Shanghai?" Fortune asked hopefully.

"No, Soochow."

"Everywhere I go I am told what I seek is more beautiful in Soochow. Everyone raves about Soochow's superior flowers, porcelains, paintings, and people."

"Since ancient times Soochow has been called Paradise on Earth." Barbarians were not allowed in Soochow. Although John Poe already knew from his spies, he asked, "And where are you headed?"

"Captain Balfour has opened Shanghai for the British. I'll be there through the winter."

"I may be in Shanghai while you are there."

"I would be honored to see you. I'll be easy to find." Then he clamped his wool cap over his brow, shouldered his umbrella, and strode back to his lodgings across town.

The mandarins approached the gate, bowing their goodbyes to Dr. Chang. They stared questioningly as Fortune's back disappeared down the darkened street. "He has no chair?" asked one. "He walks back alone?" asked another.

"The English are very strange," John Poe acknowledged. "When given a chance, they prefer to walk instead of ride. On the way through the canals when our boat was being pulled upstream against the current, the barbarian wandered the countryside and jumped back on whenever we stopped."

"As long as he wanders only within the five treaty ports," said Dr. Chang. "But before Mandarin Tai leaves, he and I must speak to you in private." Suddenly, the doctor whirled around and stared out at his grotto garden.

Jadelin ducked below the window's fretwork. She grabbed the hem of her skirt that she had rolled up to muffle the little bells. Fortune was going to her home, to Shanghai!

Dr. Chang searched the darkness and rubbed the back of his neck. He turned back to John Poe, paused, and tipped his head. "Did you hear those little bells?" he asked and stared back into the moonlight. Then he extended his arm towards the room lit by lanterns casting a low light on the thick carpets. Formal horseshoe chairs surrounded the table that had been in Dr. Chang's family for two hundred years. Its name was the Bearer of Secrets.

Jadelin turned and walked back carefully. She smoothed her dress and patted away the smudges of dirt from when she stumbled on the path. The *bak gwei* was indeed a curious creature, she thought. She hoped such men wouldn't change China. All she had known up to now was the comfortable life within the Poe household ruled by Mandarin Poe. First Mother was strict but fair, and had taught her the most intricate embroidery. Her mother, Mei, was very different from Auntie, her father's Second Wife, the singer who criticized everyone. All her brothers came often to her mother's courtyard to practice kung fu, since Mei was ranked as a Master. Most of the time, her brothers treated her like one of them, which she liked since she was the only daughter in the household.

She skidded to a bell-tinkling stop as soon as she saw Big Amah and Mei outside the women's pavilion, waiting for her with daggers in their eyes.

Four

ALISTAIR MACKENZIE

NINGPO

Fortune rose at dawn. From the food stall of a one-armed man with five fat babies and a scar-faced wife, he bought a bowl of steaming rice embedded with slivered onions and seasoned pork.

After breakfast he headed for the port to find a ship to Shanghai. He remembered his former translator, Bing, taught him that all Chinese cities were designed with identical layouts: thick city walls topped by guard stations, a bell and drum tower, and heavily guarded gates. So he oriented himself. The streets were laid out in a grid with suburbs close to the city walls and a corresponding pattern of pagoda-roofed stores, temples, and homes. Fortune noted that the only difference between towns in China seemed to be in the cleanliness of the streets and the quality of buildings. Layers of dirt and garbage had typified Amoy. But here in Ningpo, sweepers attacked dirt and trash at dawn with bamboo brooms. He heard prosperity in the air: in the vendors' bargaining sing-song, children's laughter, and energetic chatter flowing out of the tea houses. Doors were freshly painted, windows sported stylized lattices, and tile roofs sparkled in the winter sun. Even the eaves were carved with colorful creatures to scare away the evil spirits that lurked in the streets.

"You there. Are you an Englishman?"

Fortune whirled at the hearty voice, the welcome accent.

"Stay right there." Heavy footsteps pounded up the street towards him. "I'm Alistair Mackenzie. Here for the opening of Shanghai, are you?" Mackenzie's tweed suit strained against his beefy shoulders as he panted for breath.

Fortune grasped the meaty hand he offered. "Robert Fortune, official plant collector for the Royal Horticultural Society. Yes, I'm wanting to go to Shanghai." He stared at Mackenzie, startled at the sight of eyes so blue and round they resembled robin's eggs in a baked dough face topped by sunflower-yellow hair that stuck out from under a grimy bowler. Alistair Mackenzie was covered in dust from the shoulders of his rumpled coat to the tips of his leather shoes.

"I've been posted to Shanghai with Captain Balfour. A good chap, Balfour. He argued for Shanghai as a treaty port. Its location at the mouth of the Yangtze allows us access to a hundred million Chinese. A great new market. Shanghai's to be East Asia's commercial center. My ship leaves tonight. Plant collector, you say? I'm an amateur botanist myself. By Jove, what a fortuitous coincidence. Aren't plant hunters wealthy men with time and money? I can tell from your burr you're a Scot, like me. Are you famous?" Mackenzie tipped his head and peered at him, a man hungry for the sounds and speech of home.

"No." Fortune's gruff voice hid his embarrassment at the truth. "No plant collecting experience at all. But I read the writings of Joseph Banks who brought back thirty-thousand plant specimens." The formidable William McNabb at the Botanic Garden in Edinburgh had trained him when he was a lad. He admitted that the Royal Horticultural Society had given him, an inexperienced and unproven thirty-year-old, a spade and trowel, a Chinese dictionary, and detailed instructions.

"To do what?" asked the incredulous Mackenzie.

As they walked the narrow streets veering around laden shoppers and hawking peasants, Fortune told his new friend that his job was to collect fine decorative plants with the admonition that the value of the plants he collected diminished with their requirements for heat unless it was an aquatic, orchid, or produced unusually beautiful flowers. He had to collect and analyze soils, collect cocoons of the Atlas Moth, and find the plants that produced rice paper and sugar. And despite the French Academy of Sciences' conclusion in 1763 that the tea bush was so peculiar to China it could not be raised anywhere else, he was to collect samples of tea shrubs because each different kind of tea obviously came from a different type of bush. In addition, he had to prepare dried specimens, find out why Chinese mixed seeds with burnt bones, and discover how the Enkianthus grew in Hong Kong. He was to find the Peaches of Peking, reportedly weighing two pounds apiece, that grew in the Emperor's garden. And although the Society doubted their existence, he was instructed to find the blue peonies and the double yellow roses. At Fortune's insistence, they gave him a rifle and a pair of pistols, which he had to sell before he left China. In addition, he had to keep a daily journal and send descriptive letters in duplicate, by separate means as a precaution, to advise the Society of his progress.

"What have you collected so far?"

"Alas, I lost everything overboard in the monsoon. The locals stole my clothes and collecting boxes. The Chinese are the most hateful, untrustworthy people."

Mackenzie threw his arms wide. "Do you blame them? We want their tea and porcelain and silks. They don't want our opium. So we blast their coastal towns and forts and block their ports with our gunboats."

"It was settled in a treaty. They should be satisfied."

Mackenzie shook his head. "Even William Gladstone denounced sending the entire British Fleet to shoot up China as 'unjust and iniquitous.' He accused Lord Palmerston of initiating the war to protect contraband traffic. No wonder they don't trust us. We kill tens of thousands of Chinese citizens and their Emperor has to reimburse us twelve million dollars for doing so."

"Humph," Fortune turned away with a dour expression. "I don't care for politics. All I care about is lasting one year in this uncivilized country." A year was bearable if he could sail home with glass plant cases filled with the most wondrous specimens of flora and fauna. His accomplishments would be heralded.

Mackenzie threw his arms wide. He thundered, "Well, Fortune, this may be your ticket to fame. Wasn't Banks knighted? Didn't he head the Royal Botanic Gardens at Kew and become a Trustee of the British Museum?"

Fortune's forehead flushed at the thought. China was the mystical kingdom where the Celestial Emperor sat on thrones of pure gold in a palace larger than London, where the abundance of flora and fauna exceed the imagination of the civilized world, where precious tea was produced in a carefully guarded process, its secrets forbidden to all non-Chinese. England lusted for Chinese porcelains, jades, and tea.

But when he arrived in Hong Kong on the *Emu* on July 6, 1843, he had found a barren coast so diseased, healthy British soldiers died before the sun set the next day. He turned his grumpy face to Mackenzie and wagged his finger. "I have been here many weeks, Alistair, so I must warn you, my first impression is that the Chinese are dishonest with no morals. They say anything to get your money and whatever they say is untrue. These uncouth people stare at me as if I am the one who is strange and uncivilized. I swat at them with my umbrella, but still they follow as if I am an alien from the moon. They call us derogatory names like Barbarian, *gweilo*, foreign devil, *bak gwei*, white ghost, and Red-Hair. The smallest unit of Chinese money is called a 'cash,' equal to an eighth of a farthing, a pittance. Yet they bargain and squeeze every cash from every transaction." He scowled at the arguments and embarrassments he endured from the moment he stepped on Chinese soil.

"And I am here to show them an Englishman can be fair and just. Come, my soon-to-be-famous plant hunter, I was just about to explore these fascinating markets. Have you ever seen any place so exotic?" Mackenzie swept his arms to encompass the fabulous Ningpo marketplace. His stocky legs bounced with energy.

The men discovered a street lined with bolts of exquisite silk. They explored streets of jade, of jewelry, and objets d'art, while others featured utensils and bamboo mats. Streets of antique porcelain, of

Western-styled porcelains edged with gold, of lacquer ware, of arts from Japan, and of carved furniture, enticed and seduced them. Fortune rapturously desired it all. When their eyes and brains reeled from the abundance of artistry, they rested in a teahouse and sipped a smoky black tea. Then they were up again, eager to see more.

Mackenzie whipped out an unstarched handkerchief and wiped his sweating brow. He gestured down the street of silk shops where purses and aprons and shirts were made specifically in the Western style for the foreigners who came to Ningpo. "You should buy some for your mother. How about your wife or sweetheart? Maybe a wee bairn?"

Fortune harrumphed.

Mackenzie saw the hollowness in Fortune's eyes, the hole in his heart that revealed his loneliness. He himself had a wife, daughter, grandmother, sisters, plus aunts and grandaunts to buy for. But he had just arrived. He would return after surveying all that China had to offer and buy everything. "Look at this street. Statues and landscapes carved of bamboo." Mackenzie hurried into a shop where they watched a bony craftsman carve a cricket out of bamboo.

The old man held it out to Fortune with one hand and held the other flat to show Fortune what he should do. Fortune jumped when the cricket bobbed as if it were about to leap from his palm. He caressed bamboo brush holders, each different, and fingered the carved scenes of intricate waterfalls and mountains, tiny homes and tinier people. He shook his head. No, he had no money and a bamboo cricket would not qualify as an expense to the Society.

One shopkeeper said his antique porcelains were said to preserve flowers and fruit from decay for an unusually long time.

"Amazing, amazing," Mackenzie proclaimed with florid gasps at every shop. Since the 1600s when Queen Elizabeth gave the trade monopoly to the East India Trading Company, England coveted Chinese-made luxuries. Lacquered screens, porcelain vases, and figurines appeared in the fashionable parlors. English craftsmen including Thomas Chippendale copied Chinese-inspired designs. The Prince Regent's Royal Pavilion, built between 1817 and 1822 in the English seaside resort of Brighton was a turreted and domed 'Hindu' palace, an Anglo-Chinese fantasy of dragons and metallic snakes supporting chandeliers, pink and blue Chinese wallpaper, and Chinoiserie faux bamboo staircase railings in wrought iron.

Chinoiserie had been the rage in England for over two hundred years, but never had the men seen such a range of colors and decoration as in these shops in Ningpo. Mackenzie and Fortune marveled over bowls so pale they looked as if they were wisps of sky, ginger jars that danced with a hundred boys at their games, and gigantic blue-and-white platters from the Ming Dynasty. A gap-toothed merchant pointed out the figures on his gilded porcelain vases that stood half the height of a man. "Look, barbarian faces." His toothy smile was broad and inviting.

Mackenzie picked up a gilt-edged vase and cradled it in his large white hands so it was a couple inches from his eyes. He squinted expertly. "This is very fine, indeed. The hairs on these figures are brown and blond, with pale skin and light eyes."

"You buy," the vendor gestured with his hands. "Special made for *bak gwei.*"

"No," proclaimed Mackenzie. "Not for us." He placed the vase back on the vendor's table and shook his head. "We buy authentic pieces. Show us only very old Chinese things." He held his white meaty hand next to the vendor's tanned one and turned to Fortune with a grin. "I never take offense if anyone calls me *bak gwei,* white ghost. He's just referring to the color of my skin. White skin is admired as a sign of the upper classes who don't have to labor in the fields."

The men ran their fingers across the fine finish of the furniture: beds, chairs, tables, washing stands, and cabinets inlaid with ivory, decorated with scenes of Chinese life, tableaus of men, women, and children drinking tea, conversing, living lives of elegance. Their grand scale was appropriate for a country home in England, not for a parsimonious Scot who lived and breathed flora and fauna.

"I'll be here for only a year. A gardener can never afford fine things," Fortune lamented. There was so much to covet and desire in China.

Alone in his little room in Ningpo, his head reeling from the people and abundance of curiosities in the markets, Fortune curled up on his hard cot and closed his eyes trying to remember when life was not so strange. He thought back to the day his life changed--was it just a year ago--when he was proud to be the newly appointed hothouse supervisor at the Chiswick Horticultural Gardens in England.

There, the greenhouse pipes hissed with mist and steam and dripped soft plops upon the dirt loam. That day he planted a great mass of young azaleas. Caring for plants was a give and take, a communication between plant and gardener. Nature knew what it wanted, and what it needed to flourish. A gardener, mindful of its secrets could, with patience and consistency, nurture a seed or twig to a full-grown plant.

He had dawdled to stretch out his time within this pristine world. Outside, the lung-burning air stank of coal and sulfur, the smell of progress in the British Empire. London's sky was a constant sooty grey, the color of the Industrial Revolution, so it was hard to tell if the sun had set. He had been in no hurry to leave his quiet, glass-protected world. He paused when he heard a sound. Plop. Moisture, accumulating on the large, spade-shaped leaves, rolled down their tips, and fell to earth. Plop. Plop. No hurry to leave.

"Mr. Fortune, it's time. May we go?" Three youths stood before him dripping dirt from their knees and trouser hems, caps in hand. They were already stamping the loam off their shoes. Four more apprentices stood in the far corner of the hothouse where they had been plucking weeds and raking the gravel walks. They stamped to release the dirt clinging to their trousers. Stamped, impatient to leave. After long days of planting, digging, and weeding, they were eager to hit the gas-lit streets.

Fortune winced at the sound of the voices that broke his concentration. The pace of gardening, the quiet and isolation, suited his nature. He had inherited his dour outlook from the moldy stone huts of his childhood. His Lutheran family, parsimonious with words, discouraged small talk and conversation. He kept his head, capped by an odd felt hat that protected his fair head from the mists, lowered to ignore the intrusion. He knew that when he stood up he would loom over his apprentices by two heads. Behind his back, they called him The Ostrich.

He glared up from where he knelt under a palm. "I'm not done." They knew the rules; they couldn't leave until their supervisor's work was complete.

"We'll help you, sir." One wheeled over the wooden handcart by the hothouse service door. The others stacked the one hundred and fifty clay pots that had held the transplanted azaleas until all had been loaded. "We'll clean them off first thing in the morning, sir."

Fortune growled, "Then be off. Tomorrow, clean pots." He heard their laughter fade out the door. He knew they made fun of his Scottish burr, his down-turned mouth, and that they imitated his walk, all angles and knees. He looked up when he heard the approaching footfall, distinctively heavy.

The Hothouse Director, Amos Brown, crunched towards him on the gravel path, keys in hand, locking the doors behind him. "The last one out again, eh, Fortune?" Brown watched the Scot awkwardly tuck his trowel and hoe under his arm. "No sweet wife to go home to, no aged parents, no one at all? Well, 'tis best. You can't support a family on the wages here."

Fortune had looked up at the towering palm fronds, then surveyed the rest of the plants under his care as if saying a fond goodnight. "The plants are beautiful," he murmured to himself. It was the apprentices who drove him daft. He was expected to give them direction, to know the schedule of planting, cultivating, and propagating of every one of the hundreds of plants in the hot house, as well as their schedule for bloom. His men did nothing unless he directed them so he spent his time supervising when all he wanted to do was to plunge his hands into the dirt and be alone with his plants.

"My wife is waiting with a hot stew and brew, so if you don't mind," Brown thumbed the smooth metal cover of his pocket watch, a gift of appreciation from Sir Joseph Banks whose collections from Tahiti, South America, and New Zealand he had nurtured upon the collector's return with Captain James Cook. A good gardener is valuable. A great gardener is priceless.

In the workroom, Fortune cleaned off his trowels and tools. He plucked his heavy wool coat from the row of pegs by the door. It hung alone, the last one.

Director Brown waited by the door, jangling his keys. "You've been here at Chiswick for a few months. How are you settling in?"

"I'm getting used to the men."

"You've trained with McNabb in Edinburgh. The man's a legend, a gardener's gardener. I understand you apprenticed under Mr. Burchan before you apprenticed to McNabb?"

"Yes, Burchan at Moredun."

"With no training past school except in the gardens?"

Fortune nodded. Chiswick was a big change from Edinburgh. The filthy air, the traffic, the lightening-fast London English, and his men who laughed at his Scottish burr made him even more stiff and surly. But oh, the plants! And the blessed peace of the hothouse.

Brown puffed his pipe, motioned him out, and locked the door. "It was upon McNabb's recommendation that we gave you this position." The air smacked him, cold and wet. Brown pulled up his collar and appraised Fortune with a tilt of his head. "You know we're looking for a collector for a plant hunting expedition in China."

The Directors had evaluated every possible man until they read McNabb's letter.

To Director Amos Brown
Royal Botanical Gardens in Chiswick
Amos,

I received your letter regarding the Society's plan to send a collector immediately to China. I admit surprise. I thought the British Empire was still blowing up the country. But with the ink still drying on the Treaty of Nanking and the country still in turmoil, it is a sound plan to be the first to explore the Celestial Kingdom. The annual wage of 100 pounds will not entice our finest botanists to such an unstable and dangerous land. Since the collector will be restricted to five treaty ports with questionable ability to leave the ship, prevented by law from speaking the language of the natives, and facing native hostility, the Society can lower its standards. Your primary requirement should be for a healthy gardener, who knows how to propagate seeds, cultivate seedlings, and keep plants alive. He should be literate, diligent, persevering, not prone to frustration by hardship, used to Spartan conditions, and frugal. The new gardener I sent to you, Robert Fortune, might be your man. He is a devout Lutheran, of tough Scottish stock, and has no family. I agree with your opinion that he is peculiar. Perhaps his eccentricities will prove to be an asset in inhospitable China.

Yours,

William McNabb

Director Brown held out his hand and bellowed, "Congratulations, Fortune, the job is yours."

"But there's a war in China." Convinced that he didn't have a chance against senior gardeners, Fortune had applied to show he was interested in advancing. He didn't want to collect plants in strange places.

Plant collecting was the mania of wealthy adventurers. Thomas Nuttall collected hundreds of plants in America that the rest of the world had never seen before. Fellow Scot David Douglas discovered the Sitka Spruce and Douglas Fir plus hundreds of species sent to the Royal Horticultural Society before he plunged to his death in a Hawaiian boar pit in 1834. Archibald Menzies traveled the world as a surgeon while collecting thousands of species from Hawaii, Vancouver, and the north Pacific. The most accomplished of them all, Joseph Banks, collected plants, rocks, and animals in Newfoundland, Labrador, Tahiti, South America, New Zealand, Scotland, Wales, Holland, and Iceland.

"This is a mission of peace." Amos Brown secured his topcoat button and wrapped his scarf around his neck. "I'd have applied myself were I forty years younger."

"China is a heathen country. They eat dogs and monkeys and eat with sticks." Fortune felt like a stray cornered in a dead-end alley.

"China is known as the Flowery Land," thundered Director Brown. "Imagine thousands of undiscovered plants waiting for you to dig up."

He clamped his thick woolen hat on his head and grabbed his umbrella with its heavy brass handle in the shape of a gnarled root. He nodded goodnight and eagerly headed home to his well-fed wife.

That night Fortune walked home through the dim alleys of London back to his tiny, cold room. He dodged the knife-wielding gangs by clicking his heels forcefully on the cobblestones. He whipped his umbrella before him like a saber.

He should be flattered by Brown's offer. A great opportunity. A chance to rise like the stars, like Hooker, Menzies, Douglas, and Nuttall. But to be in China, to be alone in a heathen land where one couldn't speak the language was absurd.

Director Brown told him not to think of the high danger or paltry pay but of the glory. He would be part of a long tradition of horticultural collecting that began with the earliest recorded plant hunter, Hatshepsut, Queen of Egypt, who sent five large ships to the shores of East Africa, the land of Punt, for seeds and plants of the *Bosellias*, source of that precious gum called frankincense. The results of that successful mission in 1500 BC were thirty-one flourishing *Bosellias* trees in the queen's temple gardens at Karnak.

Fortune coughed and gagged in the poisonous fog of the Industrial Age that suffocated the city. He whipped his umbrella behind him at a scurrying sound and thwacked someone's leg or torso. He turned and swung again, making contact. Probably a thief, he growled, and continued brandishing his umbrella. He heard running and shouts as people scattered.

He renewed his pace towards his meager quarters. The Society would give him one year to explore 1500 square miles of Chinese territory. Like most English, tales of the exotic enthralled him: men in silk robes and black pigtails, women with shrunken feet, and the profusion of unknown flowers that decorated porcelains and paintings. In a time of soot-covered British industrialization, of clanging machines and impersonal factories, China was romance, a centuries-old Empire whose walled cities and treasures beckoned.

But how would he last a year in such a hostile country with such primitive people?

Five

GRAND MASTER PING

SOOCHOW

Jadelin awoke when the junk slowed to a gentle glide. She rolled off her cotton mat and climbed barefoot up to the deck where Benjamin steered past bridges arched high over tree-lined canals. White cranes, fishing at dawn, majestically stilt-walked, their gold-crested heads elegantly alert.

"Hey, little sister." He held out his free arm. She ran to his side and put her arms around his substantial middle, as hard and muscled as his heart was soft. She shivered. He picked up a cloak of quilted cotton he always kept by the tiller to ward off the morning dew and wrapped it around her. "What are you doing up so early?" He ruffled her uncombed hair.

"I wanted to see where I'll be hiding for the next few months."

"Afraid?"

She nodded. She pressed her chilled cheeks against the heat of his chest, which warmed her like a steaming furnace.

"The Emperor's army doesn't chase just anyone." He looked down at her and chuckled. "He doesn't realize how much trouble you are."

Mei joined them when the sun's pink and purple fingers reached through the clouds. She lifted her face to the flower-scented wind streaming across the junk's high prow. Black tile roofs loomed into view. "I've reached Heaven," she sighed. In answer to Jadelin's quizzical look she pointed out how the ornate roofs in Soochow turned up at each corner in the distinctive architectural feature called Reaching to Heaven. "It's a play on words, a pun." Whenever she saw these upturned black tiles, she knew she had returned to the heavenly place of her childhood.

"Look!" Mei pointed to a cloud of wild finches that circled a series of distinctively peaked roofs before swooping away. She imagined how free they felt when they soared, the power of their wings against the wind just as when, after an exceptionally challenging practice, she felt such exhilaration that she felt she could fly out of her skin. Her eyes rested on her daughter, how her innocent eyes took in the sweep of the elegant rooflines of Grand Master Ping's spacious buildings, and how much she had to teach her. No, perhaps it was best if her father placed her with his students so she could develop her skills under his exacting standards. She would be there for her tears. She held out her hand. "Come, Jadelin. We're getting close." Mei led her back to her trunk and shook out trousers and a tunic. She combed and tied her daughter's hair back with a blue ribbon so it cascaded in a single ponytail. "When I was your age I was free to run in trousers through the gardens with my brothers and climb the fruit trees in summer. I lived in my father's world then, so different from Shanghai."

Benjamin lowered the sails and guided the ship to the private dock. Jadelin leaned over the bulwark to watch dozens of young men in the royal blue silk of Grand Master Ping prepare to catch the lines that John tossed to shore. Effortlessly, Benjamin coasted in and they tied off.

The Poes returned the students' bows as they stepped under the hallowed arched gates into a spacious plaza surrounded by three graceful pagoda-roofed buildings with moon doors and intricately latticed windows.

Above, a hawk swooped down on the roof dispersing clouds of doves.

Grand Master Ping's black robes billowed behind him as he descended the stairs of the Great Hall on the far side of the plaza. His face was wrinkled and creased as if he had lived many lifetimes. His queue fell thick and white to his waist. Based on the spring of his steps he had many lifetimes yet to enjoy. His eyes were bright; they missed nothing. His sense of smell, hearing, and taste were in their prime. As for his libido, he had no need for the aphrodisiacs of rhinoceros horn or snake eggs men half his age imbibed to renew their life force. Throughout China he was respected as the Grand Master of Kung Fu and the philosophies of Confucius, Lao Tzu, and Buddha.

Benjamin bowed first, head to knee. "Master." He held his hands together in greetings.

"Mandarin Poe's Second Son, one of my finest students," the Grand Master acknowledged. "Welcome back."

John bowed. "Master," he said with the awe of a young man for his mentor.

Grand Master Ping clasped his hands. "I have missed you."

Mei bowed her head to the ground. "Father," she said in a breathless voice.

Grand Master Ping's tone was melodious. "Daughter. I rejoice your return." His eyes crinkled in happy crescents.

"Gung Gung." Jadelin's voice was light and lilting. When she looked up, his twinkling eyes met hers.

"My granddaughter," Ping lifted her chin and studied her face. "You grow more like your mother." He pulled back her sleeve and inspected the bruised shoulder that was now as purple as a ripe eggplant. "The birds must fly in fright when they hear you practice."

Jadelin bowed her head. How did he know she made so much noise when she sparred with her brothers that the caged canaries were scared into silence while wild birds raced away as fast as their wings could beat?

Ping gestured them to follow him up to his private dining room hushed by tapestries and scrolls. The Poes had not eaten since Ningpo. They devoured the platters of poached fish in garlic, crabs in black bean sauce, and steaming vegetables. He asked Benjamin for news of Shanghai and queried John about the Western foreigners along the coast.

Afterwards, they withdrew to his light and airy tearoom where hardwood chairs surrounded a hexagonal rosewood table. A servant placed a teapot before each.

"My teapot," Jadelin exclaimed. She fingered the finely modeled silkworm curled on its lid and rubbed the notches in the old vine which served as its handle. When she first stepped into her grandfather's tearoom years ago, she had gazed in awe at the stunning sight of hundreds of Yixing teapots displayed from floor to ceiling. Her grandfather had explained that these teapots came from a tradition of exquisite pottery dating back to the sixth century. Treasured teapots of the unusually fine, naturally colored clay from Yixing had the ability to retain both fragrance and taste. Each teapot was reserved for the use of a specific person and used only for the finest teas.

"It has been waiting for your return, Jadelin." Grand Master Ping's voice was soft and papery.

Benjamin's dark brown teapot flecked with real gold was shaped in a perfect oval ellipse with a sinuous spout.

Each side of John's hexagonal blue teapot was decorated with the relief of an auspicious flower of prosperity, and its handle resembled the gnarled vines of a plant, down to the minute insect perched in the scar of a leaf stem.

Mei's teapot could easily have been mistaken for a large cut of aged bamboo sprouting a handle of two slender green bamboo branches. She exclaimed in surprise and reached out for a spectacular teapot in the shape of a golden dragon with bulging black eyes and snake-like red scales that her father had chosen from the hundreds in the room. She held it between her palms. "Baba, I've never seen this one before."

"I need this dragon's fire to keep up with my energetic family. My favorite student Adam Poe had it made in the Imperial workshops." Mei flushed and looked down. Her father leaned forward. "Since you sent no warning of your arrival, I sense you have come in secret."

After the tea had been chosen and boiling water poured for all, Mei leaned forward while the scent of steeping tea leaves wafted in the

52

air. She wrapped her long fingers around her teapot, pulling strength from the warmth of the dense clay. "Father, two nights ago, Adam Poe risked his life to reach us in Shanghai. He advised us that the Emperor had sent his army for Jadelin. Adam raced for twenty days knowing the Emperor's Imperial courtiers and army followed a day behind him. If the Emperor's spies knew he had come to warn us, he and his entire family would have been executed." She bowed her head, afraid for his family's safety. No one was allowed to defy the will of the Son of Heaven. She looked beseechingly into her father's eyes for help. "My husband sent Benjamin immediately to Ningpo on legitimate business. No one knew we were his secret cargo."

Grand Master Ping closed his eyes and inhaled a meditative breath. Long ago, his daughter had dressed like her brothers to deceive the inquisitive eyes of the Emperor's spies, a ruse that worked for many years. One of his rivals could not resist the gold the Emperor offered for the most beautiful girls to be among his 10,000 concubines. When the Emperor's army banged on Grand Master Ping's door, he and Mei had raced down the back steps to his dock and, with twenty students rowing at top speed, escaped to the protection of one of his most powerful students, Mandarin Poe. In those days, only someone with Poe's stature and honorable face could defy the Emperor's demand for Mei. The Emperor needed Poe's support among the mandarins of Shanghai more than he needed another concubine then. But the Emperor had grown greedy and stupid.

"The Manchu Emperor is fattening his harem again," he growled. "He diminishes women to futile lives of gossip. For what? The Manchu Emperor is a sniveling weakling, only interested in bloating his overflowing stores of art. His eunuchs steal from the Imperial warehouses as quickly as he fills them. If China's Emperor had been a Han, he would never have surrendered China's ports to the barbarians." Although the British gunboats didn't approach Soochow, they had blocked traffic on the Grand Canal and cut China's main river and canal communications. For three years he had felt a disturbance in the ch'i as if a million souls were screaming. Later, he learned scores of Ching officers and their families had committed suicide rather than surrender or be raped by the British.

He leaned forward and stared at Jadelin with a piercing frown. "Have you learned enough to fend off the Emperor's army? They are after you."

"Not yet. But I fought Benjamin in a duel." Her quick answer surprised him.

Ping arched his eyebrows.

Benjamin offered generously, "She's a worthy adversary."

Mei shook her head. "Baba, when they practice, her brothers give no consideration for her tender age. As Benjamin told you, Shanghai is to be opened to the British. My husband and his sons are absorbed with building their tea trade with the foreigners while protecting our rights."

Ping waved his hand sagely. "It is better that you are here. The time will come when the only person anyone can depend on is oneself. Even I will not be here forever."

Mei's eyes widened in surprise and she looked questioningly at him.

He gestured he was fine, for now. He turned to his granddaughter. "While you are here, braid your hair in a queue and dress like a boy as your mother did until the day she married. You and your mother will train with my students. The Manchu emperor wants easy prey, not women warriors who can thrust a sword faster than his men."

"Benjamin?" He turned to his giant grandson who had listened with amusement and a great deal of eye rolling. "Have you word from Shanghai?"

Benjamin's bushy brows rose. "Imperial soldiers entered our front gates two hours after Adam left for Peking. By then, Big Amah had packed Jadelin's clothes in chests hidden deep in the hong's warehouse. Baba told them his daughter had died. The soldiers were too lazy to check thoroughly."

Benjamin had been in awe of Grand Master Ping from the day the scholar selected him for his prestigious school. From the age of five, he and his brothers studied Chinese philosophy, art, and culture and trained in the martial arts as their father had done. Their days were filled with pain and happiness, discipline and joy, serenity and study. Mei, the Grand Master's daughter, had been just another classmate then. He saw her shed tears when she failed to deflect what could have been a fatal blow. A counter blow with her own staff, and no one knew she had been weak for a second, except Benjamin.

"Useless Emperor," grumbled Ping.

"But he has the Mandate from Heaven."

"Each Treaty he signs with the barbarians removes a limb from the body of China. Soon we will have no legs or arms to move, no head to think." Ping turned to John. "My youngest grandson, you have traveled with the English foreigners."

John put down his teacup and shook his head at what he had heard and seen. "My English name makes me more like them in their eyes. They do not look down on me as much as they do my fellows whom they treat worse than dogs."

Ping's eyebrows dipped in a frown. "Perhaps the English do not treat their own countrymen so well."

John recounted the astounding sight of how the naked Fortune rode one of Landers' crew like a horse in Chimoo while Bing raced behind on foot. "Alas, they don't. But we ourselves do not always follow Lao Tzu, the Tao, or the middle path."

His grandfather nodded in agreement. Mastery of Kung Fu was incomplete without the guiding philosophies of Taoism and Buddhism. He leaned back on the embroidered cushion and nestled the celadon cup in fight-callused hands. For thousands of years, China had traded with foreigners from across the oceans and along the Silk Road far to the West. Persian faces, fair Northern European skin, big eyes and noses, as well as their uniquely distinctive attire had been immortalized in Chinese figurines and paintings since the early Northern Wei Dynasty 1400 years ago. Foreigners successfully assumed Chinese names and dress to make them acceptable, as did the Jesuits, Matteo Ricci and Ferdinand Verbiest, known as Li Madou and Nan Huairen. Ping had advised Mandarin Poe to give his sons a corresponding advantage; not only did Mandarin Poe give his sons English names to use when dealing with the Westerners and thus, increase their acceptance as business equals, but English was one of the languages in which they spoke and wrote fluently.

"Father, this tea," exclaimed Mei. She closed her eyes to concentrate on the flavor that warmed her tongue. "It flows like silk across my tongue. I can taste the mists on high mountains, the cool afternoon breeze, and the chilly nights."

Benjamin swirled the tea around his palate. "Aah, this tea must come from Longjing, a small village on the Fenghuang Hill." He turned to Jadelin and lifted his shaggy eyebrows. "A long time ago, little sister, a dragon lived there and controlled the rainfall. He was a very powerful, huge dragon. Since his water was especially pure this tea is called Dragon Well."

"Is there a real dragon?" She believed most anything he told her.

"Of course. In fact, we should find you a dragon husband from Longjing. You could fight him all day and have little dragon babies."

"Humph." She blushed. At fifteen she was an adult. Too old for such teasing.

Mei's eyes crinkled at their sparring. In most families, jealous wives and sons would have sabotaged her position as a very young Third Wife but Mandarin Poe had learned Ping's lessons well and instilled his mentor's virtues in his children.

"Interestingly," Grand Master Ping added with an intrigued look in his eye, "Longjing tea is an elixir for health, especially useful because it helps deter food poisoning." He took a long sip, closed his eyes and savored the taste. He studied Jadelin. "This is an exceptionally fine hand-rolled tea made by one of my most extraordinary students. This tea is my favorite, from the Longjing mountains in the West Lake district of Hangchow, a land cloaked by clouds and mist for long periods of time. In the Tang Dynasty, Lu Yu wrote about it in *The Classic of Tea*, the first book ever written about tea. According to legend, the most famous Ch'ing Emperor, Ch'ien-lung, personally visited the tea growing area of Longjing not only to sip tea and to write and sing poems in its praise, but to watch the process of picking and roasting." He held up his tea and inhaled. "Tea is taste, a texture, a scent. It engages all our senses."

Contentment settled on his face when he met his family's' eyes. They shared that spiritual tie that bound their hearts and souls.

"Tea is an experience," added Mei. She held her teacup with both hands.

"Tea is culture," John proclaimed holding up his teacup to toast them all. "Five thousand years of history spawning literature, paintings, and art. We drink this tea with our entire body, receive it with an open heart, and accept its calming and cleansing effects."

They fell silent, content in the moment.

"Gung Gung, I need your advice." John placed his teacup soundlessly on the lacquered tray. "During your long life you have seen how the Manchus made China a great kingdom. Now they open the doors to its demise. They believe only what their advisors tell them and their spies are afraid to tell them the truth of what occurs far from Peking."

The Grand Master raised his index finger. "The Manchu are more interested in preserving their Imperial Treasuries than in the welfare of the people. Look at the thousands of artisans in the Imperial workshops who produce the finest porcelain, painting, calligraphy, and jade for the pleasure of those living within the palace. But outside the Forbidden City," he gestured, "Han males must wear a queue as a sign of their submission. The Manchu massacre our intellectual elite when they resist." To protect themselves, the Chinese formed secret societies like the Dragons of the Mist, elite fighters who were also intellectuals and artisans, sworn to avenge and protect.

"Grandfather, in Ningpo, Mandarin Tai met the barbarian Robert Fortune at Dr. Chang's and subsequently invited him to visit his gardens. To his horror, the barbarian rudely mishandled an ancient tree the Tais had nurtured for a thousand years."

Jadelin perked up her ears while seemingly absorbed in tasting the nuances of her tea.

Ping shook his head. "Tai drew his sword, did he not?"

John nodded. "I believe the Englishman merely wanted to touch the plant, to feel the texture of the leaves and bark, for this is what gardeners do."

"But without the permission of his host? Mandarin Tai showed great restraint by not skewering him. What else?"

"He asks everywhere for the plant that makes tea."

"Ai-ya." Ping stood up, shattering his teacup on the tile floor. "The secrets of tea have belonged to China for five thousand years. The English agreed by treaty that the lands of tea are forbidden to the barbarians."

"Which makes the mandarins' request difficult for me to refuse," John said in a low voice. Everyone sat motionless, waiting.

"Which is?" demanded Ping, leaning forward on his knuckles. His eyes glinted keenly.

"To befriend the Englishman, to learn his true purpose. Fortune says he's here to collect the finest decorative Chinese plants to grow in England. But everywhere he asks about tea and how it's made." John averted his eyes so his grandfather could not read his irritation. He had gardens to study, growers to visit, teas to buy, plus a father, three mothers, five brothers, a sister, and soon, a wife. He did not want to shadow a barbarian through China.

"My grandson," Ping's voice was strong and sure. "This barbarian is forbidden to travel more than a day's journey from the treaty ports. Befriend his servants to know his secrets. Discover his true nature and his real motives will be revealed." He leaned back on his cushions, his brow furrowed in contemplation.

John bowed. "The mandarins in Ningpo will be pleased that you agree with them." This task complicated his life. The ideal life of the scholar recluse he desired slipped further from his grasp.

But Jadelin had been sitting too long. She wiggled her shoulders. "Mama, may I change? Now that we're in Soochow I don't have to wear these shoes."

Mei rose slowly like an unfolding blossom. "Please excuse us, gentlemen. We'll change and join the students in the Great Hall."

Grand Master Ping nodded his consent. "Good. I want to show you four exceptional students. Now masters in their own right, they have returned for the winter to share their skills."

Jadelin stretched her hearing to capture their words as she and her mother silently exited, so she heard her grandfather's final words, "Beautiful deceptions, aren't they?"

"No one suspects," Benjamin agreed with a chuckle.

∾

The brothers tensed with anticipation when they heard the slap of bodies rolling to the floor in the Great Hall. The shouts meant a good session was underway.

John's eyes met his grandfather's. "Please, may we join them?"

The master stood. "Come," he gestured. His silk gown billowed like a curling wave as he led his grandsons through a doorway curved like a meiping vase, peaked at the top and curved to a swell before tapering downwards like a woman's thigh.

He turned to Benjamin as the three walked along the hall. "Before we join the others, tell me how your father's Fourth Son is doing."

"His wife finally gave him the son he desired," answered Benjamin. He saw his grandfather touch his heart and furrow his brow. "Ah, yes, fulfillment of his potential. But Edward hasn't found his niche at the hong. He doesn't have the mathematical and analytical skills to assist Daniel or the people skills of his younger brother Paul who, even though he's only sixteen, excels in attracting and charming our customers. We've trained him in every job, as we all were. Baba has even sent him inland to learn about tea propagation and production. Edward is impatient and feels he should be in charge."

"I hoped his ambitious spirit would help him find what work he does best." Ping shook his head. "Such a melancholy boy. Always looking up to see who is ranked higher, always wanting to be in that first position."

"I didn't know Edward was that unhappy," puzzled John. The men stepped into the wide courtyard where the scent of flowers in the full sun welcomed them but they continued on to the Great Hall.

"You are doing what you do best, learning about foreigners first hand," Benjamin assured him. "Your information helps us adjust to the changing times. But Edward wants my job."

"That would bring disaster on the house of Poe. He lacks your heart and maturity," Grand Master Ping mused. Benjamin was the family's rock. John was annoyed with the foreigners' world, but he was best prepared for meeting the future. As for Edward, his fate was uncertain.

Long spears, curved swords, staffs, and other weapons lined one side of the Great Hall. Forked red banners and weapons stood ready on the opposite wall. Dozens of students moved in the fluid gestures of a swan, a soaring crane, a leaping monkey, a stalking tiger, and a powerful leopard. They completed their preliminary warm-ups and broke quickly into groups.

Grand Master Ping watched Mei's and Jadelin's movements as they completed their warm-ups. He taught his students all twelve styles of kung fu before assigning one appropriate to an individual's strengths and weaknesses. Since Jadelin had no one to practice with in Shanghai except her mother and occasional spars with her brothers, she perfected a style most effective for her petite body and skill. Mei had the elegant long style of a dancer. Benjamin was a master of all, able to switch depending upon the level of his opponents' skill.

∿

*M*ei closed her eyes and took a quick breath to put herself back into the days she had spent within these walls studying her father's ancient skills and philosophies, from the time she could walk until the day she fled to Shanghai. She had trained as hard any student, receiving no special privileges, to rightfully earn the rank of master.

On the far side of the hall she saw Benjamin, who had stripped down to his bare chest, accept the challenge to take on five students at once. A tidal wave of motion with staff or sword, the husky warrior drew an appreciative audience including Grand Master Ping who stood far, far back. She chuckled to remember when Adam and Benjamin, both about her age, first entered her father's school. She had been able to beat them both then; she was the 'teacher's daughter,' after all. But the brothers were strong and talented: Adam was an intuitive strategist and Benjamin possessed strength and quickness. For practice, Benjamin would take on both Mei and Adam at the same time. Now he was taking on five of her father's best.

She watched John spar with two students in another corner and was delighted to see how effortlessly he dispatched them.

In the center of the hall, the morning light speared down on four bare-chested men, two with staffs and two bare-handed. The sheen of their sweat emphasized muscled backs and rope-like calves. The atmosphere around them was taut with tension, terse and deliberate.

Mei approached her father and gestured at the four. "Baba, their moves? I don't recognize the style." She had watched her father teach many styles and himself spar with old friends, many legends in their time including Mow Chow Ching whose powers were whispered to border on black magic.

His voice was low when he answered. "These four have taken my teachings and added their own strengths. They are each masters with their own following." He narrowed his eyes and watched how his daughter made her assessment. After half an hour, he clapped once. The four approached and bowed. They breathed heavily, exultantly. Ping turned to his daughter and introduced each, their village, and training. He asked the tallest to stay. The others would continue with the dozens of students in blue practice silks who now gathered for their lessons.

"Mow Bowli, this is my daughter, the wife of Mandarin Poe. And you know my grandson, John."

The young man bowed. His voice was low and humble when he addressed Mei, "Madame Poe." He had a calm unreadable expression, but his brown eyes, as light as bamboo shoots in spring, took in Mei with respect. He had heard rumors about Grand Master Ping's daughter and granddaughter. He glanced quickly at her feet then turned to greet John. "So John's your English name? The last time I saw you, your chin was as smooth as an egg."

61

"It's been too many years, Mow Bowli," John greeted his friend. "You've gotten a little better."

Mow Bowli's laugh was hearty and inclusive. "Though not even in technique, we've always been even in victories."

"Your style is impressive," Mei said truthfully. She had followed their movements with her inner body noting their sophisticated nuances and skillful timing. She took in Mow Bowli's strong jaw, the shadow of a beard, his broad chest, sinewy legs, and long fingers that grasped the staff with as much familiarity as a calligraphy brush. He stood taller than her husband.

"I'm no match for the others," he said humbly, but his eyes were quick and intelligent.

Grand Master Ping approved his answer. "Mow Bowli is a poet in the ancient tradition of the Scholar Warrior. He returns every winter to humble my best students. He is a credit to his father, Mow Chow Ching."

Mei raised an eyebrow. "The legendary Mow Chow Ching?"

Ping laughed, delighted he could still surprise his accomplished daughter. "Yes, my dear friend, a member of the Dragons of the Mist. Mow Bowli was your son's training partner years ago."

"Please, I am a humble student and grower of tea." Mow Bowli waved off their admirable gazes. He looked directly at Mei. "If you are wondering, I do not possess the mystical gifts of my father."

Mei raised an eyebrow and looked as if she did not believe him. For whether they were embellished or not, the legends of Mow Chow Ching inspired tales of magic and the supernatural.

When she first entered the practice hall with her mother, Jadelin had lingered between a tall wardrobe and the door to absorb the unfamiliar energy and center her ch'i. Mow Bowli had captivated her with his moves, fair skin, and light brown eyes. Compared to the others his hands, swiftness, and strength were extraordinary. The minute her grandfather clapped, Mow Bowli had dropped his staff to his side and smiled directly at her as if he knew who she was even though she stood in the shadows. The moment was electric. In the next second, he had bowed his head and answered, "Grand

Master Ping," with the others as if the look they shared had been an illusion.

When her grandfather nodded, Jadelin stepped forward.

"My granddaughter." The Grand Master placed his hand protectively on her shoulder and introduced his protégé. "Mow Bowli, meet Jadelin. By the Lunar New Year we need to teach her enough to beat back the Emperor's army."

∾

*J*ohn felt the sudden change of air pressure near his head. He whirled and ducked, body aimed for attack. His eyes narrowed when Jadelin evaded his precise kick. He switched to the dominating Dragon style, but she thwarted him again, neutralizing his incoming blows and redirecting his force. He changed strategy. She focused on centerline and simplicity. Once a blow was struck, she marched him backwards with a constant barrage of swift kicks to disrupt his stance. He countered with a flurry of cycle punches that were both offense and defense, batting every attack off center and continuing in for the strike.

Grand Master Ping watched intently. His students, in formation along the walls of the practice hall, waited their turn. This was not a contest of winning or losing or of competitive victory, but the method by which they mastered their skills. One's entire heart and soul had to be in the moment.

John lunged, his face so close to Jadelin that she inhaled his breath. They circled each other. "I have been easy on you," he growled. He took deep breaths to center his ch'i.

"As have I. I don't want to ruin your reputation. If your potential bride heard that you were bested by your little sister, you would not be worthy to receive her substantial dowry." She paced her words so he wouldn't know how much she ached. Her entire body whimpered 'Please stop.' "Shall I give you another chance?" she panted. But every muscle screamed and shivered with exhaustion.

His eyes read her well. He growled, "We'll call it a draw."

They both bowed, relieved, then turned and bowed to the class.

He joined Mei, who serenely observed in the lotus position with her hands cupped at her waist. He wouldn't even try to spar with his mother. Mei excelled in preying mantis kung fu, a soft-style that evaded direct power confrontation. The footwork followed a pattern resembling the seven classical stars in Chinese astrology, a style that suited her long legs and nimble feet.

When Ping dismissed the class, Jadelin threw back her shoulders and rolled her neck. She locked her fingers and stretched her arms back as far as she could to release what felt like a heavy weight between her shoulder blades.

"Jadelin, are you hurt?" Mow Bowli leaned over and gallantly held out his hand to help her up.

"I'm trying to loosen the knot in my back," she groaned. She couldn't move.

He knelt down and ran the flat of his hand across her shoulders until he found the tenseness. He pressed. "Here?"

"Ow! That's the spot." She turned to him, eyes wide. "How did you know?"

"Your foot placement. You weren't centered. I've done it myself."

"It must have been a long, long time ago," she muttered.

He didn't say anything, just hummed. He placed one hand firmly below her collarbone and applied pressure to each vertebra.

She threw back her head. "Ouch! That hurts."

"Deep breath. Blow the air out of your mouth. That's right. Deep breaths now. Slowly."

She dropped her head forward and stretched her spine. When she closed her eyes she felt lifted out of her body into a warm cloud as the radiating energy of his hands warmed each muscle and bone. The muscles of her back unwound, stretched, and loosened. After a blissful period in which she seemed to float away, she whimpered, "Stop. I can't take any more. My bones are melting into the floor."

Mow Bowli put his hands on her shoulders and searched her eyes as if he could read her soul. "Yes. I see less pain now."

She looked into his warm brown eyes and felt their glow suffuse her body. She smiled. He understood her secret.

In Chinese society, all Han women bound their feet to achieve the ideal three-inch Lotus foot starting at around age six. Such dainty feet were considered a reflection of their capacity for pain and strong character. No man would marry a woman who did not have Lotus feet and besides, many thought the dainty sway seductive.

Unbeknownst to everyone outside their family, Mei and Jadelin's feet had never been bound. Their silky floor-length gowns revealed only the tips of their dainty Lotus Blossom shoes. Others might decry their unbound feet as hideous and socially unacceptable, but to Grand Master Ping and Mandarin Poe, it was imperative that Mei and Jadelin move with the same power and energy as a man. What appeared to be Mei's and Jadelin's three-inch Lotus Blossoms were cork forms clad in tiny slippers beautifully embroidered by Mandarin Poe's First Wife.

When Jadelin was three, her father carved the cork forms attached to the bottoms of her real shoes for her growing feet himself so she, too, could carry on the tradition of her grandfather, Grand Master Ping. But while they were in Soochow, Mei and Jadelin ran barefoot so they could feel the earth and the ground and center their ch'i.

Mow Bowli dropped his hands. "We could work on your foot placement, on that move that twisted your back. But you need a day of rest for your muscles to recuperate and rebuild. Tomorrow?"

"Tomorrow," she answered. She could still feel his breath upon her cheek and where his hands had melted her skin. "Absolutely, tomorrow."

Six

THE WINTER OF 1843

SHANGHAI

*M*andarin Poe's Second Wife rose from her bed where she had flung herself in a fit of pique after her husband's First Wife had dared to comment on her less than rosy complexion and to note that, at fifty, her beauty had waned. She had seethed through lunch then stormed to her own wing to sulk. Here, among her silks and fans, jades, and kingfisher hairpins she reigned supreme, surrounded by splendor that reflected her own magnificence.

"Madame," her maid whispered, "your son arrives soon. Let me dress you."

Second Wife stretched languorously and slithered out of her silk robe, an act she had perfected so she appeared to be a blossom opening to the sun. She used to drive Mandarin Poe wild that way, but in the past few years he was always busy with his work. She knew she was still young and vibrant, so much more elegant and chic than his childlike Third Wife. What was her name, Mei? Such an ordinary name suited that unsophisticated country girl from Soochow.

Lying naked, she lifted each leg high in the air and inspected her pale skin for non-existent imperfections. She threw her head back. How good that felt. She ran her fingers between her legs and made herself moan with pleasurable delight.

The afternoon sun hung hot and lazy when Edward entered his mother's garden of dwarfed trees and immaculate walkways. A long time ago, First Mother had brought her three sons here to visit him and Paul. The five rambunctious little boys, even as well behaved as they had been then, had given his mother, whom all were required to call Auntie, such a headache that she had burst into a fury of screams. His half-brothers were never invited back. Instead, he and Paul were sent daily to First Wife's wing to play and study.

His mother chose to approach him from a tree-covered path so the dappled shade softened her appearance and bathed her in filtered light. She had chosen a gown of complimentary pink so its reflected glow would light up her face.

"Auntie, you are as beautiful as a peony in spring." He held out his arms and bowed grandly.

"My son, only you see my true beauty. Just today, First Mother told me I'm a withered blossom." She sighed dramatically and touched her fingers to her cheek as if her fingertips could smooth out the wrinkles. "My life is over."

"No, no. See? I have a package here from one of your admirers."

"I have no admirers. I hide here in my wing surrounded by beauty. I do not wish for admirers. Only for beauty." She pursed her crimson lips into a well-practiced pout.

He smiled at the coquettish twirl of her fan. "The fame of your peach blushed cheeks has flown over these walls and captured the heart of very influential, very important admirers." He held out a package wrapped in glossy paper. "The Englishman came to the warehouse again. He brought you a gift. Twice as much as last time. He said he had heard that Mandarin Poe's Second Wife was a rare beauty and had need of this."

"Ah!" She looked away as if in thought. "I wonder what this could be." She plucked the parcel from his outstretched hand and clasped it to her breast. "You work very hard at the warehouse, don't you? Yet your talents are not recognized. Everyone reveres First Son Adam, who brings the Poes much honor from Peking. Benjamin is second only to his father in power and influence. Third Son Daniel, with his quick head for numbers and laws, controls our money and finances. Sixth Son John gallivants all over China looking at connoisseurs' gardens. You and your brother Paul work hard for your Baba and do anything he asks to win his praise. No one pays me any attention." She sighed theatrically and bent her head like a coy schoolgirl. "Your Amah raised you to be conscientious and ambitious. You think I'm silly and shallow." She lifted her eyes to him and recognized a kindred soul. "But still, Edward, you are kind to me."

"You taught me that family comes first." He saw her luminous eyes search his. They were large and glossy, so soft and wet. Her skin shone with a pearly softness that she had consulted many ancient healing texts to nurture.

"You are a gentleman," she cooed. "I thank you for your kindness. I'm so very lonely. I have nothing to do all day."

"No one will care if I don't return right away." His words revealed his hurt. His father and brothers were conferring over a barbarian's letter written in English. Of all the sons, he was the least proficient in that unmusical language; it caused great pains in his head. "Aren't I doing my duty to my family by keeping your spirits happy and light?"

Second Wife's sloe-eyed glance appraised her son. "Come, let us open this packet and see what escape it may bring us." She dismissed her maid for the day. With a glance at her son, she tottered on Lotus Blossom feet to her sitting room where silk-cushioned chairs were arranged for intimate conversation over quiet cups of tea and sweets.

Edward entered her inner chamber and bolted her door. He was not as smart as Adam, as strong as Benjamin, as quick as Daniel, or as talented as John. He was even overshadowed by his younger brother Paul, who was so handsome that men and women looked twice, struck by his confidence and beauty. How his younger brother's eyes sparkled when they alighted on something curious or interesting. Yes, Paul had the grace and charm of their mother and had even inherited her musical voice. Did anyone notice he flirted with men more than with women?

But Edward was clever and an excellent actor. For who would suspect him, dutiful Edward, raised by a fearsome strict Amah in the household of the highly respected Mandarin Poe? He was his mother's son and, like her, appreciated pleasure. All it cost was a case or two of premium first-cut tea, which wasn't even his. His anger rose. Yes, it was his! If his mother had been First Wife, as her first-born son he would have inherited everything from his father. Everything!

Mandarin Poe still enjoyed her singing and said she was as beautiful as a nightingale, when she asked. She had once been his favorite. But he and his sons were gone all day, leaving her alone with his other two wives. All alone. She wanted to be entertained and loved. What could be so important at his tea warehouse? It practically ran itself, especially now that his sons worked.

Edward opened a small, unadorned wooden chest, drew out two pipes, and prepared the drug. She loosened her robes and arranged them so her naked body appeared to be the center of a flower. Her skin glowed like an exposed pearl when she leaned back upon the silk coverlet of her bed. She held out one creamy arm for the gift he presented. By the time the afternoon sun dipped modestly below the garden walls, she felt once again that she was the girlish flower of her dreams.

∾

*M*andarin Poe lifted his arms and flexed his shoulders, relishing the cold bite of winter. From this tiled tower he had an expansive view of Shanghai's port, warehouses, and city. Crucial to Shanghai's power, the Huangpu was easily navigated except for the unpredictable ever-changing mud-banks that ensnared experienced seamen. Gigantic merchant junks arrived from as far away as Singapore and Malaysia. A network of rivers traversed by natural canals across the lush plain provided easy travel to every major city from Peking to Canton and beyond.

Bundled in furs that revealed only his stern dark eyes, he came to this spot daily, even when it snowed, to check the pulse of the overland and canal routes. He could see no movement during winter, but the invigorating wind and rain carried the scent of the inland mountains where the tea shrubs were now resting. Come spring, thousands of coolies would stream into Shanghai laden with tea and return to the interior with supplies—wood, hemp, and iron. Like armies of ants, lines of coolies headed in all directions ensured the prosperity of the Poe clan and China. It was a delicate balance they had weathered for twenty-seven generations.

"Baba!"

Mandarin Poe's eyes brightened when his Sixth Son, equally bundled in furs, approached up the slate-covered walkway. Of all his sons, John strained the boundaries of Confucian ethics, just like his mother and little sister. But Mandarin Poe indulged Mei and her children, for they were his youngest family, gifts of his mellow years. And when his headstrong Third Wife Mei decided to stay in Soochow with their daughter Jadelin until the New Year, he agreed although their absence left an abyss in his heart. He often thought that each wife reflected his life at that point in time. His First Wife was his duty, his Second Wife his impulse, and the Third, his heart.

"My youngest son. Has our visitor arrived?"

John's breath misted white and his cheeks were flushed like ripe peaches. "Yes," he bowed. When he straightened, he looked into his father's face, into the depth of ancestral knowledge honed by twenty-seven generations. His father exuded the energy of a vigorous, husky man with thick eyebrows and rough, tanned skin. His fingers were short, his palms broad. Working hands, he called them. At sixty-five he could still sling an eighty-pound tea chest onto his inspection table in one easy motion.

"We want to know his plans, approximately how long he intends to stay in Shanghai, where he will go afterwards, and what he expects to accomplish. You've arranged his interpreter?" Mandarin Poe walked with his son through the vast expanse of wings, one for each of his wives and sons. He had built sitting rooms that musicians filled with music and libraries where tutors educated his children. A courtyard on the far side of a large garden often resounded with the sound of his sons, youngest wife, and daughter practicing the martial arts of his mentor,

Grand Master Ping, a skill that Poe considered essential for developing the mind and body. His First Wife's wing was silent, as usual. She was a stately woman who relished peace while she embroidered her tapestries. She gifted all the women in his household with intricate embroideries for their gowns and shoes. His Second Wife had stormed out in the middle of lunch. No one dared disturb her when she was in her tempestuous moods.

"Cousin Li, master of dialects, will accompany him."

"Excellent," the mandarin intoned. Ten years older than John, Li's work as a trader gave him the maturity and experience to monitor the Scot.

Two guards in bear furs silently opened the double moon gate at their approach. Father and son walked past the iced over waterfalls and fish ponds, through passages decorated with panels of inlaid mother of pearl and ivory, and emerged in a sitting room. They handed their sable coats to the servant, who announced that their guest had arrived.

An hour later Fortune left, knowing nothing that he hadn't already known about Shanghai. Mandarin Poe had watched him with a penetrating gaze that was not unkind, but not welcoming. He was especially displeased when Robert Fortune said he had met his family and offered to give his daughter English lessons when she returned to Shanghai.

Mandarin Poe glared at John. He was glad Mei and Jadelin were exiled in Soochow.

∾

That night, when the moon was high overhead and the streets empty, cousin Li knocked on the heavy doors of the Poe estate. Bushy-eyed guards led him directly to Mandarin Poe's study, a quiet retreat with thick carpets and candle-lit lanterns. Li grinned when he saw John and his father. He bowed. "I have Fortune's latest report. Did you have a good visit with him?" He nodded as they described their meeting with the plant collector. "This letter will reveal what he did not want you to know." He read it to them.

Confidential Report to the Royal Horticultural Society
Shanghai, January 1844
Honorable Sirs;

It is impossible to fulfill your requests within the one-year term of my contract. Distances in China are far. I do not trust my servants to procure the plants I request unless I see for myself the color and quality of the flowers. I humbly request that you extend my contract for one more year in China.

The black-tea districts we seek are not in this area. It's too flat, too well irrigated. The rich alluvial plain of Shanghai resembles a vast, cultivated garden with the nearest hills thirty miles away. The soil is rich, deep loam and produces heavy crops of wheat, barley, rice, and cotton, plus immense quantities of green vegetables such as cabbages, turnips, yams, carrots, eggplants, and cucumbers. As an agricultural area, the plain of Shanghai is by far the richest I have seen and is perhaps unequalled by any in the world.

I sent my first shipment of plants to England in twelve Ward cases, duplicated and divided among three different ships for safety. Expect to receive chrysanthemums, the unusual dwarfed trees from Ningpo, azaleas, maidenhair trees from Shanghai, tree peonies from northern China, and seeds from my first season.

After a few months here I feel qualified to state that opium smoking is not detrimental. I have seen trade conducted by highly respectable opium-smokers, who are known and esteemed merchants. The opinion of all intelligent Westerners is that importation of opium ought to be legalized. China merely has to add a small duty, which would reduce smuggling and bring revenue to the Chinese treasury. True, opium used in excess has pernicious effects upon one's constitution and morals. But it's not as bad as portrayed in England. It's like having a drink; a person imbibing is perfectly able to function. Mr. Alistair Mackenzie, aide to Captain Balfour of Shanghai, assures me that opium from Bengal, Patna, and Benares, is always of good quality and pure. I believe the number of people who use it to excess has been very much exaggerated. Opium is legal in England as laudanum, a remedy for diarrhea. My fellows here consider opium to be less harmful than alcohol.

I now head south to Canton.

I look forward to your approval of my request to stay in China for another year. I wish to fulfill your requests and follow some leads to the black-tea districts of China.

    Respectfully,

    Robert Fortune

Mandarin Poe paced the thick Tianjian carpets with a deepening frown, his fists gripped. "He told us nothing about his intention to stay another year! He said nothing about seeking tea plants! He's a common thief," he growled. "A deceitful liar. We cannot trust anything he says." He turned to Li and John and threw up his hands in exasperation. "With British gunboats and armies in our ports we're powerless to stop him. If he is killed or disappears the British will kill one hundred Chinese in retaliation. The British are paying him to break our laws. They know China courts cannot try Englishmen. The British know he can operate with impunity because of those Treaties the Emperor had to sign to stop bloodshed and destruction."

"He rails to his people that the Chinese are ignorant and uncivilized. But I can make his life miserable, perhaps impossible to continue in China," offered Li. He nodded to the assent in their eyes.

Seven

THE TEA ROOM

"Jadelin, lower!" Grand Master Ping rapped her leg with a thin bamboo staff. "Here!" His staff tapped her back. "Your body isn't centered. You have no energy. Again!" He rapped her shoulders. Hard.

Jadelin landed awkwardly on her side when her opponent tossed her. She winced, rolled to her feet, deflected the next blow, faked a turn, and vanquished her challenger with a strategically aimed foot. She bowed to her partner, a boy her age but a head taller, and limped to her place among students who sat in order by skill and rank along the perimeter of the great practice hall.

She sent her mother a pained look to apologize for her pitiful performance. Mei showed no favoritism, but the smile in her eyes reassured her daughter.

Jadelin ached. Every muscle, every bone, throbbed. Their regimen of meditation at dawn, breakfast preparation in the kitchen, then morning practice until the sun was straight up in the sky tapped all her reserves. After afternoon studies and a light evening meal, most of her classmates curled up for the night in soft cotton quilts that smelled of the sun. She was tougher now. Blindfolded, she could fend off two attackers. She did worse without the blindfold. And when that happened, her grandfather scolded, "You think too much. Trust yourself."

Tonight after her bath, she wrapped herself in her warmest robe and walked out to the balcony off Grand Master Ping's teapot room. She leaned over the railing to inhale the mélange of scents captured in the evening breeze. No one was allowed onto this private veranda overlooking the canal unless specifically invited. Jadelin returned to the tearoom and built a fire to boil water. She lit a single beeswax candle that flickered in the winter chill that suffused the air and retrieved her silkworm teapot, wiping it with the sleeve of her quilted robe. She sensed the presence of another and turned quickly. "Mow Bowli," she whispered in surprise.

"May I join you?" Fresh-scrubbed from his bath, he was wrapped in a quilted gown that glowed amber in the candlelight.

She felt the heat rise from her toes, through her belly, and redden her cheeks. "We shouldn't be here," she answered, suddenly shy.

"Then we trespass together." From a top shelf he lifted a tall Yixing teapot, dark brown with wavy golden triangles, and placed it next to hers. "This teapot was my father's farewell gift when I first came here. Whenever I use it, I think of him and my brothers." Sadness flickered across his face. "I miss them, as we all miss our families. When the time comes, I'll miss you."

Jadelin looked down at her shaking hands. "I'll tell grandfather I wish to stay here forever."

"No, we all move on." His voice was meltingly low. "Here we learn and center our ch'i. But we live in the world outside these walls. Grand Master Ping said you must leave by the Lunar New Year." He reached into his robe and drew out a packet of tea he and his brothers had cultivated and prepared with their own hands. "Let's not think of the uncertainty of time." The fragrant tea leaves fell lightly in their pots. He covered them with boiled water. "Come, let us enjoy our tea outside." He picked up both pots and two teacups.

She pulled her robe tight against the chill as she followed him out to the moonlit water and joined him at a low table where the night air was heavy with the scent of winter. Lanterns twinkled along the canal. Their flicker reflected in the still waters.

"While we're waiting for the tea to steep, I brought this salve for your shoulder." Bowli reached in his robe and drew out a small tin. "It will relax that muscle you twisted."

"I didn't think anyone noticed." She loosened her robe and gasped sharply when the cold air hit her bare shoulder. Mow Bowli's fingers were warm against her skin. He had a slow, expert touch. The salve, tangy with sandalwood and eucalyptus oils, soothed and relaxed, just as he had promised.

"I notice everything about you." His voice was low and calm.

He's a fellow student, she reminded herself. He's just being kind. Yet she saw how his eyes drew her in, inhaled all of her with a force she could not resist. She shivered. Instinctively, he covered her bare shoulders with his large hands and sent the heat of his body through hers. She leaned her head back and gasped at the surge of warmth. She lifted her lips to his ears. "Bowli, hold me."

"Jadelin," he whispered. He pulled her robe up around her neck so she was completely covered and wrapped his arms around her.

She leaned against his chest and felt the solidity of his body, his racing heart. She snuggled close, inhaling the scent of him. "I don't want to think of leaving you." She looked up at his face, now lit by moonlight and stars. "Gung Gung said you are here only through winter."

His voice was husky. "This is the quiet time for my family's business. I must return before the spring harvest. You, too, must depart."

"And then? Shanghai is far away. I'll never see you again." She nestled further in his arms. "Promise you'll find me." She lifted her right hand to his cheek and held it there. When he kissed her palm she parted her lips in pleasure. Her voice was throaty. "Do that again." He kissed her palm and fingers until she could no longer breathe. She lifted her face to his. His eyes closed, and he kissed the lips she offered.

∾

lashy red banners with auspicious sayings in gold fluttered throughout the market the week before the upcoming Lunar New Year, which heralded the Year of the Dragon. Shopkeepers crowded their displays with budding quince, camellias, cockscombs, and magnolias. But Grand Master Ping and Mei hunted the best narcissus bulbs. "See this shape?" Mei handed a particularly grotesque bulb to her daughter.

Jadelin twisted the lumpy mass in her hand and inspected it from all angles. "But it's crooked and one-sided," she protested.

"Gung Gung will show you how to carve it. When it swells and blossoms, the bulb will look like a crab claw. It's an art." Mei laughed, exulted by the infectious joy of the upcoming New Year Celebration. Her husband had written that the Emperor's army had forgotten all about her daughter and were long gone. The Emperor's court was fighting Britain's demand to double the amount of opium they could import to China. Now they could return home, home to Shanghai.

Jadelin's heart was heavy. Mow Bowli had extended his stay until after Chinese New Year, too. And then? She shook her head. She wouldn't think about the future. She would remain in the present and enjoy each moment with him now.

∾

adelin bent her head over her cup as if she were engrossed in inhaling the delicate scent that swirled from her teacup. When she finally met Mow Bowli's eyes, she blinked back tears. "My heart aches with a thousand splinters." She already felt the pain of missing him.

"Time is never ending. Every minute we've shared is forever in our soul." He placed his fingers over her heart. "I will always be here." She covered his hands with hers. He kissed her fingers and placed them over his heart. "You are always here with me."

She wiped her tears with the sleeve of her quilted robe and snuggled closer to him in the teapot room that had become their haunt now that winter storms deluged the veranda where they used to watch the stars reflected on the water. On these evenings, they cuddled under a cotton quilt, their fingers wrapped around their steaming teapots. They talked for hours, often over a text or painting borrowed from the Grand Master's library, until sleep tore them apart to dream in their separate rooms.

Grand Master Ping entered and took down a teapot shaped like a ripe peach, the Peach of Immortality. "My children," he greeted them as if he had been expected. Jadelin and Mow Bowli immediately stood up. Their eyes widened with guilt. The tearoom was off-limits unless Grand Master Ping was in attendance.

"Gung Gung." Jadelin bowed, cleared her throat, and stared down at the painting of Guilin's misty crags in her hands.

"Good evening, Grand Master," Bowli greeted him with a deep bow.

Ping, bundled in an indigo robe that had seen many winters, smelled of sandalwood soap and eucalyptus. "I felt like joining you tonight. I hope you don't mind the intrusion of an old man." He looked around the room with a nostalgic sigh. "I don't blame you for choosing this as your special spot. This room has the unique power to soothe the soul." He had always known about their evening trysts. "For many decades I came here at night to search for answers." He took a pinch of tea from Mow Bowli's packet on the table and added boiled water to his teapot. "I shall miss your tea, Mow Bowli," he sighed, easing himself onto his favorite padded high back chair. He smiled kindly. "But your tea shrubs are in bud. Your brothers pace the processing rooms ready to harvest their first pick." He poured the steeped tea into his cup and savored its essence. "Your father, Jadelin, is also anxious for your return. He writes, 'Where is my precious daughter? The halls are quiet without her running footsteps. Her brothers are bored. They have no one to tease.'"

"I want to stay here with you forever, Gung Gung. Mow Bowli will come every winter to keep me company." Her eyes gleamed with determination. "You will miss your favorite granddaughter too much to let her leave your side." She clutched Bowli's hands.

"True, my child. But Benjamin arrives tomorrow. And your parents are choosing your husband."

No! Jadelin closed her eyes and wished with all her heart for time to stop.

Eight

Robert Fortune Heads North

CANTON

$\mathcal{L}$i fingered one of the thick English envelopes that the extraordinarily cautious Robert Fortune had sealed with wax and handed him that morning. He bent over one of the aromatic lilies in the Fa-Tee Gardens in Canton and inhaled the heady perfume of the flower's magenta and white stripped petals. When he heard the light footsteps behind him, he tipped his head to the left. "*Ah Moi*, littlest sister?" he whispered under his breath.

"Your Westerner is in the next aisle examining pink peonies," she answered in a voice as soft as a breeze in the grass. "His pattern is to examine every petal, the leaves, and the stems before he draws them." Fetching in a yellow tunic and trousers edged with red bias, she drew approving glances from the other connoisseurs in the flower garden. She looked back at her amah, an older woman who followed two steps behind holding the hands of her handsomely dressed sons, age five and seven.

Li reached into his tunic and slipped out one of Fortune's letters. She quickly slid it into a pocket sewn inside her tunic. She laughed quietly. "I must walk very straight so it won't be seen. Why is his paper so stiff?"

"They are odd people, the English. Almost every day the Englishman writes a letter. He makes two copies which I must mail by two different ways."

The jade charms dangling from the elaborate rolls of her black hair chimed as she shook her head and widened her eyes in disbelief of his eccentricity. "Uncle Poe will be happy to read this." She patted the letter and straightened. "Oh! Your man turned around to look for you. Travel safe. I'll see you in a couple of days to get the next. I'll await your message." She held out her hands to her two sons, and walked slowly away admiring the flowers as she headed towards the exit followed by her amah.

To the Royal Horticultural Society, London
February 1844
From Robert Fortune

I am now in Canton, one of the richest and most important cities in the Celestial Empire. At the mouth of the Canton River, jewel-like islands of yellow, green, and gray rise from the turquoise sea. I imagined simple people live contented on these remote islands, typified by picturesque huts, rice fields, and perfectly carved bays, in the middle of seas rich with fish. But my new translator, Li, told me the islands are inhabited by pirates who target small vessels with valuable cargo and commit acts of unchristian cruelty.

We entered the river through the impressive Bocca Tigris, the Tiger's Mouth, which is guarded by the ruins of once-mighty forts and batteries we destroyed during the Opium War. The river widens to a view of rice fields framed by mountains. Cultivated banana trees line the embankment. Sugar-cane fields come into view, then fruit trees: mango, guava, wangpee, lychee, longan, oranges, and pomelos. Banyan trees with long aerial roots, fig trees, water pine, bamboo, and willows line the banks. I found a stunning cypress with thick branches that grows straight out from the trunk before dropping with grace and elegance. It fondly reminds me of death and eternal rest. It's an excellent companion to the weeping willow that I have already collected to embellish our cemeteries and churchyards in England.

Canton's rivers teem with thousands of boats. The largest vessels are arranged in rows like streets, which are coursed by merchant vessels, ferry boats to Hong Kong and Macao, and massive sea-going junks. The thousands of families who live on the river cultivate flourishing gardens on their sterns. A layer of incense hangs over the water from their little joss houses.

I saw the famed Fa-Tee Gardens near Canton, the 'Flowery Land,' the source of many fine plants now in England. In 1819, the survival rate of plants collected by Kew Gardens from Fa-Tee Gardens was one out of every thousand plants, which brought the final cost of each plant to three hundred pounds apiece. I intend to reduce that rate with the use of the Ward cases that encase the plants in a pristine, airtight environment during shipment.

As we approached Fa-Tee Gardens, the fragrance of oleander and magnolia suffused the air. Within, families in brilliant silks, from bent white-haired elders, to babes in the arms of their amahs, strolled the pathways to admire the colorful blossoms. The Chinese cultivate dwarfed orange plants, including the mandarin orange and kumquat. The splendid red, white, and purple azaleas that grow wild in the hills of Ningpo flourish here. These plants are arguably superior to any in the gardens of the Horticultural Society at Chiswick. The impressive tree peonies from northern China are in full bloom. The Chinese revere the most unusual fruit I've seen -- a citrus in the shape of a hand.

There is one unscrupulous person to avoid. All the Americans buy their seeds from one of the old gardeners here who speaks English very well. But his seeds fail to sprout. The British officers tell me that Old Chun boils the seeds so enterprising propagators in England or America will not spoil his trade. Others think he poisons them so that they are dead by the time they are planted. I have advised all my friends in China not to buy Old Chun's seeds.

The Chinese are celebrating their New Year, which is based on their lunar calendar. Firecrackers explode everywhere and fireworks light the night.

I am beginning to develop a high opinion of the Chinese. I am inclined to trust the people of Canton as much as I do the people of the north.

Botanists have already ransacked the south, so I head north for the collecting season.

Respectfully,

Robert Fortune

Nine

TEA LESSONS

SHANGHAI

"It's time." Big Amah put down her teacup. When she stood up she blocked all the light that had been streaming in from the doors open to the garden. "Now," she insisted.

Ignoring her amah's meaty hand clamped on her shoulder, Jadelin leaned forward against the table that separated her from her new tutor. "Isn't that right?" She enunciated, "Thursday, Friday, Saturday. Did I get your 'r' sound right that time? Don't I learn quickly?"

Robert Fortune sat mesmerized, as if all the words in his head had melted away in her presence. She had imitated the Scottish rolling 'r' of his burr perfectly. If he closed his eyes, she could be any cultured woman in Scotland. Her colorful silk gown accentuated the femininity of her slim figure. He inhaled her light scent, of silk and flowers, each time she moved. Her lilting eyes enchanted him, and she looked at him as if he were the only person in the world. He felt heat build in his chest and flush his face.

"Mr. Fortune, would an Englishman understand me?" Jadelin tapped the table impatiently. "Are you awake?" She peered up at pale gray eyes rimmed by almost invisible lashes. It was as if she was looking right through his head to the clouds in the sky. She wondered why Westerners were called 'red-haired' when their hair also grew in shades of black, brown, yellow and white. They were curious people, so abrupt and colorless, who dressed in black from their hats to their shoes.

"I was concentrating on your voice," he stammered. "Very good. Clear and understandable. Excellent progress." He lowered his voice so only she could hear. "I brought you a present." All morning he had waited for the right moment. With Big Amah looming over them he had to act fast.

"What did you bring me?" Jadelin clapped her hands. She flushed, suddenly embarrassed. What could an awkward barbarian think she needed or wanted?

Tentatively, he handed her a mahogany box with pounded brass fittings from the bag that normally held his magnifying glass, spade, knife, notebook, and writing tools. "Something small, to help with the English lessons," he explained. He had inspected every shop between Shanghai and Canton for the perfects gifts to please her. His heart beat faster as she unlatched the clasp and lifted the lid.

"What delicate ivory animals. See, Big Amah." She would never have thought he would select such intricately carved miniatures. "These are the animals of the Chinese zodiac. Here's the rat—that's me. The dog—my brother John and Baba. My mother is a boar." She lifted each carving no bigger than her thumb, each nested in its fitted compartment lined with silk. "They look like they could come alive in my palm. What animal are you?"

He shrugged. "We do not follow the Chinese zodiac in England." He saw a disbelieving frown crinkle her smooth forehead. Her every expression reminded him of how lonely his life had been up to now. "Next time, you can explain each wee animal of the zodiac to me in English. I will then ask you questions. That way, we can practice conversation."

"What a practical method."

"I am happy to make our lessons interesting." He thought for a minute. "I could lend you a book to read." He held out his worn Bible. Why did time pass so quickly? Such petal-lovely skin, and eyes as deep as polished lacquer. How lovely she would look, her arm crooked in his as they walked the pathways in Kew Gardens. How exotic, people would exclaim as they watched this bonnie Chinese woman at the side of Robert Fortune. He was sure that when he returned to England, the Society would promote him from hothouse supervisor to a better position that paid well. Then he could take her home, the most beautiful flower in his collection.

"What's that?" demanded Big Amah. She squared her broad shoulders and plucked the book from Fortune's grasp. She flipped through the pages. "Ah, the picture of the *gweilo* god." She pointed at the illustration on the frontispiece with a lilac scented forefinger. She glared down at him when she handed him his book. She scolded her charge, "Your father forbids you to read such barbaric rubbish. Speaking practice is enough. Come." Her booming voice filled the exquisite study pavilion encased in dark woods, thick wool carpets, and dainty candle-lit lanterns. She snapped her fingers, and a servant appeared to escort Fortune to the exit.

"But," he sputtered. He clasped the Bible in his hands. She needed to know his God. "I shall return without fail," he called as Big Amah pushed him out the room.

"Come now, Jadelin," soothed Big Amah with a warmth Fortune would never see. "Time for play is over. Your Mama waits for you in her sitting room. Time to prepare for the biggest change in your life."

Mei motioned her daughter into the chair on the opposite side of the small tea table and motioned her maid to bring the lacquer box that contained her teas. "Are you ready to learn about tea now?" she asked. "You will marry into a family who will expect you to be versed in all aspects of your legacy." Despite the budding trees and trilling song birds that heralded spring, each afternoon she sequestered Jadelin in her private rooms to impart the knowledge tutors could not teach. Her daughter would marry into a home which, like her own, included many generations and many families. She needed to be skilled in how to run a household and maneuver family politics.

She tipped her head and smiled as she studied her daughter. Their time at Grand Master Ping's had strengthened and developed her body. Daily practice had given her a good awareness of movement and increased her grace. At times she could move noiselessly between layers of air, so silent that if one wasn't watching, she suddenly appeared in a spot she had not been a moment before.

Today Jadelin learned to judge the three levels of heated water by sound, starting with the low humming sound, yin-yang or 'baby water,' to the second way by watching the steam, to the third way which involved watching the bubbles in the water. The green and white teas could be brewed only by 'fish-eye water' when the larger bubbles replaced the continuous stream of small bubbles. 'Old man water' bubbled viciously and was too hot.

Mandarin Poe strode in just as the afternoon sun, dropping below the edge of the courtyard, cooled the air and cast Mei's pavilion in shadows. Her maid had lit twenty more candles so the room seemed to brighten the minute he appeared.

"Mandarin Poe, please join us for tea." Mei stood, hands clasped. It seemed all the light in the room glowed from her face to his.

Without hesitation Jadelin selected a porcelain teapot, thin as a leaf with a pattern of bamboo, and three matching cups. She inspected the boiling water and rinsed the pot and cups before pouring the hot water over the leaves with a gentle stream. Slowly, the tea unfolded in the agony of the leaves releasing the scent of jasmines.

"How was your English lesson with the barbarian?" her father asked. The tired eyes in his care-worn face had watched every move he made. He would never have consented except that during the New Year celebrations, Li brought word that Fortune wanted to pay his respects to Mandarin Poe. Unfortunately, Fortune arrived at the Poe estate at the same time Jadelin and Mei arrived from Soochow. He hated to disappoint his daughter's only request on the first day she arrived. And he gave in, certain that Jadelin would tire after one or two lessons with the unlikeable *bak gwei*.

"I had difficulty understanding his speech pattern at first but then I haven't had much exposure to native English speakers. Here are the ivory animals he gave me for our next conversation practice. It's good for me to hear different accents to develop my proficiency." Jadelin hoped he noticed how smoothly she paced her movements so the act of serving tea became a meditation, a prayer.

"You will have no need for such skills when you marry."

"I did well, though." She had heard her father's footsteps in the next room. And she disagreed with him. For over two thousand years, Chinese traders led caravans through desert oceans of the Silk Road and braved treacherous seas. In the marketplace she heard a mélange of languages and saw the most interesting faces drawn to the energy and prosperity of Shanghai's port.

Her father nodded. "I have difficulty understanding him but I was satisfied to see how you listened and mimicked his words. I was pleased to see the barbarian didn't lose his dour expression. Big Amah made sure of that."

"Baba!" Jadelin swallowed her laugh. "China is changing. I must be prepared for the future. You taught us that if we understand another person's language, we understand how they think."

"The Poes have survived for twenty-seven generations." His voice trailed off and he looked at Mei with an expression that made her gasp. He shook his head as if he was reminding himself to enjoy this moment with his youngest wife and daughter. He took the teacup his daughter offered and cupped it within his callused lands. "Tea is your legacy, Jadelin, our family legacy. Tea enhances our ch'i, the flow of energy through our minds and bodies. To disturb one leaves the other vulnerable to external influences. Mental tensions can produce internal energy imbalances and lead to physical disorders. That is why a person needs to be inwardly warm and relaxed to remain healthy." He inhaled. "Tea is a positive source of energy. These properties infuse into the water and refresh the mind."

He had repeated these same words to his wives, sons, and their families, each time with a passionate spark in his eyes. Today his words were too fervent. His hands shook when he put down his teacup. When he leaned back in his chair and looked up, the cloud returned to his face.

"Jadelin, it has been a long day of lessons for you. Why don't you rest now?" Mei touched her daughter's cheek. "You did very well."

Poe walked to the far corner of the room and opened an armoire. "You must have grown while in Soochow. Let's see if I need to adjust your shoes."

His daughter blushed. "I didn't want to bother you, Baba. You're so busy."

"Working with my hands is a good break and a chance to spend time with you." He handed her two forms he had customized from her last fitting. She slipped them on. With a practiced touch he felt its fit. "Too tight here?" He made notations on the fabric. "How's the base support? Do you feel balanced?" She walked across the room and back. After they had made the proper adjustments, Mandarin Poe leaned back. "Running barefoot in Soochow has developed good muscles in your feet and ankles."

"I feel strong, Baba."

"Good. Now, off you go to study your lessons." He looked up as Big Amah loomed in the doorway as if summoned by an invisible bell.

"She's become a young woman. Soon she will leave the house of Poe." Mandarin Poe's voice was both sad and proud as he watched his youngest daughter leave. She had grown tall and lithe, like her mother.

"We must find a young man who will protect her as you did me. It will be difficult." Mei motioned her maid to clear away the pots, cups, and canisters of tea. "From the moment she arrived in Soochow my father studied her movements. He observed the elegant carriage of her head and how she quickly she turns at the flutter of a bird, the fall of a leaf, the change of others' expressions. The grace of her hands disguises their power."

Jadelin stood under the frozen willow, as still as the hawk. She had stretched her hearing to embrace her parents' voices and the sadness that permeated their souls. She clasped her hands and stilled her heart so she would not miss a word.

"Then my heart can rest knowing she is able to protect herself, mentally and physically." Poe took out his carving tools and cork blanks. Together, they sat on the chaise overlooking the winter garden. He ran his fingers down the sweet curves of his wife's face and noted each faint line that added character and wisdom. "My dearest Mei, Benjamin returned from Soochow with a call from Grand Master Ping for all Dragons of the Mist to prepare themselves."

Mei gripped her hands together, centering her thumb in the middle of her palm to calm herself. "Will you go? Will your sons?"

He ran his thick palm across his forehead. He set out the forms and pattern for Jadelin's shoes and began carving. "I have no heart for politics or endless meetings with the British. It must end. For five thousand years we have cultivated tea, China's soul and heart." His frown deepened as he growled, "Now we must deal with the Western interlopers who, to satisfy their insatiable lust for our tea, ship millions of pounds of opium to our shores, addicting millions of our countrymen. When our Emperor refuses their drugs or destroys the opium illegally shipped to our ports they retaliate with gunboats, blazing cannons, and trigger-happy armies. They blast our coastal towns into submission. Militarily, we can't compete." The glow in his eyes dimmed as he thought of the struggles ahead. "Our future is uncertain. I am thankful Benjamin oversees everything at the hong now."

His shoulders slumped as if his words weighed as heavily as his responsibility. He focused on the Lotus Blossom shoe that emerged in his hands. "Every report from your son, who shadows the barbarian, tells me how futile our efforts are. Bit by bit, the foreigners chip away at our land and our government. They take what is ours. They glut our market with cheap cotton made by giant machines. Meanwhile, unrest seethes throughout the land. Grand Master Ping would not have called for us if he did not think it was time to take action, that all other paths have been exhausted. He has decided this is the only way to protect our culture and country."

"You can't leave us now. Nor can your sons." Only the finest warriors were initiated into the Dragons of the Mist, an ancient secret society of scholar warriors sworn to protect truth and justice during tumultuous times. Greatly admired, invisible to all, the legendary Dragons of the Mist brought justice to the wronged and fear to the corrupt.

"I would not leave without you." He put down his tools and clasped her hands to his. He met her gaze and held her fingers to his lips.

"Jadelin isn't married yet. No, not until she's protected would I think of leaving. But I'll accompany you when the time comes." Her lips brushed his ears. "We have a wedding to look forward to soon. Let that lighten your heart, my love."

Hidden by shadows behind the willow, Jadelin shivered with apprehension. Her grandfather had alerted the Dragons of the Mist. That would prompt her mother to get her married off, soon. Who among the ranking mandarin families would she choose? The Tai and Huang sons had come with their fathers to welcome her home, as had dozens of other sons of the highest-ranking families. She knew these clans were interested in a powerful alliance. Who was the most powerful?

Surely Mama had seen in Soochow how close she and Mow Bowli had grown. Her grandfather and mother praised his skill, intelligence, and character and he was a master in his own right. But he was not from a ranking mandarin family, even though they grew and produced one of the finest teas in far away Longjing mountains. Her heart panicked when she thought she might never see him again. She put her hand on her chest. "Mow Bowli," she whispered into the wind. "Please, come for me."

❦

*A*s soon as Jadelin heard the quickening drums, she ran up the tower to watch the bridal procession. Today climaxed months of negotiations and gifts. Nested baskets of snowy white buns had arrived from the bride's house, which the groom's house returned filled with black bean pastries decorated with auspicious words. Messengers bearing silk, tea, and gold traversed the path between the homes of the bride and groom until all the rituals had been satisfied.

A parade of musicians, queues bouncing to the rhythm of their cymbals, filled the streets. In the center of the procession, four men in blue tunics carried a red sedan chair fringed with swaying gold tassels. Little children pointed in awe. The older, wrinkled elders sighed and waved. Many followed the brightly dressed guests who walked or rode behind the palanquin. Even Robert Fortune, Jadelin saw, had followed the procession through town and was now craning his neck and scribbling in his notebook.

The Scot had been allowed another English practice session under the searing supervision of Big Amah. He had concluded the lesson by giving her gifts for their next lesson: a porcelain vase in the meiping shape painted with gold carp swimming in a pond with lotus, and a painted scroll of travelers on a mountainous trail that wound through waterfalls and craggy cliffs wrapped in mists. She explained that the jade he handed her was made to hold water so a scholar could wash his brush and that it was shaped like a Buddha's-hand citron, a real fruit that he could find in the market. He asked many questions, and she was pleased that she could answer, sometimes haltingly as she searched her growing English vocabulary. He was careful in his correction of her pronunciation and word usage. In this way, Jadelin realized that the seemingly bumbling Westerner had an eye for color and fine Chinese art.

But today, John married Flora, eldest daughter of one of Shanghai's great tea hongs within the great walls of the Poe estate. The bride was fourteen and educated by tutors from Soochow, her mother's ancestral home. In fact, Widow Tung had been saving this bride, her fourth cousin twice removed, for such an alliance.

During the great wedding banquet Widow Tung approached Mei. "Third Wife of Poe," whispered the wizened woman. Her voice was steady, honest, and serious. "Your daughter will be sixteen next year, too old for marriage."

Although Jadelin had been chatting with her Poe cousins on the other side of the room, she tuned her ears to the matchmaker's voice. She had to get back to Soochow. Mow Bowli had promised to return next winter.

Mei leaned close to Widow Tung's wrinkled earlobe that sagged with a bi-shaped jade set in pure gold. "We're willing to listen to a good proposal. But our youngest daughter has qualities that only an exceptional family will appreciate. Her husband must be of matching stature with a kind heart." And then there was the important matter of her unbound feet, which she could not mention, not even to Widow Tung.

Widow Tung looked over her shoulder and pierced Jadelin with a wrinkled glare. She turned back to Mei. "Jadelin has a soft beauty. She will bring honor to your household. You have turned down all previous proposals." She lowered her voice to a soothing tone and cupped her hand around her lips. "I heard the Emperor sent his army for her last fall. It's best to marry her off before the Emperor learns she is not dead, as your husband told them." She gestured with a finger across her throat.

The matchmaker waved a soft hand bejeweled by grateful families and spoke in a melodious voice. She was known for her honesty and, since she was literate, was able to make the most discrete inquiries into family backgrounds. "I have heard from the Mow family in the West Lake district near Hangchow. Their Third Son stands as straight as a pine and over a head taller than your husband." Widow Tung stared kindly in Mei's eyes. "I'm surprised that a non-mandarin family would want you to consider their proposal for your daughter. But Grand Master Ping himself suggested it. And West Lake is far from the Emperor's eyes."

Ten

ROBERT FORTUNE PLANS HIS
NEXT ADVENTURE

SHANGHAI

*G*iven the opportunity, a Chinese would hop on a horse, cart, carriage, or boat. Not the Englishman. He walked everywhere clutching his umbrella, even if there wasn't a cloud in the sky. Every day he hiked at least ten hours through the countryside loading flowering plants into the collection boxes strapped to Li's back. He stopped for neither noodles nor tea.

The intricate network of canals that irrigated the bucolic Shanghai plains had initially sent Fortune into rhapsodic delight. Now they turned into the barbarian's curse. No matter which path, which trails, which direction Fortune turned, just before he got to his destination a canal perversely crossed his path. He was tired of trails that doubled-back across fields and circuitous routes to destinations he could see but not reach. Bridges always shimmered just over the next field. Flies and biting things buzzed his eyes and flew up his nose. His clothes were drenched in sweat and dirt caked his shoes.

On one foray from Shanghai, the sun had dropped to a gigantic orange orb above the horizon when they saw the gates of the city. When night fell, they would be enveloped in impenetrable darkness, so Fortune picked up his pace. A mile before they reached the city gate they encountered an intersecting canal. Fortune threw up his hands and shouted, "Why? Why? I do not understand these canals." He stomped in frustration. "Is there no system? No logic in how they're laid out?"

"The sun has set." Li pointed at the last glow of the disappearing orb. "Since there is no bridge within sight we should sleep here. The nights are so dark we won't see a canal until we fall in."

Every time Fortune thought he had China figured out, an obstacle appeared, like this canal in the middle of a field. He didn't want to sleep here where clouds of bugs swarmed the typically cold nights. "Wait, I hear a small boat." He leaned over the water. "Yes, I hear the grunts of their tracker on our side of the canal. Quick," he ordered Li. "Ask the men on the boat to come closer and help us across the canal."

Li cupped his hands around his mouth. "Hello there! My master and I are travelers stranded across the canal from the Shanghai city gate. Please, take us across. We are far from home."

The boatman leaned forward in the waning light to verify that the travelers were not armed or dangerous. "I am coming," he answered in the code of the canal men who readily aided fellow travelers. He was within touching distance when he screamed, "Ai-ya! A foreign devil, a red beard!" The crew shouted to their tracker who dove into the water and scrambled aboard while the oarsman sculled swiftly to the middle of the canal.

Fortune raised his umbrella and waved his arms. "Stop! Stop I say." He ordered Li, "Quick. Tell them if they do not stop, I'll shoot them all. I'll blast them to smithereens." When Li hesitated, Fortune hoisted his gun in the air.

Li cupped his hands and bellowed in Shanghainese, "This red-bearded devil has a powerful gun. Come back, or he will make your children fatherless."

For a second, the boat hesitated.

Fortune lifted his gun and blasted the stars.

∾

*W*henever his calves felt they could not go one more step, Li thought of his bride of one year, pregnant with their first child, and remembered how much he missed the curve of her husky body against his. A hard worker from a family of textile merchants, she got along well with his parents with whom the couple shared a cottage. For the love of his family and their future, he tied on a wide-brimmed hat to protect his broad tan face and used his linguistic skills, an advantage of being born in a merchant family in the bustling port city of Canton, to serve the Westerner Fortune and gather any information from others about him. And whenever the Scot asked him to post his duplicate reports to England, Li made sure one of them reached the hands of Mandarin Poe.

Late last night after the *gweilo* had gone to bed, Li delivered the latest letter. The sentries quickly ushered him directly to Mandarin Poe's study where moonlight shone through the fretted windows and candlelight danced upon porcelains and jades.

Poe's hands clenched as he read. He rubbed his handsome brow and muttered. When his eyes met Li's they were both angry and sad. "Whenever British break the law their armies execute the Chinese who are with them. Do you understand how precarious your job is, Li? You are risking your life."

Li bowed. "I appreciate your concern, Uncle Poe."

"Please let me know if the funds I send to your wife and parents are sufficient. Fortune is off to another adventure."

"I am keen to see where this will lead." Li handed Poe a letter to send his wife to assure her that he was safe before he slipped into the night.

Mandarin Poe paced the gardens so late that only the sentries and the stars were awake. His servants boiled water and prepared him a cup of tea when he returned to his study and reread the letter Li had handed him earlier.

Report to the Royal Horticultural Society
From Robert Fortune, Shanghai
Honorable Sirs:

   I arrived in Shanghai on April 18, 1844 to spend three weeks to gather the flowers that bloom in northern China. These plants are safely stored in the gardens of Alistair Mackenzie, aide to Captain Balfour in Shanghai, who lives in a large house confiscated from a mandarin for our use. Mackenzie has drawn every different flower he has seen in China. His botanical drawings have assisted me greatly in documenting and gathering data on China's flora.

   China's beauty is beyond description. The air is suffused with a scent of flowers unknown to Englishmen. The land is covered with lush pines, cypresses, and junipers. The rich and fertile valleys produce tea, tobacco, and corn.

   My countrymen have created problems for the rest of us by going far up the canals into the interior and sounding the depths with bamboo in the manner of the Chinese. The Chinese, who jealously guard their country, complained to Captain Balfour that these men were trying to determine if their gunboats would go up the canals. Captain Balfour had to acknowledge the complaint. Their Chinese boatmen were executed.

   Consequently, the mandarins have decreed that boatmen can take foreigners down the river towards the sea or up the river no further than two miles above Shanghai. They are not allowed to take foreigners up the western branch of the river. We are limited to going only as far as we can go and return in twenty-four hours.

   However, I am determined to get to Soochow even though it lies far beyond my limit. In every shop in Hong Kong, in Canton, or any other city in the south, if one inquires about the price of a particularly exquisite curiosity, one is told that it comes from Soochow. If one orders anything extraordinary or elegant, it must be sent for from Soochow. This applies to paintings, carvings, embroideries, and flowers. If one admires a particularly beautiful woman, one is told that Soochow women are finer. This celebrated city must be China's earthly paradise.

   The Celestial Emperor's laws mean nothing to me.
   Respectfully,
   Robert Fortune

Eleven

EDWARD'S SECRET

SHANGHAI

*E*dward gripped his hands to quell their tremors. He glared into the accusing eyes of his wife. "What I do is none of your business," he barked. He knew she would shrink back from him, as she always did. His gut ache clawed at his insides. He had to feed his longing, his need. He grabbed her thin arms and yanked her into his study. "I told you not to interfere in my life. But you're always sneaking around, spying on me, moving my things."

"Never. You are my husband, father of our son," she implored. "But the other wives and children stare and whisper."

"You're lucky to have a place to sleep and food to eat," he growled. He flung open a carved cabinet. "Where is it? Where's my money? You know you're not allowed to touch anything in my study." He grabbed her shoulders and shook her so hard she almost passed out. He flung her to the floor

"I touch nothing. The servants know never to clean here." She covered her face with her hands so her tears wouldn't anger him, again. She thought of her three lost girls and hoped they had a better life than hers. Her husband had ordered the midwife to take them away after each was born. She begged the woman to give them to a good family. "Don't throw them in the river, please!" But the midwife shook her head and said that Edward paid well for her services. She could not jeopardize her family's income.

He pawed through his drawers and in disgust, dumped the contents on her head. She hunched against the onslaught of pens, ink stones, and carved seals raining down on her shoulders. "Liar! You're against me, just like my brothers and father. Everyone has an important role but me. The Emperor in Beijing confides to Adam, Benjamin lords it over us at the hong, Daniel collects our money, Paul parties with clients, and John disappears on secret missions for Baba. They have no idea how valuable I am." He thumped his chest.

"I believe in you, my husband." She pushed herself up, taking care to hide her bruised arms. She clung to the image of the young man she had married. In those days, Edward and his brothers sparred with Mandarin Poe and Mei every day before work. Laughter rang through the court-yards during their practice. After a cold bath and bowl of hot congee, the men rushed to work together. This sallow man scarcely resembled her handsome bridegroom. "You changed. Quit the British drug. People talk. They know."

"They know nothing!" he growled. He stepped over her huddled form and marched out the door.

~

A heavyset man with red sideburns stomped along the Bund, tapping each step with an eagle-crested cane. Masted sailing ships, British gunboats, and junks laden with goods coursed the busy water-way. He turned, thinking he heard a familiar voice among dozens of languages shouted at this international port. If anyone came close, he covered his eyes with the brim of his hat and turned his body as if he meant to look in the opposite direction. The elbows of his beefy arms thrust outwards as if to protect his sides. He stopped, checked his pocket watch, and clicked it shut with a curse.

"It's about time," he hissed when Edward sidled up to him. "I was ready to look for someone more reliable."

"You could try. But I am the only one who offers the quality worth the premium you charge your clients."

The Westerner brushed the lapels of his long wool coat. "Do not threaten me. Time is money. I have passage already booked." He handed Edward a packet. "The best on the market."

Edward looked around, and when he was satisfied no one was watching, opened the packet. He nodded.

"My porter will be at your warehouse at midnight."

"Make sure he comes to the back door. Alone."

"And you?"

"I'll personally deliver your shipment."

The Westerner narrowed his eyes in victory. He tipped his hat and returned to the British Consulate. Edward called for a rickshaw for the ride to the Poe tea hong. Benjamin would have locked up by now and all his brothers would be home with their families.

He relished the walk up to Benjamin's aerie when the warehouse was deserted. His brother's office was locked, but he could stand at the landing where he surveyed the vast space and inhaled the power of tea. He imagined it smelled like the far-away inland mountains of Longjing and Wuyi. When he was alone in the darkened warehouse, all this belonged to him. It would have been, if his mother had been his father's First Wife. For that, he would never forgive Mandarin Poe, Adam, Benjamin, and Daniel. It was their fault that he was not the first-born son.

He knew Daniel's books were locked up, too. And that he took the day's monies home with him each night where they were secure in the underground vault under Mandarin Poe's study. No matter. He had stored tonight's prize behind the standard-grade teas. Even he had the key for that storeroom. He got to work rearranging the tea cases. He worked with such care that when he walked out, everything looked as if he had never been there. He had even erased his footsteps.

He would return at midnight through a back door where he had relocated the most expensive case of premium tea. He was so pleased with himself that he sauntered through the markets looking for something pretty to amuse himself. The flickering lanterns of the open shops added to their mysterious allure.

He chose the lane of oddities where rare curiosities tempted the senses. These objets d'art had traveled to Shanghai from across the Silk Road, from the far corners of the Chinese empire, or from distant lands. He never felt the tremors and pains in his gut when he combed through these little stores stocked floor to ceiling. His perused each object and fingered those that seemed promising: oddly shaped jades of red and brown, grotesque masks, and cylindrical metals warm to the touch of seemingly no use at all except their tactile pleasure. At one stall, a cricket made of bamboo danced on the palm of a young man dressed in bright silks. Edward twisted his lips and walked on.

"Do you have anything special?" he asked a wizened merchant whose face was as wrinkled as a dried lakebed. Edward raised an eyebrow to emphasize he wanted something unusual. He never failed to be disappointed by the peculiar objects he was offered at this shop at the end of the lane. Most were erotic, worth a try once or twice before he craved something more titillating.

The old man studied his client, then nodded slowly. "I might." He motioned with his head to the back of the store. He opened a brocade-lined box of silver balls that tinkled when shaken. "From inland," he said. His fingers gestured obscenely as he demonstrated its use. "They will drive your lover wild."

A faint smile crossed Edward's face but he shook his head. "It's for my pleasure, old man." His eyes glistened. "Show me something that will drive me to ecstasy."

Twelve

THE TEMPLE OF THE HEAVENLY BOYS

TIEN-TUNG

Twenty sonorous gongs shuddered the darkness three hours before dawn. By the fifth gong Fortune was sure the luminous chants he heard was his choir in Berkwickshire calling him to prayers. He pinched his face to make sure he was awake. Where was he?

He clasped his head when he recalled he had convinced British Consul Thom and his two friends to see the fabulous Tien-Tung monastery in the green tea district near Ningpo. Like giddy schoolboys, they had plotted their illegal venture to the middle of the tea district. They knew this trip defied the Treaty the British had signed, which stated that non-Chinese were not allowed to travel beyond a day's journey from a treaty port. How they had laughed when their boat ghosted thirty-six li inland to where the famous peaks of Tien-Tung scraped the sky on both sides of a gorge so steep they could barely see the sky above.

But their bravado melted in the thunderous mountain storm that pounded their craft like a thousand Scottish drummers. The rain fell with such ferocity they could barely see three inches in front of their nose. By the time they docked it was storming so hard they could not see their hands.

"I'll get chairs and men to carry you," Li shouted over the storm. "The roads are flooded."

"No, we'll walk," insisted the parsimonious British.

"You can't," argued Li. But he knew better than to argue if they were all like the tight-fisted Fortune. He waved for porters to unload. With water rising to their chests, his men lifted their trunks to their heads and trotted off through the rain that was now a solid curtain of grey that quickly turned darker as the sun set behind the next peak.

The Consul and his friends looked down in dismay. "That's a river, not a road," squeaked Consul Thom. "Tell your man we need to be carried. Pay whatever he needs." Porters bearing bamboo mountain chairs sloshed to the rail and motioned the men to step down. Instead, the British took a flying leap directly onto the chairs perched on their backs. The coolies struggled to keep their footing in the torrent. Balancing the foreigners and cursing mightily, they plunged into the chest high waters.

Rain flooded down the narrow stone paths they ascended. Torrential waters cascaded down the cliff onto their shoulders. Higher and higher they climbed through the roaring storm. The downpour continued as the night grew dark as midnight, with no stars and moon. The porters trudged for hours until they reached the slippery steps of the Buddhist temple atop the mountain peak.

As he lay on his mat listening to the monks at prayer, he wondered what the golden-robed monks thought when they flung open their doors to strangers stinking of the sea, dripping rivers of water on their threshold like demons from the depths of night?

He stared at the stars through the open window and placed his hands on his breast. He was surprised at the effect the gongs and chants drifting in on the pre-dawn breeze had on his soul. How could he feel so moved by heathen voices? He closed his eyes and felt for a brief second how the gongs and chants inspired and soothed.

∾

*F*ortune found Li sitting cross-legged at the foot of the pagoda in the first glow of sunrise.

Li, his clothes damp with morning dew, rose to his bare feet in a single motion when the Scot approached. "You see how we arrived at Tien-Tung." He pointed out the path that curved around boulders, waterfalls, ponds of blooming lotus, and exquisite trees, all meticulously tended. "Tien-Tung is at the head of a fertile valley surrounded by hills. Last night, we ascended along the column of those Chinese pines and up those steps carved in the mountain."

"No, we went up a long, straight avenue."

"See how the path winds around the edges of two lakes on the valley floor?" Li, a broad shouldered man, indicated the mountains on either side, which rose a thousand feet from the lakes below. These were towering mountains, jagged-cliffs lush with large pines, firs, cypress, and elegantly swaying bamboo forests. "Temples are built on the peaks of the most beautiful mountains because they have excellent ch'i." With his right hand, Li swept his hand at the view of dazzling peaks, each topped by a temple. "But this is one of the most breathtaking mountains. See how the arched opening at each level of Tien-Tung's pagoda reveals bronze bells that diminish in size from the largest on the bottom to the tiniest at the top."

Li rubbed his chin as he observed how Fortune studied the never-ending ridges in the mist, and how longingly he stared at the dark bushes that grew on the lower sides of the more fertile hills. The *gweilo* was looking for something and his search made his ch'i cloudy and unsettled. He asked, "Do you know why this is called Tien-Tung, the Temple of the Heavenly Boys?"

Fortune thought what a great tale this would be when he returned to London and described his travels. He was the first Westerner to see this landscape. A true and historical tale of its origin would enhance the exoticism of his adventures.

Li took a breath to center himself into the moment. He extended his arms in the tradition of storytellers, which his family could claim for a dozen generations, and began his tale.

"Hundreds of years ago, a pious man retired from the world and came to these mountains called Tien-Tung. In those days no one ventured into this unknown land despite its reputed beauty. Here, surrounded by nature, his only companions the birds and animals, he decided to pray and meditate in solitude until it was his time to die. He was so devoted to his prayers he neglected his own needs. The gods, honored by his lifetime of kindness and devotion, felt a good man like him should not starve or freeze. Every day, little boys appeared bearing bowls of fresh water and the simple vegetarian food he, a devout Buddhist, could eat.

"Soon people heard about these miraculous daily visits of little boys. Did the boys live in the mountains? Did they come from the valleys? People watched day and night. They observed boys cheerfully clambering up the mountains. They returned with their empty bowls and disappeared into the trees. People tried to follow these boys but always lost their trail. No one could discover where they came from. And it was never the same little boys. Yet every day they appeared bearing fresh water and food.

"The fame of this sage spread far and wide throughout China. Disciples came to him to learn and follow his ways. Even the Emperor worshipped at Tien-Tung temple offering, at these very altars, incense and gifts from the Imperial workshop. This is how Tien-Tung, or the Temple of the Heavenly Boys, began. Tien means heaven. Tung means boy. When the old monk died, the little boys never returned."

∽

Fortune and Li joined the monks for the morning breakfast of rice that had been simmered overnight over a low fire until it turned silky and fragrant with herbs and vegetables. The monks gawked at the barbarian's stiff wool clothes and hat, his white skin, and pale eyes. They wondered at his strange speech and listened intently as Li translated. They had never ventured further than a few valleys from their home.

After breakfast, they set off in the brisk air through uncultivated lands where shrubs, vines, and trees grew in wild profusion. One young monk, his shaved head sweating profusely in the searing sun, insisted on carrying Fortune's plant box. Another monk tucked Fortune's collecting papers under his arms and dutifully trailed him about. The monks pointed out flowers and plants, explaining what they were as Fortune meticulously wrapped them in oiled paper.

Li said little but remembered all that he translated.

That afternoon they arrived at a valley blanketed by hundreds of low shrubs in uniform rows. Monks knelt beside them, weeding and watering.

Fortune eyed the glistening leaves. If he could crush them between his fingertips he wondered whether they'd exude the scent of tea. He leaned forward and extended his fingers.

"Ai-ya!" The tending monks leapt in front of him and motioned him away.

Li whirled and threw his opened hand before Fortune's face. "Get back. Sir, these are the temple's tea plants. You cannot touch these leaves. Your fingers are unclean."

"But I know these are tea plants."

"You cannot touch everything you see." Li shot him a murderous look. There was little he could do now that Fortune was in the midst of the tea plants. He took a deep breath and politely asked the monks a question, which they considered. He turned back to Fortune. "Since you are their honored guest they offered to pluck a few leaves from low on the branch."

A few leaves were a start. Fortune wrapped the leaves they gave him in oiled collecting papers and placed them in his plant box. He then gestured for the whole plant.

The monks glared, offended.

He bowed. He had time.

Before dawn a few days later, the droning chants of the Tien-Tung monks wafted up to Fortune's room at the top of one of the small temples. He relaxed into the chanting punctuated by distant bronze bells as his breath turned into icicles.

He was relieved that Consul Thom and his friends had returned to Ningpo after only three days. In fact, after the first day in Tien-Tung he had resented their questions. The others cared nothing about the unique flora and fauna of China. They hadn't even bothered to learn to use chopsticks. Instead, they stabbed at their food like animals. He hated their buffoonish jokes about the Chinese. He was embarrassed when they talked loudly while the monks were at prayers. He preferred the solitary challenge of adventure. For the first time in his life he had the distinction of being the first, the only one to see or experience something remarkable. And so he took his time collecting every plant, flower, and bird.

At first light, he pulled on all his woolens and followed the scent of the morning fire down to the kitchen.

Li, bundled in a thick padded tunic, sat at the well-worn table nearest a wood-burning stove crackling with warmth while monks boiled water for tea and stirred the morning rice porridge they called congee. He and a hunched pilgrim, each cradling a teacup in his hands, were reading a scroll unrolled between them.

"You're up early," Li greeted Fortune. His eyes were bright without the morning fog that still sat on the Scot's head.

"Not as early as you and the others," Fortune grumbled. He enviously eyed Li's thigh-high leather boots and fur hat, so appropriate for the mountain mornings. His companion, the old pilgrim cloaked in ragged furs from head to foot, pulled his hood close around his face to keep in the heat.

"Before dawn, the air is still and clear. Our prayers rise directly to the gods and heavens," Li responded. He turned back to the old man and lowered his head to speak in words too soft for him to overhear.

Fortune wondered if Li had joined the monks in their pre-dawn chants but his translator's broad face and dark eyes remained inscrutable.

The kitchen filled with quiet activity. Saffron robed boys carried in firewood for the great fires that roared under huge bronze pots. Others stirred the simmering congee. The air grew thicker with the smell of rice and pickled vegetables that had been stoked over the fire for hours.

Li rolled up the scroll and, nodding in thanks, handed it to the pilgrim. The hooded man, a cripple, stood with great difficulty before limping silently out with the aid of his thick gnarled staff. Li lifted the cup of tea in his hand to Fortune and gestured to the teapot in front of him. "Sit. This will heat your bones." Steam rose in a circular mist as he poured Fortune's tea into a plain teacup he plucked from another table.

Fortune settled his rump onto the bench and sniffed the pale amber in his cup. "Yesterday, the monks said the tea they offered would refresh us from our long walk. How can tea cool me one day and warm me the next?"

"Each tea has unique characteristics, like last night's tea, which usually accompanies a meal with many sauces. With its medical and digestive properties, it cleansed your palate so you could taste the distinctive flavors of each dish."

Fortune considered Li's words. "Do different tea bushes produce different teas?" Li's eyes warned him but revealed nothing. "Or are they prepared in a way that results in unique tastes?"

Li poured himself another cup of tea and sipped it slowly, savoring its nuances. "The Emperor has forbidden Westerners from venturing into these lands where tea is grown or produced. You know you should not be here. Nor should you ask those questions."

Fortune snorted. "I have the leaves."

"Leaves teach you nothing." Li didn't take his eyes off him as he put down his teacup. Showing restraint, the translator bowed to the monks and walked out.

Fortune pondered alone in the kitchen amidst the hubbub of the cooks and monks. Li was right. The fresh leaves didn't tell him what secret process transformed the fresh green leaves. He drew the liquid over his tongue and noticed how lightly the flavor slipped through his mouth yet warmed his belly. When he first came to China, he thought it was uncivilized to drink tea without milk and sugar. Now he abhorred the British practice. China's pure air and fresh foods had cleansed his palate. He could taste differences that made each tea unique. Last night he was served a black tea that was rich and full; it cut the gravies from his palate and enhanced the flavors of every bite. At other times the monks served light teas that invigorated him after his long hikes.

He returned to his room and laid the fresh leaves he had gathered across his palm. They were dark green and shiny with no odor resembling any of the teas he had enjoyed since coming to Tien-Tung. Was each tea cultivated from a different type of tea plant? What were their differences? How could he tell which was which? He needed Li's help, he realized. If he continued to treat him as rudely as the Consul and his friends did, he could justifiably abandon him here. He sighed. Surrounded by so much beauty he had to find some of that Christian charity that his countrymen said made them superior to the heathens.

Fortune gathered his equipment and tucked his gun under his arm. He found Li at the bottom of the temple steps strapping the collection boxes to the monks' backs. "I'm sorry, Li, if I offended you," he apologized. He shifted his feet. Apologies and social pleasantries made him appear even more awkward than he felt. "China is such a strange place and I am curious. I ask too many questions." He saw the edge of Li's lips twitch upward.

"Yes, you do." Li tipped his head and raised an eyebrow as he considered the Scot's apology. He stared at those pale grey eyes that reminded him of an empty window. Then he pointed to the top of a far hill where the pagoda's golden roof sparkled above the treetops. "The monks will take us to the Lotus Temple. If we do not dally, we can have tea there and return before nightfall."

Fortune shaded his eyes with his right hand and squinted up the face of the hill. Hundreds of birds soared from the trees in all directions. He could see no trail, no break in the blanket of crimson azaleas that billowed across the valleys and up the mountains. But he heard the alluring rush of waterfalls and bird calls in the restless winds.

"Pilgrims have come on foot to these monasteries for a thousand years." Li pointed out a few straw hats bobbing along a path on the far side of the lotus pond and disappearing in the sea of blossoms and greenery. "Come, we must leave now unless you want to spend a long night under a cold tree. It is far."

As before, one monk carried his specimen papers, another his plant box, and now a third, a box for the birds he intended to collect. Whenever Fortune raised his rifle, the monks leapt back and plugged their ears with their fingers. Afterward, they rushed to the feathered bodies and chanted prayers over the dead bird for a good reincarnation.

If Fortune had turned to look back on the path, he would have seen a crippled pilgrim, face hidden by his wide straw hat, limp slowly just behind the last tree or azalea billowing taller than a man. The old man watched Fortune pick up the birds he had blasted out of the trees and inspect their tiny bodies before carefully wrapping and placing them just so in his boxes. He noted how the Scot bent over a particularly red azalea, cradled the blossoms in his huge hands, and inhaled its fragrance; how he traced the stem back to the main plant and carefully unearthed the roots with his trowel; how he spread a handful of soil in the palm of his hand, sniffed it, and gently pinched it over and over, as if analyzing its composition and texture. He watched how the foreigner gathered a sample from the base of the plant in a clean jar, then held it up to the sun, shaking it as if to spread the ingredients so he could more clearly inspect it. He saw how the Scot took his time writing detailed notes about the flower, stem, and root system. He observed how he measured the size of the blooms, their color, how closely the plants grew, how they spread, and if a particular exposure produced more blooms than others. Was this the method Westerners used to study all things? Not much different from the methods of a Chinese gardener, the pilgrim mused.

Each day Robert Fortune and his entourage visited another temple, always situated on the most beautiful promontory landscaped with curved pines, blankets of flowers, and lakes. Around each mountain lake, some filled with lily pads the size of elephant ears, manicured pathways invited them into another landscaped paradise that took their breath away anew. As they approached, shaven-headed monks rushed out to stare. They invited him to sit under the shade of a fine cypress so they could gape at the tall stranger with the pale skin who collected flowers and plants. Li complimented the monks on their tea, its distinctive flavor, color, and taste. The monks humbly accepted his compliments, genuinely pleased that their guests appreciated their hospitality.

Each evening when Fortune returned to Tien-Tung Temple, scores of monks who had traveled many days to see the traveler from beyond the borders of the Celestial Kingdom descended from the temple's wide steps like blossoms in hues from saffron to yellow. They gestured for him to open his plant box so they could see what flowers were wrapped in his specimen papers and what birds he had shot from the skies. They asked to see his gun but few dared to touch it. They had never beheld such a contraption in their sacred valleys.

Each evening, the Tien-Tung monks set Fortune's table and chair in the middle of the dining hall so all, including the visiting monks, could observe him as if he were an exhibit in their private zoo. Fortune reciprocated by eating with relish, obvious delight, and great exuberance.

∾

"Cousin Poe."

John looked up from the array of dishes set before him on a table close to the cooking fire, the best place to be as the chill night descended upon the high mountain. He motioned Li to sit opposite. "Cousin Li, come eat with me. Cousin Wong is the chef here. See what specialties he prepares." He had doffed his wide straw hat and ragged fur cape by the fire where it steamed off the day's moisture.

Cousin Wong, bald and lean, wore the saddest wrinkled face Li had ever seen. "Sit. Sit." he commanded Li with a wave of arthritic fingers. He placed a pair of chopsticks and a bowl down on the time-weathered table opposite John.

"No, I do not want to bother you." Li bowed humbly. Enticed by the aroma-filled kitchen, his stomach answered otherwise with a hungry roar.

"No bother," Wong exclaimed. "Everyone is watching the barbarian eat my food. Hear them laughing?" A cacophony of voices carried through the thick door between the rooms.

Li's smile stretched across his face and his eyebrows jiggled when he laughed. "The monks find the barbarian entertaining. He demonstrates his dexterity with chopsticks by eating anything set before him."

"My food is irresistible," agreed Wong. He leaned forward as if sharing a secret. "But in the kitchen, the food is best." He wiped his hands on an impeccably clean towel wrapped around his waist. He dipped a ladle into one of the sizzling woks and tasted. "Ah, perfection." He used a pair of extraordinarily long chopsticks tucked into his waistband and ate from another wok. He smacked his lips. "This is ready."

"How about you, Cousin Wong?" asked Li. He swung his legs around the bench and slid in opposite Poe. He picked up the chopsticks and filled his bowl.

"I eat from every pot. I'm full." Wong patted his very firm flat belly. "You two enjoy." He plated a couple dishes from the woks and placed it between his seated cousins.

Poe and Li, ravenous from a long day in the brisk mountain air, readily complied. They sat companionably, accepting each new platter of food from Cousin Wong.

"John, you are a master of stealth." Li shook his head with admiration. He leaned back with his elbow on the table and chopstick aloft, deep in thought. "Sometimes I see a tree move against the wind or a bird suddenly startle in the sky. But I never see your physical self. You have a talent for disappearing."

His cousin nodded. He wore the rags of an ancient pilgrim as if he were still in role. Yes, he prided himself on his ability to disappear, to blend into the background. "I enjoy watching. I learn so much about his methods, how he treats plants and gathers them, how he inspects and studies them, and the tools he uses."

"I think he saw you." Li smiled softly to himself. He chuckled at John's flush.

"Impossible. He was too busy digging up plants and shooting birds. He has the kind of eyes that sees only what is right in front of him. What is he going to do with everything he puts in those boxes?"

"Make me carry them back to Shanghai."

John took a deep breath and stared at the pulsing reds of the kitchen embers. "Sometimes I get so engrossed in watching him I forget he is a foreigner. He thinks he's Chinese."

Li paused, his chopsticks suspending a healthy mouthful of tofu-shrimp in garlic sauce an inch from his mouth. He laughed so hard at the absurdity that his ribs hurt.

∞

To Mandarin Poe, Shanghai
Greetings, Honorable Uncle,

Fortune almost killed himself yesterday. He entered a dense brush to dig out a plant. He emerged, plant in hand, then suddenly disappeared. I cautiously approached and found loose rubbish had sunk into a boar pit covered with sticks and grass. The pit was narrow at the mouth and widened inside to prevent a boar from scrambling out when it has tumbled in. It was half-filled with water. Fortune lay slumped on the bottom, his head barely above water, out of my reach. His head and hands were bloody. These pits are in the most remote parts of the mountains; no one would have heard his cries for help.

It was so dark in the pit Fortune did not realize that your Sixth Son, John, fashioned a rope out of vines and pulled him out before disappearing in the woods. I cleaned the foreigner's wounds. When he awoke from his faint, he said a distinguished plant hunter fell to his death in Hawaii in a similar boar pit lined with stakes. That could have been his fate.

Since Fortune is now sailing for Chusan Island to visit Dr. Maxwell of the Madras army, he says he will not need me. Instead, he sends me to Soochow for tree peonies.

I can arrange for Fortune to have an accident in the Chusan seas, if you wish.
Cousin Li

Thirteen

VISITORS FROM THE INLAND MOUNTAINS

SHANGHAI

*J*adelin and Flora took their embroidery to a bench near the willow tree placed to capture the warmth of the September afternoon. Mandarin Poe had arranged his estate so each new family could have their own courtyard surrounded by a private wing. John had envisioned this, his own garden, as a microcosm of the universe: yin and yang, and the life force, ch'i, embodied in heaven, earth, mountains, and water. He told Flora it would take him a lifetime to perfect the plantings, but he had laid out the garden's bones: a burbling waterfall, a stream that curved under an arched bridge, and a rock lined lily pond with gold and black koi.

While her brother shadowed Fortune through China, Jadelin accompanied Flora. Her instructions were to share the secrets of how to survive the changing dynamics of the household.

Mandarin Poe's First Wife, called Mother by all, a handsome woman with huge shoulders and powerful hands, awed Flora. She learned that Mother's eldest son brought the Poes much honor since he had reached the exalted position of First Scholar in the Emperor's court in Peking. At first, Benjamin, the designated head of the family business under

Mandarin Poe, intimidated her with his broad, beefy shoulders, dark eyes, and thick, bushy eyebrows that grew straight across and curled up at the ends. Despite his swarthy appearance, she saw he was a gentle soul who made it a point to speak to each child in the household every day. She immediately liked Daniel who was quiet, respected by all, and seemed to work day and night on the business' finances to the absent-minded neglect of his wife and dozen children.

The first time Second Wife met Flora at breakfast, she eyed the bride's slim figure. "That pink gown makes you look fat," she sniffed. "Why would your family choose such old-fashioned clothes for your dowry?" Second Wife's own apartments overflowed with silk fans and gowns too numerous for her ever to wear. She waltzed to the seat that gave her the best view of the garden. She smiled pityingly over her shoulder. "Such a pasty complexion, too. No wonder you had to settle for marriage to a Sixth Son."

Second Wife's two sons, slim like their mother, had been reared and disciplined by an amah that the entire household feared. Number Two Amah, as she was called, had come from a family of northern horsemen from the windswept plains. Manchu nomads who coveted her family's herds had rode into her camp, slain the men and boys, and tossed her baby into the air, slicing him in half before he hit ground. Mandarin Poe had rescued the heart-broken woman from among the destitute beggars who huddled outside a northern city's wall. Although she tried to raise Edward and Paul to be as tough and self-sufficient as she would have raised her own son, Edward had inherited too much of his mother.

Paul entered their courtyard just as Flora and Jadelin began to yawn, their heads heavy with the scent of the wisteria vines twining counterclockwise over a decorative gate.

"Here's our gorgeous brother," sighed Jadelin, welcoming his company. Flora's maid followed with a tray of boiling water, a teapot, and three delicate white teacups.

Paul bowed to them both. To Jadelin he said, "I thought you considered John the handsomest."

"He is," she agreed with a tilt of her head. "But when you walk into a room, everyone's eyes are on you. They vie for your attention. If he wants to, John can enter a room and he's invisible."

"He can be elusive that way," said Paul with a quirky smile that lit up his face. "How is our beautiful Flora?" he asked. "Don't try to keep up with Jadelin who is too quick and witty for me."

"No one is too quick or witty for you!" The first time Flora met him, he made her laugh with his imitation of how Benjamin intimidated clients he didn't like by drawing his body up to his full towering height with a scowl and puffing back his massive shoulders. She nodded to the maid setting up their tea on a small side table and gestured for him to sit on the porcelain stool next to her. "Thank you for going through my gowns. My seamstress worked on the alternations you suggested. The embroidery panels for the turquoise gown bring out the elegance of the silk weaving. How clever you are."

Paul glowed with her praise. He took the offered seat with a wink to the maid who, with admiring glances at him, prepared and poured the tea. She served him first.

"Any news?" asked Flora anxiously. "You always know what's going on in Shanghai."

"Alistair Mackenzie took his Chinese mistress to the British Consulate's Sunday supper and introduced her as his wife." His almond eyes lilted with mischievous glee. "The British Consul's wife, Mrs. Thom, was so shocked she ordered her maid to kick out 'that Chinese woman.'"

Flora and Jadelin put down their teacups in rapt attention.

"Sai-Lin, Mackenzie's woman, asked Mrs. Thom to please make the request to Mr. Alistair Mackenzie because no lady walks through the streets unaccompanied. When Mrs. Thom repeated her request directly to Mackenzie he laughed heartily. The gossip among the servants is that Mackenzie came home in a jovial mood. He felt it was a very entertaining evening with a tale that the British community will embellish for weeks."

"The British live in our country, on land where our houses used to stand. She was rude to expel a guest because she's Chinese." Jadelin tossed her head. "I applaud Mr. Mackenzie."

"The British Consul's wife threatens to take the first boat to London. Good riddance, all her servants say."

Flora quickly turned to greet a canary's rapturous melody with a smile on her peach-cheeked face. She didn't see the shadow pass on the far side of the garden. In the next instant, John slipped behind her. "Miss me?" he whispered in her ear. He nuzzled her neck and inhaled her scent, of oriental lilies in full bloom.

"Ai-ya," she gasped. "Husband, you startled me." Instinctively, she put her hands to her belly. "Your baby leapt like a carp." She blushed self-consciously. "Did you miss me?" Her eyes lilted up in the corners like bright commas. The Poes had been pleased when they met Flora, daughter of a powerful Shanghai Mandarin. She enchanted them with her naturalness and unspoiled, good nature. Her family's status could have entitled her to marry the First Son of any wealthy family, but her Shanghainese father and Soochow-born mother preferred the security and honor of John's lineage: twenty-seven generations of Poes of Shanghai on his father's side and Grand Master Ping's legendary lineage on his mother's.

"My heart yearns for you every minute. But since you wear no jewelry or adornments, I found no gift I could bring as a token of my love." John gazed into her eyes, still bewildered that she was his wife and pregnant with his child. He kissed her fingers, as smitten now as when he lifted the red silk veil of her headdress on their wedding night. Lonely nights on the trail were the worst. Just the thought of Flora's silky skin and moist sweet lips made his heart pound deliriously.

"I have everything I desire." Her cheeks flushed and she dropped her eyes, embarrassed.

"I have kept her amused as you instructed, brother," said Paul. He stood up and bowed. "Now that you have returned, I will return to the depths of the tea hong where Benjamin and Daniel slave away under mounds of accounts. They need my levity."

"We all need your generosity and heart, Paul. I'll come later to regale you with my tales."

"We look forward to it." Paul bowed to them all and departed.

"You have grown since I left." John placed his hand on the swell of her belly.

"You've been gone two months."

"I had tea gardens to inspect, far inland." He couldn't tell her about his nomadic life among the monks and his father's personal mission. "At least they were in beautiful settings, my blossom." He ran his fingers along her apple-round cheeks just to feel their softness.

Jadelin turned her face away from the lovebirds' intimate greetings and bent her head over her embroidery. From Cousin Li's letters she surmised both men had found an edgy thrill to the game they played with Fortune.

After Flora pulled herself shyly from her husband's arms, Jadelin welcomed her brother. "I've enjoyed every letter you sent. Li wrote how you saved the Westerner's life when he fell in the boar pit." She looked him in the eye and the message she sent was clear.

"You know according to Buddhist ethics we cannot kill. I will not harm the ch'i of our family." His voice was firm and sure.

"But he, of all people, who willfully defies our Emperor's edicts and his own country's treaties for his own gain." Jadelin's fist clenched. "He deserved to die."

John shook his head. "I've replayed the scene over and over in my mind since that moment. I didn't hesitate, little sister. He has no idea he could be rotting at the bottom of a boar pit right now."

The glare she sent him could have chilled glaciers. They were raised according to Buddhist and Confucian ethics. But some circumstances demanded another course. Despite Grand Master Ping's training in discipline and ethics, she wasn't so sure she would have been as magnanimous as her older brother. In fact, she was sure of it. She picked up her embroidery and walked to the far side of the garden on the other side of the wisteria so all she could hear was the waterfall's gentle trickle into the koi pond.

Flora ran her fingers down her husband's tanned cheek. "Will you stay home now? Or must you leave? Although your brothers work long hours with your father, none is ever gone for more than a week." She turned his hands over and danced her fingertips along the rough calluses of his palms. "Nor do they spend two months living under the sun carrying heavy loads."

"Is that so, my observant wife?" John turned to her, thankful for her thoughtful change of subject. She had lived in the Poe household for less than a year, but already she knew the strengths and weakness of each person--who were her allies and who might not be dependable. She was observant and for that reason, he had to be more cautious. "You know we rely on Benjamin to hire and manage the men who guard our warehouse, shipments, and deliveries. Daniel manages the payments and credits so our business continues to grow. Edward and Paul are at the warehouse every day working with my father."

"Edward?" She leaned forward and whispered cautiously. "He's addicted to opium. He doesn't show up for work and grows pale."

"He is a source of great worry for our father."

"But you will stay home now? Your sister misses you as well. I'm not good company for her. She is a more active person."

John chuckled at his sister's flustered indignation. He knew how she rushed through her studies so she could leap through the courtyards to spar with her mother.

"I did not know where you were, or I would have written." Flora looked down, blushing again.

"I'm home for a while." John placed a flat soft package in her lap. "I have a present from your nursemaid." Big Amah tolerated no other person to look after Mei's children so Flora's amah had returned to her family in Soochow.

"My amah." She unwrapped the simple brown paper and clapped her hands with unexpected surprise. "Nankeen. Look at these designs. Feel how strong and soft this cotton is. When I was a child my amah dressed me in nankeen. I love the feel of this fabric against my skin." Nankeen, more sturdy and functional than linen and silk, hand-woven and hand-printed with artistically refined patterns and dyed with the distilled color of local grasses, had been sold along the legendary Silk Road for two thousand years. "The Emperor can wear his silk. My amah was always proud that since the Chou dynasty, her family continued to use patterns developed during the Song dynasty."

"I didn't know my wife was an expert in textiles. I must be careful what I say."

She pertly tapped his chin. "You should. Women pick, spin, weave, and produce the finest nankeen."

The willow branches above parted in the breeze and John lifted his face to the sun. On the trail, he had gotten used to the full heat of the sun against his skin and the way it wakened his primitive survival instincts. He pulled out a length of cloth and gave it to her. "Since you are an expert, what do you think about this fabric?"

Flora rubbed the thick white cotton between her fingertips. "What extraordinary weaving—so very dense and even." She held it up to the sun for a closer inspection. "This is not Chinese." She frowned at him. She called to her sister-in-law. "Jadelin, come feel the texture of these fabrics and how tightly it is woven."

Jadelin's curiosity overcame her anger. She rubbed each sample between her fingers to check the weave. She held them up to the sun but there was no variation in color. "Where did you get these?" she asked her brother.

"Cousin Li brought me these samples from Canton where the British are selling their cotton. Huge machines in England weave this fabric in long lengths."

"Machines." Flora ran her fingers along the weave. "No wonder it's consistently tight. But it's too heavy for Chinese clothes, too coarse to fall right."

"How about this?" He held out a length of blue cotton that shimmered with a sea-like sheen when he held it aloft. He lowered it into his wife's hands. She fingered its texture and held it to her cheek.

"It feels like cotton but shines like silk."

One by one he handed them more--in red, orange, green, pink, yellow and white. Flora and Jadelin were astounded. "These colors. How do they do this?"

"In Canton, the market for Chinese cotton is collapsing because English cotton is cheaper and comes in many colors. The British don't gather flowers and grasses to make their dyes. They use chemicals they brew in large quantities." Cousin Li's wife's family, textile merchants, now had to travel to villages far beyond the reach of the British to sell their textiles.

"China doesn't need English cotton." Flora rubbed her fingernails across the white broadcloth and the finer cotton sateen.

"But the English have flooded the markets of the five treaty ports. If you had to work hard for every cash you made, would you pay more for hand-made, hand-dyed Chinese-made nankeen, or would you buy cheap cotton made in England? Our handlooms can't compete. The barbarians are squeezing us. First our cotton, next our tea."

"You see, John?" said Jadelin. "Why we have to take action to protect our heritage?"

Flora covered her belly with her hands, suddenly afraid for their child's future.

John put his arms around his wife to comfort her. "But now, my dearest, I must see what news my brothers have for me. Patience, my darling. I'll return to you tonight."

"Brother, I'll come with you." Jadelin had already folded her embroidery. "Wait while I change." She caught his quizzical stare and explained, "Since I'm supposed to be dead, I dress as a boy whenever I go out. I've gotten very quick at braiding my hair into a queue." Luckily, when dressed as a man, she didn't have to disguise her feet.

ॐ

*M*ow Bowli possessed steely nerves honed by decades of training under Grand Master Ping. But his knees quavered when he faced Jadelin's father. His father, Mow Chow Ching, had extolled Mandarin Poe's reputation and warned of his legendary prowess: Poe could size up an opponent with a glance and see the weakness in his heart, a skill he used to his advantage to secure victory. Bowli took a deep breath, centered his ch'i, and bowed.

"So you are Mow Chow Ching's youngest son. Please, be seated." Mandarin Poe returned his bow and motioned his servant to bring boiling water for tea. He studied the young man who had traveled from the Longjing mountain area of Hangchow southwest of West Lake. He would never have associated short, stocky Mow Chow Ching with this tall, fair-skinned student of Grand Master Ping. He observed that outwardly, Bowli appeared calm and relaxed. Inwardly, he was acutely alert and aware of everything about him: his eyes quickly scanned the layout of Poe's study before he entered and registered the movements of everyone, including the servant who guided him as well as Poe himself. "I have been looking forward to this meeting. Grand Master speaks highly of you. Didn't you travel with my son, John?"

"Yes, he requests you forgive him for not seeing you as soon as he arrived, but he is worried about his wife. He hoped that we would have the privacy to get to know each other." John had slapped Bowli's back and wished him good luck before hurrying away. Bowli didn't mind that his friend had abandoned him, but he had hoped for his moral support.

"My Sixth Son is always dashing off. He says he wants to live in quiet retreat, to be a scholar poet, but he never stays in one place. Did you join him on his adventure?"

"No. He came to Longjing on his way back and we traveled here. My brothers and I just finished processing our second pick. We have a few weeks before we begin our third pick." Mow Bowli offered Mandarin Poe the elegantly simple bamboo box he cradled in his hands. "I had my finest tea master hand-roll this first pick Dragon Well especially for you and Jadelin's mother. We hope it pleases you." His voice was assured when he talked about tea and his light brown eyes met Poe's with confidence.

Mandarin Poe's eyes widened when he held the box in his hands. The lid rolled open with a smooth and gentle touch of his finger. He inhaled the scent that wafted upwards. "Ahh, the aroma. The mist wrapped mountains of West Lake. The high peaks of Longjing." He motioned his servant to use these leaves to prepare their tea.

"Mandarin Poe, my father sends blessings and his deepest wish that our families will be joined."

Poe read the earnestness in Bowli's eyes, but he played the stern role. "We have high expectations. Jadelin possesses unique talents. She must be protected. You know we turned down many proposals from prominent mandarin families."

Bowli looked down as if his spirits sagged. He raised his chin and met Poe's eyes. "I will protect Jadelin with my life."

"Few dare to meet Grand Master Ping's high standards. Yet he recommended you as the only suitable match for my daughter. Do you feel you are worthy?"

"I'm humbled to be in the presence of the man Grand Master recommended for his own daughter."

A smile spread across Mandarin Poe's face. The parallel the young man referred to, that Ping had chosen both Poe and Mow for the women most dear to him, was clear. "How well do you know her?" His daughter was more than a handful and wearingly persistent when she felt she was right.

"We studied together with Grand Master Ping last winter." His eyes met Poe's. That meant tears and triumphs, overcoming pain and exhaustion.

"My wife tells me you corrected some of her bad habits, shortcuts in technique she had developed."

Mow Bowli nodded humbly. "She had to adjust her balance and anticipation, but Jadelin's precision and speeds are excellent."

"Mow Chow Ching, your father, how is he?"

Bowli said his father was semi-retired, disappearing for days at a time. His sons managed the tea farms now.

"Your father gave me a beating once. We were fellow students and I was two heads taller than he."

Mow Bowli gulped.

"I was young and confident, seeking to impress Grand Master Ping with my prowess and superior skill." Surrounded by the entire school, the two had faced each other in the final spar of the practice. Poe knew he was handsome, that his fellow students were in awe of his power and talent and looked to him as their natural leader. Mow was a loner, occasionally a trickster, and many teased that since he was squat and square he reminded them of a scuttling crab. Overconfident, Poe added flourishes to his lunges and attacks, seeking to humiliate the stocky Mow and chalk up a quick victory. Within two seconds, Mow had him on the defensive. Poe suffered strikes to his chest and back. As a finale, Mow flung Poe onto his belly with such force he could not move for five humiliating minutes. Poe gasped for air, humbled and disgraced.

He knew he did not deserve to stay at Grand Master Ping's academy, not after that mortifying exhibition of hubris. He returned to his small room to pack his clothes and books. Embarrassingly trounced by his peer, he would leave forever. When he was certain everyone else was at the evening meal, he slipped into the tearoom to retrieve his teapot from the shelf where it had sat with honor for many years. He hung his head. Already, he missed the camaraderie of the school. He had let everyone down, including himself, and especially his beloved mentor, Grand Master Ping.

That night, Mow Chow Ching found Poe in his small room nursing his crushed ego. He drew a small tin from his robe. "My salve will soothe your bruises," he said. He motioned with his head for him to show him his injuries. He rubbed a small amount on the purple areas blooming on Poe's forearms. Finally, he poured an amber liquid into a teacup and handed it to a very surprised Poe. "Drink this."

"Is it poison? Will it finish me off?" Poe asked warily. He still smarted from his humiliation. With his eyes on Mow, he threw back his head and downed the bitter potion in one gulp. He gasped. It tasted nasty.

"Not unless you want it to. Your muscles need to rest and recuperate. Sleep now. Tomorrow we have a lot to practice."

Everything in young Poe's head whirled faster and faster when he fell back on his cotton mat. The last thing he remembered was the squat Mow leaning over his torso circling his hands in a slow rhythm over his muscles. Although Mow's hands hovered at least twelve inches over his chest, Poe felt their heat right down to his bones. Poe didn't wake up until the sun was high the next day. He was astonished to find that all his bruises were gone. He stretched his ache-free arms out and leapt to his feet. He felt stronger than he had ever felt in his life.

"Mow," he shouted when he found his adversary seated on the dock with a series of wet stones and knives. "What did you give me? You're magic."

Mow answered with an enigmatic smile. He lifted one of the small daggers he was sharpening, one of a set of six he carried whenever he traveled, and peered down its edge. "Your ch'i is strong but you must control your pride. Now that you know your fault, it will be harder to defeat you." He tested the blade he had just worked on with the tip of his finger and, satisfied it was sharper than a razor, slipped it into its leather case where it nested with its brothers, all perfectly balanced with hilts depicting a sinuous three-claw dragon. Then he looked up and eyed the raptors soaring slowly overhead.

From that moment on, the two were constant companions and friendly rivals. After they graduated from Grand Master Ping's school, Mow returned to the Longjing mountains of Hangchow and Poe to Shanghai. Family and business consumed their lives. Now their children brought them together.

ॐ

*J*adelin, in one of her brother's trousers and tunics that Big Amah had had tailored to disguise her feminine shape, strode down the corridors with her brother, mimicking his manly stance.

"Throw your shoulders back like you're a rooster." John eyed his sister's saunter. "And keep your thighs apart like your balls are too big for your pants," he coached. "That's better. No one will see through that disguise." With her hair in a queue to her waist and one of his old skull caps low over her forehead, she looked masculine enough, he thought. He paused at the entrance of Mandarin Poe's study. "Jadelin, I brought home a visitor who is now with Baba. Let's see if you can fool them. Ready?"

Jadelin took a deep breath and threw back her shoulders. She strode in with her brother, keeping her eyes down to hide their feminine lilt. She bowed as her brother said, "Greetings, Baba and Mow Bowli."

Mow Bowli's wide-eyed shock and dropped jaw matched hers. Last Chinese New Year when she followed Mei and Benjamin to their junk to return to Shanghai, she was heartbroken. She didn't know if she'd ever see him again.

She clasped her hands in front of her and bit her lower lip to quell her dizzying emotions. She wanted to throw her arms around him and tell him how much she had missed him. Then she saw her father scowl at her lack of manners.

She turned to Bowli and bowed. "Welcome to Shanghai, Mow Bowli. Please pardon my tears of happiness," she whispered in a contained but trembling voice.

Mei had timed her entrance to follow her daughter's. She led her daughter to a chair. "Sit, Jadelin." She patted her daughter's hand and waited until she had composed herself on the hardwood chair next to her. "Your father and I have accepted Mow Bowli's offer of marriage."

Now it was John's turn to look at his sister and friend in surprise. "You didn't say a word the entire trip from Hangchow." He slapped Bowli on the back. "Good luck!"

Jadelin didn't think her body could contain all her joy. Her head spun. Her body seemed to float. She barely heard her father say that Mow Chow Ching had sent wedding presents from his family. Their entire first pick of premium Dragon Well tea now sat in one of the reception halls along with dozens of bolts of exquisite silks for Jadelin and her family. Because of the situation with the Emperor last fall, she would depart quietly in disguise. Her luminous eyes filled with tears. She didn't care about presents or tea or silk right now. All she wanted was to be with Mow Bowli forever.

Fourteen

THEFTS AND A WEDDING

SHANGHAI

*B*enjamin paced his office. Movement helped him to think through their dilemma. In any one else's business it would have been a simple mistake: a misplaced case of tea or an error in accounting. But Daniel was positive that for the past year or two at least one case of premium first or second-pick tea went missing every month. Premium teas were packed in smaller cases. A porter would carry a single case, and only that case, all the way from the tea garden far inland to their warehouse where it was stored in an area where the temperature and humidity remained constant. Forced to relocate by the British, Benjamin and Daniel thought the problem would be resolved when they had designed a secure warehouse. Instead, the number of missing cases increased. Who, they wondered, was the thief?

He leaned out over the ledge of his loft office from where he oversaw all matters having to do with security of the warehouse, tea, and porters, and transporting tea from the distant hills and onward to their clients. He called it his 'aerie,' an appropriate name for his strategic perch that commanded a view of every window and door, every secret panel and hidden room.

Benjamin leapt down the moment he saw the four arrivals pull open the warehouse's heavy door. Who were his father's guests? The thin one might be his sister, who always dressed as a boy. A street ruffian and a tall man with an athletic gait accompanied her.

Third Brother Daniel glanced up from the octagonal mahogany table in the center of the warehouse where he correlated the lists of customers, from those who had been promised shipments of premium teas down to the various grades. He straightened his spectacles and stood up.

Paul leapt down from where he had been storing tea chests on elevated shelves off the floor, safe from moisture and vermin.

The rough clad stranger, outlined by the rectangle of afternoon light, raised his hand in a familiar greeting and eagerly strode in ahead of the other three.

Benjamin eyed his sister. "Ah," he pursed his lips and put his hands on his hips. "You look like a eunuch in training. And John, why are you in disguise as a southern beggar?"

Mandarin Poe cut through the brothers' laughter and hooting. "My sons, meet the brave warrior who will marry your sister." Her brothers congratulated Mow Bowli on his choice of a bride. They all knew him, had watched in admiration whenever he appeared at Grand Master Ping's, but only Benjamin could claim to be his worthy opponent.

"Aha!" Paul flew at John with a lightning bolt leap, right foot aimed at his brother's chest. John neatly deflected the kick and instead, flung his brother into a back roll. Paul jumped to his feet with a back flip and clasped him on the shoulder. "I see sleeping under trees hasn't slowed you down. We've missed you."

John Poe rubbed his deeply tanned cheeks and stubble. "Thanks for the test. I look like a coolie," he apologized. "You have no idea what hardships I've faced for the honor of the Poe clan. But what's this?" John raised his hands above him, at the high beams, the lofts and windows barred for safety. The warehouse smelled of fresh sawn wood.

To ensure that the major British trading merchants were prominently situated along the port's edge in the first years of the Shanghai settlement, Captain Balfour's master plan established streets, quays, and river frontage from the west bank of the Yangtze to the Yangtze Creek at the southern end, and close to the Wusong River at the northern end.

Paul explained, "The British tore down homes, temples, meeting halls, farms, craft workshops, silk weavers, cotton furnishers and dyers, wood carvers and candle makers. Even mortuaries were demolished. We had to move from the waterfront where we have done business for twenty-seven generations."

"Humph," John growled. Much had changed while he was gone.

Mandarin Poe sounded resigned and heavy. "I spend too much time with the mandarins negotiating, settling arguments, hearing complaints, and trying to preserve Shanghai's trade and way of life." He tried to remain upbeat despite the downturn in politics. The Chinese, perceived as uncivilized naïfs, were just another market for British, French, American, and Russian goods. They were treated as strangers in their own country. Demand for local nankeen had diminished among the masses in preference for cheap machine-made cotton from Manchester, England. The British openly sold Indian opium. In return, the Westerners got the porcelain, silk, and tea they lusted after.

"But the Poes of Shanghai will survive. Come," Mandarin Poe said to John and Mow Bowli, "let us show you around the new warehouse. See the ramps to the lofts, the rooms for grading, and the private cupping room." Wide and spacious, the new warehouse could accommodate the thousands of porters who journeyed thousands of miles with their precious tea chests balanced on their backs. Benjamin himself had supervised the craftsmen who built hidden storage for the finest premium teas. Daniel, who kept track of their clients, had designed rooms to keep the buyers separate and unseen. He pointed out the thick doors, heavy locks, and bolts. "Sometimes, one must run harder and smarter to stand in the same spot."

Now that Mow Bowli's marriage proposal was accepted and confirmed, Benjamin needed to address a business problem. He touched his lips and pointed up to his office. Daniel and Paul slid the great doors shut and drew the bolts. All headed upstairs to where secrets and strategy was best discussed.

∾

*J*ohn inhaled the steam curling from the surface of the dark Bo Lei, a comfort tea long used for medical purposes. He needed it now. He had questioned and evaluated the evidence. He had convinced Mow Bowli to leave his peaceful mountain mists and lakes. During their grueling return they had analyzed what he was going to say to his father and brothers. This matter had to be resolved now that their suspicions had been confirmed.

The men gathered in Benjamin's aerie. No chance of eavesdroppers here. Mandarin Poe, Jadelin, Mow Bowli, and all the brothers involved in the hong were present, except for the one who slipped out before lunch, if he came in at all. Bamboo trays of hand-made dumplings filled with savory fillings from a cousin's teahouse had been delivered and piled in steaming layers. While they ate, Daniel gave them an update of their finances. Business with the British, French, Russians, and Americans had increased their profits a thousand fold. Too busy working sixteen-hour days, they had shelved the problem of the disappearing tea chests.

John put down his chopsticks, took a long draught of tea, and looked deep in the eyes of his siblings, father, and friend. It was too painful to think they had been betrayed from within. He loathed delivering the damning evidence but the look in their faces, of trust and loyalty, gave him the courage he needed. "Over the past months, I visited each of the farmers and monks who complained of a discrepancy in the amount of tea that arrived versus the amount they sent us. I interviewed the coolies for each missing shipment. In some cases, I was lucky that the farmer himself delivered the tea."

John exchanged looks with Mow Bowli who leaned back, one arm protectively around Jadelin. Bowli nodded him to go on.

John took out a scroll and unrolled it. Everyone leaned in, eyes intent as he spoke. "Daniel compiled these figures so I could compare them with our suppliers' accounts. You see how random our loss was the first year. We thought human error caused the problem: either our miscounting or their bookkeeping. The second year, rare and valuable first picks did not arrive or were not entered in the ledger. A few second pick teas were missing or not tallied as delivered."

"To whom did they deliver the tea? And who recorded it?" asked his father.

"Fourth Brother." John kept his voice even and nonjudgmental. The unembellished truth was hard enough for them to absorb.

The atmosphere grew heavy as if a cloud had descended on their hearts. They looked from one to the other with dismay, betrayed by one of their own. Although there was a system for tracking tea in and out of the warehouse, it would be possible, because they trusted each other, for tea chests to go astray.

"I asked Mow Bowli to speak to you from his personal experience. For two years his porters delivered premium Dragon Well tea but some chests were never recorded as received. We have built our business with our growers and clients through generations of trust." John looked to Bowli to continue.

Bowli looked down at his clasped hands, long fingers more used to a calligraphy brush than planting. He glanced at Jadelin. What he said would protect her as well. "The Poes are one of the most respected families, your hong the most reputable. Our records show we have always supported each other, when times were prosperous through times of drought, even the unstable years of bandits and warlords. Only if both of us remain strong can we all prosper." He withdrew a small scroll from his robe and unrolled it, pointing out the numbers of tea chests from each pick they had shipped to the Poe's hong in the past ten years. "Two years ago, you claimed you received only half our first pick. We assumed bandits had taken their share. When you told us only half of our second pick had arrived, we assumed the tea trail had become more dangerous because of the British. We heard how their gunboats blew up our coastal towns and barbarian soldiers roamed everywhere, inflicting destruction. But last year, you received none of our first pick. For safety, we selected our most loyal porters to carry them here. All insisted that the tea had been delivered and showed us the signed receipt we requested. The Fourth Son signed it. For our second pick we instructed our porters to insist on a receipt from anyone but the Fourth Poe Son. We were paid in full for that delivery." He touched his chest and bowed his head before he continued. "It pains me to bring my future brothers this bad news."

All the while, Daniel rubbed his jaw with one hand as he ran his fingers down the columns, comparing the Mow's figures with his tally. When he looked up, his eyebrows sagged. "What do we do now?"

Mandarin Poe's head drooped. "We repay the growers for their loss." The evidence had been circumstantial at first: a farmer complained he hadn't received payment for tea he claimed delivered, tea meant for them mysteriously appeared in the warehouse of a competitor, and the opium addiction of Second Wife and her eldest son, Edward. Their lust for opium exceeded their honor.

The worry lines on Daniel's brow deepened as he calculated the financial impact. Like hundreds of thousands of Chinese families, the Poes had been cursed by British opium.

Each morning Mandarin Poe woke eager to work alongside his sons in their new warehouse fragrant with the scent of premium teas, to enjoy the success of many generations of Poes. But in the afternoon his energy waned, especially when the Taoutae of Shanghai called another meeting to deal with the demands of the foreigners. This problem broke his heart. His eyes turned to steel when he looked around the room. "We'll trap him when he least suspects it."

∾

"Once you enter the house of Mow, you no longer belong to the house of Poe." Mandarin Poe's voice, uncharacteristically gruff, caught in his throat. He frowned to cover his emotions. He had seated her at his side during dinner so he could impart the last of his fatherly wisdom. He shifted his gaze to Mow Bowli seated on his other side.

Bowli coughed awkwardly. He could barely taste the exquisite Shanghainese delicacies that servants carried out in endless mouthwatering profusion. He hated farewells and would have preferred to depart immediately for the Longjing mountains. But Jadelin had asked for one last day with her family. Her brothers, taking advantage of Bowli's strength, immediately elicited his help at the hong to clear space for the chests of tea that would arrive within a week.

Second Wife arrived for the banquet in silky splendor, glassy eyed and pale. She sat with her son, Edward, and his solemn-eyed wife and son. The Fourth Son did not meet anyone's eyes nor did he give his blessings to his sister and her future husband. He was seated at the rear of the dining hall, close enough so he could see all the Poes, and far enough to not ruin anyone's mood.

Mandarin Poe turned to his daughter and confided, "I wonder if Mow Chow Ching can still fight all of Grand Master Ping's students at once. It used to be a weekly ritual when we were students. Grand Master Ping would send everyone barehanded against him. Your future father-in-law possesses extraordinary peripheral vision and almost supernatural reflexes. To the casual eye he appears to be a slow fellow." The mandarin tapped the side of his head. "A deceptive mannerism." Then he frowned. "I also remember that he has an incredible power of illusion. You're never sure of what you're seeing with Mow Chow Ching." He patted Jadelin's hand.

His daughter's eyes widened at the warning. She picked at her food, trying to stretch time.

Mandarin Poe sensed her distress. He whispered, "Bowli's father may frighten you at first. Never doubt him. He's one of your grandfather's closest allies."

∞

*A*s the Mow junk sailed the magnificent Huangpu River, skirting the hundreds of boats that coursed to and from Shanghai, Jadelin kept her eyes on Mow Bowli's handsome face. She could barely breathe when she gazed up at his strong brow and sculpted cheekbones. He draped one arm around her shoulder and pointed out the broad plains of Shanghai coursed with well-tended farms and crystalline canals with cloud-covered mountains in the distance. When they reached the Grand Canal the water and sky seemed to expand as China unfolded in an ever-changing landscape of sharp peaked mountains. The air grew warm and thick. The mountains grew taller and soon scraped the clouds from the sky.

They were welcomed into Longjing by cymbals, dancing musicians dressed in red, and three days of wedding banquets. It seemed as if the entire village had been invited.

And then they were alone.

∾

*J*adelin waited for him on the edge of the marriage bed in the pavilion he had built just for her. When he lifted the red veil of her elaborate headdress, she dropped her eyes. He held her face in his hands and slowly kissed her eyes and lips. Smiling, she removed her layers: the red tunic and skirt of silk embroidered in gold thread with the dragon and phoenix, the auspicious symbols of husband and wife. She stepped out of her purple silk pajamas, dropped the white halter and silk under things that clung to her skin, and lifted off the red headdress. She unclasped her hair so it cascaded down and surrounded her body like a black cloak. Then she held out her arms.

Outside, the bamboo rustled as the night winds blew. Waves of wind gusted through the grove in a sensuous, trembling rhythm. The nightingales in the garden heard his moans, her virgin gasps, his endearments. When he bent her backwards to take her deeper, she arched like the willow, arms gracefully reaching back to accentuate his pleasure. She was enticed, entranced, and bewitched.

The night closed around them with promises of many more pleasures. The wind softened and above, the trees rustled as if they, too, were suffused with the love that grew in the house of Mow.

Fifteen

THE TRAVELER FROM BEYOND

THE GREAT WALL

SHANGHAI

*S*hanghai bloomed with such brilliant colors in spring that the city's growing population of foreigners and bustling businesses were distracted by the efflorescence of flowers and scents. Just beyond the city walls, colorful and fragrant fields of vegetables, wheat, cotton, and fruits stretched to the horizon.

When Cousin Li entered John Poe's courtyard on this hot Shanghai morning, the soft rhythm of flowing water and the chatter and song of birds gave movement to the stillness. He shook his head when he saw his cousin bent over a gnarled and twisted pine tree only a foot high, yet over a hundred years old. "A beautiful day for gardening," Li called. He waited by the red moon gate for acknowledgement before stepping over the threshold.

John stood and gestured with the tiny clippers in his hand. "A gift from Doctor Chang. Exquisite, isn't it?"

Li shrugged good-naturedly. "I like my trees tall and upright, like me."

"Yes," his cousin chuckled, "an excellent character trait." He lowered his voice. "Not like me?"

"Your honor and loyalty has many layers." Li smiled at his young cousin. John balanced complex obligations towards his wife, the Poe clan, and the study of classical Chinese gardens while he dodged and shadowed Robert Fortune when all he really wanted was a quiet life with his family, books, and gardens.

"Wisely stated. Come, let us enjoy the fine tea we received just this morning from a monk who lives high in the distant mountains. It grows on cliffs so steep monkeys harvest the buds of the wild bushes." He gestured to the hexagonal huanghuangli table and chairs set in the shade of a tile-roofed gazebo.

Li ran his coarse fingers along the rich grain of the chair back. "It's too fine for me to sit on. I'm a rustic person of humble tastes."

"My hearty and persevering cousin, this chair is of a tropical wood so hard it maintains its finish while developing a rich patina. For six generations my ancestors have used and abused it. Its imperfections accentuate its design and timeless beauty." A servant appeared with warm water and a soft towel. John wiped off his clippers, dusted off his hands, and washed before joining his cousin.

In his travels, Li had noticed how furniture preferences differed according to the availability of woods and materials. In the south, Chinese preferred more ornate carvings. The foreigners liked inlaid mother-of-pearl and gilt gold. "The Scot thinks I understand him." He accepted the tea John handed him with both hands and inhaled its fragrance.

John held out his teacup to toast Li. "We're pleased that Fortune trusts you implicitly."

"At times the foreigner's behavior bemuses me," began Li. "In English, I think you would call him eccentric."

"Aren't all foreigners eccentric?"

"Let me tell you a strange tale. Captain Balfour lent Fortune a pony so he could expand his exploration into the countryside and return by nightfall, in accordance with the new regulations for foreigners traveling in our country. On that day I didn't accompany him because he sent me to a garden to buy a peach tree. He still searches for the tree from the Emperor's gardens that produces two-pound peaches.

"Long after dark, he and his pony returned exhausted, hungry, and caked with mud. He said that on the way back, all the bridges they crossed were in such poor shape the pony's feet plunged through the rotten planks. A couple of bridges disintegrated while they were on them, pitching Fortune and his pony into the mud. By the time they returned all the inns were closed. I asked Fortune if I should find him something to eat. 'No,' he said, 'but the pony needs food.' All I found in the market was a large pot of boiled rice and a pair of chopsticks. The animal ate ravenously. Then Fortune pulled up a stool and ate from the same pot." The Scot had stroked the animal's head and soothed him in a tender voice, assuring him that he had done well that day and now he could rest.

"How extraordinary." John put down his tea and contemplated the odd behavior of the lanky Westerner. He couldn't imagine the Scot cared more for the well being of his animal than for himself.

Cousin Li leaned back and looked up at the sky as if he were rolling back the days, weeks, and months he had spent with the misanthropic Scot. "He used to be demanding and imperious. Suddenly he's morose and distracted. Even more startling, he lowers his head and walks with smaller steps, not like his fellow British who act like they command the earth. Something has chastened him into a new humility. The people who live inland have never seen a foreigner like him. They stare at this awkward man with skin as pale as the moon, who tries to speak to them in Chinese. To avoid endless questions, I tell people he comes from beyond the Great Wall."

John rubbed his forehead. The foreigner was assuming more and more Chinese mannerisms. Yet, he defied every decree of the Emperor in his quest for flowers and tea. "He is just one man, but more like him will come. Soon foreigners will storm Peking and seize control of China."

Li shook his head and brushed away the idea with a grandiose sweep of his hand. "The Son of Heaven will always rule," he proclaimed. "It's up to us to ensure the Emperor remains on the throne. We have a daunting task. As a citizen of the British Empire this man moves with impunity within China, confident that his country's gunboats sit in our harbors with loaded cannons and trained armies. British officials displace our people along our waterfront. Their people desire our silk, tea, and porcelains, and now our flowers. In exchange for our treasures, they flood our cities with their cheap goods and drugs."

John considered his cousin's opinion as he slowly sipped his tea. "The more we learn about the British, the better prepared we will be to defend our culture and country. What's the barbarian doing now?"

Li described Robert Fortune's vigorous forays to explore Shanghai and vicinity by foot and pony. They rose when the frost still covered their blankets and visited every nursery to look for newly bloomed flowers. "He has stored all his plants in the gardens of Alistair Mackenzie who lives in a large house confiscated from a mandarin. He often refers to the drawings Mackenzie has done of every flower he has seen in China to document and gather his data on our flowers."

Li leaned forward. A frown deepened across his wide forehead. "This morning Fortune asked me to arrange for a boat and crew ready to depart in the morning with enough rice for several days. 'Why?' I questioned. 'We need food for only one day.' I reminded him that by decree of the Emperor, foreigners can only venture as far as one could travel and return within a single day from one of the five treaty ports of Canton, Amoy, Ningpo, Shanghai, and Foochow."

Fortune had thrown up his hands impatiently. "I know, I know. Tell the boatman I like to get off and walk around the countryside. Tell him no one will get into any trouble." He then slunk off to the market where anything and everything could be procured.

Li winked at his younger cousin. "Are you game for another adventure?"

"Does it result in disappointment and failure for the *gweilo*?"

"Most assuredly, it does."

∾

R obert Fortune inhaled the morning air layered with floral perfumes. If sensuousness wasn't a sin, he wished to be a bee so he could plunge into the brilliant banks of flowers and savor each delicate bloom. He was especially enraptured by tree-peonies in dark purple, lilac, and crimson. He had never seen such wondrous colors in all his years at the Royal Horticultural Gardens in England.

The minute he returned to Shanghai he had gone to see Jadelin. He had brought her a scroll painting that Mackenzie claimed was by a seventeenth century master. He looked forward to hearing her explain it to him in her soft, sweet voice. He imagined the flutter of her eyelashes and the smooth curve of her cheek as she concentrated on the exquisite landscape.

Instead, Third Wife Mei entered the candle lit reception hall where he stood clasping and unclasping his sweaty palms. In a long aqua tunic edged with green bias, Mei addressed him. "How kind of you to call upon my daughter, Mr. Fortune. She no longer needs tutoring."

"May I see her to say hello," Fortune stammered. Did he offend her in any way? If so, he didn't mean any discourtesy.

"My daughter lives far away. I doubt you will ever see her again. But the next time I write her, I will let her know you called." Mei called for tea to be served and, noticing his alarmed expression, asked him to please sit.

He perched woodenly on the edge of his chair. He looked lost, as if he didn't know what to do next. "What province is she in?" he inquired. He would reroute his expedition to find her.

"One where foreigners are not allowed." Mei asked about his travels but his answers were vague. After one cup of tea, Mei thanked Fortune for calling and motioned Big Amah to show him out.

Every nook and cranny of Shanghai now brought loneliness and disappointment. Perhaps Madame Poe had not been truthful to keep him away. He rushed from garden to garden hoping to see Jadelin, to glimpse her face or hear the sound of the tiny bells stitched to her hems. Frustrated and despondent, he yearned for an adventure. The riskier the better.

At the end of the day he strode to the boat Li had arranged for their trip clutching his satchel containing his most precious items: magnifying glass, guns, pen and ink, writing paper, and a change of clothes.

∾

*T*he canal rippled with the wakes of sculling sampans, barges pulled by wiry muscled trackers, and junks with bamboo mat sails billowing in the wind when they set off. Li sat cross-legged at the stern. They passed miles of lush, well-tended lands, past villages where smoke curled from cooking fires, wiry peasants hand-tilled the lands, and children tended cows, chickens, and ducks. The riverbanks were lined with thickly growing reeds, willow trees, and herds of water buffalo. Normally, Fortune would have jumped up at every change in the landscape, eager to hike the muddy hills and pull up every flower and plant. But this time he moped in the gloom of the sampan's covered shade.

When the sun headed down towards the horizon, Li told Fortune it was time to turn around. The crew did not want to be beheaded.

"Tell the boatman we continue to Soochow," Fortune ordered.

Li's eyes widened. "You cannot go there. Soochow is beyond the limit decreed by the Emperor."

Fortune insisted. "I'll give you an additional five pounds to persuade the boatmen to go on to Soochow. Tell the crew I shall double the amount I promised them."

"Our boatman knows the Emperor's edict. You will be reported the minute you enter Soochow."

"No, I won't." Fortune's pale eyes glimmered. He opened his satchel and pulled out a gray mandarin's robe, a satin skullcap, and a long black queue of real human hair. He slipped on the mandarin's robe, then sat on his bedroll and put on the skullcap and black satin shoes custom-made for him in a street stall a few days prior.

"A *gweilo* mandarin," gasped Li. From the shore, he might pass. He thought how much five pounds would mean to his own wife and children in Canton, especially with the collapse of the cotton trade. Would the boatmen risk their heads for a doubled fare? He looked back at the dozens of boats plying the river. Cousin John Poe, shadowing them from the cover of a small boat among dozens of other small boats behind them, would observe the transformation and advise the mandarins. When they discovered Fortune further than twenty-four hours from a treaty port, his own government would arrest him. This was the solution to their problem with the tea-hunting Scot. He provided the means to get himself deported.

"Ai-ya," the boatmen yelped when Li told them what Fortune wished to do.

"Hush," Li warned. "The Emperor's spies lurk everywhere." He assured them that the *gweilo* would not be detected. The boatmen were intrigued, especially by the financial reward.

In the shade of the sampan Li covered Fortune's head with steaming towels. While his hair softened, he sharpened Fortune's blade and tested it by slivering a leaf. When he was satisfied, he shaved Fortune's head in slow even strokes. Then he attached the queue to the cap and positioned it on the Scot's head. He stepped back to appraise his work. He laughed. The scoundrel!

"Do I look Chinese?" Fortune wasn't sure his deception would work, but he hadn't expected laughter. A wry face perhaps, or a shrug would have been enough.

Li pointed to the surface of the brass water basin he had used to rinse off the sharpened razor blade. The water was dark and still like a mirror.

Fortune turned his head to the right and left to admire his reflection. "Don't you think, Li, that the European's facial features are very similar to men from northern China?"

Li couldn't stop laughing. "Perhaps someone from the far, far north."

The boatmen gasped, "Ai-ya. Who is this mandarin?" What had happened to the *gweilo*?

In his mandarin robe and queue, the Scot bowed, hands folded humbly before his waist. "Call me Sing Wa," he said in Chinese. The crew laughed so hard their knees wobbled, their sides ached, and tears spurted from their eyes. They had a new passenger, Sing Wa, a mandarin from the far, far north, from beyond the Great Wall.

When they docked for the night, Li slipped out and found the person he was looking for in the sampan tied up a short distance behind them.

Sixteen

A THIEF IN THE NIGHT

espite his authentic disguise as Sing Wa, a traveler from 'beyond the Great Wall,' Fortune felt awkward and self-conscious. Well-traveled Chinese, like the Cantonese who dealt with Westerners, could expose him. Li said that as long as he did not speak, he might pass; Fortune understood a few words of Chinese but could not carry on a conversation. He spent his days sitting on the bow of the boat as they passed numerous large towns and walled cities. He looked imperiously ahead, but his heart sped every time they passed near shore or close by another boat. Either he did not attract any attention, or his disguise worked exceedingly well.

Two nights later when they pulled up near the ancient fortified city of Cading, Fortune watched to see how people reacted to his appearance. As in most towns, shoppers hurried through the market buying vegetables and meats, men hefted sedan chairs or were being carried themselves, little girls tended younger siblings, and boys studied in the Great Ancestral Halls. Porters carried towering baskets of vegetables, cotton, silk, and boxed goods balanced from bamboo poles across their shoulders. People thronged over bridges in groups or singly. None turned to stare at the tall Englishman. No one yelled, "Ai-ya, a barbarian," or pointed in horror shouting, "*gweilo*, a red-haired foreigner."

John Poe sculled his small sampan close to where Li had ordered Fortune's boat to be secured, the end-tie of a small dock at the end of a long line of fishing boats. He had memorized the urgent message that cousin Li had handed to another cousin in a passing sampan with his own orders to race to Shanghai. As their boat tied up at the end of the dock outside the ancient walled river town, he focused on the tall man in gray, hands clasped at his waist, who intently watched the crew. One boatman was preparing rice while another swept the deck clean of the day's dirt.

The air smelled fragrantly delicious when Li leapt off. He maneuvered around the boats tying up for the night on his way to the city wall, entered through the gates and walked straight to the marketplace. The massive city gates would close at sundown and there was no time to dally. He felt the presence of another close by his elbow and the scent of the incense that Master Ping burned at his ancestral altar in Soochow. He turned his head slightly to the right. A young boatman in faded nankeen, head shaded by a huge grass hat, stood behind him. "You got here quickly," Li said, keeping his eyes on the vendor who was weighing out a pound of pork on his hand scales. "Are you alone?"

"Yes." John smiled. Li was no-nonsense. A reliable, observant man.

"Your plan?"

"To discourage him. To make him turn back. Are he and the crew heavy sleepers?"

"I'll make it so." Li paid the meat vendor with a few copper coins. He glanced at his cousin, a twinkle in his eye, eager to do mischief.

"I'll be humbly grateful." John handed him a small packet.

"We must do what the Emperor will not. He does not see the threat as we do. What word from Shanghai?"

"My father says the hongs are alarmed that Fortune travels to the tea growing areas in defiance of the Emperor's decree. But the Emperor replies that he will not censure Fortune or the British Consul for fear of the British gun boats and armies."

The cousins shook their heads and muttered, comparing observations and strategies. By the time Li returned to his boat the crew had neatly coiled the ropes in their proper places and the day's equipment was stored.

The men prepared and ate dinner. They heard the guards shut and bar the city gates. Armed guards lit the torches that blazed from the towers. Calls and answering whistles of the night patrols reverberated from the top of the city walls. Beyond the walled fortification, the countryside disappeared in darkness. One by one, lanterns were dimmed until the canal was swallowed.

John Poe needed no light at midnight to scull next to the boat at the end of the small dock. No one heard when he side-tied his boat, which had been padded at the rails with cotton batting. He stepped noiselessly over the prone forms of the boatmen who slept on the deck under the stars. When the men muttered in their sleep, he paused. He lifted the window above Fortune's head. Silently, he thanked Li for greasing the hinges. He slipped through the window and landed effortlessly onto the cabin floor. He was quick now. Guided by Fortune's barbarian odor, he reached under his bed. One by one, John hoisted his boxes and trunks through the window and loaded them onto his boat.

Smiling to himself, he sculled silently back to his mooring.

ᐳ

The sickening sound of wood against wood, hull against hull, tossed Fortune off his mat. Crash! Screech! Branches scraped the cabin roof like bare fingernails. Boatmen screamed and became entangled in the low-lying trees. The boat took a turn and bumped another. "Ai-ya," the crew shouted, "wah, wah, wah!"

Fortune rubbed his chilled cheeks and scowled at the wind whistling down through the window over his head. Hadn't he closed it? He opened his eyes and thought he saw stars overhead. Stranger still.

Everyone was bumbling sleepily on the deck now, including Fortune with his nightdress flapping like a sheet in the brisk wind. His boatmen pushed away from the other boats jammed against them like nestling chicks, apologized for crashing, and shouted to others to throw them a line. They cursed and screamed when they found their tie lines had been severed.

Li lit a lantern and helped the men inspect their vessel inch by inch. Fortunately, except for the sliced lines and minor scrapes to the hull, nothing was amiss.

Satisfied, Fortune went back to sleep. When it was time to get dressed in the morning he reached under his bed for his clothes. He dropped to his knees and peered under his bed. "No," he shouted. He stood up, scratched his head, then sat back on the bed, and looked up at the open window above his head. "No, that's impossible."

Li, who always slept on the deck under the stars, heard the Scot's vociferous shouts. He had finished washing his face and hands with the fresh smelling soap his wife had made and dressed in clean tunic and trousers. He liked an early morning bath when few were up and he had the river virtually to himself. He called to the Scot, "The crew says everything is in order."

"But, it's not."

Li slipped on his shoes and swung into the cabin. He furrowed his brow at Fortune's befuddled look.

"Everything's gone," gasped Fortune. He gestured at the bedding piled on his mat. "All my trunks, my clothes, my journals. Everything."

"Look under your bed where you stowed them," suggested Li with his hands on his hips.

"They're gone." The Scot's mouth moved open and shut like a fish gasping for air. His shoulders drooped.

"That's impossible."

Fortune dropped to his knees and waved his hands in the emptiness. "You have no clothes?"

"Only what I'm wearing. I've lost everything."

Li eyed Fortune's pale hairy legs sticking out from the bottom of the thin nightshirt. "Then we best turn back to Shanghai. You can't travel like that."

Fortune's voice withered, small and defeated. "How could every-thing disappear? I was sleeping right here." He crawled back on his mat and pulled his blankets up to his chin. "I would have heard if someone had come in. Wouldn't I?"

"We'll return to Shanghai immediately. I'll send word to Consul Thom that you've been robbed and beg that he provide you clothes and immediate passage to England." Li spun on his heels and left to discuss the change of plans with their boatmen.

The boatman sounded happier to be heading home to where it was safe. It was fate that severed their lines in the middle of the night. The *gweilo* would find all his things back where he came from, where he should have stayed.

He had come so far, Fortune grumbled. His Chinese disguise had worked. Now he was naked, penniless, bobbing in the middle of the canal on a boat that didn't have enough lines to tie up to a dock. He couldn't do any fieldwork without his magnifying glass, tools, books, pens, and paper. And his journals. He moaned at all the work he had lost. He cuddled on his pillow like a baby. If he weren't a Scot he would cry.

Outside, Li and the crew simmered the rice for breakfast. Their voices were eager, anxious to return to Shanghai as they hoisted the sail. The wind swept across the water and caught, filling their sail with power. The crew sat back on their haunches to enjoy the ride home.

"Wait!" Fortune leapt from the sampan's cabin, his white nightdress flapping around his knees in the breeze. "Look, I found my money under my pillow." He held up his purse and jingled the coins. "I have enough to make a complete set of clothes and pay the boatmen. We can go to Soochow."

"But you have no tools to collect or write."

"I can improvise." Fortune ducked into the cabin but the saddened crew could hear him laughing.

Li decided that if he had to dress Fortune, he was going to do it his way. He gave instructions to the crew to boil water for the barbarian's bath while he went back into town. He approached the high ramparts of the fortified town of Cading and walked through the markets until he came to a little store where silks and cottons were neatly arrayed. The tailor, a smooth-shaven man, sat at the entrance with a cup of tea. On the table at his side were a pair of long sheers, a lacquer box of very sharp needles, and an elaborate display of threads in every possible hue. At the back of the shop, his father, now almost blind, stitched the strong, invisible seams for some of their oldest clients who appreciated his workmanship. By his side sat the tailor's wife and daughters, simply attired in dark blues and plums, who made the intricately knotted buttons and frogs that fastened their creations.

"Tailor, I need clothes for my master who is this high." Li held his hand up to about six feet. "This wide." He extended his arms about six inches past the tailor's own shoulders. "He is in a hurry, for he was robbed last night."

The tailor had heard many strange tales in his long career. He shook a face creviced by wrinkles and clucked sadly. "Times are dangerous. Strangers prey upon the unwary. You pick the material. I'll make him a proper robe by the time you have walked around the market place once." The tailor pulled out appropriate colors and displayed them with a flourish. For five generations his family had manned this very shop creating both elegant and sturdy robes for the citizens of Cading. He was not the cheapest tailor, but his measuring eye was the most accurate.

Li surveyed his stock and picked a medium weight cotton of dark gray. "He is a man of means but does not want to attract the attention of the mandarins."

"Then we shall make his knots of the same color, not contrasting. The stitching will be simple." The tailor tapped his head to mentally note the specifications. The wrinkles radiating from his eyes lilted up. "Anything else?"

"Make the hems sturdy, for he is a man who likes to travel by foot." Li was anxious to get the rest of his errands done. Across the road, he saw a boatman in indigo trousers and shirt enter a small corner stall where he ordered a bowl of wide noodles in a steaming broth sprinkled with finely chopped green onions and cilantro. The boatman quickly scrutinized the other patrons, three bombastic fishermen and two querulous old men, before he sat at a small table with his back to the wall and a view of the market. Li turned back to the tailor who had already whipped out his long-bladed shears and a drafting pattern. "Can you recommend a reasonable shoemaker?"

After Li met with a slope-shouldered shoemaker, with stops to purchase a queue and cap, he headed to the small noodle stall across from the tailor shop. He bought a bowl of noodles and joined the boatman sitting against the wall.

"If you fail as a tea merchant, you will never starve with your talent as a thief," Li muttered under his breath.

John Poe laughed. He kept his eyes on the street and the tailor shop. "When are you turning back?"

His cousin surreptitiously scanned the faces around them. His voice was low. "We continue. His money was under his pillow."

John turned to his cousin with a start, eyes wide. "A pity," he sighed. "Didn't you think it was a nice touch to steal everything under his bed? Was he discouraged?"

"Mournfully so. I had him ready to return to England," Li snorted. "We had already hoisted the sail." The two continued to plan while Li savored his noodles with simmering beef bones and vegetables.

∿

"*E*verything off, sir," commanded Li. "I'll not dress you until you wash like a proper Chinese." Li himself used the soap his wife made for him before and after every meal and completely bathed his body, even if it had to be from a mountain stream, every morning and night. But the barbarian seemed to loathe cleanliness. It was a disgusting aversion, especially when seven men had to share a small sampan.

Fortune sat on his bed and spluttered in protest, clutching his thin nightdress while the boatman poured pots of boiling water into a pan at the stern. "But I'm not dirty."

"You have not bathed in a month. Your water will be warm for twenty minutes. Here is soap and a washcloth. Give me your clothes."

"I can't go out there naked. It isn't decent. I need privacy."

"Your stench isn't decent. I've had the men put boxes around the stern so no one will see anything important unless you stand up." Li handed Fortune's nightclothes to the cook to boil.

The Scot walked out in the sun, blinked, and crouched by the pot of steaming water. He held the soap to his face and inhaled as if trying to discern its scent. Vigorously, he soaped and scrubbed his body. "I'm not done," he protested when Li stood over him.

"Scrub every inch," Li said with an inspecting scowl. "I want to see clean skin and no dirt between your toes and fingernails."

Fortunes scrubbed until he turned as pink as a boiled pig. He took extra care between his legs, which, Li noted, looked well fleshed even in its flaccid state. The cook brought a pan of warm water for Fortune's face and hair. The thin cotton towel wasn't adequate to dry his hairy body so Fortune sat, his hands covering his lap, in the sun behind the barricade of boxes. And when he stood, finally dry, his blond hairs glittered in the sunlight as if he had been sprinkled with gold dust.

☙

*A*s soon as they passed Cading their little boat shot out into a broad and beautiful canal. Hundreds of Chinese boats of all sizes, most under sail, skimmed across the broad, smooth waters. Curved roofed pagodas rose like filigreed ornaments from the picturesque peaks. Buddhist temples dotted the lush lands. Rice paddies undulated to the horizon. From all directions they heard the clatter of hundreds of waterwheels powered by barefoot women flushing the rice fields with fresh water.

Now properly dressed, Fortune asked Li to explain the wondrous canals and the serene landscape that stretched to the horizon.

Li pointed out the highlights. "Twenty-two hundred years ago The Grand Canal was used to ferry Chinese troops between the Yellow River and the Huai River Valley, the distance of 250 of your miles." Succeeding Emperors expanded The Grand Canal so rice and other tribute from the fertile plains of the south could be sent to Peking. Over five million people worked on the canal at one time under Sui Dynasty Emperor Yang

Ti in 604 who built 1,500 miles of canal in six years. He did not to tell Fortune that during construction, two million workers were reported 'lost' and it was unknown whether that meant they fled, fell ill, or died.

They crossed a beautiful lake fifteen miles across and entered another canal lined by weeping willows, passed under graceful bridges curved like half moons, and skimmed past quaint villages and prosperous towns.

The unmistakable scent of blooming flowers, lush greenery, and the rich, moist earth of Soochow welcomed them long before they saw the peaked roofs, curved up at the corners, Reaching to Heaven. Walls topped with black tiles tantalized him with secrets of gardens within. In the trees, birds competed with passionate trills. With a light breeze, the little boat skimmed the clear surface joining others headed for the Venice of the East. Like dancing fireflies, thousands of lantern-lit boats glided along the riverbanks and under the delicate bridges. By the time they moored under the city walls, the moon had reached its peak among the stars. The men secured the boat with multiple lines to avoid a repeat disaster and were asleep within minutes.

∾

*ortune woke with dawn's first light. He washed Chinese style with soap, washcloth, and cold water following Li's example. The finely woven cotton of his new robe felt softer on his skin than his English woven broadcloth shirts and trousers. Li took some time placing the mandarin hat with the attached queue on his head and adjusting it so it looked natural.

"Do I look Chinese?"

"No. But few people here have seen a white person. They will think you are from a different part of China, perhaps a Mongol or a Hun, or afflicted by disease."

Fortune followed Li ashore, mimicking his gait. His eyes darted anxiously as they crossed a bridge over a wide canal flanked by ancient willow trees. He warily watched the sleek-haired citizens in their bright silks and elegant jewels who leaned over to watch fine junks and boats ply the canals landscaped with willows, pines, and flowers. Although he had passed as Chinese in the countryside, he fretted that the inhabitants of this sophisticated city might not be deceived. He felt the tingle in his spine, that rush of excitement and adrenalin; he was the first Englishman to walk undetected through the most fashionable city of the Celestial Empire. Even Li had forgotten him. His translator leaned over the side of the bridge with his face lifted up to inhale the scent of flowers, silks, and sumptuous richness that infused the atmosphere.

He had done it. If he learned enough Chinese to get around by himself, he might be able to travel unfettered and undetected.

Then he saw the pack of dogs cruising both sides of the street, sniffing people and doorways. Throughout China, Chinese dogs were known for their uncanny ability to detect Westerners as far as half a mile away. Chinese dogs had chased and attacked Fortune from Hong Kong to Canton, from Foochow to Shanghai.

"Li," Fortune shouted in panic. He dodged down an alley and spied another pack of dogs cruising from doorway to doorway. He rushed around the corner, running to the left, and then to the right. No matter which street he took to escape, dogs roamed, dogs slept, dogs guarded doorways, or dogs approached, tongues lolling. He cowered behind Li and tried to still the fear that pounded in his head as he inched along behind his man. At an achingly normal pace, they passed a dog guarding a silk shop, walked past snarling monsters chasing a larger one with a stolen bone, and stepped over restless pups cavorting by the noodle shop.

"You see, sir," Li glanced at him with a knowing sweep of his arm at the lolling canines, "you have washed off your Western stink."

They crossed many bridges, each more beautiful than the last, while the air off the water grew sweeter with floral scents. Li stopped at the peak of a moon bridge within an especially exquisite garden and indicated with his hand into the distance, "Do you see that pagoda rising above the mists in the west? It's actually over a mile away, far off in the country." Li gestured over the curved dip in the garden wall to the hills beyond. "We call it the 'borrowed view from afar.' This view will continue to evolve as it has for over three hundred years." He was surprised at how many details he remembered from that time long ago when Cousin John Poe had guided him through this 51,000-meter garden. Its serene beauty, centered on a central pond with pavilions, terraces, chambers, and towers representative of the classic gardens of the Ming Dynasty, stunned him anew.

Fortune squinted at the distant mountains and saw how the juniper and cypress within the walls framed the pagoda as if it were part of the garden's landscape.

Three finely dressed women with their attendants paused a few feet away. Tiny silver ornaments inlaid with turquoise kingfisher feathers shivered in the thick rolls of their hair when they turned to watch a waterfall tumble down artistically eroded limestone rocks into a lake. The scent of their gowns rose sweetly in the wind that fingered the folds of their silks. A stab of regret crossed Fortune's face as he watched how their oilskin umbrellas cast soft shadows on their fair, smooth faces. He bent forward to hear their voices. None were as tall as his beloved Jadelin, nor as fair, nor as dainty.

Observing the Scot's sudden interest, Li asked, "Don't you think the women in Soochow are the most beautiful? Like fresh flower petals, their eyes are bright as sunlight on the lake and they move like the bamboo in the wind." The Scot looked at him with a startled look, as if Li had read a secret within his heart. Ah, thought Li. A man in love.

As they sailed away from Soochow, Robert Fortune, emboldened by the success of his disguise as Sing Wa, a traveler from 'beyond the Great Wall,' stood on the bow of his little boat. Since they had arrived under cover of night, Fortune wished to experience the full beauty of the famed city from the tree-lined canals. Although Soochow at night was a breathtaking kaleidoscope of glowing lanterns, its lush landscaping was even more astounding when the flowers opened their scents to the sun.

One particular series of curved-roof buildings caught his eye. Perhaps it was the hawk circling above it in elegant spirals or perhaps it was the gleam of the black tile roof against the white clouds behind it. Willow trees draped from the terraces to the water with a sway in the gentle breeze. Alas, he could not make out the flowers behind the openwork tiles surrounding the terraces, just flashes of bright pink, yellow, and red. He wondered if there were people watching because he saw the movement of blues and brilliant greens. He was unaware that Mei, in a cobalt blue gown edged with emerald green, was pouring tea for her father, a very rare tea called White Mist of Phoenix Mountain. Jadelin sat across a small rosewood table from Mow Bowli, who had just raised a celadon porcelain teacup to his lips and acknowledged Grand Master Ping's advice upon his newly married state.

All eyes turned to watch the traveler in grey on the bow of his boat stare intently at each graceful tree, dainty flower, and glossy shrub. Although dressed in the robe and cap of a mandarin, something about him did not look right. At that moment Grand Master Ping, Mei, Jadelin, and Mow Bowli knew exactly who he was and that he should not have been there.

Seventeen

A Scot In Chinese Attire

ortune tucked his hands into the sleeves of his mandarin robe in the manner of the Chinese as he headed towards the home of his friend, Alistair Mackenzie. Instead of striding aggressively as he would through the streets of London, he walked with short, sure steps which he found more compatible to the flow of a mandarin robe and slippers. He tipped his capped head modestly forward so his queue swayed down his back.

He stared directly at his friends and tried to catch their eye. But they brushed past as if he were invisible. He laughed at how easily he could move among Westerners without being noticed. The close-knit community of British, his fellow countrymen, looked through him without a flicker of recognition. How easily he could deceive.

To his surprise and convenience, he found the mandarin robe much more comfortable: warmer on cold evenings and cooler on hot afternoons. His legs never chafed or bound when he hiked and he enjoyed greater freedom of movement.

When Mackenzie opened his front door, Fortune whisked past him into his parlor and sat down in the wing-backed chair by the front window. In Chinese, he ordered Li to have the coolies bring in the rest of his luggage.

Mackenzie raised his arms and shouted out in alarm. A few stunned minutes later he exploded with roars of laughter. "What have you done to yourself, Fortune? Gone Chinese?"

After a fitting at Weatherby & Sons Clothiers, Fortune was properly attired with an umbrella, wool trousers, collared and cuffed cotton shirt, and a heavy wool coat. He put on a top hat to cover his partially shaved head. He avoided the Poe estate and tea hong. To soothe his disappointment he decided to leave immediately to hunt for flowers in Ningpo and return when the azaleas bloomed in Shanghai.

∾

*A*fter he posted Fortune's mail, Li met Mandarin Poe and John in the quiet of the Mandarin's study to plan their next strategy. The men waited until the soft-footed servants, who brought in the boiling water and their favorite teas, soundlessly closed the carved doors.

"Here's his latest letter, Uncle," said Li. He slid out the tissue-thin pages and read it to them.

Confidential Report to the Royal Horticultural Society
From Robert Fortune. March 1845
Honorable Sirs:

There is no country more agreeable or healthy than northern China. The air is bracing, the sky generally clear, and mornings are delightfully cool. Vegetation grows with rapidity, surpassing anything I had ever witnessed in England. By the middle of April, deciduous trees and shrubs will be covered with leaves. The barley is in full ear, and the oil plant, Brassica sinensis, has massed golden yellow on the hillsides and plains where the air is perfumed with its fragrance. My objective is to collect the finest plants to take back to England.

I lost no time in visiting all my former acquaintances, mandarins, and nurserymen to make my selection whilst the plants are in full bloom. I have added tree peonies, azaleas, viburnums, daphnes, roses and many other plants of great beauty, all new to Europe. Many of these plants can only be verified by the color of their flowers.

It is absolutely necessary that I visit the different districts three or four times each spring. For this reason, I request to extend my contract with the Royal Horticultural Society for another season. I must be sure I procure the best plants for my collection and properly prepare them for travel. I have found specific plants of extreme interest in Shanghai, Chusan, Ningpo, and other ports of the interior, which necessitates traveling great distances.

I have received the optical instruments I requested as gifts for those who have been most helpful to me. Although the Chinese feel there is nothing outside of China that they need or want, optical instruments intrigue them, especially the miniature magnifying glass for fieldwork.

Respectfully,
Robert Fortune

"The Westerner is going to stay another year." Mandarin Poe rubbed his aching forehead, which seemed to crease with deeper wrinkles as each season passed. He picked up his teapot shaped like a double gourd and poured out his tea, a dark rich pu'er tea known for its medicinal properties. He sipped slowly and felt its soothing heat warm his body. "How is this possible? He dislikes China." He remembered the awkward man with eyes so pale one felt they were looking through to the sky on the other side. "Will he never leave?"

"I myself do not understand, Uncle," Li answered as he poured oolong tea from a teapot incised with a bamboo pattern. He shook his head at the fits Fortune threw whenever he got frustrated with the Chinese. "Every time he enters a new town, encounters different people, or comes up against something he does not understand, he rails against China's uncivilized ways. He never trusts the prices I translate for him and insists he can get it for less. John can attest to the Scot's disgruntled nature. And now he dresses as a Chinese with a queue. You look surprised, Uncle Poe. Can you imagine how amazed I was when I saw him in a queue and robe with satin slippers on his hairy feet?"

John nodded. He refilled his teapot covered with raised plum blossoms. "Baba, I received a letter from Mow Bowli and Jadelin describing in detail how Fortune sailed through Soochow."

Li shook his head at the foreigner's boldness. "You saw how he stood prominently on the deck in his Chinese disguise to observe the gardens and canals. I did not show my face. I didn't want to be identified when the Emperor's spies recognized him. He's now headed to Ningpo to collect flowers. He plans to be back when the azaleas bloom in a few weeks."

Mandarin Poe got to his feet and paced the thick Chinese carpets. "Make him leave. Destroy his plants." He suddenly turned and faced John and Li, his hand on his heart. "I'm sorry. I wish no evil to anyone. It is wrong to kill or harm any living being. But this man's very existence threatens our people, our country, and our future." He sat down again and looked to them both for answers.

"We'll make his life miserable," John promised.

His cousin put his hand to his heart with a smile that promised mischief.

Eighteen

THE ILLEGAL VOYAGE

CHAPOO

*F*ortune fumed at his stupidity. He had timed his itinerary in each city to catch the blooming season along the coast. In Ningpo, each nursery offered dozens of flowers that intoxicated his senses with brilliant blossoms and scents. He had blissfully collected and packed these precious treasures. Now he sat on the edge of the cot in the rooms Li had arranged and double-checked his calendar. He had three days to get to Shanghai otherwise he would miss the azaleas in full bloom. His miscalculation meant a whole season in Shanghai might be lost.

He put on his felt cap and smoked glass spectacles which protected his pale eyes from the clear blue skies of China and walked outside to find Li. He saw his translator walking back between the rows of restaurants where steam curled out of rooftop chimneys bearing the scent of hearty soup stocks. "Where have you been? I need you," he shouted.

"I told you I was going out for a while. You said you had no need of my services then," Li grumbled.

Fortune scowled. "I need you to get me to Shanghai in three days." He flung up his arm and gestured him to hurry back.

"We'll be there in eight to twelve days," corrected Li.

"Three. Otherwise all the flowers I'm interested in will be past their prime. I won't be able to see their true colors in full bloom."

"Then we should have left ten days ago."

"I have a plan," the Scot hissed. He shut the door and cleared a space on the small table where he had laid out the accouterments he used to study plants. He unfolded the map he had drawn of China. He had marked where he had found the best flowers and the areas he wished to explore. "If we return the way we came," he indicated the route with his finger, "by the time we get to Shanghai all the blossoms will be brown and wilted. However, the fastest route, a distance of three-hundred li upriver including a change of boat in Chapoo, will take only three days."

"You are not allowed to travel more than a day from the five major ports."

"As a Chinese I can take the inland route. We leave immediately. Pack my things." Fortune clamped his jaw and waved Li away to do his bidding.

Alarmed, Li sent a message by runner to Mandarin Poe in Shanghai.

When Fortune and Li arrived in Chinhae at the mouth of the Ningpo River, Li headed for the dock where the upriver junks were loading. He dodged sweaty, bare-chested sailors and hailed the boatman who stood at the bulwark, shouting out orders to quick-stepping coolies bearing crates of cotton, pottery, spices, and fruits balanced from bamboo staves across their back. "Cousin Pang," Li hailed.

"Cousin Li," Pang answered back. This weathered salt, in a faded nankeen shirt, trousers of indigo blue, and hand-woven straw sandals, grabbed Li's arm. "Uncle Poe told me to expect you." He whispered low. "Your *gweilo* wants to go to Shanghai through Chapoo. Chapoo is not a treaty port. What if someone finds out I have a Westerner aboard?" His almond eyes pursed into radiating wrinkles. He was a responsible family man of fifty, born to the sea like his father and grandfather before him.

"Chapoo is a Tartar town; they don't heed the Emperor. I'll make sure the *gweilo* pays you a good price." Li clasped his cousin's arms with a reassuring grip. "He'll be disguised as a Chinese mandarin. Don't worry. We prepared a surprise for him in Chapoo."

"I do this because Uncle Poe asks, and I honor our ancestral ties." Pang's forehead scrunched into a network of frowns at the foolhardiness of the adventure. He scanned the river and noted the quickening pace of his fellow boatmen as they prepared to catch the tide. "I hope this barbarian will not change my fortune. We set sail as soon as you board."

Pang's passengers arranged their bedrolls and luggage along the sides of the central cabin with an open space down the middle. No one seemed concerned when the pale-eyed mandarin pointed out the spot he wanted and motioned others to move aside. With much bowing and soothing words to those who were already settled, Captain Pang made a space for his latest passenger and his many boxes. Finally, Fortune was settled in an area protected from the elements with a bedroll to sleep on. Li would sleep under the stars as he preferred to do, where he could smell the scent of China's rich earth, the bamboo forests, and winds riding the waterway.

A small motion caught his eye. Then many odd movements. He peered closer at his fellow travelers. Suddenly he yelped like a slaughtered lamb. "Li, quick, help me move! Everyone's got lice!" He pushed his trunks into a perimeter, a barricade against the vermin that crawled and jumped from the folds of his fellow travelers' trousers, tunics, and jackets.

Later, a dwarf, whom the other passengers treated with respect and deference, set up his pallet across from Fortune. His trunks were neatly tied with leather straps, as fastidiously neat as the man.

Fortune, his legs and arms drawn in like a turtle, took stock of his fellow passengers as Captain Pang and his crew cast off. Most were dressed like inland city dwellers in dull colors, except for the dwarf who wore a fastidiously clean Chinese robe. Fortune made a note that Li should have his clothes properly laundered when they got to Shanghai.

A storm hit that first night. Pang couldn't hold the boat steady through the rough, wind driven waves. The next morning everyone awoke in a jumble of belongings, bedding, and queues.

Hastily, Fortune reconstructed his barrier. Then he stumbled out on the open deck and sat as far away as he could from anyone else to methodically pluck off the lice and vermin and flick them into the river. He envied Li who slept on the deck in the open air dreaming of stars and a fresh ocean breeze. Li must have been the first one up for he had already bathed and smelled as fresh as his wife's soap.

After a hearty breakfast of simmered rice with fish and vegetables, the passengers staked out their positions on the deck with blankets. All day they dozed, smoked, and chatted while they watched the passing landscape of small stone farms, water buffalo grazing along the river bank, and rolling hills. Only the dwarf sat alone, content to smoke his pipe and contemplate the scenery. When the sun rose to a steamy noon that barely cooled in the afternoon, the opium addicts in their silk gowns drifted back into the shade of the cabin.

That evening they approached a town alive with flapping banners and beating gongs, drums and cymbals. The passengers pressed to the rail, pointing and shouting happily. As soon as Captain Pang docked, everyone headed for the colorful lanterns that surrounded an open-air stage lit by lanterns.

Afraid to be recognized for what he really was, Fortune chose to stay aboard. The dwarf gestured to the bright lanterns and festivities. "We are extremely lucky to be here on the one night a traveling troupe is performing. One doesn't always get the opportunity to see Peking opera," he said kindly. Dressed warmly with a cloak over his perfectly tailored gown, he had expressive round eyes and a generous mouth. "I'll take you. You will enjoy it."

Li thanked him on his master's behalf, but his master, who came from beyond the Great Wall, did not like crowds. By now everyone, including Captain Pang and the crew, had deserted the boat and joined the throngs in the glowing plaza, drawn to the grilled meats and steaming soups offered by the vendors.

The dwarf nodded sympathetically and suggested they should follow him to a good spot. On a deserted knoll overlooking the plaza, he gestured with his open arms that here on the soft grass they could sit and watch. The men had clear views of the dazzling costumes, close enough to see the expressions of love and jealousy blazing from the faces of the performers and the dizzying acrobatics as they leapt, danced, and fought across the bamboo stage.

Their new friend drew out his tobacco pouch and shared it with them. He said he was on his way to one of the businesses he owned up the canal. His family was in Ningpo and oh, how he missed his little ones while he was gone. His sons, six and ten, were taller than he. "This will be a rare treat for our visitor from beyond the Great Wall. Peking Opera, one of China's great cultural treasures, goes back almost a thousand years." And the story? A favorite called the Hibiscus Fairy.

"The actors' faces are painted such garish colors!" Fortune screwed up his face with distaste. The expressions were unsettling: exaggerated, strange, and unrealistic.

The businessman answered with a hearty laugh. "Yes, they add to our enjoyment. Even from afar we can see how each character feels." He lit his pipe and inhaled with great pleasure. When he leaned back he exhaled an exotic spicy smoke. His eyes twinkled as his arms encompassed the performance. "From the colors and the way the face is painted, we, the audience, can tell the truth about a character. Let me tell you the story as it unfolds there on the stage."

"A long time ago," their companion began, "there was a beautiful garden. There's the gardener, coming in with his hoe. He's watering the flowers one by one. He sees the hibiscus. Oh, he wishes this beautiful flower were human so they could talk of poetry and beautiful things. That night, the wind carries in the perfume of the hibiscus. See, she enters, the Hibiscus Fairy in her human form, a woman who has come to visit her admirer. You can tell by her elegant robes and elaborate hairstyle that she is a virtuous, kind lady. Notice her long pale fingers, how gracefully she moves, and the ribbon-like sleeves she swirls around her body like the wind. After she departs, the gardener writes her a love poem.

"Suddenly, a thunderstorm threatens the garden. The gardener runs out to protect his precious hibiscus. The Hibiscus Fairy is deeply touched by his devotion. She is about to appear to him again when the spirits of wind and rain kidnap her.

"Wah! The Goddess of the Hundred Flowers is furious that the Hibiscus Fairy dares to fall in love with a mortal.

"Unaware that his beloved Hibiscus Fairy is being held prisoner, the lonely gardener leaves to study with his uncle. On his way over a mountain pass, he comes across a sickly hibiscus plant. Something about this plant touches his heart and he wants to stay to nurse this particular hibiscus back to health. But he must continue on his journey. The Hibiscus Fairy appears and tries to follow him.

"Wah! Look at the Banana Spirit who leaps upon the stage. He tries to stop her. He says, 'I'm a better match for you than the human.' His vibrantly painted face--bright green and black--means he is larger than life." The dwarf leapt to his feet in excitement and pointed dramatically. "Look at his imposing costume. See his tall shoes that allow him to tower over everyone. See how he possesses the stage. He grabs our attention. Meanwhile, the gardener arrives at his uncle's house and finds they have arranged for him to marry his uncle's daughter. The Hibiscus Fairy appears to him the night before the wedding and pleads for him to run away with her. They will cross the river and get as far away as possible. As you can see by his pale virtuous face, the gardener is a humble man, more natural looking than the Banana Spirit with his green flame-like cheeks.

"The Banana Spirit, disguised as a boatman, anticipated that the lovers would run off. Halfway through their trip across the river, he turns back into the Banana Spirit dressed in bright green with that fantastical headdress of gold leaves. Wah! What a battle." The dwarf leapt in the air and threw his body dramatically into each gesture. "The Hibiscus Fairy cries for help from her fellow flower spirits. Those dainty spirits come at once. They fight the Banana Spirit and the Tree spirits who come to his aid. See how they leap into the air, five against one, with swords and staffs. See how the flower spirits trick the Banana Spirit and Tree spirits and fling them overboard? Now free from persecution, the Hibiscus Fairy and the gardener run off into the country and find happiness." Their new friend sighed, his hand to his heart. With a white cloth he wiped the perspiration that had beaded his forehead during his energetic narration.

"This was better than any performance I have seen in England," enthused Fortune. Caught up in the story and spectacular costumes, he had cheered and booed the fantastic creatures on elevated platform shoes, their shoulders padded to supernatural proportions, as they leapt and fought. Weapons flashed long and shiny while curved feathers sprouting from their armor accentuated their somersaults and aerial battles. Most surprisingly, the pentatonic singing, usually jarring to Western ears, blended beautifully in the crisp starry night.

At dawn, when the last cymbal and drum were silenced, the Hibiscus fairy and fellow flower spirits vanquished the Banana Spirit and Tree Spirits. The heroine and her gardener somersaulted off into the countryside amidst the audience's cheers. Fortune thanked the businessman and they shuffled with the other passengers to the boat.

◌

The next day, Captain Pang anchored his junk in a muddy bay near Chapoo. Li, Fortune, and their luggage were lowered in a small boat and rowed close to shore. The two hopped out and shouldered their trunks. The businessman smoked his pipe and waved, his round face wrinkled in a smile.

From Chapoo's gate tower, John Poe watched Fortune and Li trudge barefoot and muddy up the embankment followed by a half dozen coolies Pang had coaxed from shore to carry their luggage. A pushing crowd of a hundred gawkers met them. John had met with the mandarins of Chapoo. He had assembled the hordes. And in a few minutes, Fortune would enter the gates unprepared for a disastrous delay.

◌

Fortune wailed, his voice barely audible over the crowd that pushed forward with bug-eyed stares. "Li, what do I do?" Up to now, locals hadn't given him a second glance. Here in Chapoo, crowds pushed forward to touch his skin and pull his hair. Some pinched and scratched to see if he were real.

It didn't take long to locate where the Shanghai-bound boats were docked. But every time Fortune approached a prospective boat to inquire about passage, the masses pushed aboard with him.

The boatmen were furious. "You're sinking my boat. Get back," they yelled. They shook their fists. "Go away white-devil. Off! Get away you *gweilo*." Because of the close-packed crowd, every boat had denied him passage. Even worse, the mass of curious Chinese had grown so unwieldy he couldn't move.

"You must ask the mandarins to help you," Li yelled. "Only they have the power."

"But I'm not supposed to be here." Fortune wanted to sit down. He wanted a cup of tea. Li's voice sounded far away. He couldn't breathe, couldn't move, and couldn't think.

"The mandarins are not to know that I helped you get here, remember? You know enough Chinese words to make yourself understood. Tell them you got here on your own. Look at me. Look me in the eyes so I know you understand. Follow me."

Jostled, pressed in by bodies, Fortune wiped the sweat from his face with an already filthy cuff. He shoved his elbows out and shouldered forward, fearful and desperate. He didn't want to go to the mandarins. They would gladly take him to Shanghai, after they arrested him. Consul Thom would deport him back to London. All his work, all his dreams, lost. All his suffering would have been for nothing. The humiliation was unthinkable.

∾

They inched towards the mandarin's towering gate flanked by scowling Foo dogs the height of a fully-grown warrior. Crowds pressed against Li as he pounded the double doors with his fists and explained to the sword-wielding guards that an Englishman needed the mandarin's help. Come, he gestured to Fortune with his head, keep close to me.

The scowling guards kept back the crowds with whips that snapped like cracking spines. Denied their quarry, the hordes screamed. After the doors slammed shut behind them, Fortune stared at Li, too terrified to move. Only after Li assured him this was his only way out would the Scot enter the mandarin's reception hall where high backed chairs were arranged across an austere back wall lit by matching lanterns. Marble floors amplified the feeling of isolation.

"Tell your master I request the honor of meeting him on an urgent matter," Fortune explained to the bearded sage who inquired the purpose of his visit. The old man, dressed in silky black, looked Fortune up and down as if inspecting a roast pig he might buy. He stroked his wispy white whiskers as he puzzled over the European sporting a queue dressed in a mandarin robe. Then he disappeared down a silent corridor with gravity and frowns creasing his wizened face.

The Mandarin of Chapoo, a man of tremendous wealth and power, was not pleased to see this stranger. When he had met earlier with John Poe, son of the honorable Mandarin Poe of Shanghai, John had confirmed that the mandarin would be recognized for his loyalty and honor when he arrested this barbarian and turned him over to the British Consul. An irritating, unpleasant task. He had passed his fiftieth birthday with no problems with the Emperor, and he wished it to be so until his honorable death. He thought of his dozen children, his vast lands and honorable name, and how well he wielded his power.

Fortune made several low bows, which were politely returned. "Mandarin, I'm in a great hurry to get to Shanghai. I've been trying to engage a boat but can't succeed without your assistance. Will you help me?"

The mandarin repeated, as was the custom, what Fortune had said in Chinese. Out of respect, he asked how old he was. Fortune thanked him for his inquiry, told him his age, and asked for his. Fortune repeated his request for assistance in getting a boat to Shanghai.

Where have you been in China, asked the mandarin politely. How did you know there was a way to Shanghai through here? Why have you come to me to get a boat? Fortune answered some of the questions and found it convenient to not understand the rest. While the mandarin and Fortune parried, the mandarin's brother arrived with the rest of

Chapoo's highest ranking mandarins resplendent in the fine robes and insignia.

The five mandarins excused themselves to a private room. When they returned, they told Fortune that they had arranged free passage for him to Shanghai on their own boat and would send another boat with his luggage.

Fortune bowed low. "You are kind to grant me this honor." He knew the mandarins would take him directly to the British Consul in Shanghai where he would be arrested, fined, jailed, and deported. He thought of the fantastic masks of the Peking Opera which reveal but also hide a character's true nature. He would don the mask of subservience and humble gratitude to counter the mandarin's mask of generosity and kindness. With many bows and reiterated thanks, he apologized. "I can't accept so much kindness from you. I'm able to pay my own expenses. All I request is your permission to hire a small boat with three or four men which will enable me to get to Shanghai."

The Mandarin of Chapoo stroked his thick black beard and narrowed his lilting eyes. "We could not inconvenience you on your first trip to our town. We have a boat ready to take you comfortably to Shanghai. We insist you accept our humble offer. This is the only way we can ensure you will arrive in Shanghai. You have experienced the unpredictability of the mob. They will not let you leave unmolested." He was losing his patience with this stubborn Westerner. He would never directly accuse him of being illegally in Chapoo; that might bring the wrath of the British gunboats against his prosperous town. His men were no match for the militarily superior British Navy. No, one had to tread like a sparrow on snow when dealing with Westerners; one never knew how many guns they carried.

Fortune bowed again. "Thank you for your great concern for my well-being. Your gift is too great. I must pay my own way."

After many refusals and counter offers, the mandarins again retreated to their private room. When they returned they insisted he accept their final offer. "Shanghai is far from Chapoo. We can't guarantee you will arrive in Shanghai as you desire unless we send our own soldiers with you for protection."

Fortune sighed. "There is no need for your concern in this matter. I have a gun which I use for my protection."

"Gun!" The mandarins recoiled. They quickly conferred. As their last offer, Fortune could go on his own boat, paid with his own funds. They had an officer and his servant who were going to Shanghai, and they would be grateful if he would allow them to accompany him. They would find him a boat and a captain and ensure he could board safely.

A boatman, hard and lean, wearing sturdy sandals and trousers and shirt of indigo nankeen, arrived before nightfall. The two mandarin brothers, visibly relieved, insisted that they accompany Fortune, Li, and their coolies with the trunks, to be sure the barbarian left Chapoo. The crowd that followed Fortune to the boat was immense, but quiet and civil as long as the guards wielded their whips like thunderbolts.

"This is too fine a boat," complained Fortune when they approached the dock.

Li pushed Fortune aboard. "Pay whatever the boatman asks!"

Undetected in the crowd that followed, John Poe cursed. Immediately, he leapt aboard a swift boat with a Chapoo merchant that the mandarins had secured for him to tail the fine boat that carried Fortune to Shanghai.

Nineteen

A VIEW OF THE FUTURE

SHANGHAI

" I failed." John knelt at his father's feet, head bowed, palms clasped. Many times he had begged his father's forgiveness. Some of his transgressions had brought Mandarin Poe to rage that this son would never make it past puberty: a Ming vase shattered by a boastful kick, prized peonies trampled by horseplay, fireworks tossed over the wall after midnight, or stowing away on a junk headed for Soochow when he was ten.

Poe knew his son's youth and power, and it broke his heart to hear frustration in his voice. In a rich voice, low and soothing, he stroked his son's head. "Mow Bowli sent this rare Dragon Heart Mountain tea just this morning. An unusually strong and mellow first-pick that is too rare to share outside the family. You will feel your heart beat with courage and your resolve grow strong." Mandarin Poe's private study, shuttered against Shanghai's winter chill, was warmed by the sparkle of jade and porcelain. The two walked across the thick carpets to a window that framed the view of a hundred year old pine tree, thick barked and artfully pruned to the height of five feet. Moss covered rocks lay at its base. From the two chairs positioned for the best view, they could sip their tea and admire a still pond that reflected the reverse of the scene against a cloudless sky.

Tracking Robert Fortune for months outdoors had added to his son's robust resilience and fleshed out his physique. As for himself, the mandarin felt long hours conferring with officials, both Chinese and Western, had withered his reserves. He approached seventy. When he lay down for his nap after lunch, he couldn't get up until sunset.

"Sir?" A baby-faced young man put down a lacquered tray with a porcelain teapot and variety of teas. Another youth brought in a layered bamboo tray with a metal drain on the bottom. A third, older and more muscled, entered noiselessly with a teapot of boiling water. He accepted the pewter canister of tea from the mandarin and prepared the tea, then stepped back. The other two returned with tiny rice cakes. When the tea had steeped, the older boy poured for both men and stepped back into the shadows.

John Poe cradled the teacup in his tanned palms and inhaled the clean scent of the mountains. So fresh, so pure. He inhaled it deep in his lungs so it would cleanse him from within. How tired Baba looked; those furrows across his brow had deepened, and his skin tone had slackened emphasizing the sadness that occasionally swept over him as if a dark cloud had blown across a restless sky.

With reluctance, John detailed his exploits among the Ningpo tea-growing areas of the monks and how cleverly he had tracked the Englishman's explorations. His acted out how he slid through the window above Fortune's bed and stole all his belongings, including everything secured under his bed. His father laughed at his son's boldness, then gasped, incredulous that the *gweilo* had the temerity to hide his money under his pillow. John was proud of the deal he had struck with the locals of Chapoo and was sure Fortune had created his own trap. He bemoaned how Fortune had outfoxed the mandarins of Chapoo. By luck, ignorance, or plain tenacity, the Westerner persevered. Not only did Fortune collect flowering plants and tea shrubs, he had seen how the Chinese turned fresh leaves into the various teas, and walked through the nankeen producing areas. The Scot had also discovered how mulberry bushes were cultivated and silk worms nurtured. His plans had been creative. Had they worked, Fortune would have sown his own seeds of destruction. He could have gotten himself deported.

John had been careful to be sure the Scot did not die because had he done so, the British would immediately have blamed the Chinese. They would have used it as an excuse to blast their way from Ningpo to Chapoo with their gunboats and superior military weapons. That would have brought destruction, death, and probably another war, which would lead to more concessions for all the foreign powers in China.

Mandarin Poe groaned. "The only one way to absolutely stop him would have brought the fury of his country to destroy ours with their gun boats and armies. Then they would have sent more like him. No, the tide is shifting. They will keep returning to take what they want."

"Then what is the purpose, Baba?" John's voice raised in frustration. He wanted to crush the teacup with his bare hands, to feel the thin porcelain shatter in his grip. Quickly, he put it down and buried his face in his hands. "I tracked him over land and water. I lived under the stars and in crowded pilgrim inns. I bribed people to give him misinformation, stole his clothes and tools, and exposed his disguise, which churned local sentiment against him. I negotiated a deal with the mandarins of Chapoo for his arrest."

Mandarin Poe placed his hand on his son's shoulder. "We'll find a way to tame the Western appetite. Maybe not in my lifetime. Maybe not in yours."

"No! I have seen how he thinks." John clasped his thumbs to palm to center his ch'i. "I shiver to see we possess the same perseverance and attention to detail," he winced, pained at the realization. "He's ingenious and focused." John sat up and gripped his father's hands. "I should have left him for dead in that boar pit. He'd have died of exposure and starvation. No one would have known. Why couldn't I have let him rot?" He voice rasped sorrowfully.

Mandarin Poe put down his tea and ran his finger down his son's cheek, still warm and flush with youth. "All life is sacred, no matter how small and seemingly insignificant. We cannot kill. His government would have found a way to blame us. They might have retaliated with their gunboats, taken more land, slaughtered more of our people, and squeezed more concessions. You were honorable, my brave son." His voice was low, broken.

Tears welled in his son's eyes. "I can't bear to see how we have been crippled within our borders."

Mandarin Poe leaned back, tapping his fingertips, his face calm. "Perhaps Grand Master Ping is right to call for the Dragons of the Mist."

The Dragons of the Mist. A secret society dating from the Ming Dynasty, a network of skilled scholars and martial arts masters, summoned only in times of turmoil and crises. Legends recounted how the Dragons of the Mist used their skills to depose the unjust and right the wrongs of the powerless. Some, like Mow Chow Ching, had extraordinary powers. Some called him a conjurer, an illusionist, a master assassin. Mow Bowli might answer the call. But could John bear to leave Flora and his babies?

Mandarin Poe waved his hand in the direction of the Shanghai plains. "Some have already retreated to the mountains to prepare their bodies and spirit. My task, your task, is to do everything in our power to maintain the ch'i in our lives, to ensure the prosperity of our families, government, and country. To this end, Li has proven to be a shrewd ally and confidante. Despite all the barriers he threw in Fortune's way, he pleases the Scot. He reports that Fortune is in the midst of his final sweep of the five treaty ports to gather flowers before heading back to England. Warlords roam our countryside and unrest is growing against the Emperor. Perhaps they will solve our problem. But before you return to Flora's side, come with me. I have news from the Longjing mountains of Hangchow."

ॐ

In black fighting silks, Mei stretched her arms over her head then quickly lunged forward, leaping straight up in the air as if she were a crane taking flight. She landed on softly bent knees and twirled quickly on her toes at the sound of their approach, arms poised in front of her face, fingers extended exactly at eye level. Her eyes never left them as she pivoted her body to keep them in line of attack.

"Mama," whispered her son. Never one to waste an opportunity, she was using their movements as practice, as moving targets. He bent his knees slightly and raised his arms into position. Mother and son parried, moving lightly across her garden walks, leaping over the bridge and back against the waterfall.

Her voice was low. "Do not fear, my son. I'll not humble you in front of your father." She laughed, knowing he enjoyed the game as much as she. She straightened her spine and dropped her hands to her side. She looked from one to the other and smiled at their expressions. "I will protect both of you with my life." She looked to her husband. "That mysterious look in your eyes tells me you have a secret."

"Then you will not be surprised to hear that Jadelin is expecting a baby. I received the message from Mow Bowli accompanied by one of the finest teas I have ever tasted. His family assures us that their family healer confirms that our daughter has maintained a healthy appetite, and the baby will be strong."

Mei clasped her hands to her chest in joy. Her eyes glazed for a second with a far-away look, a remembrance of her own first pregnancy and the delight of bearing life. John clasped his father's hands to congratulate him on the pending birth of another grandchild, then excused himself to share the news with Flora.

But Mandarin Poe worried what kind of world this baby would inherit. With a weakened Emperor beleaguered by armed Western countries ravenous for China's treasures, what would be left for his grandchildren?

A month later, death would shatter the family he had spent decades to build.

Twenty

THE EMPTY PAVILION

SHANGHAI

Benjamin and Paul returned to the warehouse at midnight. They hunkered down in the tea storage area and waited in darkness so dense they could not see each other's face. At three when the first cock crowed, a figure entered through a small back door known only to the brothers. Cloaked in black, the figure adroitly maneuvered through the maze of tea chests. He cocked his head, frozen motionless as if checking for sound. Then he swung up to a shelf used for lesser teas and lifted a tea chest hidden behind another. He leapt down to reverse his route towards the exit.

Benjamin felled him with a single blow. Paul caught the tea chest in his arms. The chest that the thief had secreted contained one of the hong's premium teas from far away in the green tea hills. This single tea chest was worth ten times more than any other in their warehouse.

The thief leapt to his feet and confronted his attackers with a flurry of strategic kicks. He had hoped to catch the defenders off guard and at least, escape with his life.

Benjamin used his senses to guide his attack but quickly realized that the thief had also trained blindfolded at Grand Master Ping's school. He recognized the crane style that was well suited to his Fourth brother's long arms and legs.

"It's mine!" The intruder growled. He continued his defense against Benjamin's blows and leapt to the exit over the tops of tea chests.

"It belongs to the hong," snarled Benjamin. His younger brother was a wily opponent, quick and strategic, but his labored breathing meant he had lost his edge. He bounded after him and landed a strategic blow that flipped Edward on his back.

"I could have owned all this if my mother had been the First Wife," wailed Edward. He had run out of steam. He glared at Paul. "Traitor," he hissed. "The brothers of First Wife have taken what could have been ours."

"We are all brothers. We have all been given the same opportunity to excel," replied Paul. He felt betrayal and humiliation.

"You're a nothing," spat Edward. "Benjamin uses you. Everyone knows you prance with men as well as women."

"Don't listen to him," Benjamin said in a sad voice. "Opium has melted his brain."

Paul tied Edwards's arms behind his back with a braided cord he had brought specifically for this and angrily knotted it tight. "Don't ever talk against Benjamin. Our brothers have treated us with more generosity and honor than some of us deserve."

The next day, a dapper Englishman in a long overcoat tapped on the barred front doors of the Poe tea hong with his silver-tipped cane. He sputtered through his carefully trimmed mustache and insisted that No, it was impossible that Edward Poe was not at work. He was positive Mr. Poe had arranged for him to pick up a shipment. See, he had brought a coolie with him. No, he would not give his name. Unsatisfied, he returned daily with increased agitation.

The Poes couldn't lock Edward up in the warehouse; it was a place of business. And Mandarin Poe did not want the negative ch'i of his son to disrupt the harmony of his household any more that it already had with the death of his First Wife. So Benjamin bound his brother's arms and legs and sailed him up the wide and busy Huangpu River to a cousin's house far, far away.

Without his drug, Edward's body quaked with fever and trembled uncontrollably. Sweat poured from his skin as he writhed, eyes open, fearful of the demons that stuck their fingers through his itchy skin. His cousin's family tended their fields, chickens, and pigs during the day, and the neighboring farms were at least two li away so no one was bothered by his screams. Their cousin assured the Poes that during his calm periods, they fed Edward nourishing foods.

Deprived of Edward's opium, Second Wife became too fragile to move. To avoid scandal, the family herbalist prescribed a potion so she would remain asleep although she flailed wildly in dreamless delirium.

∾

*W*hen the professional mourners with their heart-rending wails, spirit-chasing cymbals, and doleful gongs departed, the cold halls of the Poe estate vibrated with silence.

Mandarin Poe stepped into his First Wife's wing for the first time since her funeral. The servants had removed all the mirrors so her spirit wouldn't be tempted to return; she must move onward across the Seven Bridges of Heaven. He fingered her beautiful embroideries, proof of her detailed artistry and discipline. Dozens of three-inch shoes that once graced her Lotus Blossoms lined her wardrobes. He picked up one of his favorites, a pink satin embroidered with blue and white songbirds, and remembered how the husky woman with broad strong shoulders swayed silently towards him on those little feet. The ache in his chest grew until he felt the chasm rip his heart. She had anchored his life and family for forty years. He stumbled into the garden, clutched his chest, and shouted, "Mei. Mei!"

He slumped on a bench by the pond and covered his face with his hands. He felt old. He had hoped that he would be able to bask in the golden glow of his success and accomplishments. But the Confucian ethics of the five human relationships which guided social harmony had shattered within his family and business.

Mei found him on the bench by the fishpond with a porcelain bowl of fish pellets in his left hand. Dozens of hungry goldfish, each a foot long, puckered the surface with open mouths. "My husband, are you feeling all right?" She knelt, hands on his arms, a frown on her alabaster-smooth face. He nodded for her to join him on the bench.

"Mei, what am I to do? The harmony of my household has been shattered." His voice sunk into his chest "My Second Wife should take First Wife's place in the hierarchy of the family, but she chased the tail of the dragon with her profligate son."

She averted her head so he couldn't see the shock on her face. It was worse than that, but nothing was discussed that wasn't honorable. The truth was never discussed, but everyone knew.

His eyes, luminous as if he fought back tears, searched her face. His large rough hands caressed her long fingers. "Mei, you must take charge of my household."

She leaned forward to catch his choked words. Unsure she had heard correctly, she took a deep breath to control her voice. Her answer was tender. "I have no desire to outrank your Second Wife." She bowed her head, heartbroken that her lord had been forced to take such drastic action.

"She is gone in spirit and mind. All she and her son desire is the British drug." He lifted his fists to the clouds and yelled so loud the swallows flew from the roof tiles in alarm, "I curse the British. They destroyed my family!" His dark eyes flashed as if twenty-seven generations of betrayed ancestors railed within him. "I had a strong house. I had a strong family and a good name. Now I discover my own son is a thief."

Poe bowed his head. His queue, now coursed with white, shook when he seethed and inhaled sharply through his teeth.

"You have five devoted sons to continue your legacy," Mei consoled him. She sat, hands together, patiently waiting for him to respond. "You have tremendous 'face' in Shanghai and a presence in Peking through your eldest son, Adam. Your business thrives."

"Yes, it is my fate," he said. He looked at her quick, expressive eyes. "Our fate." She still had the power to make him feel he could master the world. "Move into the First Wife's wing as befits your station. I want you to have her embroideries and jewelry. Burn her personal effects."

"As you wish. But with your permission, I'll divide her jewelry, her legacy; among her three sons." She looked around at the older woman's garden, which reflected a classical, refined taste. "Please, I wish to remain in my wing. I like my gardens and pavilions. They hold so many wonderful memories for both of us." She traced the side of his face with her fingers and rested her fingertips on his square, strong jaw to coax a wistful smile from his tired face.

"Come," she whispered. She took his hand in hers and led him back to her courtyard where the birds twittered playfully in the trees. Sunlight played through the leaves of the overhanging trees and danced in patterns upon the stepping-stones that led to her room. She waved her maids to draw the shutters when they entered. She kissed away his protests and gestured for her bedroom doors to be closed. They wished to be alone.

"I am old," he protested. She pushed him onto her bed with her forefinger.

With her eyes fixed on his, she slowly undid the buttons of her tunic, untied her trousers, and unfastened her camisole. She stepped over the silks pooled at her feet and lifted her arms before him, skin still the color of alabaster, muscles toned, and breasts soft in his hands. "I came to you at sixteen and you taught me that love overcomes fear. You are a good teacher and lover." She reached for his tunic buttons and undid them one by one. Then, with two fingers, she slid his trousers off. They fell in a puddle onto the floor.

He undid the clasp of her hair and pulled her down so the scent of her waist-length hair enveloped them like a shield against the world. "Oh, Mei, my dearest love," he whispered.

"You are not old," she laughed softly. She ran her hands down his body and caressed him until he arched his back. "I will not hurt you," she warned. "But I am deadly."

"I have trained longer than you," he panted with need and passion.

"I am in better shape," she gasped when he rolled her under him.

"Then I must pleasure you until the sun goes down." His voice was husky now, almost out of control.

"And I will make you gasp for breath until it rises again," she moaned. The afternoon sun sank slowly and the night stretched in luscious waves. But for the two, all thoughts of family and tea and the dastardly plant hunter dissolved in their heat.

Twenty-One

THE PIRATES

MIN RIVER

*O*blivious to the angst he caused, Fortune headed up the Min River searching for tea plants and exciting new flowers in Foochow. He had a dozen new glass boxes built in Mackenzie's gardens while he was in Shanghai to protect the plants he had collected thus far. Despite the spring floods, he had waded in waist-deep water in his quest. He felt he had discovered one of the great tea lands of China, collected every different plant, and shot every kind of bird possible. The sun was relentless, over a hundred degrees in the shade. Now he was covered with oozing sores.

Still weak from his forays through spring floods and the summer heat, Fortune hobbled along the waterfront dodging swarms of men and coils of oiled rope as he begged, cajoled, and bargained for passage to Shanghai. The valley exuded the scent of the fresh cut pine harvested from the forests that blanketed the mountains upriver from Foochow, rafted downriver by bare-chested men, and stacked along the Min River. These rafts were loaded and stacked on every available vessel to improbable heights and widths. Junks lashed with timber up to three times their normal width massed in the Min for the voyage north while their captains sent envoys to the mandarins of Foochow to request a convoy of war junks to protect their fleet from the pirates that swarmed like mosquitoes off the coast.

Every ship he approached refused him passage. After a week, Fortune decided he would forcibly board one of the junks with or without the captain's consent. He sent Li to the waterfront to scout for a loaded junk ready to sail.

He propped his gun and umbrella in the hall while he packed. He nestled each tea plant in oiled paper in special collection boxes. Dead birds were wrapped in a separate container. It must be over a hundred degrees, he panted. He straightened from his task of boxing flowering plants and dried flowers and wiped his fevered brow with the back of his hand. He was so weak he couldn't stand for any period of time. He jerked in alarm when he heard the clatter of many footsteps at the door.

When Li threw open the door and entered with a dozen tanned ruffians wearing their queues wrapped around their heads, he grabbed his gun. The wiry seamen in thick leggings and loose white shirts impudently poked at his boxes and trunks. Their fierce expression as their piercing eyes examined him looked as deadly as their knotted arms.

Li indicated their leader with a tip of his head. "Captain Wing will take us to Ningpo."

Sun-hardened Captain Wing swaggered close to inspect Fortune on all sides as if he were a roast duck he was considering for dinner. He sauntered around their half-packed belongings. Now that he had seen the *gweilo* for himself he told Li, and ascertained that he looked harmless, he would take them to Ningpo. He asked Li to point out which trunks were his and his men would carry them aboard.

Relieved, Fortune thanked him profusely in Chinese. "This," he pointed to a stack of trunks. "And that. And those trunks."

Captain Wing, who was broad and thick-shouldered, turned in surprise. "You speak Chinese," he said in a gravelly voice. His smile revealed teeth as white as sun-bleached bone. He held out his hand for Fortune's matchlock. He hefted it to feel its weight and ran his leathered palms up and down its seven-foot length. This was the first musket he had ever seen up close. "I hope your gun is a good one and you have a great supply of powder and shot."

The Scot looked puzzled. "I'm sure there is nothing to shoot on our sail up the coast."

"Oh yes, you will have something to shoot." The captain aimed at the opposite wall and awkwardly peered down the barrel with one squinty eye. "We are likely to be attacked by the *jandous* who swarm the islands of the East China Sea. I take you only because your man says you have this gun and will shoot all *jandous*." He lifted the gun to his shoulder where it wavered dangerously. "Pow, pow, pow!"

At this his crew shuddered and hurried out with Fortune's luggage on their backs muttering, *"Jandous, jandous, jandous."*

"Jandous?" Fortune furrowed his brow.

"Pirates," Li translated. "The *jandous* are the bloodthirsty pirates who lay in wait in coves along the coast. Unless all these cargo junks travel in an armed convoy, *jandous* will attack, kill the crew, ransom the rich, and steal the cargo and ship."

Captain Wing's thick brows knitted ruefully. He thrust the gun in Fortune's hands and leaned forward, his salty breath hot on the Scot's ear. "They swarm like locusts to plunder our ships. You shoot them."

"No pirates will attack us. I'll make sure they will repent it." Fortune waved one arm gallantly in the air and slung his rifle over his shoulder. Chinese were anxious and high-strung, too concerned about protocol and obedience to those of higher authority.

"The *jandous* will change your mind," growled Captain Wing. He waved to the rest of his men to follow him with the barbarian's luggage.

∾

That first night, Fortune leaned over the bulwarks, listening to captains and crew call across the still, starlit night. The junks sat low to the water with logs towered high on the decks and lashed on all sides so they were now three times their normal width. Under full sail, the overburdened junks had lumbered to the mouth of the Min River and joined a convoy of one-hundred-and-seventy similarly encumbered behemoths.

Fierce hawk eyes painted boldly on their bows symbolized the fearless-
ness of their captains and crew.

Over the slap of the waves, he heard a lone captain sing his lament that they nested like unguarded baby birds waiting to be plucked.
Another's song bemoaned the futility of his wife and children offering
incense and flowers every day to the sea gods for his safe return. To the
rhythm of bobbing lanterns, others recited poems of riding home on the
benevolent sea, of loneliness, of fear and hope. These were noble voices,
enduring voices, of men who had sailed the seas for thousands of years
through changes of rulers and emperors. Compelled by love of the sea,
family, and duty, they ventured into danger once again.

And what compelled the Scot? No one pined for his return. Fortune
nestled his head on his arms and let the wave of the boat carry him in
his daydreams back to Shanghai. Of all the creatures on earth, Jadelin
with her alabaster face and saucy wit had enticed and entranced him. His
pulse quickened just thinking of the tinkling bells on her hems. But she
lived far, far away. How foolish, he rued, he had been to think Mandarin
Poe would let him take his daughter to England. She would have been
the crowning jewel in his collection of exquisite Chinese treasures.

In the morning the sea captains sent another delegation to the mandarins. Surrounded by heavily armored soldiers, the powerful mandarins
peered down from a carved teak platform on the deck of their largest
war junk. Smoke curled from the fretwork of towering bronze incense
pots standing at each corner of the platform so the mandarins, dazzling
in their peacock hats and silk robes, resembled gods.

The captains, dressed in their cleanest tunics, humbly requested a
convoy of war junks to accompany their cargo of valuable wood from
the forests up the Min River. Captain Wing pointed out that it was in
the mandarins' interests to ensure this cargo arrived at its designated
ports. Without these revenues, the mandarins would never fulfill the
Emperor's demands when his armies came to collect the taxes. The
mandarins again demanded a price greater than the profit of their cargo.
Frustrated, the captains returned to their junks, resolved to sail together
without protection as a single fleet. Safety in numbers.

While Li slept on the deck with the crew under the shooting stars and an iridescent moon, Fortune curled up below deck on his cot. He heard the fleet call out to each other in the night, a roll call of clans and families. Their haunting voices carried across the water to be answered and repeated throughout the night. They prayed for fair seas and favorable winds, the only conditions in which junks could sail. In the morning the convoy would depart en masse.

But in the morning a Siberian gale blew down from the north and did not let up for two weeks. Unable to sail, the overburdened junks bobbed at anchor on the rough seas.

Stressed by inactivity in the cold, wet ship, Fortune collapsed with fevered sweats and shivers. Pus and infections plugged his ears. When he closed his eyes he imagined the sonorous bells of the church near Kello in Berwickshire announce his demise. In his dreams the church doors, weathered even in his childhood by moisture and sun, swung open to reveal the shimmering Gates of Heaven. His travels were over. No, not yet, he pleaded. He should be on his way to London, where he would be acclaimed for discovering many new plants that he had personally introduced to the Western world. He hadn't yet been awarded fame and wealth, or a knighthood. He couldn't die without saying goodbye to his Jadelin. Then he fell down, down, down into his grave. He gasped for air and swatted away the shovelfuls of dirt that followed his body into the darkness while the bells continued to toll.

In his lucid moments he ruminated on the gravesites he explored in China. He couldn't decide which he preferred, the remote horse-shoe shaped monuments facing spectacular views or the spacious coffin houses laid out according to the principles of feng shui for the eternal pleasure of the deceased. He wanted the funeral cypress to droop over his tombstone. Would he be buried among the decorative flowers he collected? Or tossed overboard?

He never knew that Li ordered a servant to bathe him daily to remove his stink. Three times a day they had to wash the pus that sealed his eyes closed.

Finally, the winds calmed and the echoing calls across the fleet of junks confirmed their readiness. The captains and crews double-checked their sails and lines of woven bamboo. With fists full of sandalwood incense, the men lined up on the most level spot of their log-covered deck and bowed humbly, three times in each cardinal direction. They repeated their offerings to the gods for benevolent winds and enveloped their masts in clouds of heaven-bound incense and prayers.

The night before they set sail Captain Wing loomed over Fortune's bed to see if he was still alive. "You have your gun and pistols ready? You have plenty of powder and ball?" He looked to Li who nodded that all was ready.

Fortune feebly raised his head. "You joke with a dead man, Captain. I can barely see."

"I'm serious." Captain Wing's cargo, his crew, his family, his entire net worth was at risk. "I only took you because your man said you would shoot the *jandous*. You promised!"

Li raised his hand to calm the man. "Captain Wing, Mr. Fortune might be persuaded to rise from his death bed if you agree to drop us off at Chusan Island on your way to Ningpo." That would get them to Shanghai three days early.

Wing calculated that the detour to Chusan Island would cost him only a couple hours. He heard the clamor of fear spread like the plague through his crew. He would be willing if the barbarian used his guns.

"Sir?" Li was ready to return to his rosy-cheeked wife and children in Canton. "Captain Wing agrees to take us to Chusan if you will use your guns against the pirates."

Gain three days for firing an unreliable old musket? Fortune dropped his head back. "My guns are ready and I'm prepared to beat off any pirate who may attack," he rasped with a theatrical wave of his hand.

The brown eyes sunk in the Captain's grizzled face. "As soon as we enter the East China Sea the *jandous* slip from their hiding places. Four or five at a time will attack and try to separate one ship from the others." He pointed at Fortune for emphasis. "I will see you on deck."

An ebullient mood swept the fleet with the first rays of sun. The sails of one-hundred-and-seventy overburdened junks snapped as they filled with air. The hopeful fleet set off together under billowing sails and the tide. Each junk jockeyed for clear air to maintain speed. Within hours, they abandoned their plan of mutual protection and separated into groups of three or four who could sail at comparable speeds.

Around four in the afternoon a call came from the crow's nest, "Five *jandous.*" Five sleek ships shot out from where they hid among the lush islands dotting the coast.

Fortune had been dreaming of hiking through hills of azaleas and camellias on Chusan with the brisk breeze sweet upon his fevered face. He dreamt of Chinese cities with hundreds of flower ships, of antiques and silks, and of the tinkling bells on the hems of Jadelin's gowns. He woke to Captain Wing's bellow.

Wing's face was two inches from his, florid with excitement. "Five *jandous.* Are you ready?" He pointed to the two pistols and the matchlock lying on Fortune's trunk. "Are they loaded?"

Fortune groaned, "You imagine every junk to be a pirate ship. We're only fifty miles from the Min."

Wing shook his clenched fists. "If we haven't given you passage you and your plants would be rotting in Foochow. Get up!"

Fortune rolled to the edge of the cot and crawled on his hands and knees to his guns. He took the supplies Li handed him and, propped against a trunk, cleaned the nipples of the gun and pistols and put on fresh caps. He rammed a ball on top of each charge of shot and shoved a pistol in each side pocket. He wobbled up on deck. The fresh air shocked his feverish skin and he drew back with a cry. Li hoisted him up by one arm and propped him up against the rail.

"Take a look," said Li. He held up Fortune's small telescope and pointed a short ways off. The five pirate ships were so close they could see the snarling crew loading their deck cannons.

"I can't fight all of them," Fortune wheezed. Everything he saw whooshed in and out of focus. "What kind of defense do we have?"

"The crew is below gathering stones from the ballast," said Wing. He kept his eyes on the pirate ships and barked out adjustments in course to his helmsman.

"Stones? What for?"

"To throw at the *jandous*."

"They're throwing stones?" Fortune gasped in despair. "My musket can't shoot anything further than one hundred yards. They have to be right in front of me to hit anything."

Li peered through Fortune's telescope. "Cannons line port and starboard. They will have killed us all by the time they get in your range." Still lightheaded, Fortune grabbed the side of the junk and steadied himself. "Take a deep breath of fresh air," counseled Li. "It will give you strength for your fight ahead. The *jandous* will spare the crew. You, they will throw overboard." He thrust the gun in Fortune's hands. "Fight or die."

Fortuned edged his way towards the wheel. From a distance of three hundred yards, the nearest *jandou* fired a broadside shot with its port guns. The first volley was short.

The crew flattened themselves on deck. Captain Wing and his helmsman stood fast to keep the wind in their sails. The pursuers gained rapidly. The second shot landed under the stern.

"Now," Fortune ordered the helmsman, "keep your eye fixed on me and keep sailing. The moment you see me fall flat on the deck, do the same." He aimed his gun at the captain and helmsman. "My gun is nearer to you than the *jandous*. If you leave your post, I shall shoot you."

The third shot whizzed through the sails. Fortune, Wing, and the helmsman flinched but maintained speed. The pirates bore down on the laden junk hooting and yelling, sure of victory.

At thirty yards, the pirates had reloaded and were ready to rake the deck of the junk. They approached fast on the junk's stern prepared to put down their helm to position their cannons.

The moment Fortune saw them tack he shouted, "Fall." The pirates' cannons showered them with splintered shards of mast and ship.

"Now, mandarin, now," the crew shouted. "Shoot!" They wailed they would never survive another broadside.

With the pirates celebrating victory only twenty yards away, Fortune raked their decks fore and aft. The pirate helmsman was the first to die. Those who weren't dead hit the deck and let the air spill from their sails.

With the pirates stalled dead in the wind, Captain Wing powered away with a full wind in his sails.

The next pirate ship picked up the chase. It pursued as boldly as the first, raking their decks with gunshots twice and peppering their sails.

"Shoot!" The crew pointed at their pursuer. "*Gweilo*, shoot now!"

The pirate ship closed in. They were so sure of victory the scraggly crews were practically dancing.

Meanwhile, the first pirate ship regained control and followed with their ragged sails streaming like banners behind them. Three others in their fleet joined the action.

Captain Wing repeated their previous maneuver. As soon as the second pirate ship had tacked for the final attack, Fortune emptied all his barrels at their helmsman. When he crumpled, their sails spilled their air causing the ship to turn into the wind where it floundered.

"*Jandou* to leeward," shouted Li.

The crew groaned.

"No," shouted Captain Wing. He squinted at the vessel. "It's my cousin. His junk must have been captured. The pirates onboard will be unarmed. They are headed for their den where my cousin, the ship, and passengers will be held for ransom. If the ransom is not paid, the ship will be stripped and burned. We don't have enough guns to save them. It is their fate."

The crew held their breath as they scanned the sea. They saw that the other pirate ships had witnessed what happened and had given up the chase. Captain Wing's crew leapt from where they hid and leaned over the bulwarks. They taunted the disappearing pirates by flinging stones and words of bravado. They turned to Fortune and praised their foreign savior. Some knelt at his feet in reverence. But the hero, exhausted and feverish, stumbled down to his sweat-soaked cot and crumpled into a deep sleep.

In the evening, they came upon a fleet of anchored boats. Seeking safety, Captain Wing dropped anchor for the night in the midst of the fleet. They would continue at dawn.

∾

*S*tillness startled Li awake. He propped himself up from his bedroll on the deck and cocked his head. He heard the creak of the wooden hull and the anchor chain, the moaning wind in the mast, and the crews' snores. Why didn't he hear the watchmen from the other junks, their whistles, and the answering calls from ship to ship?

He leapt up and peered into the night. He saw nothing but the emptiness of the sea stretched all around them. The other junks must have been waiting for the rising tide to enter a nearby river and sail to safety. Alone and vulnerable, Captain Wing's ship sat low in the water. He woke Wing who roused his crew. But as soon as they hoisted anchor and the first rays of sun reached over the horizon, six pirate ships swept out of a cove.

Captain Wing shook Fortune awake from another sweat-swamped nightmare.

"No. No more *jandous*," moaned Fortune. He swatted away the captain.

Wing grabbed Fortune's fevered wrist and shook it. "Get your guns ready," he growled. "You will fight six swift *jandous* with guns on port and starboard." The captain noted his passenger's pallor and how his limbs curled around his body like a dying man. Then he left to tell his crew to hide their valuables under the floorboards as before.

"Li, I can't fight six *jandous*," Fortune moaned. He thrashed his limbs to the edge of the bed and struggled to raise his head. "Help me, Li."

Li was already dressed and ready for action. He stowed his bedroll and considered their options. Fortune was one man with a musket and two handguns, but the pirates didn't know this. He bent over Fortune. "Get up, now. I know you don't think you can repeat your performance. But what if the pirates thought our ship carried many foreigners who were armed with guns like yours? They want an easy victory, not a battle against an army of barbarians."

"We don't have an army of barbarians."

"They don't know that. Here are your clothes. I'll meet you up on deck." Li flung open Fortune's trunks and carried all of Fortune's spare clothes up to the deck where he chose the tallest of the crew. He put a wool coat on one, collared shirts on others, and a wool jacket on another. He handed Fortune's umbrella to the tallest and told him to wave it about when the pirates closed in. Then he gathered all the short levers used for hoisting sails--at a distance they looked like firearms--and armed the recruits.

Fortune staggered up to the deck, dressed and armed with his gun and pistols. He laughed when he saw the crew. When they lined the deck, 'firearms' clearly visible, they looked like foreigners prepared to defend themselves against any attack.

Li ordered them to stand tall and to let the pirates see them. He pointed to the first pirate ship that drew close. "They can't hit you from where they are. Stand fast. Do not fear. Do not fall to the deck." When they were close enough to see the villains' expressions, Li ordered, "Stare them in the eyes."

But at the first broadside attack, the imposters threw down their arms and dove for the deck. Pirate cannons riddled Wing's sails again and again. For the final, disabling attack, the pirates tacked to aim their portside guns. But before they had a chance to reload, Fortune emptied his musket fore and aft killing their helmsman with his first round. The pirate ship spilled its air in defeat and stalled.

Captain Wing scooted away with the wind full in his sails. His crew leapt from their hiding places shouting praise to the mandarin Fortune and his great guns. They leapt up and down. Then the shout rang from the crow's nest. "Two *jandous.*"

"Ai-ya," the crew screamed, "not again." They grabbed their 'arms' and waved them in the air. Suddenly the pirates, seeing armed foreigners manned the ship they pursued, slipped back and away.

ॐ

he morning horizon was clear, the sky empty of pirate ships as Fortune, weak and feverish, watched Li pack their trunks. They would arrive at Chusan in two hours, enough time to disembark and seek out Captain Landers who would take them to Shanghai.

Li stopped and cocked his head. "Listen. Hear the change in the motion of the waves? The ship has changed course," he hissed.

Fortune looked up from his cot where he had hoped to take a nap. Without a word, Li handed him his musket to use as a cane and helped him up to the deck where Captain Wing, dressed in his second best shirt and trousers, stood by his helmsman.

Fortune staggered forward, face to the wind. "You've changed course for Ningpo. You promised to take me to Chusan harbor if I used my guns."

Wing dismissed him with a wave of his hand. "We had a two week delay caused by the mandarins and the weather. You can easily find a boat in Ningpo to take you to Chusan."

"We had an agreement."

"I've changed it."

Li loaded the musket and handed it to Fortune.

Fortune aimed it at Wing's head to check his sights. He then clasped his gun across his chest. "British gentlemen never break promises," he rasped. "I'll stand here by your helmsman. I'll not be responsible for my actions if he steers off his course to Chusan."

Twenty-Two

FORTUNE'S FAREWELL

SHANGHAI

*F*lora grabbed Jadelin's hands when she and Mow Bowli entered the courtyard of warriors and held them out to survey her blooming figure. "How radiantly you glow." A low fringe of thick black bangs framed Flora's eyes, lilted up at the corners and shadowed by exhaustion. She had pinned up the rest of her tresses as if she had been rushed or tired. "I hope your stay here, with the uproar of my little one, won't discourage you." Motherhood had rounded out her own body and softened her aristocratic high cheekbones. With a tip of her head she motioned towards her son cradled in Mei's arms. Big Amah hovered protectively beside her.

Jade smoothed a belly that swelled like a ripe melon under her blue tunic. "He'll have company soon." Her face seemed to beam with its inner secret and she moved gently so the bells in her hem tingled like rolling wavelets. "Mama is looking forward to teaching her grandchildren to leap like crickets in combat as soon as they can stand."

"May you have a hundred sons," John congratulated Mow Bowli. He laughed when the father-to-be uncharacteristically blushed, proud and embarrassed by the attention. He noticed that his friend kept his senses attuned to his wife's movements, as she did to his. He had seen the same sensitivity between his parents, Mandarin Poe and Mei. They had turned their heightened awareness, useful in combat and uncertain times, to strengthen their bond. The gossip among the mandarin families was that Mandarin Poe could have arranged a better marriage for his youngest daughter. They were wrong. Jadelin and Mow Bowli were perfectly suited, and he wished them a long and prosperous life together.

Mei hugged her daughter. "How I've missed you. Was the journey smooth?" She smiled up at Mow Bowli, happy he was the one to protect her daughter. Bowli assured her their sail up the Grand Canal and the Huangpu River had been smooth and uneventful. They had enjoyed a crisp autumn wind and the sight of farmers busy with their last harvest before winter.

"And soon, you and Jadelin will have a treasure like this." Mei swayed her grandson back and forth in her arms, his cheeks trembling against her pink tunic like two bowls of jelly dribbling trails of drool.

"Your gown," protested Flora.

Mei looked apologetically over her shoulder at Big Amah. But Big Amah would wash Mei's gowns a thousand times as long as their home was graced with babies.

Flora rubbed her tired shoulders. She craved one good night's sleep, a few hours of solid rest. How she looked forward to the long nights of winter.

Jadelin jiggled her nephew's chunky cheeks and teased that he looked like his father. Her brother, who denied ever being layered in soft fat, beamed at his son as if he had conceived, carried, and delivered him himself.

They were unaware that one of China's greatest threats had entered their midst.

∾

*W*hen Mandarin Poe's servant entered the courtyard of warriors with the mandarin's request that the men join him in receiving Robert Fortune, Jadelin had asked if she could come, too.

"No!" Big Amah was aghast. "One glance from the white devil will make your baby a hunchback. The shock might even cause you to lose it."

The young woman was too educated to believe Big Amah's superstitions. She assured her she would remain where she was to keep harmony. After all, Big Amah had been Mei's amah since birth and considered her children her responsibility, too. She could be a wildcat when it came to defending her charges. "Big Amah," Jadelin sighed. "The journey has tired me. I will rest." She motioned her servant to follow her.

"Yes, you must get lots of sleep," Big Amah insisted. "Flora, too, will nap. Since neither of you need me, I will escort your mother. I do not understand why she wants to see this *bak gwei*. She has seen him before."

∾

Two years ago Robert Fortune would have strode into the secondary receiving hall at the Poe estate and sat down in the most comfortable chair. Now he knew to stand and wait for his host's direction. In preparation for this visit he had assiduously bathed with sandalwood soap and donned freshly laundered underwear, socks, and trousers. Yu had brushed and aired his coat so it, too, smelled of sunshine. Two years ago he was a gruff barbarian who didn't make a step without his translator or a decision without arguing with him. But today he had confidently left Li to accept his shipments of wood, glass, and dirt, and to supervise the workers building more glazed plant cases in Alistair Mackenzie's garden.

Fortune bowed to Mandarin Poe, to John, and again when he was introduced to Mow Bowli. To Mandarin Poe he said in Chinese, "Thank you for your hospitality." He switched to English. "I have a gift for you from the Horticultural Society in England. This German telescope is fitted with fine glass lenses." With two hands, he handed the polished wood case to Mandarin Poe who slid open the clasps and slowly lifted the lid.

Poe lifted the telescope with a firm grasp and took it over to the open window. He peered through the eyepiece and twisted the focus. "Aaah. Very good," he exclaimed to his son and son-in-law.

As the men peered at wonders far and away, there was a rustle in the exterior corridor of silk as delicate as butterfly wings. Mandarin Poe looked up and motioned to his servant to bid Third Wife enter so she could add her grace to the company of four very serious men. Mei, in pale blue silk embroidered with peonies, entered behind Big Amah.

Fortune bowed to Mei but took not a step closer. "Third Wife of Mandarin Poe, I asked my employer to send me a memento for a powerful mandarin's wife. This is something that ladies in England desire most for their precious face powder." He reached deep in his pocket and presented her with a leather box. When opened, it revealed within its padded interior a cosmetic case of intricate design and detail made by England's finest silversmith.

John accepted it for his mother. She nodded to him and indicated he should inspect it, which he did before handing it to her where she sat on the far side of the room, Big Amah at her side.

Mei held up the cosmetic case and admired how it sparkled in the candle light, how it shone in the palm of her hand like the full moon in October. She handed the silver case to her husband whose somber expression did not change. "I must reciprocate your generosity," she said. She tipped her head at Fortune who was now flushed and red.

"Oh no," Fortune stepped back. "I did not expect anything in return. My gift is a trifle, not worth much."

"As is this." Mei handed her husband a small silk pouch which he inspected before handing to Fortune.

A small crystal bottle slid out of the pouch onto the Scot's palm. "Ah, a snuff bottle. I have never seen one like this." One of the most prized possessions of British and Chinese society, these fashionable containers for snuff, the smokeless tobacco introduced by the British for its reputed medical properties, reflected the taste and wealth of its owner. Fortune hefted the tiny bottle in his hand and felt its weight. "Crystal. Painted with the exquisite Chinese peonies." The Scot cradled the snuff bottle in his huge hands and marveled at the intricate painting done inside-out by a master using a brush with a single hair. The miniature flowers seemed to bloom and glow, shimmering with a life and energy of their own. "I shall treasure it forever. It will remind me of China's exquisite flowers and of your family's generosity." The bottle was still warm with Mei's body heat when he pocketed it.

Suddenly, Mei turned imperceptibly towards the garden window, toward the sound of tinkling bells.

At the same time, Fortune quickly looked out the window. Was it she? He could feel Jadelin's presence. He was sure he had seen the shadow of blue silk behind the willow. Then a servant, who entered to serve a delicate tea, mild and smooth with a jasmine finish, in porcelain as thin as eggshells, distracted him. The aroma and taste was as delicate as gossamer.

"This is most excellent. Do you mind if I ask where it was grown?" asked Fortune. He inhaled the fragrance and tried to imagine the mountains, mist, and soil that would produce such a flavor.

John lowered his voice and stared at the pale eyes of the man he had tracked throughout China. "Jadelin's husband brought it today. His family grows some of the finest teas, far inland."

Bowli noticed the pained look Fortune sent him and how the tea trembled in the Scot's large hands. To ease the awkwardness of the moment he said, "My wife told me you are a man of great fortitude. We heard that you saved your captain's vessel from the pirates despite your own illness. Please, tell us of your adventures."

Fortune stammered that actually, he had been so sick at the time, he didn't care if he lived or died. But at their insistence, he told the tale of his perilous voyage from Foochow to Chusan and how he had successfully repelled the pirates, once, twice, three times!

When Mandarin Poe refused a second pour, Fortune knew that was the signal for him to leave. He bid them all farewell, then followed their servant out.

After Fortune's shadow had disappeared down the corridor and his footsteps faded past the front gate, Mandarin Poe asked John Poe and Mow Bowli to stay. Cousin Li had arrived. "I wish you to listen as well," he said to Mei, "for you view the world with a different eye." He then turned to the window and said loudly, "Please come in, Jadelin."

His daughter stepped into the candle-lit room and warmed her hands by the porcelain stove that was, thankfully, filled with glowing coals. "Thank you, Baba. Your garden is very cold this time of year."

"Jadelin!" Big Amah's eyes grew large and her face turned red. "Your baby!"

"Don't worry, Big Amah." Mow Bowli stepped forward and placed an arm around his wife's shoulders. "My wife is a strong woman, thanks to your care. She's seen the barbarian three times before and has built up defenses against any evil spirits that he many carry."

Big Amah grumbled that yes, she had taken very good care of her and because of that, her unborn child would probably not have any ill effects. "But still," she grumbled, "You should obey me." Her fierce glare could have melted glaciers.

After Mei ordered a servant to bring Jadelin a warm shawl, Mandarin Poe invited them all to sit closer together now that their guest had left. He ordered fresh tea and teacakes just as cousin Li entered.

Li's broad face lit up. "I am honored to meet your husband at last, Jadelin. Unfortunately I was working far inland at the time of your wedding. You are a fortunate man, Mow Bowli." He clasped the younger man's strong hands and nodded with approval at the calluses of the martial art master and tea grower. "If Jadelin had been married to any of the mandarin sons in Shanghai, she would have had them cowering at her feet." He smiled teasingly at her.

"Cousin Li," said Mandarin Poe. His sad face looked like he wished for a miracle. "What news do you bring?" He gestured to a huanghuangli horseshoe chair his servant placed at his side with a side table for a freshly poured cup of tea. Li sat, glad that he always dressed in his finest clothes when he visited his Shanghai cousins.

He reported that he was taken aback by how single-mindedly the barbarian pursued tea plants from the monks and farmers. Fortune continually asked questions about the manufacture and production of tea and took detailed notes, with drawings. He openly defied the mandarins of Foochow to find the tea plants that grew beyond the hills despite the extreme heat and floods that sickened them daily. He detailed how the barbarian traveled through China's silk territory off-limits to non-Chinese, questioned the peasants about the mulberry bushes and asked to see their silk worms. He worried about the many detailed missives Fortune sent to his country and was glad the Poes had received the duplicates. "His plan is to depart within the week as soon as his plants are safe in their glass cases," Li concluded. "He plans to have glass cases built for all his plants and send them via two different ships to England."

"He's a cautious man," confirmed John Poe. "Too wily for our traps."

"All the tea plants he sent last spring from Hong Kong to Shanghai died," said Li with a growing smile. "I apologize, Uncle Poe. But I was responsible for their demise."

Jadelin laughed. "Do you have any more surprises for him?"

"I will try to take the tea seeds he got from Ningpo. But that will be difficult because he carries them on his body with his papers."

Mandarin Poe sighed, his heart heavy with worry. Every week brought new problems and demands from the Americans, British, French, and Russians for quality tea at lower prices, threats from the Emperor to take the land under his warehouse for barbarian use, and new laws favoring the foreigners to the detriment of the locals. The British continued to ship over 22,000 cases of their Indian opium into China a year. Millions of addicts continued to die.

Their only consolation was that Fortune would return to England and never return to China's shores.

"My final task is to accompany him to Canton, where he sets sail for London," Li said. He longed for home, for the warm southern winds, fresh savory foods, and the embrace of his family.

ॐ

*I*n Mackenzie's garden, Fortune stood over the eighteen glass cases he had newly planted with the tea plants he had found on his inland forays. He wore his Western clothes now, with a flat-topped felt hat covering the parts of his head he had shaved. He had packed away his queue and Chinese clothes to show his British sponsors to what lengths he had gone to obtain all the flowers, plants and bird specimens as they had requested. He motioned to Li when his translator entered the garden. "Get coolies to carry them to the ship for Canton. Once they're aboard I'll seal them. But until then, make sure no one touches them."

"Shall I check to make sure they have enough moisture for the voyage?"

"Their soil was moist when I planted them, but yes, check them just before the coolies carry them out. Be careful of the tea seeds I planted between the plants. I want to see if they'll germinate on the voyage." With that final instruction, Fortune dusted off his hands.

A few days later before dawn broke in Shanghai, Li inspected the plant cases, the eighteen plus the eight Fortune had previously planted. He sliced a thin line between all the plants and seeded it with finely ground salt, then carefully watered all the plants so they would survive at least until they had departed China. It didn't make any difference then when they died.

∾

Li lowered the coolie hat that he wore to shade his eyes from the bright December sun. All day he had watched eighteen glass plant cases loaded onto the *John Cooper.* The captain stormed furiously when the coolies lined case after case of plants on his poop deck. The men argued, but Fortune shook a sheaf of important looking papers in the captain's face, which he said were orders from the Royal Horticultural Society. The Scot fussed with the crew about the cases' placement until they were positioned to his specifications. Then he sealed the case joints with narrow strips of canvas dipped in a boiling mixture of tar and pitch.

The week before he had watched Fortune direct coolies loading eight similar plant cases on another England bound ship.

Li sighed with relief when the *John Cooper* with Fortune aboard, finally sailed down the Pearl River towards the sea. He was sad about one thing. He had failed to steal the last packet of Robert Fortune's tea seeds.

Part Two: 3 YEARS LATER,

1848-1851

Twenty-Three

THE DRAGON WELL

LONGJING MOUNTAINS

*J*adelin stared up at the saucer-like eyes and toss of the huge head that dared her, with a defiant snort, to mount. Those eyes sparked with an intelligence she couldn't read, couldn't understand. "I've always been afraid of horses," she muttered to Shanli through gritted teeth. Horses seemed to have an uncanny awareness of everyone and everything around them. Consider how they pricked up their ears and flicked them. They were constantly in motion: their tails swayed and their skin rippled. They shifted their weight, stamped their hooves, bobbed their heads, neighed, and snorted. And their power! The first time Jadelin saw her husband race his brothers, Shanli and Chongli, on horseback the earth shuddered as if it would crack asunder.

She wiped her sweaty palms on her tunic and clenched her toes within her new leather boots to gather courage. Her shaking fingers stroked her mount's neck. The horse's skin quivered; she knew the rider was stalling.

"She's a Mongolian breed, sturdy and nimble," Shanli reassured Jadelin. He had led her mare, a dappled brown with a white blaze across her forehead, from their stables downwind, away from their tea shrubs and sheds. He waited, reins in hand. "You'll find her comfortingly mellow, and she knows the way home from anywhere in the West Lake district of Hangchow." He let the horse sniff Jadelin while he whispered soothing words in the animal's ears and combed her mane with his fingers.

On cue, the Mongolian snorted and stamped her feet. She flicked her tail, impatient to be off. Bowli lifted Jadelin up on the saddle and fitted her feet in the stirrups. With Shanli leading and her husband and Chongli following, Jadelin decided not to worry. After all, the men promised to go slowly. And her horse knew the way home. The brothers mounted their stallions and all four trotted up the dirt trail.

They rode the main road through the West Lake district and stopped at farms where they were welcomed as old friends. These families had cultivated their tea shrubs in the same prized location for many generations so the bonds among them were tight. They were delighted to see Bowli's bride riding with him and his brothers. The other Mow wives didn't like to ride and anyway, they were too busy with cooking, their gardens, and the children.

Early in their marriage, Bowli had sensed Jadelin's frustration and boredom with the daily routine. Her major responsibility was to oversee the laundry, easily done in half a day. She had read and reread her brother John's almost daily missives. She yearned for his adventures as he shadowed Robert Fortune through China. Thankfully, the plant hunter had sailed home. Letters from Shanghai assured her that her parents and brothers were fine despite the swell of French, Russian, and American merchants settling in Shanghai. Missionaries arrived monthly determined to turn the Chinese into Christians and save the souls of those whose civilization dated back five thousand years.

So Bowli decided she should ride with him and his brothers on their weekly visits to their neighbors. It was the best way to teach her about the premium tea growing areas of the Longjing mountains of the West Lake district of Hangchow and the culture of tea in the area. On a horse, she would see things differently and, since she had never ridden, she would welcome the challenge.

Their first rides covered the oldest part of West Lake, the villages surrounding the Lion Peak Mountain rising a thousand feet above sea level. The best Longjing, or Dragon Well tea, came from areas named according to their descending quality: Lion, Dragon, Cloud, and Tiger. The Mows grew tea in the Lion area that yielded the highest quality.

As they rode, Shanli recounted the legend that when K'ang-hsi's grandson, Emperor Chi'en-Lung, and his vast and colorful entourage came to West Lake, the monks from the Hu Gong temple under the Lion Peak Mountain served him tea prepared from their eighteen tea shrubs. The Emperor was so impressed by its complexity he gave these plants Imperial status.

When they rode past the gilt and red Hu Gong temple which emitted billowing clouds of sandalwood incense, Shanli pointed out the Emperor's imperial guard by the eighteen ancient tea trees growing out of the cracks of the steep cliff. "In a month the buds and tips will be ready for harvest," he explained. "The Imperial guard ensures no one will touch the Imperial tea shrubs and that all the tea from those plants goes to the Emperor."

"Shanli, is there really a Dragon Well? Or is the tea from West Lake named after a legend?" Jadelin asked. When Benjamin told her the tale long ago, she had envisioned a dragon with bright green scales and curved talons swooping over the land. As she grew older and no one admitted to seeing a dragon, she felt sad that the dragons must have had died out long ago before she had the chance to see one herself.

"Most definitely there is a Dragon Well," answered Shanli. The brothers naturally deferred to him, the eldest. A detail oriented leader, he explained everything and anything until everyone understood what needed to be done. Kind and knowledgeable, he had shown Jadelin how tea was grown and picked. He taught her that the highest grade was picked in the first two days, which yielded the fattest and sweetest tea shoots. As the climate warmed, leaves grew faster. The tea had to be picked quickly, cleanly, and consistently with no broken leaves. Old leaves, fragments, fruits, and other unwanted bits were thrown out during the drying process.

The three rode further along the path between peaked mountains and fragrant rows of tea shrubs until they came to the crystal clear natural spring called Hu Pao Quan. The water flowed smoothly out from the rocks without bubbles: not too fast, not too slow. They slid off their mounts.

"The best tasting tea is made from the water of this spring," Bowli explained to her as he tied their horses to a hitching post. He held out his hand for hers and they entered the teahouse built near the natural spring. Slender columns lined the delicate wood building. Both rustic and elegant with clean lines, it looked like it had nested in this spot for centuries.

Shanli ordered from the old woman who greeted them at the tea house's well-worn entry. "Tai Shee, Longjing tea, please."

Although her face sagged with deep wrinkles, and she looked at least a hundred years old, the tiny woman with the neatly pinned white bun stood erect and undaunted by time. She smoothed the front of her tunic with tiny hands. "Mow Bowli, Mow Chongli, and Mow Shanli, I'm honored to see you." Tai Shee pursed her lips and tipped her head. "I have not seen your father for many months."

"He is visiting friends," answered Shanli. Their father spent longer periods with Grand Master Ping now. China's history abounded with legends of distinguished men who retreated to seek a scholarly life of meditation. The Mows let their neighbors assume Mow Chow Ching had chosen this path.

A furrow deepened across Tai Shee's forehead as she opened her eyes wider. "Is it true, the stories I have heard about him?"

"What stories are those?" asked Chongli. He cloaked his wary eyes with a friendly smile.

Tai Shee opened her mouth, then thought better of it. She shook her head and motioned them to a table set off by itself with an excellent view of the spring. "Idle gossip. Please, sit." She returned with a tray of porcelain cups and a bamboo container, a tea tray and a teapot. She waited while the brothers checked the tea leaves. They approved their appearance and fragrance. Only then did she rinse the leaves in the pot, discard the first pour, and fill the pot with water. Then she bowed and left the four to enjoy their tea and the view.

Bowli poured. The brothers again checked the color and the fragrance.

"This tea has a light jade color and a mellow flavor," Jadelin noted. The brothers nodded.

"Would you like to see the steeped leaves?" asked Shanli. He nodded to the teapot and Bowli offered it to her.

She lifted the lid. "They are very long with pointed tips." She looked up and saw Chongli's smile wreath his face.

"A distinctive feature of Longjing tea leaves," said Chongli. "These are very fine, undamaged and whole."

Jadelin had never tasted Dragon Well as refreshing as the tea they enjoyed that afternoon overlooking the spring. She looked from Shanli to Changli to Bowli. The brothers understood each other so well. Each complemented the others. She could not imagine one without the other two. The four grew poetic and philosophical as the afternoon light turned blue. They had ridden for hours and the menacing clouds churning around Lion Peak turned darker by the minute. The men seemed in no hurry. In fact, they waited until it started to rain before getting up.

Only then did Bowli ask her, "Would you like to see the dragon in the dragon well?"

Jadelin laughed, incredulous. "You're teasing me. I thought Dragon Well was a flowery euphemism."

"Come!" He grasped her hand and led his wife outside. Shanli and Chongli followed a few steps behind. Bowli led her to the uncovered well so carefully maintained there were no leaves, no insects, no bits of twigs or dirt anywhere near it. Its smooth rim was constructed of stones that had held their position for centuries with no mortar. The rain fell steadily.

"Look in the well, Jadelin. What do you see?"

Jade observed the surface of the water dimpled by raindrops. She checked the depths for the flash of an eye, a flick of a tail, a claw. Nothing.

She rested her hands on its rim and leaned far over is surface. She turned to Bowli. "What am I looking for? An illustration? A carving?"

Bowli held her shoulders. "Let me hold you." He put his arms around her waist and held her tight against his broad chest so she could lean out. "How you look is important. The water in this well is very dense. After it rains, the lighter rainwater floats. Now, soften your eyes and look at the surface of the water. Relax your back into my hands. Gaze lightly."

Jadelin let her weight fall into his arms. She softened her focus so the water seemed cloaked in mist. All she could hear was the gentle tap of the rain on the wall of the well and her own breathing. She felt the warmth of Bowli's arms surround her body and the beat of his heart, strong and steady. She took a deep breath and emptied her mind.

"Oh," she whispered. With her eyes and mind relaxed she could make out the sinuous boundary of the lighter rainwater floating on the dense well water. It emerged out of its watery realm with the ears of an ox, horns of a deer, claws of a tiger, scales of a fish, and eyes of a rabbit. It curled and swirled on the surface of the water, claws outstretched.

He helped her to her feet. "Benjamin was right, wasn't he?"

She faced him, triumphant. "Yes, he was."

"Someday, we'll come when there's a full moon," he whispered. He held her hands and kissed them tenderly. "On the night of the full moon, we'll return to see the dragon in the Dragon Well chasing the reflected moon, the Pearl of Wisdom." His eyes held hers.

Yes, she promised. She looked forward to that romantic moonlit night.

In great spirits, the men picked up the pace, skirting the parts of the path that the rain had turned to mud. The sun broke through the mists and flooded the sky with golden shafts. At last, the house of Mow appeared low on the horizon.

Shanli shouted a challenge. Bowli and Chongli answered. The brothers bent forward and raced towards home.

Jadelin didn't think they expected her to join in. After all, her horse knew the way. By now she knew her little Mongolian; she was nimble and fast, the hardy quick breed that carried Genghis Khan and the Mongol hordes in their conquest of all the lands from the eastern shore of China, through the lands along the Silk Route, and far and wide across the lands of Western Europe. She clutched her horse tight with her thighs. "Hai!" She slapped the Mongolian's sturdy flank. Her horse took off after the men as if she had been waiting for this chance all her life. Jadelin lay flat against her neck so they became one compact animal racing in the wind. The farms whizzed past and the mud flew. The wind whipped their eyes.

Bowli looked back, surprised to see her gaining on them. He shouted to his brothers who slowed for an instant.

Jadelin kept her head down. "Faster, faster my Mongolian princess. We'll beat these men." Faster she galloped. The brothers' split second pause favored her.

Bowli let up, but Shanli grinned and bent over his horse as she passed. Jadelin heard his horse at her back. The house of Mow was in sight. Shanli's horse's stride was greater than the Mongolian's and when the path narrowed their horses bumped.

Jadelin momentarily lost her grip and slipped off her saddle. "Faster," she yelled, "faster." She grasped for the reins, holding tight -- half on, half off. The Mongolian, a horse trained to continue the course even if it lost its rider, raced on. By now, Jadelin's eyes were so splattered she couldn't see. She heard Bowli yell to Shanli and Chongli.

With a herculean effort she pulled herself upright just as Shanli splattered to the stable ahead of her. Her horse slowed to a trot and headed for the water trough. She was so covered in mud she looked like a parcel tied to the back of her splattered mount.

The brothers trotted over and dismounted. "Are you all right?" They laughed, but it was with admiration and respect.

Bowli gently unkinked his wife's hands from the reins and lifted her out of the saddle. He laughed. "How could you expect to beat Shanli on his stallion?"

She blew a strand of muddy hair out of her face. "I had a chance."

Shanli looked at her husband with a very pleased expression. "If anything were to threaten the house of Mow, I believe Jadelin would avenge us all." He lowered his head and when he looked her in the eye, she felt he saw right through to her soul. "You have a killer instinct, Jadelin."

Twenty-Four

THE BARBARIAN RETURNS

SHANGHAI

Cousin Li followed the steady line of coolies bearing tea chests on their backs to the Poe's tea hong. Hundreds of chests arrived daily on the backs of coolies from the inland mountains to perfume their warehouse. Even the tea buyers and coolies stopped the moment they stepped into the cavernous space to inhale the mélange of scents— bitter, smoky, citrus, floral, light, full, and sweet. The finest and rarest teas would be sold in the cool of the morning before dust stirred on the bricks.

From his post at the central table Daniel tracked a thousand different teas from as many tea gardens. Paul inspected and directed the incoming coolies and tea chests. Benjamin approved the storage of each chest as they were delivered.

On a polished zitan table, John Poe prepared the inventory lists in English since his talent was with the foreign buyers. In consideration for the relationships they had cultivated over generations, the brothers scheduled the Westerners after the Chinese had placed their orders.

Out of the corner of his eye, he felt cousin Li's broad-chested shadow slip sideways through the side door nearest to him. "Li, what brings you from Canton?" he asked softly in Cantonese. His cousin hated leaving Canton's famed restaurants and cooks for any period of time even though his business took him to every corner of China from the Gobi desert to the tropical coastline.

"A thousand greetings, cousin." Li's large brown eyes swept swiftly across the warehouse. On the other side of the building his uncle, Mandarin Poe, conversed with two buyers in silk gowns fastened with jade buttons, their hands poised over a wooden crate that exuded the scent of chrysanthemums when the winter sun touches their luscious blooms. "I have come a long way," he sighed wearily.

A servant brought hot water and teacups while John cleared his desk. He chose a pewter tea canister from a small chest and prepared their tea while the two shared their news. Li, his elder by ten years, had a natural talent for adapting his persona to fit the regional nuances of the Chinese, from the coasts to the interior, from Shanghai to Hong Kong, while keeping his eyes and ears alert to any news and trends that might affect his family or business.

Li accepted the tea with thick-fingered hands and inhaled its toasty flavor. It was a smoked Bo Lei to calm the ch'i and enhance digestion. "I'm honored. This is your favorite."

"Yes, I seem to desire it these days," acknowledged John. "It brings back memories of a simpler time." When he was very young, he would accompany his father to tea houses where the banter of his father and his cronies and the taste of steaming trays of dumplings piled one atop the other was enhanced by the smoky Bo Lei cha, the Pu'er tea known for its medicinal qualities and ability to increase the flow of ch'i.

Li sipped while he listened to his cousin bemoan how European buyers insisted on high quality tea at low prices.

"They have no respect for the expertise of the tea farmer, the care he gives his plants and the quality of his harvesting process, the coolies who walk hundreds of thousands of miles with heavy tea chests strapped to their backs, and the hongs who have paid the farmers in advance to ensure they can maintain standards of quality." Less scrupulous tea merchants met the low prices by mixing in twigs and tea dust.

Li heard similar complaints from businessmen throughout China, from the little storefronts along the road stands to the wholesale exporters in Canton. All he could offer John was his compassion and understanding.

"Do you still want to be a scholar recluse studying gardens and paintings?" asked Li.

"It sounds peaceful, doesn't it? A scholar's life of philosophy and art. My goal recedes further in the distance now." John shook his head. "I think my sister is close to that life now. Her life flows with the growing and harvesting of tea, with the lives of her husband's family and her children. She has time to retreat in the quiet, mist-shrouded mountains of West Lake."

"I don't think she's the type to retreat from anything. She could never sit still long enough," said Li. His eyes crinkled with memories of Jadelin's saucy answers and how mischievous she looked when dressed as a boy to deceive the Emperor's men. He took a deep breath and leaned forward. "Cousin, remember Robert Fortune, the plant hunter from England?" A crease between his arched eyebrows was the first sign of concern on his normally inscrutable face. Unlike his Shanghai cousins' slanted almond eyes and pale complexions, his was a tan Cantonese face with soulful round eyes.

John frowned. "The barbarian plant hunter?" He remembered Fortune's blond hair crammed under a flat felt cap, his bushy sideburns, and how his pale eyes darted possessively whenever he spied a flower or plant of unusual beauty or color. "You saw him sail off. He is gone."

Li shook his head and his brown eyes sagged. "I traveled north to tell you I saw him disembark in Hong Kong. He has returned."

John jerked up his head. A feeling of apprehension flushed through his body. "When was this? Are you sure it was him?"

"Positive. The dockhands transferred his luggage to Captain Landers' ship headed for Shanghai. Just before they set sail, he requested one of the officials to post a letter to Shanghai. Fortunately for us, he still posts duplicates. The official is my wife's cousin." He handed his cousin a thick envelope.

John weighed the letter in his hands. "Baba and my brothers will be most interested. Come. I'll have lunch brought upstairs to Benjamin's office where we can read and discuss this in private."

∾

*B*enjamin slid the warehouse doors shut at noon after all the buyers and coolies had left. The aroma of roast pork dumplings and sizzling vegetables over thin noodles in a savory gravy wafted down from his office where his father and brothers feasted with Cousin Li. He patted his stomach. His herbalist had suggested he cut back. But no one could resist the trays of food Cousin Won carried over from his restaurant next door. Meetings and decision-making required discussion over a good meal. He double-checked the doors and secret entrances before he ascended to his office.

He stepped into the aerie, a large room that commanded a clear view of all the activity on the floor of the warehouse. From this lofty position, Benjamin observed each entrance and exit and all the windows. In the center of his strategically placed office his father, brothers, and cousin sat at a rough-hewn table. Their chopsticks darted from the platters of food to their bowls of rice as they laughed and joked.

"We started lunch as you suggested," said Paul. "We're trying to eat it all so you can maintain your svelte figure." The others guffawed and shook their heads at that probability.

Benjamin's stomach growled loud enough for his brothers to hear. "Move over," he nudged John. He sat down and proceeded to scoop a sizeable serving from each platter into his bowl with lightening chopsticks.

After the food was gone, the chopsticks silent, and all were satiated, Mandarin Poe turned to each of them. It was time for business. "Cousin Li has come from Hong Kong with news that the plant hunter has returned. He will read the letter Robert Fortune has written to his friend who works for the British Consul of Shanghai. Then we will decide what to do."

Li read.

To *Alistair Mackenzie, assistant to Captain Balfour, British Consul, Shanghai*
From *Robert Fortune, Curator of the Chelsea Physic Garden*
My *dear friend Alistair,*

I accept your invitation to stay with you whilst in Shanghai and to store my plants in your garden.

I arrived in the Bay of Hong Kong on the evening of August 14, 1848 on the Peninsular and Oriental Company's steam-ship "Braganza." Before we could tie up, two long boats powered by fifty oarsmen scooted alongside. Amidst vociferous shouting from the competing boats, one built by the English and the other by Americans, each was loaded with mail and newspapers bound for Canton. They raced up the Pearl River like silver arrows through the water to be the first to arrive. I watched until the shushing of the oars faded and the vision of racing oars vanished in the moonlight.

It was a clear moonlit night that one finds only in China. On this evening, warm and balmy, scarcely a breath of air fanned the water that sparkled as if blanketed by polished gems. Vessels from all parts of the world lay at anchor; their dark hulls and tall masts loomed in the distance. The view was bounded on all sides by rugged and barren hills.

Whilst in England I missed this most about China: its ability to continually surprise me with the unanticipated. In England, one is bound by rules and laws and schedules. In China, I never know when I'm going to arrive, whether I'll be waylaid by a new flower, stopped by a crumbling temple or exquisite view, mesmerized by a wedding party led by gongs and banners, or witness a mail race. The path is never direct, the way is never straight, and the objective is never easily obtained.

I'm a stranger in an exotic land, alone with my wits. The curious Chinese scurry up the street and stare as if I'm from the moon. The shopkeepers and workmen squawk at their customers in their rough singsong language. Horses and oxen pull produce carts and products of all sizes and shapes through the city streets lined with tile-roofed buildings whose corners curve upwards. The smell of strangely spiced food exudes from bakeries carried on peddlers' backs, from little shops two arms-length wide with no seating, and from ornate teahouses where men with birdcages spend their mornings drinking tea with friends. My body quivers to be astonished once again.

When the East India Company asked if I would return to China, I told them I had no intention of reliving the deprivation and hardship in that country. They offered me five times what the Royal Horticultural Society paid me for my first trip, plus expenses. Posing as a collector of decorative flowers, I'm to obtain the finest tea-plants and seeds, Chinese tea manufacturing equipment, and native tea masters who can produce tea in the north-west provinces of India to supply the needs of British India and England.

We conclude the Chinese are healthy because they drink only tea. Tea is essential to improving the health of natives in our India colony but they can't afford to pay China's price. We have calculated that if India can produce its own tea, there will be no negative impact upon China's trade. Sir George Staunton calculates that the Chinese grow such immense quantities of tea a sudden failure of demand from Europe would not cause any material diminution of price in the Chinese markets.

Her Majesty's government believes this is our destiny.

I have lived in China for three years, visited all five treaty ports, and can convince anyone that there are many wild plants in the Anwei and Bohea tea districts that I have not seen. I speak a little of the language, can use chopsticks, and can talk about plants and flowers with nurserymen and connoisseurs. I have grown my hair so I can wear it in a queue to perfect my disguise when I venture inland. The Chinese will never suspect me.

I am the perfect tea thief.

Your devoted friend,

Robert Fortune

Mandarin Poe, John Poe, and Cousin Li strode into the carpeted receiving hall of the governor of Shanghai, the Taoutae. Silk lanterns highlighted the beams of the ceiling painted with landscapes of China's fabled interior. Beneath this splendor, the Taoutae welcomed his loyal friends and served them a fine green tea from a mountain that sprouted one hundred waterfalls every spring. The Taoutae listened carefully as Mandarin Poe summarized Robert Fortune's letter.

"What do you wish me to do?" asked the Taoutae. He folded his blue-veined hands. His thick white queue and unwrinkled skin belied his seventy years. Although his reflexes had slowed and he could no longer fight off five intruders simultaneously with his bare hands as he once did, he was in his intellectual and political prime. He wished China, especially Shanghai, to prosper.

Mandarin Poe's voice was urgent. "We must convince our Emperor to stop him. The last time Robert Fortune was here, he obtained tea seeds and plants. With the backing of his government, he's returned for more. The last time he cursed our country with his presence, my nephew Li obtained his daily missives to England. This is his latest letter to his friend here in Shanghai. In this letter he writes he is posing as a plant collector to steal China's tea plants, methods, tools, and the men who can turn leaves into tea. Sir, listen to Li who saw the barbarian arrive in Hong Kong with his own eyes and obtained this letter."

The Taoutae held out his hand towards Li to approach.

Li bowed. "Sir, the last time he was in China, the barbarian disguised himself with a queue and a mandarin's gown. He successfully entered Soochow, which lies beyond the twenty-four hour limit. In the rural areas where they have no exposure to outsiders they did not realize that he was a Westerner. They freely shared information about tea and silk production."

The Taoutae gripped the arms of his polished chair and turned to the senior Poe. "Is there any way to get rid of him without bothering the Emperor?" He growled softly, "How can we erase him from the earth?"

"For every European killed, even in an accident, five Chinese are beheaded," Mandarin Poe reminded him.

The Taoutae slumped back. His grip on the arms of his chair turned white. He inhaled the calming scent of jasmine that infused the hall and exhaled slowly. Finally, he lifted his head and sat tall in his chair. His voice was grave as he considered their options. "Ten English gunboats sit in my harbor. The French and Russians have ships with cannons larger than we have ever seen and armies with superior guns. Every day the Westerners ask for more privileges while they continue to import over twenty-two thousand cases of opium every year from India to weaken and kill our people."

Mandarin Poe's brows dipped in a contemplative frown. "Respected Taoutae, the British broadcloth collapsed our cotton market, starving thousands of farmers, weavers, and merchants. They must not do the same with our tea." With European gunboats in their harbors and British armies in their seaports there were no favorable outcomes for China. "Our legends say that the Bodhidharma gave us tea when he tore off his eyelids so that he would not sleep during meditation. Tea is the blood of China. If we lose our secrets of tea, we lose our heritage and the legacy of our ancestors."

The Taoutae rubbed his forehead as he paced the thick carpets. "He will hire a translator and a coolie. We must have his eyes and ears." Both mandarins turned expectantly towards Li.

Li crossed his fisted arm over his chest. "I will do what I can. In disguise, he passes reasonably as a Chinese and has learned enough Chinese to understand what people are saying. According to the Treaties, Chinese laws do not apply to British subjects. He has no qualms about breaking rules to travel to forbidden areas. On the other hand, if he is injured or hurt, Chinese will be killed in retaliation. We don't want to give the foreigners an excuse for another 'Opium War.'" He looked to John who immediately nodded his assent. "He will not suspect we are sabotaging his efforts. That is the only way."

The Taoutae groaned. The past decade had made him wish for a contemplative life in a quiet garden overlooking a remote mountain stream.

Twenty-Five

TRACKING BEYOND THE LIMIT

AMOY

*L*i scrutinized the crew of hardened Amoy seamen scurrying up and down the masts, securing sails and lines when the boat docked in Shanghai. He recognized the scents of a long voyage, salt-washed sails and lines sunbaked in the wind. There were few passengers so it had been easy for him to spot the tall Scot.

"I know all the nurseries and gardens in northern China," Li reminded Fortune. They stood face to face on the dock while coolies unloaded the cargo that bobbed on thick bamboo poles across their shoulders. More lines radiated from the Scot's eyes and the blond hair peeking from under his flat-topped Turkish hat was coursed with white. He still wore bushy sideburns down the side of his face.

"I know, I know. But I went through all your nurseries and gardens the last time. I need to discover new flowers." Fortune pushed his small, smoked lenses up his long nose with his index finger and tapped the ground with the tip of his ever-present umbrella for emphasis. He was pleased to see his former translator Li, but he couldn't hire him.

Li stared into Fortune's pale eyes to discern how much of what he said was truth. "And where will you find those? You have been to all five treaty ports."

"I'll walk through the countryside and see what I can discover."

"I know the hidden valleys and paths along the coast." Shanghai had changed. Since Fortune left three years ago, twenty-four merchant firms, three of them American, had opened in the international concession. There were now five foreign retail stores, twenty-five private residences, a church, a hotel, a dispensary, and a clubhouse at the racetrack. A volunteer committee had been set up to oversee construction of buildings and wharves along a section of the Huangpu River they named the Bund, the Hindu term for embankment. Tens of thousands of new Chinese merchants lined the streets.

Fortune waved him off. "I can't go back on my word. I didn't know you were available." He didn't want him to know that Alistair Mackenzie had hired a coolie and a translator to accompany him into the great tea district of Hangchow. Unused to dealing with Westerners, these men did not know about the laws and treaties that limited Fortune's movements as Li did. Tze, an old man, was stupid in many ways, but his back was strong and broad. Young, energetic, and strong, Wang was the perfect translator since had had been born in Hangchow, where Fortune intended to purchase his first tea plants.

"Wait. You can post these letters for me." Fortune thrust two envelopes and a handful of cash in Li's hands. "This is a task I always trusted you with."

Li's face remained professional and unrevealing. "Travel well, Robert Fortune," he said with a bow. He glanced quickly at the letters in his hand before disappearing in the crowd of hawkers, shoppers, and seamen to meet John in the teashop on the street of birds.

∽

The cousins watched Wang and Tze as the afternoon light waned and dusk blurred the figures on the approaching boat tied along the riverbank. Fortune's men were easy to spot because the two were trying so hard to not attract attention.

"They are loading his trunks into that small boat headed for Wang's ancestral village in Hangchow," Li pointed out. Darkness fell quickly on the river.

"So the barbarian travels into the heart of the green tea growing area where Jadelin lives."

"There's no chance he'll see her," Li assured him. "He'll stay close to Wang's village which is on the river where lower quality tea plants grow. The Mows grow tea in the Longjing mountains."

John Poe pondered Fortune's strategy. The Scot had chosen evening, the best time to slip aboard without attracting the watchful eyes of the mandarins' spies.

"Look, there they are now, creeping through the shadows with exaggerated steps. Fortune is getting on the boat." Li chuckled when the barbarian turned to Tze, both arms raised and his hands gesticulating in utter frustration. The evening wind carried his angry voice. Li whispered to his cousin, "I told their boatman that one of his passengers was a *gweilo*, a Foreign Devil, hoping to discourage him. But he said he was paid in advance. What's that I hear? Fortune is berating Tze and Wang for bragging to everyone on the dock that they were accompanying a foreigner even after he had sworn them to secrecy. He knows the authorities beheaded four boatmen last month for taking three Englishman inland to see the silk district. He will not trust them now. A good beginning, isn't it?"

John shook his head. "Everyone needs rice to eat. Even the threat of beheading doesn't daunt them." Fortune motioned his men aboard the little boat and the bare-chested crew cast off, poling quickly into the current.

"The boatman will make Fortune pay extra to keep his secret when they reach the twenty-four hour limit." Li pointed up the river. "Our boat is there." The two stepped from shadow to shadow and blended into the night.

～

*O*n the morning of the second day, Wang curled into a ball with a soaring fever and diarrhea. Every ten minutes he hung his butt over the water. He groaned like a sick water buffalo.

"But who will dress me?" Fortune demanded. He shook out the creases in his mandarin gown, shaped the skullcap with his fingers, and unpacked his soft Chinese shoes.

"Tze." Wang moaned to the old coolie, "You must shave the master's head. I cannot hold the razor steady."

"I'm no barber," Tze wailed. "I don't know how. I never shaved heads." He waved off the razor Wang held out. "I have broken hands. See? Too many fights. Crooked fingers."

"Tze, you must. See how my hand shakes? Ai-ya!" Wang ran to the side of the boat and dropped his drawers again. "My guts are coming out. Ai-ya!"

Fortune unwrapped the long queue he had used on his previous forays into China's inland. He glowered at the younger man. "Wang, I order you to get well immediately. Tze is not shaving my head." The Scot had hired him because he was strong and cheap, not for any finesse, which he doubted he possessed. He covered his head with one hand and batted away the ex-wrestler who brandished the razor blade as if he intended to peel a banana.

"You have no choice," Wang gasped. He held his head over the water and dry heaved. "If Tze shaves you before you dress there won't be as much blood on your clothes."

Fortune sat rigid trying to watch the bucolic scene sailing past as Tze prepared for the task. Cotton plants waved in the warm breeze, farmers walked their blooming fields, and long-legged cranes fished along the shoreline against a blue washed sky.

The old coolie washed Fortune's scalp with hot water to soften the stubble and flourished the razor. And each time the barbarian shrieked, the boatmen peered in and marveled at the rivulets of blood. "Ai-ya, very bad, very bad," repeated Tze.

Finally, the tall Scot emerged from his cabin to the amazement of all. As 'Sing Wa,' a traveler from beyond the Great Wall, he looked to the west where the land was intersected by rivers and canals which connected all the towns in the province. Now he could travel these canals to Soochow, Nanking, and, via the Grand Canal, to China's capital of Peking, or to the Tarter city of Chapoo. But for now, he headed southwest with a fair wind along the grassy banks to the great silk growing area of Hangchow.

The next day the skies poured waterfalls of rain and slathered the river with fog. Unable to go any further, the crew huddled around a single fire.

Wang bent over Fortune, who lay in the only protected area of the boat. "Sir, someone needs to stand watch at night." Not wishing to be robbed again while he slept, Fortune volunteered Tze for duty with severe admonishments to be vigilant.

By dawn Tze, who kept watch within the cabin, and the captain, who watched the stern, were both snoring as loudly as the rest of the crew. So they did not notice that John Poe and Li had passed their boat in the night. When the cousins heard the snores, they tied up and bedded down, snug, warm, and dry in their enclosed sampan.

೦ಌ

Tall masted junks skimmed the Grand Canal from the inland tea growing regions and the coastal silk and cotton districts. The mighty ships converged in Hangchow, the ancient city in Chekiang province, where thousands of coolies transferred thousands of tea chests from their backs to river junks headed for the magnificent cities of Soochow and Shanghai. They unloaded silk and cotton and lead from the coastal junks onto their backs for the mountainous trek inland.

He was bounced across town in a bamboo chair balanced on the shoulders of two porters. Like a bird in a cage he was carried through orderly suburbs into a well-paved city with gardens, under ornately carved arches, and past gilded Buddhist temples. Shops glittered with gold and silver, jades, ancient porcelains, bronzes, and carved bamboo.

His stomach growled when they passed the teahouses and food stalls. Weak with hunger, he ordered Wang to stop. But single-minded

Wang, leading the gaggle of coolies bearing their boxes and luggage, would not stop until they got to the quiet inn on Green River where he could arrange for a boat upriver to their destination.

At the inn, Tze and Wang secured his belongings. Fortune gestured to the innkeeper he wished to eat. As the innkeeper directed, he walked up a floor to where tables and chairs were set for merchants to smoke long bamboo pipes and discuss the news of the day and the state of commerce. Warily, he eyed the other customers to see if they stared, raised any eyebrows or shouted alarms. But no one took any notice of the long nosed barbarian dressed in a queue and mandarin robe. Satisfied, he pulled out the long bamboo pipe Wang had purchased for him before they left. He had practiced smoking on the boat ride and found it much more gentle and soothing than the harsh Manila cheroots his fellow British were so fond of. He relaxed with his pipe and listened hungrily to the sounds of chopping and sizzling from the kitchen. Minutes later, attendants motioned the men to get up so they could set the table. One by one, steaming dishes were placed upon the table. One by one, the guests were called and requested to sit down as each place was set with a bowl and pair of chopsticks.

But when the innkeeper shouted, "Sing Wa, Sing Wa," Fortune struck his head with his fist. Fool, he groaned. How long had it been since he used chopsticks with proficiency? Three years. All the way up the river he had dropped rice and shoveled his food into his mouth as if he were a child. If the other merchants saw him struggle they would quickly deport him down the river. He would be arrested and his men beheaded.

Fortune bowed to the innkeeper and shook his head. "I shall dine when my servants return," he apologized. He stumbled downstairs and sank onto a bench by his trunks. Faint with hunger, he leaned forward in despair with his arms around his stomach.

John Poe and Li, who had been reclining among the tea chests and trunks on the lower floor with the other servants, leapt to their feet. Disguised in faded indigo tunics and trousers with cotton scarves tied across their forehead to absorb sweat like the tea-carrying coolies, they had hoped to taste the steaming rice and the vegetables simmering in the woks. But Tze and Wang might return any time with news they had secured a boat and their quarry would be on the move.

Hours later, Tze and Wang returned with porters for the trunks and their master, Sing Wa. The starving Scot was hoisted on a chair and off the procession headed to the river.

Wang and Tze loaded Fortune on a flat-bottomed cargo boat carrying twenty passengers where everyone slept on the open deck. Fifteen men pulled the boat upstream with braided bamboo ropes strapped across their shoulders. Naked except for woven bamboo shoes, these trackers followed one behind the other along narrow footpaths that had been worn into the riverbeds or carved into the cliffs by generations of their predecessors.

"Why don't they wear clothes?" asked Fortune. Coming from Victorian England, he found the men's nakedness offensive. In his entire life he had never seen a nude except as depicted by Greek and Roman statues.

Wang shook his head at his master's ignorance. "Sometimes the tracking path is under water, sometimes along the river bank, and sometimes on the cliffs. You see how wet they get? They have learned through hundreds of generations that wet clothes chafes their skin raw. It is more comfortable and healthy to work naked. If their bodies bother you, don't look. No one else does."

The trackers worked as a team. They grasped thick ropes and slings across their shoulders and bent, heads down almost to their knees as they slowly pulled the barge against the current. One man sang a plaintive song while the others stepped to his strong musical beat. Their nude bodies sparkled in the waves like polished bronze.

As they headed inland, the hills rose in starkly ridged and furrowed summits broken up into peaks and cones, some low, some thousands of feet high. All stood rugged, barren, and wild.

The boat's pace was so slow that every morning after Fortune had bathed and donned his Chinese disguise, he leapt off and climbed the nearest hill to estimate how far the boat would go that day. If there were many rapids, he wandered far. If the river looked smooth, he stayed close to the banks. He collected many plants. He was especially happy with a beautiful palm tree that he asked Wang to carry.

"This tree," said Wang as he tied its fronds close to its trunk for transport, "is useful. We make rope and cables for our junks from this part." He indicated the hair-like bracts. "You can also weave them into bed bottoms. Since it is water repellent, they can be woven into hats or cloaks like the ones our coolies wear."

Fortune shook his head. No, he didn't want the tree for its usefulness, but for its beauty. "They will look lovely in the gardens in the south of England."

"But it is so useful." Wang shook his head. Why grow something you can't eat or use to make something?

At each patch of rough water, all the boats slowed. A flotilla of small boats waited in the shallows. In each boat stood white haired men and women called river beggars. Land beggars stood in the shallows. All held out a basket at the end of a bamboo pole. The boatmen filled the baskets of the land and river beggars with rice. Fortune felt ashamed at how the British at home treated those too sick or old to work, whereas the Chinese honored and respected old age. Then he felt very proud that everyone thought he was a Chinese from beyond the Great Wall.

John Poe and Li followed just a few boats behind, always changing their distance behind their prey. The trip thus far had been uneventful but action would begin once Fortune got to the tea growing areas. They would have to destroy whatever he found and be sure he got back to Shanghai alive and unhurt.

Twenty-Six

MOW CHOW CHING

LONGJING MOUNTAINS

"*N*o, my love, it's too dark to get up." Jadelin grabbed Mow Bowli's arm as he rolled out of bed. She craved the heat of sleep and sex radiating from his body. The bamboo grove behind the house rustled as if to seduce them back into each other's arms. "See, the sky still belongs to the moon." He scooped her up and carried her outside where the wind whistled around the peaked eaves of the courtyard.

"My dearest, the water has iced over." She pointed to the wooden barrel that collected the rain running from their roofs. He knotted his hand and whipped down with his fist. Crack! He scooped out the ice with his bare hands so they could wash. She gasped when she plunged her hands into the water and washed her face. She gasped even louder when she stepped into her fighting silks, so cold and slippery against her skin warmed hours before by her husband's hands. She caught him watching and flushed with pleasure. Then it was her turn to watch him slip off his robe and get dressed. Moonlight accentuated the definition of his muscles. She couldn't resist running her fingers along his neck, across his shoulders, and down his arms. No matter how hard she trained, she could never develop such hardness and strength.

Bowli and Jadelin stepped into the central courtyard where Mow Chow Ching and his two eldest sons were already warming up. Lanterns lit with scented beeswax candles surrounded the perimeter of the court-yard built in the style of the West Lake district known for its exquisite gardens and peaked tile roofs. The first time she met her father-in-law, Jadelin wondered how such a small square man had produced such tall sons, lithe as bamboo, who towered two heads above him. And how, she wondered, could Bowli's father, although the same age as her father, look decades younger.

As soon as they entered, Bowli and Jadelin bowed to Mow Chow Ching. Then the five stood, hands clasped, eyes closed to center their ch'i before their patriarch led them in a Tai Chi practice from his days with Grand Master Ping. Whether sheathed in mist or chilled by frost, they disciplined their minds and bodies so they felt only the warm core of their soul sending its power through their bodies.

When dawn finally warmed the courtyard with pink rays, they joined the other wives, children, and amahs in the kitchen which was already steaming with pots of congee. Unlike the house of Poe, the house of Mow had no servants. Besides the patriarch and his sons and their fami-lies, only ghosts and legends inhabited the halls, gardens and pavilions built generations ago.

Sweet Amah, a tea picker before she married and had babies of her own, brought Jadelin her baby to nurse. Her husband Wu, now the Mows' senior tea master, had worked in their tea sheds since he was a child. There he had mastered the ten hand movements unique to pan-roasted Longjing, Dragon Well tea. Both Sweet Amah and Wu treated the Mow babies as their own, coo-cooing and singing folk songs.

"My children," Mow Chow Ching bellowed in a strong clear voice. He lifted his stout arms for attention. Everyone looked up from their congee and tea in surprise. The mellow energy of the Mows was the opposite of the hearty arguments and energetic rough housing that typi-fied the 'discussions' of the Poe brothers. No, at the end of the day the patriarch and his three sons would sit in the main hall or central garden and serenely sip tea that the eldest son had chosen minutes before.

Arms akimbo, his forehead still flushed from the morning tai chi, Mow Chow Ching surveyed his family and took in their expectant faces. Bowls of congee, steaming rice porridge accompanied by five different dumplings and condiments in porcelain platters, lay untouched on the table worn with the patina of generations. "My children, I bid you all farewell. By this time tomorrow," he spread his arms high and wide, "you will be eating your congee together. Only I will not be here," he exulted.

The family jumped to their feet so abruptly that the babies cried. Only Mow Bowli remained seated. He bowed his head, composed and calm, the only one unsurprised.

"Baba, are you ill?" Eldest son Shanli stepped to his father's side and held his fingertips to his pulse. He tipped his head in concentration. "No, your ch'i is strong and healthy."

Mow Chow Ching clasped Shanli's shoulder to reassure him. "For fifty years I have loved and guided my family. Now I'm embarking on an adventure alone. You are more than capable to lead our clan. I'm confident you and your brothers will continue the thousand year success of the house of Mow."

"Why are you leaving? Where are you going?" asked Second Son Chongli. "Will you return from time to time or send word so we won't worry?"

Mow Chow Ching's eyes met Jadelin's. "It may be unwise to write." Then he sat down leaving his sons and daughters-in-laws to ponder his sudden announcement. They each clasped his hands in theirs and bowed in honor and reverence, as did all his grandchildren. Mow Bowli and Jadelin were last. Chow Ching put one arm around his youngest son's shoulder and the other around Jadelin's and drew them close. "You know I have been called. You know how to find me." He whispered in Bowli's ear. "One last practice today?"

∾

A year after Jadelin became his Third Son's bride, Mow Chow Ching stepped back from running the family business. He even declined to accompany his sons on their daily inspection through the lush rows of tea shrubs. Occasionally he appeared in the tea sheds during processing but disappeared as quickly. He had trained each son for a role that best suited his talents.

Eldest brother Mow Shanli was happiest walking the mist shrouded tea shrubs at dawn when the cold air was muffled by dew. From the scent and texture of the leaves he could tell which had the correct amount of rainfall and night soil and which tips were ready for harvest. He inspected the tea sheds where his workers sorted, dried, and rolled the tea before packing. He checked the leaves as they dried and monitored how they were rolled. After the workers wearing special booties packed the tea, he gave each tea chest a blessing for that was the last they saw of their precious tea once the coolies lifted the chests onto their backs and carried them over the hills to Shanghai to bring pleasure to those who could afford the finest.

Before her babies came, Jadelin would join Shanli on his morning walks. She learned that tea thrives at high altitudes, where there is plentiful rainfall, humidity, and a moderate climate. Their misty tea garden, nourished by flowing streams, had excellent drainage.

Second Brother Mow Chongli had a talent for choosing the pickers with the eye and dexterity to cleanly pluck only the bud and top leaf. He remembered how quickly each worked, their strengths, and whether they were steadfast and loyal. He saw whose fingers were best for plucking tea leaves and noted when these fingers started to slow. He soothed the tears when pickers who had reached puberty had to advance to the tea sheds. He trained those whose nimble hands had a talent for creating perfectly compact balls of tea that exploded with the unique aroma and taste of their fine Longjing tea.

Bowli encouraged Jadelin to try her hand; if tea was to be her life, she had to understand every aspect of how the tender buds became a prized drink. The quality of the tea came from experience: knowing when to pick, which was ten days before Ching Ming for the premium first pick, to how to wither the leaves, and when to roast to stop the drying process. They could do one kilo of high grade tea a day. It took

80,000 tips to make one kilo. Once the process was started they couldn't stop, even if it meant they were turning and drying leaves ten to fifteen times until dawn the next day. During the six weeks involved in harvest and production they rarely slept. When the tea was pan roasted, the whole valley was redolent with the scent. It was their aphrodisiac.

Everyone deferred to the tea masters. Their badge of honor was their leathery hands, evidence that they spent at least three years mastering the ten complex hand movements to make Longjing tea. These men, respected and valued, possessed the Mow's treasured tea secrets.

Of the three brothers only Mow Bowli had been trained and educated by Grand Master Ping. His brothers relied upon him to watch their expenses and profits, to monitor the tea markets and prices for the Mow family which, for a thousand years, had refined the planting, growing, and making of tea to an art. He knew how many tea pickers arrived before dawn, how many baskets of tea they plucked, and how many pounds of tea each harvest produced. He tracked which buyers paid a fair price. Because he was an excellent listener, he was most effective in negotiating with the tea hongs. Their tea was sold to the most discriminating buyers.

By the time Jadelin finished cleaning the kitchen with her sisters-in-law, Shanli was walking the tea fields and Chongli had gone to the tea sheds. Sweet Amah had taken the children to be washed and dressed. Jadelin returned to her rooms via the large sitting room where the children and their tutors worked on their lessons. The main corridor decorated with bronzes and scrolls led to other corridors which opened into the separate courtyards of her father-in-law and the three sons. A large sitting room, bedrooms, private sitting rooms, and a study surrounded each courtyard. She entered Mow Chow Ching's courtyard and watched from the shadow of a column.

Mow Bowli and his father, each bare-chested, their queues wound out of the way atop their heads, leapt and parried, rolled and kicked as gracefully as choreographed dancers, each in their unique variation of the ancient martial art. Time stretched. Air hung suspended.

Suddenly Chow Ching's right hand made contact with Bowli's, a movement so quick Jadelin only assumed it from the sound. As if it were a signal, both men sprung into the most intense action she had ever witnessed between colleagues. She couldn't tell if they meant to kill each other. They flew with power and speed, often with such strength that the other was knocked to the ground. But each sprang back lightly to his feet. They ran up the walls to leverage height and the power of gravity while the other placed precisely aimed blows. Jadelin's hands flew to her chest. Should she jump in to protect her husband? Or would her presence distract Bowli and get him killed? She never imagined Chow Ching could move so fast; his persona was of sluggishness, which matched his solid, square shape.

With a sudden movement, Chow Ching pinned Bowli with two fingers at his jugular. "Much improved, my son," he commended. "It could have gone either way."

Bowli leapt up and handed him one of two cotton towels folded on a garden stool next to a two basins of clean water, one for each man. "You know I didn't hand you this victory." His chest, neck, and arms glistened and the veins of his neck pumped strong and hard.

Chow Ching's eyes met his son's, and together they laughed with satisfaction. When he had finished washing off he took out a set of sleek daggers. He held them blade up and threw a towel in the air. The towel landed on the blades and slid to the ground in evenly sliced quarters. He strapped the daggers to his thigh.

Jadelin loved watching her beloved, no matter what he was doing. She never tired of watching him leap with the grace of a panther and slip through the air like the wind. His chest heaved with exhaustion now, a sensuous sight. She gripped the column that had hidden her and thought of what pleasures they would enjoy later. Her father-in-law's demonstration, however, left her in awe.

Without turning around, Chow Ching lifted his head and said, "Jadelin, come join us for tea." He walked over to the round table that sat in the shade of a gazebo and covered it with the strips of his towel so it once again looked whole. He turned and faced her. "Jadelin, what are your favorite tea cakes?"

Bowli, his face and upper body still wet from his washing off, turned in surprise when she stepped out of the shadows. He had not yet perfected the sense to feel the unseen, like his father. He caught her quizzical look and tipped his head indicating that she should answer truthfully. So she named the rich plum-filled crusted buns from Shanghai, the lotus seed tarts from Soochow, and a thick buttery cookie cousin Li once brought from Canton.

"And you, my son?"

"I know it's out of season, but I'm fond of the black bean moon cakes with double yolks that are made only during the Mid-Autumn Festival," said Bowli. "And the crusty buns filled with creamy custard from Lantau Island."

"And I have a craving for the filled Japanese rice cakes called mochi. One of each flavor." Chow Ching whirled around and held his hands over his towel that was now whole, clean, and dry. He grabbed a corner and lifted it to reveal every treat they desired, fragrant and fresh, a bounty of each artfully arrayed on porcelain dishes.

He motioned to the three chairs around the table. "This may be the last time we drink tea together." He clapped his hands. Wu appeared with a tray of boiling water, a tea set, and a box of tea. Chow Ching sat and gestured his son and daughter-in-law to join him.

Jadelin followed her husband to the table. Was this a sample of Chow Ching's extraordinary power that her father had warned her about? And if she ate what Chow Ching magically produced, would it destroy her ch'i? She sat with her chopsticks clutched in her fingers and watched the men feast with relish.

"No, it will not affect your ch'i," Bowli reassured her; he had read her mind. "My father is your grandfather's student."

With great ease Mow Chow Ching prepared their tea from a small dark cake of Pu'er. "This is a vintage year, almost twenty years old. You'll enjoy the robust smoky flavor. I have saved this treasure to savor on my last day in West Lake." He desired this last moment with them, this time of reflection and togetherness. They would never have another opportunity.

Warily, Jadelin tasted the delicacies beautifully arranged on fine white porcelain. She sipped the tea and tipped her head. "This tea has a complex taste, like none other." She put down her chopsticks and dabbed her lips with a napkin. She plucked one of the Japanese rice cakes and bit into it, savoring the creamy filling. "I can see why you love Japanese mochi. Its texture and light sweetness is an excellent contrast to the Pu'er." She tried the custard filled flaky buns, and the moon cakes, and all three of the foods she had requested. Even her favorites tasted far better than she remembered. She put her hand to her stomach. Yes, she was getting full. This was all real, not an illusion.

Chow Ching nodded with an encompassing gaze that seemed to see more than just the two before him. "I wish only happiness for the both of you." His voice broke as he gazed upon Bowli's face. He gripped his son's shoulder and squeezed. For a second, Jadelin saw sadness cloud his face as if he had seen into the future and mourned the vision.

∾

*T*hat night they lay entwined, half-asleep, lulled by the creak of the wind and flutter of bat wings. Suddenly, Jadelin awoke. Their bedroom was wrapped in darkness and rustled by the wind. Bowli reached for her and said in a hushed voice, "It's time." He ran to the next room and grabbed his sleeping son in his arms, soothing him with endearments. Jadelin plucked their infant daughter from her basket and rushed after her husband, down the main hall to Mow Chow Ching's courtyard.

Shanli, fully dressed as if he had been expecting the moment, nodded when he met them. His wife arrived with her arms around their three sleepy-eyed sons. Chongli, bare-chested with a floor length silk robe belted around his waist, held the hands of his son and daughter. His wife clasped her baby to her chest. All entered at the same time, as if they had been summoned by an unseen force.

Mow Chow Ching stood in the center of his courtyard and nodded to them all. He glowed in the moonlight as if he were lit by a hundred candles. Each of his family bowed one last time and wished him well on his quest. One by one, he put his hands on their brows in blessing. "My children, be happy that I have the strength to answer the call," he said with a beatific expression. His sleek daggers were strapped to his thigh under a simple Chinese robe and he wore leather slippers with thick soles. Then he threw a long fur cape around his shoulders and slung a small leather bag over his shoulder. Before their eyes he was transformed into a wandering sage. He grasped his staff with a core of iron, nodded to each of them and turned. His body faded into the ether. He was gone.

Twenty-Seven

THE SUNGLO HILLS

*A*n ancient legend recounts how long ago in the beautiful lands called the Sunglo hills in the far-away province of Kiangnan, a Buddhist monk of the Fo sect taught a Kiangnan man named Ko Ty the art of making tea. Whoever drank Sunglo tea felt his heart fill with serenity and contentment. Its taste was seductive, tantalizing, and bursting with earth's sweetness. The monk became rich and abandoned his profession. Ko Ty, the man he taught, is gone. Only the tea's legend remains.

Many feared the area, believing it was bewitched. Some said the imposing cliffs had entrapped spirits who now longed for the companionship of man.

By the time Robert Fortune arrived in the Sunglo hills, the magical tea shrubs had been neglected for so long they crawled over each other in an orgy of woody branches. The monks of Fo who had many temples in the rugged hills harvested the tender tips that yielded just enough to satisfy their private use.

"Listen," said Wang as their boat move slowly upstream pulled by naked trackers on the narrow path carved in the cliff above. He cupped his hands and shouted his name into the wind. "Wang." Above them, sky-scraping cliffs shaped like prancing horses and dancing dragons rose so high above the river the men felt like ants beneath the clouds.

Everyone on the boat was startled as Wang's name echoed "Wang, Wang, Wang, Wang, Wang, Wang, Wang." As if dozens of men repeated his name all along the course of the river, the cliffs sang over and over, "Wang, Wang, Wang, Wang, Wang, Wang, Wang."

"Impossible." Fortune craned his neck and stared up at the majestic cliffs and mountains. He felt disoriented by soaring cliffs pressed in on all sides. "There must be a scientific explanation."

Wang shook his head. "It has always been so. Legend says some men choose to return to these beautiful mountains after they die. If you shout out to them, they will repeat your words over and over and over." He waved his arms the length of the river. "You heard their spirits."

"The dead go to either Heaven or Hell."

"That's where you barbarians go. When I die, I'll return here, for this is where I was born," said Wang. He left Fortune to sit on the bow and drink in the curve of the river, the nuances of shading in the cliffs, and the birds that rode the thermals along the peaks.

When the river mist behind them swallowed the cliffs, Wang pointed upriver where docks were built along the shore and low buildings nestled between the tree-covered banks. Rows of crops neatly defined the land. He stood at the bow and directed the boatmen to shore. "Come, Mr. Fortune. I'll take you to my house now."

"My son, my son!" Half the height of his son, old Wang ran with his arms flapping wide. His wrinkles wreathed an exuberant smile wet with tears. He grasped his son by the shoulders. "You're home!" His face was as brown as the dirt that covered his woven sandals and the land he tilled dusted his shirt and trousers.

Wang wept like a dutiful son. "Baba, this is my employer, Sing Wa."

The elder turned to Fortune and bowed. He had been well off at one time but, like others in his village, worked harder for less. Wang's mother, a similarly shriveled woman barely five feet tall, apologized that they had little to offer him.

Fortune assured them he needed only a roof over his head.

That was all he received.

For three days it rained with such ferocity he could not step out of the cottage Wang's parents shared with four other families. Since each had their own kitchen but no chimney, lung-choking smoke filled the interior before seeping out through the cracks in the doors and windows. Fortune lay on the floor to breathe. Once, he stepped out the door for air. In a minute, he was soaked and colder than before.

The weather cleared on the fourth day.

"Come, Wang," Fortune gasped. He thrust his magnifying glass and clippers in his pocket and grabbed his umbrella. He flung open the front door and inhaled so many deep breaths he got deliciously lightheaded.

In the countryside, Wang asked farmers for information about the cultivation and manufacture of tea on behalf of his esteemed client, Sing Wa, a visitor from 'beyond the Great Wall' who spoke a different dialect and could not make the request himself.

Fortune plunged his hands deep into the rich loam that covered the well-drained hills and nodded with appreciation at how well the soil was nurtured. He praised everything he saw and sampled. And since he was with Wang, a local Hangchow boy, farmers sold him anything he wanted. They explained how they plucked the top two leaves for some teas, only buds for others. The drying time, whether the leaves were rolled into pearls or left whole, and the packing procedure, were unique to each grower. The resulting teas might taste as light as the morning mist, sweep a velvety twist across the tongue, or fill the mouth with full-bodied lushness. They could process their own tea but for greater quantities, only an experienced tea master had the skill to coax the finest taste and aroma from the fresh tea leaves. All told him that the finest tea masters came from the Longjing mountains of the West Lake region.

∾

While Li kept his eye on Fortune, John Poe explored the tea gardens. He inspected how the tea plants in each garden were grown and the sheds where tea was stored and dried. He met the tea preparers himself and discussed their harvests. He warned them that a Westerner was asking questions and buying tea plants and seeds. No one he talked to knew of the Emperor's ruling that foreigners were banned from entering the tea growing areas.

"He has purchased plants and seeds," Li moaned to his cousin as they slurped bowls of broth and dumplings at the only inn in Hangchow. They sat before an open window in the rustic timbered building with a view of the river and tea gardens that terraced the landscape. The air smelled wet and musty, but the cool breeze kept mold and mildew from taking hold.

A jolly widow and her equally jolly daughter, Lily, ran the inn. The daughter had been married, confided her mother who had instantly warmed to the two men with city manners. Lily's mother-in-law would beat her with a broom whenever her husband left the house. Since he tended their tea garden alone and processed the tea himself, he was always gone from the house. She was happy her daughter had left her husband and returned to run the inn with her, especially during the harvests when the village was swamped with coolies.

"Want more?" Lily asked the two. She had a towel slung over one shoulder and a clean kerchief around her hair. She greeted everyone with a huge smile as if no one deserved to be unhappy. "I see you like my dumplings. Made them myself." In the afternoons while her mother rested, Lily both cooked and waited on customers. She always made sure that Li and John, the nicest guests she had ever met, were served first.

"You look pretty when you smile, Lily," complimented John. He didn't see any evidence of bruises or beatings.

"That's because I'm no longer married. I tried to treat my husband and his mother with respect according to the Confucian ethics, but she called me terrible names and said I didn't work hard or fast enough. My husband would not stop his mother from beating me. One day I grabbed that broom out of my mother-in-law's hands and broke it. With my bare hands! I told her it was a good thing it wasn't her neck. I packed my belongings, found my dowry money that they had not spent yet, the cheapskates, and came home."

Li and John sat open mouthed.

Lily laughed. "Shocking, isn't it?" she whispered. "My husband and his mother came here and pleaded for me to return. They promised they would take good care of me." She winked. "I'm no fool. I'm 'too slow' for my mother-in-law but I can cook and clean for this whole inn." She picked up their empty bowls and flicked her towel to wipe off their tables. "I am so happy not to be married. Mama and I are our own bosses. No need for husbands."

Li conceded, "You and your Mama are the happiest innkeepers we have met." John agreed.

"Say," she leaned towards Li, "You know that stupid Wang you've been following around? His father just booked passage for four to Nechow. From there, the strange looking man who's digging around the tea plants and bothering all the tea farmers is going to Shanghai."

∞

Robert Fortune and the Wangs were on their way downriver to Nechow at last, but the river rushed loud and wild. It was so difficult to navigate that they had to anchor fore and aft at night.

When they had been three nights out, a sudden gust blasted open the door of the sampan's cabin and peeled off the roof. The wind tore the boat from her moorings and spun her towards the rocks. The crew poled and sculled to get to shore while the Wangs lashed the roof to the hull with ropes. The boat flew before the wind with the current, turning like a top. Finally, the crew ran her ashore and secured her on a sandbank.

Six days later Fortune and the Wangs reached Nechow where they rafted up with dozens of other boats and houseboats. During the last meal of the day, they heard a rush of water and a great noise. A wall of water loomed so high it blocked the sky. The wall roared and grew broader and darker. Everything turned as black as a waiting grave.

∞

John Poe and Li lost Fortune's trail on the river their first night out. When the winds gusted like a typhoon, the two cousins, securely anchored in a snug and sturdy sampan, watched Fortune's boat blow away. They would never catch up to the barbarian now. But they knew his route.

They entered Nechow just as the flood tide blotted out the sun. Hundreds of people on bobbing boats screamed, *"Jan-shui, jan-shui."* The black wall of water picked up the vessels and whirled them like tops. Women screamed for their children as hulls bobbed like corks and smashed into each other like eggshells. Masts and lines tangled while boxes and baskets were swept from decks. Poe and Li hung on as the thick brown water of the flood tide swelled and roared like a thousand tigers, plunging day into a night deafened by a thousand screams.

When the flood tide receded, everyone quickly took their bearings. Boatmen yelled to each other to untangle lines, mothers counted children, and everyone fished possessions out of the water. .

"Look," said Li under his breath. "Rafted up at the far end of those covered sampans. See the tall gangly figure that stands gawking at the boats floundering in the middle of the river?"

John's smile stretched mischievously. "We'll tie up just past the boats at the first clear spot. Make sure we have the outside tie."

Li chuckled. "Shall we go ashore and hear what they have to say?"

John whispered, "Perhaps we should go in disguise as well."

The cousins disappeared under the blanket of dusk.

ஒ

*A*s soon as they were tied up for the night, Wang and his father leapt off the boat to look around.

"Come back," Robert Fortune shouted to their disappearing backs. "We need to clean this mess." His plant boxes and supplies were scattered and jumbled. Plus, they had to mail his daily reports to the East India Company. He shouted for Tze, but he, too, had immediately run ashore to look for something to eat. Their boatmen were sorting out the tangle of lines and cargo, a task involving a lot of shouting and cursing, which would take them through the night if they intended to sail tomorrow.

As far as he could see up and down the river, boats were rafted up six to eight deep. Women had stopped screaming at the other boats and were now cordially inquiring after their neighbors and lending necessities to the other mothers. Boatmen assisted others to right their rigging and their cargo. Wet clothes hung from masts and lines like string puzzles across every surface. Drying clothes flapped in the river breeze like a thousand flags.

The Scot bent over his plant cases and propped their glass lids open. He sopped up the condensation that had accumulated on the interior, straightened the plants that had been tossed sideways, and smoothed the dirt. As far as he could tell there had been no river water intrusion.

"May I pass, kind sir?"

A white haired crone, bent under the weight of her load, stood on the boat next to Fortune. She indicated with her head the boat on other side of his where five children had stripped naked and were gleefully chasing each other in and out among the clothes hanging from the makeshift clotheslines, leaping from boat to boat as easily as if they ran on land.

When he had straightened fully, he saw there were actually two old women, each balancing a bamboo pole with buckets of drinking water on either end. He drew back when the second, a warty-faced hag with a dark complexion smiled a toothless grin at him and cackled good-naturedly. Their wet clothes made them look even more pitiful and bedraggled.

Fortune nodded and stepped aside so they could pass.

"Ai-ya," shouted the first ancient crone. Her threadbare shoes slipped on the wet deck and she fell backwards onto her companion. Both threw up their hands and with that upward thrust, all their water flew up into the air and drenched Fortune and his plants anew. The women fell on the deck in a tangle of limbs, buckets, and poles.

"Ai-ya," wailed the second, "our water." Both moaned and massaged their bruised knees and backs. "What do we do now?"

They looked up at Fortune's stunned face and widened eyes. They hobbled to their feet. "Sorry, kind sir," wept the first white haired crone. She turned to the warty-faced one. "We must go all the way back to town to get more water."

"Sister, give me your hand," moaned the second as she grasped her pole and empty buckets.

"Wait," said Fortune. "Grandmothers, if you're going into town, could you mail these letters? My servant disappeared as soon as we docked."

He emptied a handful of cash into the elderly woman's outstretched hand. "That's exactly enough." He paused and looked from one wrinkled face to the other before putting two more coins in her hand. "For your troubles."

The two women nodded and shouldered their poles and buckets. They shuffled from boat to boat and onto shore. They looked back and saw the tall mandarin bent over his boxes, totally absorbed in his plants and dirt. He had offered no help when they fell. They walked along the river in the direction of town for about half a mile then boarded a large covered sampan.

They handed their bamboo poles and buckets to a tall boatman with leathery wrinkles and an ebony queue wrapped atop his head. "Thank you," they said with a bow.

"What did you need two pounds of salt for?" he asked as he stowed the equipment along his bow and secured it with a tie.

"We had to water some plants," cackled the warty-faced woman. But now she stood up straight and tall. She slipped off the baggy wet clothes, shook them out over the side of the boat, and handed them to the boatman along with her warts. The white haired crone handed him her hair and wet clothes as well.

"We're performing in Shanghai," the tall boatman said. "Will we see you there, John Poe?" His voice was powerful and theatrically rich.

"Most likely," John answered. Then he raced his cousin to their boat tied at the end of the raft of boats.

Twenty-Eight

CHINESE NEW YEAR 1849

SHANGHAI

ortune peered through his smoked spectacles at the messenger standing at the snow-encrusted doorway. A good six feet tall, the stranger had slanted eyes, long black lashes, and a porcelain complexion. Snow dusted his fur cap and matching sable cape. His English had a warm accent with a slurred R, and his voice was commanding, strong, and self-assured when he asked, "Robert Fortune?" He brought an invitation from John Poe of Shanghai.

Fortune winced when the cold air hit him. He motioned the man in. Although Shanghai was at the same latitude as Egypt, it sat in the path of the Siberian winter winds. At least Mackenzie's house was warmer than the unglazed rooms in which he first wintered in Shanghai. Recalling the embroidered tapestries that covered the Poes' walls and the thick rugs that muffled his footsteps, he anticipated that they kept their coal stoves roaring.

The messenger closed the door behind him while Fortune wrapped a wool scarf up to his eyes. "There is no need to bring your translator since I'll escort you," he assured the Scot. He fingered Fortune's wool coat and shook his head.

"British wool is warm," Fortune snapped, although it didn't insulate him as well as he would have liked. Even indoors and bundled in a black wool jacket with a felt cap, the Scot was freezing. Mackenzie's servant continually opened their windows at night for fresh air, even during winter. He envied the Chinese dressed in layers of sumptuous furs which gave them the appearance of padded bundles. Children were carried on specially warmed bricks and wrapped in layers of quilt in the arms of their amahs. Even the poorest dressed in warm furs like rabbit and wolf.

Fortune prided himself on being a brisk walker, but he had trouble keeping up with the fur-clad messenger who strode effortlessly through snow so thick it muffled the sounds of the street. He slipped on the ice so often his guide had to wait for him at each of the arched gates to catch up. When they arrived at Poe's brass-banded red doors, Fortune saw the white walls of the Poe's estate stretched as far as he could see and loomed even more imposing in the clear winter day.

They were ushered into a courtyard that even during winter, looked lush with dwarfed pines and towering brass vases antiqued with centuries-old patinas. To the right, left, and ahead, the red moon gates that led to the different halls were closed. The messenger conferred with the sword-bearing guards. He whipped off his fur coat and hat and handed both to a servant who quickly appeared and disappeared. Then they were off again, through passages lined with red columns.

John Poe glanced up from his desk, a seventeenth century scholar's table of honey-toned huanghuangli wood. He rinsed his brush in the jade water bowl, tapped gently, then dried it on a cotton blotter before placing it to dry in a brush pot carved with a landscape that matched the water bowl. He pushed back his yoke back chair, a Ming design with an s-shaped curve in the tall splat, a pattern which could be traced to wall paintings dating to the sixth century in the Buddhist cave temples of Dunhuang.

He stood to greet his guests and bowed in greeting. "I heard you had returned to China. My brother Paul had no problem finding you?"

Fortune whirled swiftly to face the messenger. He turned back to John. "He did not tell me he was your brother." He flushed, remembering the dismissive manner in which he treated him.

"In China, one must assume everyone is related." John motioned a young boy of twelve in quilted blue cotton to serve tea for three on a small square table that matched his desk in grain and patina. The fangzhuo, as such a table was called, was depicted in Song dynasty paintings but this replica was a recent seventeenth century Ming. Horseshoe chairs, comfortably rounded, were pulled up and the men invited to sit.

John's expression was inscrutably neutral as he watched his guest's face. "When did you arrive in China?"

"I arrived in Shanghai a couple of days ago."

"Aah," said John. Fortune hadn't answered his question. "When we parted over three years ago, you said your farewells to our country."

"I didn't think I would return. The collection I brought back was received with acclaim in England. The plants that survived thrive in the Royal Kew Gardens and in the greenhouses of some of the greatest estates in England. The Royal Horticultural Society promoted me to curator of the Chelsea Physic Garden. People invite me to talk about my experience in China." He found that people were so fascinated by his tales, they ignored his surly, dour personality.

"My deepest congratulations. So now you are a famous man, successful and well known in England. You must be happy." John lifted his teacup and inhaled the delicate scent of White Dragon Tips. He nodded to Fortune. "What are your plans while you are here?"

Fortune paused to choose his words. "The exquisite flowers of China amaze all of England. They could not imagine the colors and blossoms of your peonies, azaleas, and camellias. China is truly the Flowery Land. So I have been sent to seek more flowers to introduce to England's gardens. I intend to revisit the five treaty ports and see what plants I can collect." He rubbed the curved arms of a chair that would be considered an antique in England, but not in China with its five-thousand-year history. He looked out on the pines in the garden courtyard beyond the fretted windows and hoped John would give him a tour of his new garden.

Fortune clasped his hands and asked, "Your mother and sister, are they well? I was hoping to continue your sister's English lessons."

"My sister lives far inland now."

"What place is that?" He leaned forward ready to change his plans to find her.

"It's unlikely you will ever see her again." John noted the Scot's dismay. Surely he hadn't hoped to continue his friendship with Jadelin. He walked over to his window and gestured for Fortune to join him. "There is a stark beauty in a winter garden. This is the time for the three friends of winter: the pine, the bamboo and the prunus. Notice how the pine and bamboo remain green while other plants wither. In winter, the prunus reaches full bloom. We admire such resilience." He turned as if struck by a novel idea. "Chinese New Year is a time for family and friends. This year it's January 24th according to your calendar. We would be honored if you would join us one day during the festivities to celebrate with our family. Paul will fetch you when it's time."

Paul's face was impassive, his inscrutable almond eyes bright. He exchanged a look with John and bowed to their visitor. "And now, Mr. Fortune, I'll be happy to escort you back to your dwelling."

Fortune bowed. "I observed how we came. I would like to explore on the way back. There are many new shops that caught my eye."

"I hear you collect our Chinese antiques with as much passion as our flowers," John said. "I bid you farewell until the New Year."

Fortune followed his host's brother along the walkways lined with red columns to the round red moon gates manned by three armed guards. He bowed again to Paul Poe and disappeared down the chilly streets of Shanghai.

"He's a thinking man." Paul sat back, content to watch his brother who had returned to his desk to compose his letter to Jadelin with a fine fox hair brush. Paul, the Fifth Son, only a couple of months older than John, found his passion was for beautiful things, for fine art and music, scintillating conversation, and satisfying friendships. He admired his brother's strong, smooth calligraphic hand, unlike his own impatient strokes.

John met his eyes and tipped his head in thought. "Yes. He's been here for many months exploring the tea-growing areas forbidden to foreigners." He shuddered to remember the boat ride to Hangchow, the three rainy days in the village and the long boat ride back tailing the barbarian. "There's nothing beyond our borders that China needs, thus the British grow poppies in their Indian colony to poison us so they can buy more Chinese tea which gives Indians and British health and strength." John put down his brush and clasped his hands in thought. "I hope it wasn't humbling for you to retrieve this foreigner."

"Thank you for giving me the opportunity to observe how Westerners live." Every window had been shut tight against the cold so the smells of the kitchen, unwashed bodies, books, furniture, and mildew festered into a ripe odor reminiscent of wet dogs. Every horizontal surface was packed with Chinese porcelains, sculptures, jades, and lacquer ware. Every room he peeked into was filled with carved Chinese chairs inlaid with mother-of-pearl, porcelain vases four feet tall, and stone Foo dogs. Paul shivered with distaste. "But," he smiled. "I practiced my English on him, and he had no problem understanding me."

His brother nodded approval. "If we learn to speak their language, we are closer to understanding how they think. That is one of China's problems." John held out his two hands, palms facing each other. "We are like this with the barbarians; we think and speak in different languages." He washed his brush, gently reformed the bristles to a hair-thin point, and hung it to dry from an ornately carved brush stand. "I've finished this report to the Emperor for father to review with the mandarins of Shanghai." He rolled up the scroll and threw his fur around his shoulders. "We'll deliver it to him at the hong."

"You trust me to go with you?" Paul watched his brother rise to his feet but he remained seated.

John sat back down. "What's troubling you?" Inseparable as children, John and Paul could be found wherever there was mischief. The rest of the time, they studied together or chased each other with abandon. "We've never had secrets."

"Do Baba, Benjamin, and Daniel trust me?"

"Of course. We couldn't succeed without you."

"Edward betrayed us." Paul could barely say the words.

"He did it for himself and his own pleasure. What does it have to do with you?"

"I felt soiled after we caught Edward in the act. As if I were a reflection of his weakness." Paul looked down, embarrassed. "We have the same tainted mother."

John rested his hands firmly on his brother's shoulders. "You're not him. Look me in the face. We all trust you. We love you, Paul, as our brother, our confidante, and an important member of our family and business."

Paul took a deep breath and rubbed his forehead. "I worry about letting you down."

"You won't." John pulled his brother up. "Come on, we have an important mission to do, together."

∞

Wrapped in mink, sable, otter, and fox, the Shanghai Taoutae and five tea hong merchants swept into the warehouse. The guards stepped aside as the mandarins passed into the fragrant dusk, the sanctuary of tea. Light from clerestory windows near the roof lit the crated teas meticulously packed in unscented wood. The small crates held premium teas, borne one-by-one on the back of a coolie. Here the crates would be opened for the first time since they were packed at their source thousands of miles away. Mandarin Poe and his sons would brew a sample and allow their senses to soak in the aroma, taste, body, and soul of the tea.

Today's meeting was of a different nature. If England succeeded in cultivating and producing their own tea, China's tea trade and its economy could collapse.

"The Emperor has legal grounds to deport Robert Fortune under the Treaty of Nanking. The Englishman has ventured further than one day's journey from a treaty port many times," Mandarin Poe advised his colleagues. His voice was deep and troubled. "I have detailed reports from my Sixth Son and my nephew Li that the Englishman has gone as far as the Sunglo hills. The barbarian entered the Hangchow district. He walked through tea gardens and bought great quantities of tea seeds and plants. We weren't able to destroy all of them."

"Ai-ya," the others muttered. Their great shoulders shook with anger. They were a formidable group. In black silk tunics edged with dark-colored bias, they represented power, wealth, and great lineages in the Ancestral Halls. "He must be stopped."

"He has done the same in Kintang, in the Chusan Archipelago," added Mandarin Poe. "This barbarian studies everything about the plant, from the amount of sun and shade it receives, the amount of water it gets, and the slope of the hill. He notes how and when the leaves and buds are plucked, and the method of drying and preparation. He saw how they are packed and transported to preserve their freshness."

"Let's kill this barbarian and destroy his plants and seeds," growled the eldest. "Yes," added another. "No one will suspect an accident in the countryside he loves to roam." A couple added their agreement. Others muttered their concern.

The Taoutae growled, "And risk another disastrous war and unfavorable treaty upon China?" He stroked his white beard and sadness grew in his heart for the troubled legacy his children and grandchildren would inherit.

After Mandarin Poe read John Poe's report to them, the merchants agreed that it accurately detailed the barbarian Fortune's success in accomplishing his mission and the economic threat it posed to their country. "I'll send this directly to the Emperor through my First Son," said Mandarin Poe. "Hopefully, he can return for Chinese New Year with the Emperor's response."

"May he have a swift and safe journey," the others agreed.

ॐ

*T*he skies, a miserable gray, sucked Fortune's mind of all joy and thought. Collar up, shoulders hunched against the wind, walking the streets of Shanghai diverted him from winter's boredom until his 'collecting season' began in spring. He fingered the curves of Mei's crystal snuff bottle secreted in a pocket close to his heart, and relished the visceral pleasure of its weight and curves.

He treasured her snuff bottle as a memento of the pleasurable hours in her house, despite the looming presence of Big Amah. The assertive lilt of Jadelin's voice and the sparkle in her eyes still filled him with longing. When he returned to England, all other women, especially in London, seemed colorless and bland. So he rubbed its sensuous curves with his fingers and conjured up the image of his beloved.

The elbowing crowds of shoppers swept him into stalls filled with blooming flowers and plants symbolic of prosperity and luck for the coming New Year: magnolias, double blossomed peaches, blooming prunus, camellias in shades from white to deep red, and towering branches of red berries. Everyone was in a holiday pitch, eager to bargain so they could settle all debts by the New Year. Businesses would close for the weeklong holiday. Everyone would wear new clothes and celebrate ancestral and familial ties in freshly cleaned homes decorated with an abundance of red flowers and auspicious blessings written in gold on red. Every stall exhibited flowers forced to flower in the dead of winter. How did they accomplish this? Azaleas! Roses! Quince! Even the exquisite mountain peony blooms were tied in a special way to keep them from opening until the right day. When he saw the small potted trees covered with kumquats, the oval golden fruits symbolizing wishes for prosperity and wealth for the New Year, he had to buy two, one to tuck under each arm.

The blue sky shone with a crisp winter glare when Paul Poe knocked on Mackenzie's door on the fifth day of the New Year. The trees were bare, the streets caked and frozen. Yes, he would wait inside while Fortune changed.

Paul took a deep breath of fresh air and stepped into a parlor piled with Chinese rugs and overstuffed English furniture. He removed his fur hat, brushed off the fresh snow, and unclasped the jade buttons on his fur cape. Hat in hand, he inspected the Chinese vases and decorative figurines from the 17th and 18th century that crowded every table, bookcase, and horizontal surface. He pulled back the velvet drapes in the next room to get some light. Ah, he exclaimed. The long dining table was covered with porcelain bowls and figurines except for a tiny space set aside for two men to eat. He could see that Fortune and his friend were interested in old pieces, not the ones currently in vogue, especially not those created for European tastes which featured family crests, thick gold edging, and European faces. He inspected each one and verified their markings.

Tu, Mackenzie's house servant, appeared and asked if Paul would like some tea while he waited.

"Greetings for the New Year," Paul answered automatically. "No tea for me in the house of a barbarian."

Tu tensed his narrow shoulders. "Mr. Fortune has an excellent collection of teas from his travels inland," he offered.

Paul took in the servant's baggy tunic, his eyes veiled in subservience. He walked over to the young man and asked kindly, "Do they treat you well?"

"It provides rice," Tu answered with a guarded voice. During the Opium War the British had gunned down his father and uncles when they stepped out of their favorite teahouse. He despised the British. At least he wasn't bent in half carrying hundred pound loads along mountain trails or plunged into icy river water to track boats upriver. He was only an hour's walk away from the room at the edge of town where he lived with his mother, three aunts, and two sisters. Mackenzie was a hearty man who worked in his garden or shopped for antiques when he wasn't at Captain Balfour's office. Robert Fortune was a solitary creature, particular and fussy. Few visitors meant no extra work for Tu, their only servant.

"What does Mr. Fortune do while in Shanghai?" asked Paul. He lifted Tu's face to his.

Tu said he noticed that since Fortune had arrived, no one was allowed in the garden except the workers who built boxes of wood and glass that the Scot planted himself with plants and seeds. The Westerner gave the instructions to the workmen himself, in Chinese. No one else was allowed near his plants or plant boxes. Every few months, coolies came to deliver the boxes to ships headed for Hong Kong. Workmen were making what looked like a very large shipment or series of shipments. He heard these would be sent to India. Yes, the Scot had brought home many shrubs. No, he did not know that the Emperor had decreed that Westerners were forbidden from entering the tea-growing areas of China and were not allowed to speak Chinese.

"Does your master get much mail?" Paul stroked the young boy's cheek.

"Occasionally." Tu tipped his head in thought. "Mr. Mackenzie is teaching me English. I can read a few words. Is there anything in particular you're interested in?"

"I would like to see any letters Robert Fortune sends to Mr. Mackenzie."

"Fortune writes to him often when he travels."

Paul slipped him a small bag of coins. "This will help your mother prepare for the New Year. Come to the Poe tea hong whenever you have any news for me. Anything you need, let me know. I am your friend. Sssh, hush your tears. Mr. Fortune returns." He patted Tu's back reassuringly before turning at the sound of Fortune's approach.

❧

*M*andarin Poe reigned over the New Year feast flanked by his six sons, nephew Li, and the barbarian Robert Fortune. He looked over at similarly set round tables where his wives, daughters-in-laws, their children, and cousins dined. He was content on this, his seventieth New Year, for business had grown one hundred fold, most of his living sons were married, and he had many grandchildren to continue the Poe name for generations to come. He had Robert Fortune, a dangerous enemy, indebted to his hospitality and generosity. Squabs, roasted ducks, shrimps, fish, duck, chicken and heaping bowls of steaming vegetables, some carved in fanciful dragons and birds, glistened before them. Yes, he concluded, life seemed auspiciously abundant.

He looked sadly at his Second Wife's pale face. She leaned to the right, too weak to sit straight. Her addiction had sucked her energy and beauty. She would not last long now. She and his disgraced Fourth Son were the blights upon his family. His fist tightened as he swore again against the drug that had polluted his household.

As Alistair Mackenzie advised, Fortune brought a New Year's gift to the banquet. When Fortune gave Third Wife Mei the miniature kumquat tree, she had held it out to her husband. "Look! Look at this present the White Devil gave me." No one had given her a potted tree before. She was a firecracker of changing expressions from delight to amusement.

Fortune could not remember which sons belonged to which of Mandarin Poe's three wives. He noted that the Poe sons would check often on one brother, obviously sick, who sat with his wife and son on a far table.

The Scot bowed to handsome men and women in beautiful bright silks edged with embroidery or bias. The women sparkled with jade, pearls, and rubies. Gold hairpieces inlaid with kingfisher feathers bobbed flirtatiously when they walked. The men wore burgundy or dark blue silks that reflected the light of hundreds of lanterns and candles throughout the rooms.

He greeted burly Benjamin and his sons who would soon equal their father's stature. John's wife enchanted him with her shy, downcast eyes. Only one person was not caught up in the frivolity; a woman with translucent skin and glassy eyes sat alone with her attendant. Meanwhile, he couldn't keep up with the concurrent conversations. All the Chinese words he had ever learned had slithered out of his head. He deeply missed Jadelin: her sassy looks, quick retorts, and endless questions.

"Li, a prosperous New Year to you," Fortune greeted his former translator. He was surprised to see him until he remembered Li was a distant Poe cousin.

"And a prosperous New Year to you, too. Where have you been collecting?"

"Here and there. My last trip ended badly," Fortune admitted.

"I'm sorry to hear that," Li commiserated. Actually, he was happy to hear him admit his disappointment. In Sunglo, in the Hangchow district, Li had paid the elder Wang to overcharge Fortune for the boat ride to Ningpo with the intention of depleting the Scot's resources so he would run out of money and be forced to return empty-handed. He had hoped little irritations would grow to major obstacles and eventually the foreigner would give up and depart. But Fortune proved to be tenacious.

"I'm headed for Hong Kong shortly," said Fortune. "Unfortunately, neither my translator nor coolie speaks the southern dialect." He lowered his voice, not wanting to sound too anxious. "I'm headed for the Fa-Tee gardens in Canton. Are you available?" His pale eyes blinked anxiously.

"What a coincidence. I'm headed south right after the New Year." Li toasted Fortune with his teacup.

&

To ensure his officials' allegiance, the Emperor decreed that their wives and children would remain his hostages in Peking while the men returned home for the New Year. Reluctant to expose his family to the intrigues of court without his protection, Adam had not observed a traditional New Year celebration in Shanghai since the Opium War. Because of China's tenuous political state and the important issues pressing in Shanghai, Adam journeyed home. He arrived with fellow mandarins from Shanghai on one of the Emperor's fastest junks via the Grand Canal. Prior to New Year's Day, he had paid his respects at his mother's tomb, met with the Shanghai mandarins to discuss the Emperor's business, conferred with the Taoutae, met with Captain Balfour, and considered the petitions of various governors in the area. After the most important family celebrations he would return as speedily to his family.

His father had warned him that Robert Fortune had been invited for the final banquet.

"Our enemy," whispered Mei. She had entered the inner parlor where Adam stood in darkness to study their guest.

He turned to her and bowed before he took her hands. "More arrive every day, from every Western country, wanting pieces of China. The Emperor's advisors argue continually about what to do, so he does nothing. The Westerners perceive his inaction as weakness," he said.

"What do you advise him?" she whispered.

"If the Emperor stands firm, they attack. If he agrees to their demands, they take more. If they disobey the treaties they signed and we fight back, they bomb our coastal towns with powerful cannons and destroy our people and buildings." He sighed. "We want peace. How can we negotiate peace with people intent on conquering us?"

Mei turned her head aside and clasped a hand to her breast. "This is the New Year." Her luminous eyes met his. "For your father's sake, let us be happy that the Poes are together and alive. Our business survives." A shadow crossed her face. She smiled at him. "Happy New Year, Adam Poe. May prosperity and health bless you and your family."

From his father's table, Adam studied each face with nostalgia. Familiar faces had aged, some with a rapidity that shocked him. For the first time Mandarin Poe, whom they all considered healthy and ageless, looked worn. Tired lines radiated from the corners of his father's eyes and his pallid skin sagged at the jowls. Brothers Benjamin and Daniel spoke with more gravity and care. How he missed their playful banter. Edward had been returned for the family's New Year's banquet. His robes drooped on his sallow frame and his sharp intellectual edge had dulled. His wife and son were unusually quiet.

His youngest brothers, just out of their teens, seemed the most lively, the most engaged. Practically a newly wed, married for four years, John had two sons. He doubted that Paul would ever marry.

How he missed Jadelin. The family didn't seem the same without his teenaged sister's saucy banter or the tinkling bells stitched to her hems.

He was surprised to see Mei sitting in the place of his own mother but, it was to be expected. His father's Second Wife, pale and distant, did not eat. Even when he approached to wish her a fortuitous New Year, she looked at him without recognition.

He returned Robert Fortune's bow when they were introduced. He had many questions for him, but not here, not when the family celebrated the most important time of the year, a time for good thoughts, good foods, and family.

༜

*e*arly the next morning, Adam asked his manservant to pack his trunks for his return to Peking. He had said his goodbyes to all except one. His father had been melancholy and unsure he would live to see his eldest son's return. His brothers proudly clasped his shoulders in farewell. Now he strode into Mei's wing and requested her maid to announce his arrival. He would wait here in her garden. Still wrapped in winter, her peonies were leafless stalks and the koi pond shimmered with a chill breeze.

"I thought you had sailed away with the dawn," Mei exclaimed in surprise when she met him in her garden.

"And not say goodbye to my childhood love?" he whispered. "Tomorrow is promised to no one."

"Do not call me that. I'm forty-five, a grandmother. My forehead is creased with worries about our family and household." She felt herself drawn to his dark eyes, to the memory of their youthful innocence and dreams reflected there.

"You have the radiance of a woman half your age." He touched his fingertips to her lips to shush her denials. "Your beauty glows from within."

To cover her embarrassment, she called for tea to be served in her formal sitting room where a hot stove and pots of boiling water warmed the room to the temperature and humidity of a tropical forest. "Come, let's get out of the winter cold. Now you sail home to your beloved family in Peking. I've enjoyed hearing about your wife and children. You must be so proud. I wish I could see them," she said as they walked indoors.

"You wouldn't like Peking. The court is rife with intrigue." He described the grandeur of the Forbidden City, the rigid formalities that had to be observed, and the paranoia that ruled their lives. His wife was a quiet woman, much like his own mother. His First Son would take the Civil Service exams this year. His Second Son, who wasn't a scholar, had joined the Emperor's guards. Both daughters had married sons of fellow officials, creating good alliances for him and his family.

Mei's maid closed the doors when they entered and drew the curtains to keep in the warmth.

"Adam, you return infrequently in these traumatic times." Mei took a satin-covered box out of a tall cabinet with doors of carved latticework. She rejoined him at her tea table. "These were your mother's. Your wife as First-Daughter-in-Law should have them."

Adam took the familiar box from her hands and placed it on the table in front of him. Taking a deep breath, he lifted the lid. "Ah," he exclaimed. "I remember these." He examined the long necklaces of perfectly matched jades, the thick jade bracelets covered with the patina of time, and the large bi-disk earrings that had been his mother's favorites. He felt the jades warm with the heat of his hands. Suddenly he felt the impact of his mother's loss and how much he missed her. He blinked back tears.

"I divided your mother's jewelry equally among her sons. Your wife is statuesque like First Mother and can wear jades of this size."

Adam nodded. He slowly closed the box and clasped it tightly on his lap. He nodded at the maid serving them tea and waited until she withdrew. "I don't wish to seem ungrateful, Mei, for kindness rules your heart. But Peking's artisans produce fashionable gold and jade jewelry in the Imperial workshops. The court is so competitive my wife could never wear these without ridicule. These are old fashioned, out of style."

Mei shook her head. "Adam, your mother was a good woman. Her spirit, her ch'i, resides in these family jades. She would want you to pass them on to your wife and daughters."

"Will you wear them in honor of my mother and me?"

Mei shook her head. First Wife had generously embroidered hundreds of shoes for Mei and Jadelin. Mei would not take what was rightfully her son's. Especially Adam's.

His voice grew husky. "In my mind you are always the opponent I could never beat at Grand Master Ping's."

Her laughter tinkled like a thousand stars. She lifted the teapot. "Let me pour you tea, mandarin. You embarrass me with your lofty image."

"I speak the truth. How many people think you and Jadelin are sisters, even now?"

"I am a grandmother. Jadelin married into the house of Mow. She has a daughter and a son." She smiled at him and let her silence speak what she could never express aloud. The sun rose higher in the sky, but they could not bear to part. He clasped her hands in his as they talked. Time melted away. Their smiles revealed the close friendship of their youth which had lasted through decades of change.

"Madam," her maid warned, "Mandarin Poe arrives."

Mei straightened. Now there were two Mandarin Poe's in her sitting room, her husband and his First Son. "You must go," she whispered.

"I will, after I say goodbye again to my father."

At that moment, Mandarin Poe strode through the corridors, his step firm on the thick carpets. When he saw his son stand and bow, the tired lines on his face melted away. "My son, when we said goodbye at dawn I thought I would not see you again." His eyes went from his son's face to his wife's. "I understand why my son would linger. And I see she has given you your mother's jewelry."

Adam clasped his father's shoulder. He hadn't meant to be so obvious, nor had he meant to compromise Mei's position. "It was my fault. We started talking of long ago days and childhood memories melted away the time." He held his mother's jewelry box out to his father. "I explained to her that my wife would not be able to wear these in Peking. Could you keep these as your grandsons' legacy from their grandmother?"

Mei clasped a hand to her breast when her husband's face drooped with despair.

Adam bowed to them both. "Now I must depart, or the Emperor will send his spies for me."

"I'll accompany you to your boat, my son. I want to hold your fine face in my eyes until I can no longer distinguish you from the mist. The next time you return I may not be here." The mellow tones of his voice cracked.

Adam clasped his father's shoulders. "Baba, never think that."

Mei clutched her heart. "My dear husband, you have the strength of a lion. You will live for years." But she worried when he came home at midday and could not rise from his nap until sunset. Her anxious eyes swept from him to Adam.

Adam made a quick decision. "I want both of you to see me off so I can keep you in my eyes until I can no longer distinguish you from the mist."

Twenty-Nine

JADELIN

WEST LAKE TEA GROWING AREA

Mow Bowli's courtyard was simple with uncomplicated plantings and a raised pavilion. Jadelin appreciated its wide space open to the sky for here, after her morning chores, she taught her children Grand Master Ping's basic moves which would build their strength and agility. They would have to pass the same rigorous tests of all students sent to study with their never-aging grandfather. She looked up now from her brother's letter and closed her eyes to imagine each scene that described their Chinese New Year's feast. All her brothers, including Adam and Edward, had returned home for the celebrations. Mei had been touched by Robert Fortune's gift of a kumquat tree. As the Westerner requested, John passed on his message that he wished Jadelin much happiness; he wanted her to know that she was always in his thoughts. He also hoped that some day they could continue her English lessons. Impossible, Jadelin scoffed.

She stood and called Sweet Amah to bring her children. "Time, my darlings, to practice." She gave them each a hug. "Let's take off the jackets so you can move freely." Her children followed her every move.

"Leap. Now bend like the willow, soft but strong. Be purposeful," she instructed.

Her son, tall for his age with cheeks as rosy as baked buns, cried and lowered his arms. He pointed to his mother's face. "So sad, Mama."

"Yes, Danli." Jadelin bent down and ran her fingertip down her son's plump cheeks. The angle of light upon her children's faces had reminded her how long it had been since she had seen Baba, Mama, and her grandfather Ping. Her heart ached with longing. Her daughter, startled by her brother's tears, stopped in mid-pose with her hands out to her side and whimpered. Jadelin cradled her with an arm and cooed, "Sweet baby Butterfly. Sssh, everything's fine."

"My three hearts." Mow Bowli strode in with his loose-limbed gait. In a loose cotton tunic and leggings, he had come from the fields and still smelled of the sun. He laughed and quickly joined his children in the moves he knew well.

Jadelin tossed him a challenging look, raised one arm in an arch, and placed her other hand on his shoulder. She swung her body to earth like a crane touching earth and arched backwards so her head touched the ground.

"You are my life," he answered, following her movements. "If you find it within your disciplinarian heart to take a break, I have called for tea to be served." They moved as one through the exercise.

"Ah," Jadelin turned lightly on her toes and clapped her hands. She welcomed a break, especially now that he had arrived. At the signal to stop, the children stood in place and bowed. Quickly, Jadelin tipped her head to her husband and raised an eyebrow in expectation.

He bowed. "Thank you, my wife, for the lesson."

The children followed his example.

"As a treat for all, a very fine tea." Bowli swept his hand towards his study which opened out into the garden, for winter's chill still scraped the air with icy fingers. Soon they would emerge from the quiet time in his business. Last year, all three pickings had been sold for excellent prices. Seeds had been harvested and stored. The ground around the shrubs, which would rest until spring, had been raked and mulched. The tea sheds were bolted and all their tea making implements were locked away. He had enjoyed the short days of winter, of study and poetry, and the long winter nights spent cuddled under a goose down comforter. He opened a pewter tea container and held it out to his children to smell. "A very rare white tea sent from Soochow. I wanted to compare its soul to our Dragon Well."

Jadelin lowered her eyes, even more heartsick now for the ones she loved in Soochow, especially her grandfather.

Bowli lifted her chin to catch the shimmer in her eyes. "All is well there," he whispered. Then he turned to his son and daughter.

"There is a tale about this white tea which is called White Peony Flowers," he said. He placed a pinch of tea in each teacup.

"A long time ago one of the Emperor's young officials could not stand the corruption in court." He paused to explain to his children, "Corruption means bad things that government officials do that are not good for the people or country.

"Sad and disillusioned, the young official resigned. He left Peking with his mother. As they traveled, they became aware of a wonderful scent that brought peace to their hearts. They stopped at a temple and asked the monk, 'What makes the air here so fragrant?' The monk told him that eighteen peony flowers grew in the middle of the lake next to the temple. The young official and his mother walked out to the lake that sparkled like crystals and saw the exquisite white peonies that grew there. 'My son,' said the mother, 'let's build a house here.' So they did.

"One day his mother got very sick. The finest doctors brought their best herbs to heal her, but nothing worked. She only got worse. After a long walk to another doctor far away, the young man fell asleep against a willow tree. In his dream, an old man with a long white beard told him his mother would get well if he cooked a carp with a new tea. As he walked home, the young man wondered about his strange dream. When he got home, his mother greeted him with a tale about her strange dream. It was the same.

"The son knew he must do as the sage in his dream instructed. So he bought a fat golden carp at the market. Then he wondered what he was going to do about getting a 'new tea.' Just then, the skies darkened. Thunder boomed. Lightening slivered the air. The eighteen peony flowers in the middle of the beautiful lake shimmered and exploded. When the rain cleared, they had turned into tea shrubs with leaves covered with white hair. The young man rowed out to the middle of the lake and, as he plucked the leaves of these plants, thanked the gods. He prepared these leaves and cooked these 'new tea leaves' with the carp for his mother. When his mother recovered, she told her son, 'No matter what happens, promise me you will care for these tea shrubs.' Then she turned into a goddess, an Immortal, and flew away."

While Bowli told his tale, Jadelin poured boiling water over the tea in each of the four gaiwan tea cups. She strained out the water to cleanse the leaves, then filled the cups again and replaced their tops to let them steep for three minutes. When the tale concluded, she showed her children how to lift the cover off the gaiwan and to set it carefully in its place at the side of the teacup. "The fragrance of white tea is faint so you must hold your cup like this with both hands and bring it close to your mouth before you drink. Notice its lingering fragrance, like a song that stops yet you continue to hear the music. Wait for the taste to come to you."

Danli swished the tea in his cheeks. "Mama, it tastes sweet like an orange," he exclaimed.

Bowli's eyes expressed his pleasure. "Feel the sweetness slide down your throat, my son." He turned to Jadelin. "A connoisseur. Our son has a discriminating palate."

"Not surprising with such genealogy on both sides." Their dark eyes met with a single thought.

After their tea, Sweet Amah took the children for a bath and a nap. When the children protested, their father kneeled down and chucked them both under their chins. "Mama and Baba will also take a nap," he said. "We will come and get you when we get up." Assured by these promises, the children left.

With the shades drawn, the doors slid shut, and the heavy curtains closed against the outside world, the air was soft with the scent of tea and jasmine. Bowli put his arms around Jadelin and slowly pulled the sash from her robe. She bent her head to nuzzle the heat of his chest against her cheek. She felt his blood quicken as he ran his fingers through her hair.

Time stopped. Although the sun dipped towards the horizon, their bedchamber boiled in love until they could scarcely breathe. They clung to each other in the afterglow and drifted asleep.

Thirty

OLD CHUN OF THE FA-TEE GARDENS

ortune and Li had eaten very well all the way on their boat trip from Shanghai because of a peculiar arrangement that the captain had with the merchants of Hong Kong. If any perishable stock, which he carried for free, looked likely to die, the ship had the right to consume it. To the passengers' and crew's culinary delight, the decks had been stacked two layers high with cases of pheasants, woodcocks, hares, ducks, geese, and teals.

Fortune spent every waking minute on the Hong Kong-bound ship wiping dust and moisture from his plant boxes and scolding the sailors to keep their distance. In that busy port city of Hong Kong, he arranged for the loading of all those plants onto a British square-master bound for Calcutta. Now he was back in Canton for the start of another flower-collecting season.

"First thing, Li," Fortune said after he had secured lodgings in the cheapest rooming house he could find, "I'm determined to get Old Chun to tell me how he packs his seeds."

"Why should the most famous seed seller in China share his secrets with you?" asked Li. He strolled comfortably in his favorite city, inhaled

263

the scent of Canton, of pork buns and shrimp dumplings steaming from open air restaurants, of freshly harvested rice, fish, chicken, and pork simmering in earthy garlic sautés.

"I have lived in China for four years collecting plants and flowers and can speak the language." Fortune brushed the front of the Chinese robe that he now wore all the time. He was confident that neither the Chinese nor Westerners seemed to think the sight of a tall Westerner in Chinese dress with a queue was out of place. "I'm determined to coerce Old Chun into the truth. I want him to admit that he boils or poisons the seeds to make sure that their flowers cannot be grown outside of China."

Old Chun greeted all his guests at the entrance of his famous garden in a robe of blue nankeen with hand-knotted frogs. He wiped his square hands on a white cotton towel, which he neatly folded and placed on a potting bench amongst his plants when Fortune and Li approached. He hailed them as old customers.

"Old Chun," Fortune cajoled the husky old man. "I used to come to your gardens twice a year. I was always a good customer." Dressed in his mandarin queue and robe, he hoped he made a good impression addressing him in Chinese.

Old Chun's eyes, beads hidden in a sunburst of wrinkles, wisely watched his customer. "How can I forget? You always want a 'best price.' 'Cheaper, cheaper' you tell me. You want to know where every flower comes from and in how many colors. Endless questions."

"Remember the plant I gave you the last time I was here?"

"Oh yes, very curious purple plant. You see? Here it grows." Old Chun gestured to a plant that ended in spikes that curved like miniature monkey paws.

"You are the only one in China with that plant from Australia, another country with a climate similar to Canton. So you see, I'm your friend. One thing I have always wondered is how you pack your seeds. Will you take your friend to your seed room? I want to see the whole process from beginning to end."

Old Chun led them to the middle of his garden to a pagoda-roofed shed where swallows nested in the dark rounded tiles that curved up at each corner of the roof. He unlocked the door and led them inside. The walls were lined with shelves filled with small intricately labeled porcelain bottles. "Sit down," he gestured Fortune to a small bench. Li leaned cross-armed against the doorjamb to watch Old Chun's familiar ritual. "I'll explain to you how I pack seeds because I have known Li all my life, and he is an honorable man. Because of his good 'face' I will tell you what I share with no one else." His ebony eyes, as deep as pools of ink in the dusty light, met Li's. The two had accompanied their fathers to the teahouses of Canton since they were toddlers and Li had kept Old Chun current with details of Fortune's forays throughout China. To the seed seller, the British were vultures, always with their hands out: grasping, taking, wanting.

Fortune sat back, his pale eyes darting guiltily at Li before turning his attention to Old Chun. "Li is honorable and trustworthy, Old Chun," he agreed. "I trust him implicitly."

Chun nodded. "Good. He deserves your highest respect." Satisfied he had made his point, he picked up a porcelain bottle. "First, I gather the best seeds from the plants. Then I gently fill these small bottles, one with each kind of seed." He held up both empty and filled bottles to illustrate. "I seal the bottles and pack them into these specially padded boxes, ready for shipment to Europe or America."

Fortune raised his eyebrows. "Yes, I have bought many boxes of those seeds from you. But, what is that nasty substance you put in the bottles along with the seeds?"

"Burnt rice," answered Old Chun. He opened a sealed bottle and poured the seeds out into his open hand. With a small bamboo twig, he separated the rice from the seeds and held up his palm to Fortune's face to show him. "If I did not mix rice ash with the seeds, worms will eat them." He explained that Canton's tropical climate encouraged mold and mildew. Burnt rice was a desiccant; it absorbed any moisture that might ruin the seeds.

Fortune's forehead crinkled as he pondered this information. "Don't be angry, Old Chun, but we were convinced you did something to destroy the vitality of the seeds." Since none of the seeds they bought ever germinated, all the gardeners in England were positive the grainy substance he packed them in was crushed arsenic.

"You Westerners don't understand that it's difficult to preserve the seeds of trees and shrubs in the south of China. In our warm, moist weather maggots will eat seeds if they're not properly protected. Also, consider the age of the seeds. How long does it take you to arrive in England? Five months. By then, they are no longer fresh. My seeds are alive. They must be treated as such. You buy my precious seeds carefully sealed in airtight porcelain bottles. After a five-month voyage you wait until it's the right season to plant. By then, my living seeds are dead." He shook his head with disgust. "You think you know everything about plants. You have no respect for the knowledge of others. I have heard the lies you tell about me. You dishonor my good name."

Fortune pursed his lips and sourly remembered how vehemently he had denounced Old Chun in China and England, even implying that the seed seller boiled his seeds in poison. "From now on, I'll insist that everyone must plant your seeds as soon as they receive them. And I'll tell them that Old Chun of Canton endeavors to do his best to make sure they arrive in good condition."

"That would be honorable." Old Chun's sarcastic tone was unmistakable. He glared at the embarrassed flush that spread from the barbarian's cheeks down to his pale throat, and the guilty bob of his Adam's apple.

"Do you have anything new to show me?" asked Fortune, trying to make amends. "I'm putting together another collection."

Chun stood up and waved them to follow. He was a businessman, a renowned cultivator of fine decorative plants and would maintain his professional manner with this white ghost, *bak gwei*. Out in the bright Canton sun, he locked his seed shed and led them through his garden. His broad back stretched the sturdy Chinese cotton of his tunic as he swung his arms. His stout legs strode quickly among his beloved plants. He was proud of his chrysanthemums, the gardener's favorite winter flower. Although past their blooming prime, they revealed their topiary shapes of horses, deer, and pagodas. He had planted cuttings of various plants directly in pots filled with a mixture of soil taken from the bottom of his water-lily pond mixed with old night soil from his manure tanks. The result was luxuriant dark-green leaves.

"I take good care of all the plants I've collected," Fortune assured Chun. He described how the clever English built glass houses and intricate networks of hot water pipes to grow plants in all kinds of weather, how they monitored temperatures hourly and adjusted the steam to raise or lower the temperature. He had supervised a dozen apprentices in one of these glass houses in England. He expected Chun to congratulate him for his horticultural skill.

Instead, Chun looked incredulous. "What a lot of work!" He shook his head and waved his hand to dismiss such thoughts.

"We are diligent." Fortune shrugged. "We pay attention to the needs of each type of plant, but many freeze or turn limp."

Chun shook his head at the excesses of such flower-crazed people. He gestured to his own little house to the side of the garden's front gate. "In China we use a charcoal fire to keep warm and straw to stop leaks in the doors and windows." This simple philosophy had succeeded for many generations. "If we're happy, our plants are happy."

Disappointment darkened Fortune's face. The practical Chinese succeeded where English ingenuity failed. But a minute later an exquisite bloom as pink as the blush of sunrise caught his eye. "I must have every new plant in your collection," he said. He was delighted and charmed, already scheming to get the best of Old Chun.

Thirty-One

POE WAREHOUSE

SHANGHAI

*B*enjamin Poe nodded to the two sword-wielding guards flanking his warehouse's brass studded doors. Heavy browed and bearded, these tall men from the Yellow Mountains had proven their loyalty for four generations. They stiffened their broad shoulders and nodded they were ready and the area clear. Benjamin unlocked the iron bolts. They threw open the warehouse doors. Daniel and Paul fell in step behind their brother and inhaled the early morning scent of carefully stored crates of tea.

Workers arrived to set up their stations in weighing, maintenance, cupping, and security. In the back kitchen, the cook lit the wood he had prepared in the stove the night before. He would maintain three different temperatures of boiling water required to steep the teas for the tasters.

Benjamin unlocked each of the storage areas while assistants double-checked inventory. He ordered men to carry teas scheduled for export to the secure dock where Daniel prepared invoices. After the crates were prepared and labeled, he chose the coolies to carry them to the ships bound for America, England, Holland, and other ports.

By the time the sun shone over the tiled rooftops of Shanghai, the coolies who had walked for thousands of miles from the towering Wuyi Mountains arrived. Some carried a single premium tea crate on their back, and others balanced two tea crates from a bamboo pole. Their footsteps stirred motes of tea dust in the beams of sunlight from the clerestory windows.

"It's about time you showed up," Benjamin bellowed from his aerie above the warehouse floor to the lone figure in the open doorway.

The visitor motioned that he'd be right up and patted the leather folder under his arm. His silk Chinese robe fell neatly from his broad shoulders and barely rippled with his long strides. He waved to Daniel, who looked up from his abacus without missing a beat as he calculated outgoing orders from his desk commanding a view of the floor. The youngest Poe brother bounded up the wooden stairs and through the aerie's open door. "Got it. Five-year contract for tea from Anderson of America. They're a tight-fisted group," he huffed.

"As tight as Daniel?" inquired Paul. He had run up the stairs behind his younger brother.

Benjamin huffed with exasperation at his younger brothers, beefy fists on his wide hips. "How so? I was in the meeting two weeks ago with Baba when we learned five other tea hongs undercut us in price. Last week Mandarin Mah boasted that he and his eight sons hosted Anderson's delegation of twenty plus a dozen influential officials at a banquet. Servers in Ming costumes brought out new delicacies every two minutes for eight hours. Anderson signed the contract in front of Mandarin Mah. And now you claim we have the contract? I don't find your joke amusing."

John lifted the flap of his leather folder. "Has Anderson been back to Mah's warehouse to inspect the teas? Has Mah been around to gloat recently?" His raised eyebrows accompanied a hearty laugh when he handed him a neatly rolled sheaf of papers tied with a red ribbon secured with a wax seal.

Benjamin's burly fingers quickly untied the documents. He studied the signatures and grunted his approval.

"So my lead paid off?" The side of Paul's mouth twitched in an angelic smile. It was hard for anyone to not be in a good mood in his presence. He exuded charm, elegance, and graceful bonhomie.

"Yes, your nights of erhu playing with Anderson's heir melted his father's resistance," John replied.

"Anderson's eldest son is a sensitive man and musically gifted. He wants to study violin in Paris. His father's business bores him, and financial spreadsheets give him a headache," Paul confided. To Benjamin he added, "I do all I can for the Poe family without complaint." Again, he smiled.

"Humph." Lines creased Benjamin's forehead above his bushy eyebrows

John closed his leather folder and tucked it under his arm. "We couldn't have done it without Paul's efforts," he nodded gratefully to Paul. To Benjamin he added, "I didn't want to diminish the perceived value of our teas with a price war. Old man Anderson's rigidity softened during negotiations the past two days. He even plied me with the finest whiskey, which I refused. I need my brain as keen as Mow Chow Ching's dagger blades."

Paul lifted his eyebrows and tipped his head. "I'm sure the father wanted to find out what you know about his son, to plumb the depths of your discretion." He faced both brothers and bowed respectfully. "Nothing scandalous happened, I assure you. However, the heir of Anderson finds great delight with men of lesser morals. I will never compromise the House of Poe. The threat of impropriety is always more frightening for Westerners."

Benjamin chuckled. "Everybody does whatever you want them to do. Jardine's policy is to buy from all the hongs so they curry his favor as the most powerful Taipan in Hong Kong. But this year you tell his company they have to buy their premium oolong only from us, and they do, cutting out the others. You seem to go anywhere and talk to anyone."

"I find it more challenging to make friends than enemies," acknowledged Paul. "I presented my offer to Jardine as a shrewd business opportunity. People see me in the image they wish to see."

"We all have been very busy." Benjamin raised the signed contract. "We can fulfill our pledges to our growers for the next five years. Baba will be pleased." The brothers sighed heavily, for Mandarin Poe grew weaker each day.

John peeked out over the growing cacophony of the warehouse. "Now that you have the contract, I better help Daniel."

"Good. He wants to get the morning orders out so he can give all his attention to the incoming shipments." He indicated the ledger books on his desk. "I'm scheduling the new orders and shipments now." He looked to Paul. "What's your schedule for the upcoming week?"

"I'm working on five American delegations who have invited me to lunch and dinner meetings. I have a couple of late night musical evenings with British prospects." Paul relished his role. He usually arrived home at the same hour his brothers woke up. Over steaming bowls of congee, sliced meats, and vegetables, Paul passed on whatever information he had gleaned from his night soirees. He not only alerted them to new business, he kept them abreast of the political and business situation in China vis-à-vis the Western powers.

"I don't know how you do it," said John. Work and family exhausted him. He tried to spend time with his father, who missed both Edward and Jadelin and forgot First Mother was gone. But John never forgot his responsibility to the House of Poe and that they counted on him to close the deals and get new tea contracts from the customers that Paul worked so creatively to cultivate.

"The Russian ambassador's secretary is having an affair with Emory's wife," Paul whispered as they headed down the stairs.

"Emory of Emory & Broderick from England?" Benjamin followed his brother out the door. His cauliflower ears were so keen he could hear the whir of hummingbird wings a mile away. "Emory's shopping for green teas. Said we're too expensive. I told him we guarantee our quality, unlike some of the other tea hongs he's visited. Cheapskate."

Paul looked back at him with a conspiratorial smile. "His neglected wife is coming to a private soiree my friends are hosting. She's bringing her lover. Her husband's so concerned about social propriety, who knows what he might do to keep that potentially scandalous information from being known?" He gave John a penetrating look. "I'll arrange for you to meet him with a contract."

John returned his look with a nod. "You keep the contracts coming so Benjamin can fill and empty the warehouse while Daniel counts the money." He raced down the stairs.

Benjamin watched the two, both energetic and enthused about the challenges of the tea hong, before returning to his aerie. Both used their skills and talents differently. Paul was the creative extrovert whose personality drew others to confide in him, to share the secrets they'd tell no one else. His innocent expression assured all that he was their friend and confidante. John's Western confidence and business acumen persuaded their customers that they were dealing with 'one of their own.' Their teamwork ensured that the House of Poe would survive unless the Emperor agreed to more unequal laws imposed by the Western powers. Benjamin frowned to focus his thoughts on his ledgers. In the teahouses he overheard threats of civil unrest. Travelers brought word that warlords amassed mercenary armies and already had control of some areas far from the reach of the Emperor.

"Heaven is high, and the Emperor is far away," Benjamin repeated to himself. Everyone on the street was repeating it now. It seemed the Emperor of China was indeed uncaring. The Mandarins of Shanghai's repeated entreaties to stop Robert Fortune's forays into the tea growing areas were ignored. Li reported silk worms and mulberry trees, banned from export according to treaty, among Fortune's shipments and still the Emperor didn't act. Meanwhile, British gunboats continued to patrol their coast and blockade key ports.

Benjamin stared at his ledgers. They must make the most of what they had now, to do as much business as they could and save for the future. There were no guarantees that in five years China would have a tea trade if the Englishman succeeded in growing tea in India.

Enough digression, he growled to himself. He had ten hours of work that he intended to do in half the time, so he attacked the first account with vigor. Below him, the industrious sounds of business soothed his soul. He touched his breast and did a silent prayer, like the one he did each morning as he lit the incense at the front and back door altars to the God of Wealth.

Coolies arrived by the hundreds. Now that the morning's shipment had left the warehouse, Paul, John, and Daniel could focus on the incoming tea chests. They inspected each case and marked them on Daniel inventory before their own men stored them in the appropriate storage locker.

"How's Jadelin?" asked Daniel. He was the quietest brother, but the one who most keenly felt change. Her departure had left a hole in their lives.

"She's a busy wife and mother," answered John. Her letters were less frequent, and she was not as interested in hearing about the daily Poe business as she had been when he was tailing Robert Fortune. "How's business on your end?"

"We've grown tenfold. With all the new business you and Paul bring us, we sell tea from our growers at premium prices." They never mentioned it to Flora or Mandarin Poe or Third Wife Mei, but they knew it might not last. The new rules imposed by the British were like a noose around China that could cut off their breath at any time, so the Poes had been storing gold for those lean times.

"Alternative plans?" asked John.

"Working on them," answered Daniel in a low voice. "We'll talk tonight."

Thirty-Two

SING HOO, MAY 1849

"Get up, sir. Fi de, fi de."

When Fortune opened his sleep-puffed lids, two almond shaped eyes pushed up to his face. "Where's Li?" the Scot demanded. He struggled to sit up and clear his head of his recurring dream. Once again he had entered the mist-shrouded graveyard of his childhood church in Berwickshire. This time he saw his name on one of the crooked moss-covered tombstones. Fear chilled his bones and froze his steps. He had reached out with his fingers to trace the letters of his name carved in the cold marble when he was startled awake.

"You sent him away. I am Sing Hoo, mandarin. You hired me because I have been to the Bohea Mountains, more correctly called the Wuyi Mountains, where Li said you were not allowed. You want to see where the tea grows and to smell the air scented by millions of tea bushes in bloom. Only I have the yellow mandarin flag, gifted me by my previous employer, which melts all obstacles and can get you into the forbidden areas." His new guide had a strong forehead and above his barrel chest, a toothy smile brightened a tanned face. He had ears that stood out like jug handles from a big round head. His lips were porky like his cheeks, neck, and fingers. He was a squarely built man, bossy and impatient, who would stand his ground against a horde of Mongols.

"Get up. Put on your 'outward man,'" Sing Hoo ordered. "I laid out your clothes." He placed a stool in a clear space among the ropes and boxes that crowded the deck. As with most boats for hire on the canal, it was the home of a boatman and his wife with a small crew. He sharpened his razor on a leather strip with a teeth-biting, nerve-shearing shrup-shrup. "I boiled water to shave your forehead. Come along. Eat later. Dress now. Chop chop."

He harrumphed when Fortune sat down on the crate he set out for him. He immediately began shaving the Scot's head with alacrity, leaving a circle of hair at the top. The remainder of Fortune's hair, now shoulder length, he wove seamlessly into the glossy black queue that Fortune had bought on his previous trip. When Sing Hoo was satisfied, Fortune's queue fell neatly down his back. Sing Hoo then dressed the Scot in his mandarin robe and hat to complete his transformation into Sing Wa, a traveler from beyond the Great Wall.

"You will do," Sing Hoo nodded briskly. He eyed Fortune up and down with a critical frown. "When we reach Nanche, I'll buy a summer hat which will make your appearance more perfect. That hat is for winter. Wrong style." He shook his head. "Tsk-tsk-tsk."

Fortune clasped his hands in front of him as the Chinese did, which he found to be a comforting position and, he thought, made him appear more Chinese. His brazen plan was to travel up river, then two hundred miles over mountainous country to the forbidden tea plantations of the Wuyi Mountains where the finest black tea grew. Despite his careful planning he felt afraid and for the first time, truly alone. He attempted to increase his confidence by shuffling around the boat in his Chinese slippers as if he, too, belonged to the 5,000-year history of the Chinese. He peered imperiously down his long nose at the sidelong stares of the captain and his wife. He narrowed his eyes over the river and studied the network of canals that allowed one to go anywhere, everywhere. A strangely scented wind pushed against his body. He didn't recognize the smells of the land they were entering. That night the dull and dreary evening wrapped him like the shroud he wasn't ready for. The rain fell heavily as darkness smothered the canal.

In the morning they coasted up the waterway until they came upon fifty boats in queue to go to the next level. Each had to wait its turn to be hooked to a windlass and drawn up an inclined plane to the next canal. Fortune took this opportunity to sit in the shade and write while Li squatted on the deck scrutinizing the other boats while they waited.

But one boat captained by a bully with a brash voice and a shock of wild hair came up behind them. "Out of my way. Move! Move! Move!" the ruffian ordered. He poled and sculled past all the other boats, bumping and wiggling until he was almost astern.

Fortune fumed. They had waited a long time in the hot sun like everyone else. Although he resented someone barging ahead he didn't want to call attention to himself. He tucked his head down as if in thought.

But Sing Hoo swaggered to the stern. He puffed out his broad chest and raised his large-knuckled fist. "You can't pass this boat," he shouted. He motioned his boatman to push their boat's bow diagonally against the bank to block the intruder's passage. "Push! Do not let this offensive person pass." He threw his body into his exhortations to his crew to defeat this man of a thousand vulgar names.

"Oh, but I will get through," growled the interloper. He bared his teeth and slammed his boat against their bow. He hadn't been schooled in the politeness of Confucian ethics.

"You can't pass this boat," growled Fortune's boatmen. There were rules that governed the sea and rivers and canals, including courtesy and right of way. The crew planted their poles and leaned forward to stop his advance.

On the stern, Sing Hoo frothed into a frenzy, thick hands on his hips, legs solidly planted. "Do you know that there is a mandarin on this boat?" he bellowed.

Fortune cringed.

"I don't care for mandarins. I'm in a hurry," snarled the bully.

Cackling, Sing Hoo whipped out his small yellow flag and hoisted it up the mast. "There!" He pointed his meaty finger at the triangular flag at the top of the mast. "Will you pass now?" he challenged.

"Wah, I'm sorry, honorable mandarin," the blustering boatman wailed with repeated bows. "Please forgive my rudeness. I'll wait my turn." He plopped down on the stern of his boat, eyes down, hands nervously twitching on his lap.

Sing Hoo turned to Fortune. He laughed at his slack jaw and surprised expression. "You did not believe me, mandarin. You see what this little flag can do?" From Shanghai to Peking this flag had protected the Imperial Mandarin he served from insult and interference. When Sing Hoo returned to his own province, the old mandarin had presented it to him as a parting gift. Wasn't the barbarian lucky to have hired Sing Hoo with his Imperial Yellow Flag?

When it was their turn, the crew attached the two ropes connected with the windlass to their boat. They were drawn up the inclined plane and launched on the higher canal. From there they cruised and ascended still more canals of the amazing Chinese waterway.

China was in the budding throes of summer. Streams gushed down steep ravines and exploded with hundreds of waterfalls. The rains had transformed the hills and valleys into infinite shades of green exuding enticing floral scents. The crisp morning air vibrated with mating calls and bird songs from every tree, bush, and meadow.

Fortune kept his eyes on the distant mountains. They must be closer now, for they were sailing up the Green River that led to the hills of Hangchow where the finest green teas grew.

At the first of many swift rapids, the crew dove naked into the water with braided bamboo ropes and clambered ashore to track the boat upriver. The captain set a drum on the bow and knotted a cloth over his head against the sun. He pounded a rhythmic beat that his lead tracker picked up with a plaintive lament, eerily primitive, which reverberated off the cliff's walls. His men, nude except for the ropes looped around their shoulders, groaned with each step along the narrow path as they fought the swift current.

Sing Hoo pointed to the thin ribbon-like footpaths carved along the cliff face. "The ancient song the trackers sing recounts the heroic deeds of our people, of their strength and wisdom. For centuries, trackers have pulled boats up China's rivers. You see the narrow footpaths carved into the sheer cliffs? Their ropes have worn their own story into the rock face." He rocked back on his heels. How he loved sharing his knowledge of China's five thousand year history. True, he wasn't a scholar, but he had been a good listener and absorbed his grandmother's stories, which wove magic in the late nights. And the itinerant storytellers, masters of ancient legends and myths, conjured up whole worlds with words. He wondered if this pale-eyed visitor could hear the difference in the ancient beats and songs of other trackers pulling boats, and how they echoed up the river, weaving their various laments together like a musical tapestry.

At the end of the rapids, the trackers dove into the water and pulled themselves aboard. The men lay on the deck, panting and heaving, before falling into a deep sleep. The boatman and his wife did not ask them to do any more that day. Instead, they steered out of the river into a small creek where they tied up for the night.

Just before twilight, more and more boats crowded into the little creek, crashing and bumping as they jockeyed for a space. The boatman's wife leapt up with her rice bowl and chopsticks in hand and harangued every boat that touched their sides. As the creek filled with boats, more women screamed for others to be careful until the air reverberated with shrill voices and oaths.

Sing Hoo shook his head as the men ate and watched the women battle. "In this area, women scull and pole equally with their men. They manage the boat and consider it their home. That's why they're so upset." With his rice bowl he motioned to the creek jammed hull to hull where seemingly no boats more could fit. "It rained earlier and the boat people anticipate a mountain flood. This side creek is the safest place." Eventually, the creek was so solid with rafted decks one could walk from one side to the other and upriver as far as one could see.

Two hours later a wall of water thundered down and swelled the creek over its banks. The raft of boats rose precipitously, wavered in the watery rush, and crashed one against the other. The breadth and length of the river was filled with the roar of the water, screams, and the sickening sound of splintering wood.

∾

$\mathcal{T}$he air was still cool with dew when they landed at the Green River headlands. Grass swayed on the hills above undulating rice paddies that cascaded down the hills like glistening steps. Trees and shrubs bowed with the weight of last night's rain.

Fortune gazed in amazement at the towering green mountains sweet with the inland breeze. After all these years of dreaming and hiking, thwarted expeditions and bumbling misdirection, he had reached the Wuyi Mountains. He squinted through his smoked spectacles to see the treacherous trails that curled up and over the mountains. Two lines of men moved in opposing directions along the twelve-foot wide path, one a continuous line of coolies carrying tea trudged down towards Green River. Heavily laden coolies headed in the opposite direction. Their pace was steady and robotic.

Sing Hoo immediately took off and returned with porters bearing a special bamboo mountain chair to carry Fortune up the steep incline and sharp turns of the Wuyi Mountains. He commandeered more coolies to carry Fortune's boxes, then maneuvered his procession into the unbroken stream of coolies headed inland bearing cotton, lead, and other goods from the coast. Thousands of coolies wearing wide-brimmed bamboo hats to protect their heads from the searing sun, bearing only tea chests, surged towards them along the route carved in granite. For tens of thousands of miles these coolies trudged past each other like endless armies of ants.

Just when Fortune's head hammered from bouncing under the sun on the mountain chair and Sing Hoo dragged, too parched from the dust of the road to lift another foot ahead of the other, they arrived at an inn at the side of the road. Here the men collapsed on any chair or log in the shade. A woman would give each man a stoneware teacup with a healthy pinch of tea and pour freshly boiled water. The men who had carried Fortune on the sedan chair squatted on their haunches and accepted at least three or four refills of hot water before rising to their feet.

"We have gone thirty li, a good distance," panted Sing Hoo. He vigorously wiped his sweaty face with a cloth tucked in his sleeve. He caught the innkeeper's eye and gestured for more hot water. "Do you know how I know this valuable information?" Fortune wearily raised an eyebrow and shook his head. He, like everyone else, was layered with dust. His back ached and his eyes stung from the glare and dirt. Everyone sat with heads bowed as if gathering strength for the next leg.

"All inns are one li apart. We are at the thirtieth, so we have gone thirty li. Sing Hoo is a valuable guide, is he not?" He considered maintaining his employer's good mood part of his job.

"Just get me to the Wuyi Mountains." Fortune wiped his dust-caked face with a stained sleeve. He rinsed his mouth out with a mouthful of tea and spat on the dirt like the others. He watched the never-ending lines of coolies until their motion made him dizzy.

"Never fear. Now, if you are refreshed, we will resume our journey." Sing Hoo bowed to their hostess, counted out Fortune's cash for tea for his entourage, and thanked everyone around them for their hospitality with profuse bows.

The Wuyi Mountains were formed when the sky sucked the land into the clouds with powerful gasps during a violent volcanic eruption. Millennia of erosion had shaped the winding river valleys flanked by columnar and dome-shaped cliffs. From these rugged peaks, sacred to the Chinese, hermits and priests had levitated into the heavens.

At the first mountain pass, Sing Hoo threw open his arms. "Look! Have you ever seen anything so fine?" Fortune gripped the sides of his bamboo chair balanced on the shoulders of two skinny men and squinted up at the mountain peaks piercing the sky six to eight thousand feet above. The thin morning air iced his pale gray eyes. Masses of turbulent clouds stabbed by irregularly fragmented crags glowed as if gilded with gold while others loomed with foreboding gloom. Below him, the River of Nine Bends wound through thirty-six exotic peaks where the fabled prince Tseen-Kang once lived with his two sons, Wu and Yi.

The travelers fell silent as they approached the high mountain pass at the border between Chekiang and Kingsee provinces. Sing Hoo motioned the coolies to lower Fortune to the ground. "Mandarin," said Sing Hoo. "Every mountain pass is dangerous." He indicated with a quick nod of his head at the fortified towers that flanked the pass. The thick gates were open but each traveler had to pass the scrutiny of the sword wielding guards. Leather armor plates covered their body, arms, and legs. A helmet topped by a plume magnified their height. "The most ferocious men are chosen to guard these mountain passes against invaders and trouble makers. When we pass the checkpoint, cast your eyes down. If they ask you any questions, I will answer." He gave each of their coolies a pep talk. When he felt they were ready, he motioned Fortune back up on his chair.

Fortune bowed his head. As Sing Wa, a traveler from the north, he was convinced that his 'inward man' was as Chinese as his 'outward man.' Hadn't he discarded all his European mannerisms for China's higher level of civilization and politeness? Consider the chopsticks, the most useful and sensible utensils. Leaving the gross cutting of meats and vegetables to kitchen servants, he could pick up a single grain of rice, pluck out dainty morsels, bite-sized and ready to eat. There were no utensils more versatile for eating except fingers. Forks and knives were barbarous. As for his drink, he preferred Chinese tea and light wines to the stronger alcohol that Europeans preferred. And he found the long bamboo Chinese pipe more refined, more relaxing, than the Manila cheroots of the Westerners. After dinner, when the innkeeper brought him a wooden basin of warm water and a wet cloth, he would clean his face, neck and hands, Chinese style. He was sure his actions convinced everyone that he was as Chinese as they were.

"Sing Wa, Sing Wa," Sing Hoo's hiss broke Fortune's reverie. "Keep your head humble. Think like your outward man. Remember, after we pass the guards of Chekiang up ahead we must pass the Kingsee guards on the other side. I have my yellow flag ready but I prefer to slip through without problems." He glowered at the chair bearers who discretely kept their eyes forward and expressionless.

"No, mandarin." His porters stopped him from remounting. They pointed at the narrow trail clinging to the high mountains and shook their head.

"The trail is now too narrow and steep to safely carry you," Sing Hoo explained. His breathing was labored in the thin air. "We must all walk now." He gestured for the coolies and Fortune to follow.

Even the tea bearers fell silent to save their breath; they paused every few yards to rest their loads. Long trains of coolies wearing loose cotton trousers and tunics and thick-soled sandals of straw met and overtook each other at each undulating turn. The majority of the northbound coolies balanced a tea chest from either end of a single bamboo pole across their shoulders for the twenty-four day trek to Shanghai.

Sing Hoo explained that premium teas were carried singly, strapped between two seven-foot bamboo poles lashed together at one end. The coolie balanced both poles on his shoulders and hung onto the open ends in front of him. When he rested, he put these ends on the ground and leaned his single tea chest up against any wall so it would never touch the ground.

At the next mountain pass, fortified towers flanked an arched door-way carved like the gates of a great city. Fortune lowered his head and tucked his hands in his sleeves as if he were in meditation. Every guard Fortune had seen thus far was fearsomely broad and husky like these dressed in black leather with bronze fittings. Instead of helmets, they braided and tied their polished hair in a striking topknot. They brandished spears with red and gold ribbons woven around their shafts.

"Sing Wa, think like your outward man," warned Sing Hoo. Their coolies shuffled silently, eyes down, cowering behind Sing Hoo, who was uncharacteristically silent. He looked quickly up, then hissed to the Scot, "The guards watch!"

∾

*T*he Wuyi Mountains scraped the sky with tapered fingers, each pass revealing peaks more dramatic than the last. Now that he had seen them, Fortune felt that only the worthy, people like himself, should be allowed to behold the strange and exotic flora and fauna that grew inland. Each time the guards at the gate motioned him through a mountain pass, he harrumphed triumphantly, certain that he was the first Westerner to behold these towering peaks encased in mist, the high tumbling waterfalls, and the rushing rivers that coursed through the lush valleys. These guardians had given him the privilege of entering inner China. He reveled in his deception.

"Sing Hoo," he hailed from his mountain chair perch one morning. They had gone at a good clip the past few days. "There's supposed to be a famous monastery here. Find the trail."

"What trail? There's no trail." Sing Hoo gestured with both arms to the thick growth that blanketed the steep mountainous side of the trail.

"Set me down," Fortune ordered. He stood with his feet wide, the mountain air cool against his legs, and pointed to the peak. "Ask everyone how we can get there."

Eager to please, Sing Hoo asked other travelers if they had heard of the monastery. A few of the more seasoned travelers pointed towards the tallest mountain peak. Yes, there was a famous monastery in the clouds. No one knew how to reach it. Even Fortune joined his porters and coolies as they parted bushes and hiked up dead-end trails to scenic spots. The temperatures rose quickly in the high-altitude mountains. Finally, Sing Hoo shouted success. His exultant cry brought a relieved sigh to the weary porters and coolies.

"It's barely wide enough for my foot!" Fortune stared in disbelief at the dirt tamped between the rocks.

"See the little toe holds carved in the rock? 10,000 steps. We can do it. Everyone follow me." Sing Hoo, once again in charge, attacked the vertical path. "Too steep for chair," he told Fortune. "You walk like everyone else."

They started off gallantly at first, stopping every few steps to gulp air and fan themselves. The trail was so steep they found it better to crawl on their hands and knees. With the sun intense upon their backs, they slipped and grappled upwards until their fingers and toes could no longer feel the rocks.

Up they climbed, up, up up, until the wind brought a cool smell, the scent of a forest. "Aah," the men sighed. They stepped into a small, luxuriantly landscaped wood, cool, and peaceful. Hydrangeas, azaleas, wild roses, and brambles grew lush and heavy with scent. Japanese cedars and evergreen oaks with glossy leaves grew from the manicured forest floor. Insects buzzed, zipped, crawled, and flittered everywhere.

Sing Hoo unbuttoned his golden livery so the breeze could cool his overheated body. "See the golden temples, how they glow in the sun." He pointed at the temples which rose up one behind the other in three tiers crowed with gold. "We'll soon have tea. Come now, pick up those feet. Up, up, up!"

They followed the bank of a lake perfumed by red and white lotus blossoms rising from the muddy water. Sing Hoo knelt at the edge and washed his face with the clearest water he could find. He straightened and buttoned up his livery. He indicated to Fortune that he should smarten up as well. The men trod a smooth dirt path along rows of well-tended tea shrubs planted up the sheer mountain where a series of golden temples glowed in the sun, each gilded complex stepped higher than the last.

As soon as Sing Hoo entered the first temple, a round-headed boy, who seemed to be the only person about, scampered off. He returned with a wizened monk, shaven and tall with calm eyes and a peaceful visage. He raised his thin eyebrows, looked inquiringly at Fortune and Sing Hoo, then at the dusty porters and coolies slumped behind them. "How did you find us?" he asked in a voice deep and distinguished. "We are hidden among the peaks."

"Honorable high monk." Sing Hoo bowed low. "The fame of this fabled monastery reached the distant country beyond the Great Wall where my master lives. He traveled a great distance from his far away land to see for himself the beauty and serenity of your monastery." His threw his arms wide in a grandiose gesture. "My master humbly begs that we might be accommodated with food and lodging for a few days. He will reimburse the temple for all expenses."

The old monk pulled out his tobacco pouch while Sing Hoo recited his salutations and, after rolling it between his thumb and finger, presented it to Fortune. The Scot pulled out his own Chinese pipe and joined the monk in a smoke. More monks appeared now, curious about the visitors to their hidden monastery.

The little boy brought tea. The Scot inhaled the fragrance and admired the bronze color. He nodded his pleasure to the head monk who explained that a temple topped every mountain here. Altogether, there were nine hundred and ninety-nine Taoist and Buddhist temples, some so renowned for their tea that their entire gardens, called Imperial Enclosures, were reserved for the Emperor's Court. The best tea grew in some of the most inaccessible places, such as summits and ledges of precipitous rocks, conditions that added to their taste and complexity.

"How do you possibly gather those leaves?" Fortune leaned forward, notebook in hand.

"Sometimes we throw up chains to knock off the top leaves. Sometimes we use monkeys." Behind them, the monks laughed among themselves.

"Monkeys!" Fortune's eyes widened.

"Some of our tea grows straight up the cliff. The monkeys that live there are protective of their bushes. We throw stones at the monkeys. They break off the tips of the branches and throw them down to us." Again, the monks broke into peals of laughter.

❧

*S*onorous chants floated through the mists that wrapped the mountaintops before dawn. A low drum and single chime punctuated the ethereal voices.

When rays of sunlight touched the land, it awoke. Birds sang, insects whirred, and the cries and roars of monkeys and tigers billowed from the forests. Low voices and the sizzle of woks over wood burning fires emanated from the kitchens. Saffron-robed monks left to tend their tea gardens.

Fortune's growling stomach woke him as soon as the scent of long-simmering congee reached the small room where he slept. He dressed and stepped out in time to glimpse monks wearing cone shaped hats and capes disappearing into the trails.

"Why are you up so early?" Sing Hoo stumbled out behind him and rubbed his aching shoulders that still hurt from carrying plant boxes 10,000 steps up to the monastery complex. "The sun won't rise for an hour or two."

"Where are they going? And why are they dressed like that?" Fortune asked. He didn't want to waste a minute. There was so much to see here.

"When not in prayers the monks tend their tea plants. The hats, capes, and sandals they weave from bamboo protect them from the sun and rain."

"Bamboo," muttered Fortune. The wind blowing through the thick bamboo grove behind the temple was the last sound he heard the night before.

"Bamboo fronds are strong and repel rain. Very sturdy. The stalk is strong and the tender bamboo shoots are delicious. You ate them last night." Sing Hoo laughed when Fortune looked perplexed. "Chinese are like bamboo. We bend in bad times, but we always return to our upright path. Flexible in adversity."

While Sing Hoo arranged for his explorations through the Wuyi Mountains, Fortune explored the temple complex. He held his head humbly like the monks did as he walked the corridor. Sing Hoo had explained the various Buddhas and Boddhisatvas in the temples they had previously visited and, knowing the Buddhist penchant for peace, felt it was safe to wander on his own.

In the largest temple, he hid in a passage supported by massive wooden pillars to watch an old monk with long earlobes and sad, sloping eyes. The monk approached a huge, wooden fish slung from the roof, and struck it several times with a wooden pole. Its deep sound reverberated throughout the building. The large bronze bell in the tower above rang three times and in a rustle, monks approached from all directions.

Before the altar in the middle of the temple stood thirty-foot statues of the Buddha of the Past, Present, and Future, ornately carved and gilded. These golden Buddhas were flanked by painted statues of other deities aged by the patinas of time and incense.

Monks lit candles and long incense sticks at the altar. As stillness settled over the vast temple hall, hundreds of monks entered, heads bowed, hands clasped. They knelt on the hassocks arranged in even rows before the altar, bending low several times while the large bell tolled solemnly. Then all was still.

One monk struck a bell, another a drum. The tones reverberated through the void. They chanted in haunting rhythms that varied, sometimes accompanied by the mellow tone of a wood drum. An hour later they rose and walked in two processions that curled around each other and ended with all before the great altar.

At that moment the screen that hung before the large door was drawn aside, and sunlight filled the temple. A golden-red bolt of light hit the golden Buddha. The statue shimmered and slowly expanded until Buddha's topknot touched the peaked ceiling.

Fortune drew back behind the pillar, suddenly frightened. He had come to China as a Christian who looked down on the heathens. Yet he knew fear when sunlight hit the golden Buddha and it miraculously grew before his eyes, a magnificent and awe-inspiring sight. He trembled, humbled by his insignificance. The more he saw and experienced China, the more he doubted the superiority of his beliefs over the other. Buddhism touched him in a spiritually peaceful way. The Chinese were not as his countrymen portrayed them to be.

The next day he hiked out to the next hill and looked back. The sun shone so brilliantly upon the temple that its tile roof sparkled as if covered with precious gems.

∾

ortune hiked from dawn to dusk. He collected tea plants, flowering plants, and soil samples. He shot birds and chipped rocks. He studied and noted details of everything he collected and packed them in the collection boxes strapped to Sing Hoo's back.

On the last day, they climbed to the peak above the temples to get a wider perspective of the rugged cliffs and valleys of the Wuyi Mountains, the fertile glens, and the hills dotted with tea. Far away to the north, the Wuyi Mountains stretched from east to west forming an impenetrable barrier between Fukien and the rich and populous province of Kiangsee. He looked down upon the lines of monks returning to the temple. He asked his man, "Sing Hoo, these monks spend more time on their tea than they do in prayers. They're supposed to be religious, not consumed with earthy concerns like tea plants."

"I cannot believe you are so ignorant," answered Sing Hoo. "When you get up, they have already been meditating for three hours. Some meditate all day, some all night. Tea is part of the Buddhist faith. When they cultivate and process the tea, they are meditating, concentrating on the act. They are not thinking about production or profits. Drinking tea increases their ability to meditate longer with greater attentiveness."

This shamed the Scot into silence. He had seen the head monk sitting motionless from the time he left in the morning until he returned at night. One could never sleep in such an erect position, but he had never considered how one had the stamina or strength to do so. "Well then, Sing Hoo, if they're not concerned about earthly delights, what about that lake we followed to get here? I've seen the monks go there often, some to sit, some to watch the fish, and some to work on the plants. Beautiful flowers and fat fish are frivolous joys. That's not religious."

"You are truly a stupid sir. The lotus flower is sacred to Buddhists. They remind us that no matter how horrific life is, purity and beauty emerges, just as the pure lotus blossom emerges from the murky layers of mud that cover the bottom, just as a pure soul rises up from the murkiness of life to achieve enlightenment. The goldfish are a symbol of prosperity, in spirit as well as material wealth. The monks tend their lotus ponds and goldfish which are symbols of what we must remember in our hearts."

"I'm observant enough to notice that you Chinese are a contented and happy race. Every one laughs when they're working in the fields. I've even heard monks sing as gaily as the birds in those old gnarled trees around the temple."

Sing Hoo looked at him in furrowed surprise. He shook his head at those curious observations. Singing and laughter always lightened a heavy load and shortened a backbreaking task, especially among friends. He glanced again at the Scot's dour face. Perhaps his kind didn't joke or laugh or sing. Since the Westerners sailed into China's ports, the Chinese had less to sing or joke about. It felt good to see that inland, his people still did.

On the way back to the temple, they came upon the natural cavern where nine high monks had been interred. The Scot reverently ran his fingers around the boulder that sealed its opening. He sighed to see the smoldering incense sticks, newly placed, and the numerous stubs buried in the sand of the altar before it. "What a wonderful spot," he sighed. "A perfect spot for everlasting life."

The high monk of the temple came with fresh incense while Fortune stood there. He said there was room for one more in this holy spot; he looked forward to joining his fellow monks there. Fortune clasped one hand to his chest. "This is like a dream or a fairy land. How I wish I could find a grave like this." Beautiful graves in rustic settings stirred his romantic image of death and moved him to tears. He staggered and sat down to take in the image of a peaceful hereafter as twilight cooled the air.

Sing Hoo shook his head. Throughout their travels, Fortune had gravitated to graves and tombs with similar sentiments, pointing out trees that conjured dignity in death or bent in a mournful way as if they were grieving. Such a melancholy person, or perhaps it was the way of his people. "Sir, are you all right?"

Fortune put his hand to his heart and wiped his tears. In the still night he heard a gong and bell from the distant temples. He imagined the monks at their devotion. He looked up and watched the rising moon. He had stepped into a scene that grew more magical with each breath. He looked across the valley to where the woods were dark and dense. Below them, the lake sparkled like a thousand jewels. How could he explain he felt more himself here than anywhere else he had ever been?

Thirty-Three

BROKEN PROMISES, BROKEN BAMBOO

"I cannot put one more seed in your boxes," Sing Hoo declared. "See how heavy. You collect too much." He shook his head as if Fortune were an errant child. "Time to go. We have to carry all this." He swept his hands at the tower of boxes packed with pressed leaves, seeds, and skinned birds. "The way is long and mountainous."

Fortune knelt over his boxes and ran his hands over each, remembering the glorious days he had spent collecting some of the finest tea shrubs in these remote mist-covered mountains. "This has been a fine place."

At dawn, Fortune bid a heart-felt farewell to the kind monks before he and his laden coolies followed Sing Hoo back down the precipitous footpath. They rested at the bottom of the 10,000 steps for a long time to gather their strength. Then they hiked up another hill for two miles to get to Tsin-Tsun, the great market for black tea in the hills overlooking the Stream of Nine Windings, the northern district, which reputedly produced the best souchongs, and pekoes which rarely reached Europe.

"Let's stop here." Sing Hoo pointed to a Taoist temple that commanded a sweeping view of the convoluted turns of the Stream of Nine Windings. "Very good for resting. Very good tea." He gestured Fortune to follow him into the little teahouse and motioned to the coolies that they could take their tea outside while guarding their boxes.

A Taoist monk and his equally wizened wife, who looked as ancient as the temple they tended, seated them on the porch. A peculiarity of the stone temple was that it was built against the cliff, and from high above, rivulets trickled down the rocky face to form a continual waterfall over the huge rock ledge that protected the temple and the adjacent house. The monk's wispy queue trembled as he laid out teacups, dispensed the fresh black tea, and poured out the boiling water.

"Is this not good?" enthused Sing Hoo. "One of the finest black teas. Very fresh. And such a peaceful site. Here we are surrounded by perpetual rain overlooking the Stream of Nine Windings." He tipped his head at the waterfall spilling over the ledge around them and flourished his hand at the sweeping view. "Are you not pleased with Sing Hoo?"

Fortune wrapped his dusty fingers around his cup and eyed every patron. "Sing Hoo," he whispered. "Do you see any Cantonese who might recognize me as a Westerner?"

"Just because your nose is long, your eyes are the color of the sky, and your skin looks like washed rice does not mean you are anything special to look at. For centuries travelers from the West who wear strange clothes of all colors and styles, footwear, and headdresses have traded within China along the Silk Road. Past Emperors even 'collected' such travelers for the amusement, entertainment, and enlightenment of the Imperial Court. Many foreigners, like the Jesuits, dressed like the Chinese, just as you do. As long as you behave yourself and have manners, no one cares."

Fortune took a deep breath and sat back. The peacefulness of this spot, the view of the convoluted Stream of Nine Windings and its craggy mountains, and the gentle trickle of the waterfall that encased the Taoist temple soothed his muscles and sun-addled mind. He looked around and saw that everyone sat as if in meditation, refreshed by the tea and soothing sound of water. "Sing Hoo, we only planned to rest here, but I like this place. Is it safe for us to spend the night?"

"A wonderful idea," enthused Sing Hoo. He had peeked into the main temple and seen that the old monk was so poor he couldn't afford candles to burn at the altar. A shame. This remote location, despite its serene beauty, didn't draw enough travelers. Yes, they would build much good will for this life and the next if they spent the barbarian's cash here.

Fortune gave the monk money for the room and board of his men, then left to explore. By the time he departed two days later he had purchased four hundred tea shrubs. The Taoist monk even dug up a few of his own shrubs and wrapped them in moss and oil paper to protect them from the sun so Fortune would remember his waterfall-covered temple at the Stream of Nine Windings.

Now that Fortune had seen the Wuyi Mountains, he considered his return. The easiest way to transport hundreds of plants plus trunks of flower samples to Foochow was to return the way he came, via the river Min, a four-day journey by boat. As long as no one arrested him as a foreigner illegally traveling beyond a day's journey from the coast, which Li warned him was the case, he itched to explore. He traced a path on a hand-drawn map to the town of Pouching-hien, across the Wuyi Mountains, and down their northern slopes to the province of Chekiang.

Sing Hoo held up the map. "Very interesting, this map. You drew it yourself? Hmmm. I have done this route before with the mandarin." He traced it with a fleshy finger. "It will take four days to go two-hundred-eighty li over a high mountain road to get to Pouching-hien. On the third day after leaving the Wuyi hills, we will be at the foot of a high range of mountains and the source of the river Min." He handed it back. "You will see a different China as we ascend those mountains."

"That's the way we will return." The tea thief's back tingled and his heart beat faster at the thought that he would be the first Westerner to search out the rare flora and fauna of these lands.

They traveled cautiously, alert for tigers and wild boar in the dense woods of lancet-leaved pine and deep green firs that covered the mountains beyond the Wuyi. Streams flew over rocky precipices and showered them with mist. They were lost in a jungle of eighty-foot pines before they met the waters of the Min. Flocks of red bill pies, light-blue with long tail feathers tipped in white, flew across the ravines with their tails spread. Jays, pheasants, partridges, and woodcocks perched high in the trees. Heavy clouds rolled in as the sun sunk towards the horizon and doused them with rain that fell steady and hard. Their thunderous pounding was deafening by the time Sing Hoo led them to an inn.

The porters and coolies who had traveled with them from the Wuyi Mountains were now eager to get off this wild and lonely mountain road. Soaked and exhausted, they would return home to their villages as soon as they were paid.

Sing Hoo watched his protégé and puffed with satisfaction from having transformed the *bak gwei*. What great tales he had to tell his grandchildren about the barbarian Robert Fortune, the white ghost who thought that by changing his outward man to Sing Wa, no Chinese could tell he was a red beard, a foreign devil. What about his big, long nose? His pale eyes the color of a cloud just before the spring rains? His long face, hairy hands, and skin the color of rice?

Wah, Sing Hoo thought, what I must do to make a living. He had served a great mandarin to the Emperor. And now this barbarian paid what he asked, went where he told him, and did as he advised. Sing Hoo looked up at the towering mountains and thought how much better to walk the great Wuyi Mountains and enjoy the hospitality of innkeepers and monks than hustle for work in the city to support his dutiful wife, parents, grandparents, and five children.

Yes, he was a good guide, a wonderful guide. Even the barbarian admitted that his travels had gone much easier since Sing Hoo entered his employ.

"That's because I immediately explain to all the innkeepers that Sing Wa is a mandarin from beyond the Great Wall," Sing Hoo had explained. He looked at the Scot to be sure he saw how exacting he was as he monitored the coolies carrying Fortune's boxes into the room he had arranged. "You see how the coolies and innkeepers bow with obsequious piety? Very good, yes?"

"But when we walk down the road, even before we get to the inn, why do people bow?" asked Fortune.

"Because I am wearing the yellow livery I wore in service of the Emperor's mandarin. Everyone knows only those of the Imperial Court can wear this shade of yellow. They know I wield great power." Sing Hoo's voice rose triumphantly. "And now, mandarin, you can go to sleep. I will guard your room."

"That's not necessary," protested Fortune. "You can sleep with the coolies."

"No, I do not sleep. I have been trained to be ever vigilant. I trust no one, not even the Buddhist monks we stayed with. Let me tell you how valuable I am." Sing Hoo told him about one city famous for its silk in which the mandarin he served had been bothered by four men who pushed and yelled while they smoked and gambled in the dining hall. "I assured my mandarin that I, Sing Hoo, would guard the mandarin's door myself. The mandarin exclaimed that it was impossible for me to stay up all night. I was steadfast. I did not sleep. The next morning, three of the men paid their bill and left. The innkeeper was puzzled to find that they left a huge trunk. Hoping to find precious tea, silks, or other fine treasures, he opened the box and discovered the body of the fourth man. The victim had died violently."

Sing Hoo raised a meaty fist. "I will protect you from harm. Who knows what can happen to you if men discover you are a white ghost?"

Exhausted and cold, Fortune handed Sing Hoo the cash to settle with the porters and coolies and went to sleep. He woke with a start. His walls shuddered with heavy thuds and angry voices. He pulled his thin blanket tightly around him and recalled the story Sing Hoo had told him about the four travelers at the inn and the one who had been left behind a box. Sing Hoo was outside guarding his room, wasn't he? If Sing Hoo were murdered, Fortune would never find his way home. Westerners weren't supposed to be in this area, so no one would think to look for him here. He pressed his ear to the door and heard Sing Hoo's shouts accompanied by more thuds and screams. He sweated and agonized in the dark. Should he go to Sing Hoo's aid? But what if he got hurt? If Sing Hoo was dead, Fortune might be killed, too.

Desperate to know, he flung open the door. Sing Hoo, his yellow livery askew and torn, had backed against the wall. The coolies and porters who had carried them from the Wuyi Mountains flew at him with fists while others brandished staves. His stout guide fought back with his hands and feet, splattering the opposite wall with his assailants' blood and teeth. Again and again they flew at each other, cursing and screaming like banshees.

Fortune dashed back to his room. He drew out one of his guns. The barrel had rusted shut. He threw it against the wall. Useless. The battle cries escalated. He ran back out. "Stop it." He brandished his unloaded matchlock. "Stop now!"

The most battered coolies held their blackened eyes and bleeding jaws. They shouted, "Tell your man to pay us."

Fortune gripped his gun and waved a clenched fist. "My man paid you." He had given Sing Hoo all the money he owed them.

"He shorts us 300 cash per coolie. He's a cheat!"

"No, I do not keep any money from them," Sing Hoo shouted. His sweaty jaw was clamped like a bulldog, and he crouched in a fighting position ready to take them all on.

Fortune raised his gun to silence them all. "Pay them, Sing Hoo," he thundered. "Pay them what I promised. I'm not going to die for a shilling."

Sing Hoo insisted he had been fair.

"Listen to your master, you old cur," snarled the mob. "Pay up, you cheat. We know you tell him a higher price and pocket the difference."

"I paid what you deserved." Sing Hoo thrust out his jaw.

"Did you pay them the right amount?" Fortune demanded. Sing Hoo looked away. "Pay them what we agreed." He stood with his gun across his chest as Sing Hoo handed 300 cash per man. After calm was restored, Fortune yanked him into his room and locked the door. But outside, the coolies and chair bearers continued to grumble. Sing Hoo leaned against the door and ground his teeth, moaning over every detail of their plot to ambush him the minute he left Fortune's room.

Between his coolies and chair bearers plotting against Sing Hoo and the sickeningly sweet fumes from the dozen opium smokers who had been awakened by the melee and were now chasing the dragon's tail next door, Fortune couldn't breathe or think. He would never get any sleep now. At dawn, the exhausted Scot rolled off his cot and sent Sing Hoo to hire coolies and chair-bearers to take him over the Wuyi Mountains to Chekiang.

At midday, Sing Hoo returned alone. "I went to every inn, every tea house. Every man we hired already spread the word through town not to work for the white devil," he moaned. "I try hard, offered to pay up front, but no one will work for us."

"Are you sure you went everywhere?"

"Even across town to the furthest inn, to the poorest section of town."

Fortune fumed, "It's no use trying to get a chair and coolies here." They had to move on.

Sing Hoo's round face sagged with remorse. It had started to rain while he went from inn to inn looking for men to hire. Now the streets were flooded. Fortunately, on the way back he purchased a couple of strong stout bamboo poles and had figured a way to carry all the loads himself.

Fortune looked disgustedly at the solid curtain of rain. Even wrapped as snugly as possible and huddled under his umbrella, he knew he would get soaked. But Sing Hoo, his legs bowed from the load he balanced across his shoulders, shouted, "I can manage. I'll take you to Chekiang as you wish. I am a good guide. Follow me. I know the way."

Stranded days away from Shanghai with hundreds of tea shrubs that needed to be properly planted, seeds that needed to be kept dry, and a collection of dead birds, Fortune had no choice but to splash through the deluge and follow. Their only hope was to find an inn to hire coolies and a chair. By the time they stepped out the water was up to their waist. A mile out of town, Sing Hoo's bamboo poles snapped.

"No, not now!" Fortune stomped concentric waves of mud in all directions. Watching his trunks, plant boxes, and clothes bob in the muddy water, he understood why a man might kill. They were in the middle of a flooded rice field with no buildings or people in sight. He lifted his arms in consternation. "Why? Why, Lord? Why now?"

Unfazed, Sing Hoo squinted through the rain. "Sir!" He pointed up the road to a shed. "Look, a shelter. Towns build them to accommodate travelers, just like us. Come, we'll take your things there. You will stay dry. I will go to the next town for coolies and a chair. I am a good guide."

With great trepidation but no other alternative, Fortune followed. He stuck his head into the shelter and staggered backwards. The most pitiful beggars had crammed into the shed for the night, each exuding a more odious stink. He kicked at a few to move so he could get in. While Sing Hoo ran to the next town, he wrapped his coat tight around himself to keep off the lice and vermin and tried hard not to breathe. If Sing Hoo could not get a chair and coolies, he would have to walk over the pass on foot. He would have to leave his luggage behind, including the best tea shrubs he had just obtained from the Wuyi. Why? Why hadn't he gone down the river Min to Foochow? That was the way he had come so why did he insist on returning a 'different way?' He dropped his head in his hands and despaired of his hubris. If Sing Hoo never returned, knowing how angry he had made Fortune, he would never find his way back to the coast. He didn't even know exactly where he was.

Sing Hoo did not return that night. Nor the next day. Night fell and Fortune followed the darkness into despair. He dragged through another sleepless night. Still it rained, constant and heavy with no break in sight.

Another day passed. No Sing Hoo appeared. Fortune buried his head deeper in his coat. Sing Hoo would not return. He knew Fortune wanted to kill him. Fortune would die in China, his body unclaimed. He was stranded somewhere in the middle of China.

The next day his spirits sunk lower. Thirst and hunger was the least of his worries now. Many long hours later when his hope had disappeared with the sun, he heard splashing steps. He stepped out expecting to be disappointed.

"Sing Hoo! Sing Hoo," he rejoiced. "You returned with coolies and a chair." He raced out into the rain; his steps created waves that soaked him even more but he didn't care. The coolies lifted Fortune's trunks from the mud and porters hoisted the Scot on their shoulders. Up they climbed, through narrow mountain roads chiseled in the steep mountains, through mountain passes with towers, past sharp-eyed guards in leather and bronze. Up, up up.

At the peak of the last pass, Fortune could not bear to leave without looking for the last time at the Wuyi Mountains, the pinnacle of his adventure.

Thirty-Four

ALISTAIR MACKENZIE, APRIL 1850

SHANGHAI

Sweat and steam wrapped Shanghai that April day when Fortune returned. After months of threshing his own paths through mountainous vegetation and scrambling up and down steep terrain, the ease of civilization confused his senses. He walked the packed dirt roads and stared at the homes, teahouses, and stores. He didn't even bother to look his countrymen in the eye to see if they recognized him. He knew they wouldn't. He didn't care. All he wanted was to store his treasures behind the high walls of Alistair Mackenzie's garden, where he had the privacy to prepare his plants and seeds and birds for London.

Mackenzie's servant Tu, clad in an immaculate gray cotton robe, opened the door. Fortune waved in his porters as he usually did. "No, no," Tu commanded. He held out his hand to stop the dusty procession of dozens of men bearing plant boxes, trunks, and bundles tied with bamboo twine. "Come," he motioned the porters. He led them through the side gate to the garden. "Put them here," he pointed to a small area not covered by plants or pots. Then he pointed to Fortune. "You, please, come this way." He left Fortune in the foyer and left to fetch Mr. Mackenzie.

Fortune frowned. His friend was getting peculiar in his old age. There was not a weed, brown leaf, or wilted bloom in his entire yard. Obviously, he had hired a gardener who had changed the space into a properly landscaped garden. In the house, the windows, flung wide-open, took him aback. A breeze stirred the floor-sweeping velvet drapes in the parlor. The dining table, normally cluttered with porcelains, jades, cloisonné, and other fine antiques Mackenzie and Fortune had collected, was cleared. A single figurine of blue and white porcelain was reflected in the highly polished surface.

He ran his hand along the mantle. Not a speck of dust anywhere.

"Fortune, you've returned. Welcome back," Mackenzie bellowed. He held his arms out in welcome. "You are in disguise as a long-haired English-Chinese person again." He laughed at his own joke. Alistair himself smelled scrubbed and sun-dried; his shirt and trousers were pressed, and his blond hair was cut short and neatly combed.

"I knew you wouldn't mind if I bunked with you for a few months. The porters put my boxes in your garden," said Fortune. "You must have hired a chef. You've got a belly on you. And it looks like you've got a valet, too."

"I've made many changes. But let's see what you've brought." Mackenzie good-naturedly headed out to his garden followed by an anxious Fortune who eagerly opened his boxes to share his treasures with his friend. "Good God, what's this?" Mackenzie bent down and ran his finger over the leaves.

"No," Fortune shouted. He swatted away his friend's hands. "No. Sorry. Never touch the tips. Those are the leaves they use to make tea. Sorry, old boy. Delicate plants." He lowered his voice. "*Thea bohea*. From the black tea district of the Wuyi Mountains."

Mackenzie nodded. "I should have guessed. Forbidden territory." He laughed heartily as he dusted off his hands and clasped his friend's shoulder. "Well, my garden's yours, as you know." He tucked his chubby thumbs into his vest and puffed his chest. "My wife and children will join me in celebrating your return."

"Wife?" Fortune stared at his friend with an astonished look.

"I've maintained a separate household for her so I can keep up appearances at the Consulate, but then I thought, why pay double when she can take care of me here? Plus, we have two children now. It's good to have a strong father figure for the bairn, you know."

"Mackenzie!" Fortune sputtered.

"Every British trader here has a Chinese wife, Fortune. You know that no one here's a saint. Surely for all the years you've been in China, even if you're a Lutheran…"

"No, I haven't." The delicate image of Jadelin flashed before him. He had thought of her as something he might 'collect' like a rare peony. He hadn't thought of her in that vulgar way. She was different, a rare and beautiful specimen. "Anyway, I'm leaving. No plans to return."

"You've been here since Captain Balfour opened up Shanghai in 1843. You said you wouldn't be back the last time. You'll return sooner or later. A woman would soften those crusty edges of yours. Sai-lin has made an honest man of me."

"But you have a wife and daughters in England."

Mackenzie leaned in and confided with a satisfied chuckle. "In China, a man can have as many wives as he can afford. It's a sign of prosperity. We were married Chinese style."

"You're a Christian."

"Aren't we all?" Mackenzie shook his head at his friend's attitude. China changed everyone it touched. Fortune had changed more than he could imagine, probably more than he dared admit. When Fortune donned a Chinese robe, he acted differently, as if he considered himself part of that civilization, more sophisticated and learned than the Englishman he was.

At dinner, Fortune stiffly nodded to Sai-lin, a porcelain-skinned beauty. She was gentle with Mackenzie and the children. She and the children wore pretty embroidered tunics and trousers, she in somber hues, a contrast against her fair skin, while the children wore playful colors and embroidered hats with tiger faces. The children had a fetching combination of features. The girl, almost two, had a hint of her father's blond hair, his round eyes and her mother's rosebud lips. The boy, now

THE Perfect TEA THIEF

three, was a mischievous tyke who resembled his mother except he had his father's startling blue eyes. Fortune tried not to stare. There were scores of Chinese-British children in Shanghai.

His eyes were drawn to an exquisite jade in the shape of a lock which hung from the boy's neck. He looked up to see Mackenzie's eyes on him with an amused look on his face.

Mackenzie nodded at his son. "Boys from the all the wealthy families wear jade locks to 'lock them to earth.' You know the mortality for bairn, even in England. The carving on the lock symbolizes the family's wishes. We wish him prosperity and a long life."

Fortune turned down his lips. "Isn't that heathen superstition?"

"Not at all," answered Mackenzie. He smiled indulgently at his son. "It's what all parents, British or Chinese, wish for their children."

Over the next few days, Fortune watched how Mackenzie cradled his daughter in his arms and how he ruffled the shiny black hair of his son when they played ball. As the weeks went on they seemed as normal as any British family. At the table, bread and butter were served with bowls of steaming Chinese-style vegetables and meats and rice. They ate family style with chopsticks. The children spoke English to their father, Chinese to their mother, and they acted better behaved than any of his schoolmates. Would this be the family life he would have had if he and Jadelin...? No, he could never imagine. He was a confirmed bachelor with a nomadic life. But against all reason, Jadelin continued to haunt him with the scent of silk in the freshest morning breeze and the glow of each dawn.

❧

Tu unlocked the garden gate for Sing Hoo who entered with porters bearing lumber and glass. He gestured them to proceed to where a carpenter and his assistants studied the drawings Fortune laid out before them. Sing Hoo in his yellow livery found a cool spot in the shade where he stood with his hands clasped behind his back.

"These cases must be airtight and watertight," the Scot admonished the workers. They assured him they would be built as he instructed. But he hovered so close to the men, every time they reached for a tool they bumped into him and muttered a string of Chinese curses.

Mackenzie stepped out in the garden to see what his friend was up to. "Fortune, you're only in their way." He motioned him to join him in the shade of a flowering magnolia where he held a pinwheel aloft with one hand and with the other, clasped his son's hand. "The craftsmen know what they're doing better than you do. Your man can supervise, can't he?" He knelt down and held the pinwheel so that it caught the wind and twirled with a whistling sound. His son's fat cheeks shook with laughter, which delighted his father so much he clasped him to his chest and covered his face with kisses.

Fortune joined his friend and son at the table Tu had set with tea-cups and tea. He unbuttoned the top button of his starched shirt and wiped his brow with a clean white handkerchief. It was good to be back in civilization, especially when he could have a houseboy like Tu to tend to his needs, he sighed.

"So tell me, what did you discover on your expedition?" Mackenzie turned to Tu to thank him as he prepared the tea and poured cups for each. He lifted his tea to his lips, inhaled the aroma, and smiled with satisfaction. "Did you find the black tea plants and the green tea plants?"

"I did," Fortune smiled at his triumph. "I found the *Thea bohea* that produces the black tea and the *Thea viridis* that produces the green."

"Now that you have the plants, how do you propose turning them into tea?"

"I observed how the Chinese manufacture tea. We can replicate the process in our Indian colonies."

"Do you have the tea masters? The specialized instruments, woks, and ovens they use? Who in India has the expertise and skill?"

Fortune waved his hand to dismiss the concern. "I'll find the best, the absolutely best tea masters in China to teach the natives in India. I've been advised that the most experienced and skilled tea masters come from the Lion area of West Lake, an area I have not been able to explore. Since these tea masters are loyal, it will not be easy to hire them away. Plus, they must bring their equipment so we can duplicate them."

"Do you have a plan?"

"My man, Sing Hoo, has certain tokens of power from his previous employer." He nodded his head towards Sing Hoo, who stood with a regal air over the carpenters. "I've asked him to take care of it," Fortune harrumphed. Sing Hoo was only too happy to do him the favor, for a fee, of course. On the other hand, the success of this task was a way for his man to redeem his reputation. The Scot put down his tea and eyed his workers' progress. "But first, I need to get the plants and seeds I collected into good loam. Last year all the seeds I sent to India failed to germinate. However, some of seeds I planted between seedlings germinated by the time they reached the Himalayas."

"How are you getting them to India?" Mackenzie had seen Fortune hunched over the dining table for hours studying the routes. No ship had a poop deck large enough to accommodate the number of plant boxes he planned to build.

"Captain Landers is taking the lot to Hong Kong. From there I'll send them to Calcutta via four different vessels." He had calculated the distances and times and allowed for vagaries in weather and sea conditions. He had chosen four ships, each traversing a different route which increased his probability of success. He turned towards the house. "Tu," he called.

"Mr. Fortune." Tu approached from the house and bowed. His chest and arms were now muscled and he had developed into a handsome young man with high cheekbones which imparted an aristocratic air.

"Tu, I have another letter to send to England. I can't afford to have Sing Hoo leave right now. We are in a rush to finish."

"Of course, sir." Tu bowed and tucked the letters under his arm. He was on his way to the Poe estate anyway, since he and Paul were spending the afternoon in the country with friends, sons of rich mandarins. Mandarin Poe compensated him generously for the letters Fortune wrote to Mackenzie. He would be pleased to read these.

Thirty-Five

SIGHTING THE TEA THIEF

LONGJING MOUNTAINS

*S*hanli, the eldest Mow brother, raced his horse to the grower whose tea gardens bordered his. Their families had been neighbors for more than ten generations and, like all the tea-growing families in West Lake, protective of their lands, people, and plants. While walking his lands one afternoon, his neighbor had spied a stocky figure in bright yellow, arms akimbo, surveying the lands from a mountain lookout as if he owned them. Shanli was now seeking the source of the rumors circulating around the West Lake district that this stranger was walking from village to village in the yellow livery of the Emperor. This outsider had approached the most noted tea growers and asked who the finest tea masters were. Just for their promise to come with him, the interloper offered many strings of cash--a hundred times what growers paid their workers--and many more bags of cash once they started work in India.

SHANGHAI

John Poe held the reins of his prancing horse with one hand and pounded on the barred gates of the hong with his fist. As the guards

swung open the gates, he stamped the dust off his leather leggings sending up clouds of loess that clung everywhere, from his forehead to the
back of his leather tunic.

Benjamin Poe leapt down from his aerie. "John! We were worried."
His thick eyebrows twitched like fuzzy caterpillars and his ebony gaze
seared into his brother's eyes. Every day he had scrutinized the incoming roads until he intimately knew every clod of dirt that blew in with
every traveler, coolie, and dog.

John Poe unbuckled his saddlebags and handed the reins of his frothing
horse to one of the guards. "I have ridden him hard for a month. Groom
and feed him well." He asked his brother in a low voice, "Is Baba here?"

"With business grown a hundred fold and so many foreigners in
Shanghai, he does loathe to leave." He lowered his voice. "Baba's presence, even lacking his normal vigor, reassures our clients."

John frowned. "We need to talk."

"We'll meet in Daniel's office. I'll get Baba and Paul." Because he
handled money, Daniel's office was isolated and secure. Mandarin Poe
could no longer manage the climb up to Benjamin's aerie so they chose
his office for their meetings.

Unlike Benjamin and John, men of constant action, Daniel preferred
the solitude of his accounting table where he tallied shipments and sales,
debts and payments, from dawn to dusk. He reminded everyone of a
tall gray crane. Despite his quiet manner he was as good-natured as his
plump wife. He smiled quietly when his brothers teased that he had
the most children—twelve—and tolerated their jokes about 'still waters
running deep.' He prided himself on being dependable and accurate,
able to track trends and anticipate changes in the tea market and their
clients. His children had all married before they were sixteen, thanks
to his late mother's astute matchmaking. His sons worked under his
brother Benjamin in security and logistics, an aspect of their business
that had grown more critical.

"Baba!" John strode quickly to his father's side as soon as he entered.

Mandarin Poe, leaning on Benjamin's thick arm for support, grasped
his Sixth Son's shoulders. The brothers had written that their father had

been so worried, he had not slept soundly during his youngest son's absence. Every delicacy Mei enticed him with to build his health and rejuvenate his strength soured his stomach. His lusterless skin sagged with the weight of his worry. His silk robes hung from shoulders that used to ripple with powerful muscles. John lowered his voice and asked, "Baba, what is this sadness on your face?" He wanted to hug him to his chest and infuse him with his own youthful energy.

Mandarin Poe clasped John's face between his rough hands. "Every day without you I worried." John winced to feel how his father's once-powerful hands shivered like autumn's leaves. "Your brothers assured me you were safe, but when barbarians attack the power of the Celestial Empire, no one in China is safe. Any perceived slight brings immediate unequal retaliation. We live in fear within our own borders."

"Fop See Wong made this tea for you from his own plants. It will rejuvenate your ch'i."

Daniel cleared his table and set out five glazed Chinese tea cups decorated with an over glaze of brown mottles from the celebrated kilns of Jingde, part of their collection of Song Dynasty tea cups. He held out a chair and the four brothers helped seat their father before joining him. They relished this rare private moment together.

"I'm seventy-two this year," began their father. He thumped his chest with a clenched fist. "I feel my days grow short. So I apologize for skipping the pleasantries and asking after your health and long trip, my son. I know if there is anything I need to be concerned about, you will be truthful. Tell me what you learned."

John bowed his head and took a fortifying breath. He would not cushion the bad news. "Mow Bowli told me tea bearers up and down the tea route from the Wuyi Mountains have sighted Robert Fortune and his guide Sing Hoo."

Paul's finely arched eyebrows lifted. "That's more than four days' journey inland," he exclaimed.

John turned to his brother who shared a keen interest in the Westerners. "When he wants to, his 'outward man' is Chinese. He dresses like a Chinese, speaks our language, and imitates the walk of his man

Sing Hoo. The inland people have not seen many Westerners. His man tells everyone that his master is from 'beyond the Great Wall.'" John's gaze slowly swept his brothers. "He purchased thousands of tea plants and shipped them to Hong Kong. Now he seeks the best tea masters who can transform the leaves into tea. And he has offered to buy all the tools to make tea."

"He wants our tea masters too?" groaned Mandarin Poe. He rubbed his furrowed brow and shook his head as he searched his son's eyes for answers.

"His man Sing Hoo boasted that he could have easily gotten such men from the coast. But Fortune wants only the best; he has sent Sing Hoo to find the most experienced tea masters."

The men of Poe sipped the tea that exuded the smoky undertones and rich flavor of the green tea that was processed into tiny pearls. It should have had the power to sooth their troubled hearts and give them hope. But all they could taste was disaster.

Thirty-Six

THE FINAL SWEEP, DECEMBER 1850

SHANGHAI

*W*inter in Shanghai was infinitely warmer and more comfortable now that Sai-lin and the children lived with Alistair Mackenzie. Fortune grumbled about the open windows and fresh air. He complained about how much bother it was to watch his manners in front of the bairn. Yet, Fortune had to concede that his accommodations were the best he enjoyed in China. Sai-lin had had all the windows glazed with glass for the health of the children, and her chef served belly-warming meals with the freshest ingredients from the markets.

One overcast day when Sai-lin and the children played in the garden wrapped in furs, Yu received a letter for Fortune which he discreetly read before handing it to the Scot.

"Alastair, I have word from India," Fortune exclaimed. Sai-lin and the children ran in to hear what the men were shouting about. The children were frightened, at first, to see their father's tall, awkward friend literally dancing around their parlor. "They received my plants."

Alistair looked up from his month-old British newspaper.

Fortune shook the letter in his hand. "It's from Dr. Falconer of Calcutta and Dr. Jameson in Allahabad. My tea plants arrived in Calcutta.

They asked that I come immediately with Chinese who can teach the Indians how to turn the leaves into proper tea."

Now that the end was in sight, Fortune, accompanied by Mackenzie, would scour the shops for the finest antiques and crate them up.

Yu ran to the Poe tea hong to deliver the news to Paul Poe.

Sing Hoo sent word that he had found the best tea masters, men knowledgeable in the art of manipulating tea leaves. They were the best, absolutely the best men to be found in China's finest tea growing area. Also, Sing Hoo would collect all their implements for the manufacture of tea.

Fortune prepared to pack his plants, meet Sing Hoo and his tea masters in Ningpo, and proceed to India.

LONGJING MOUNTAINS

"An outrage! Call the men!" Shanli's shouts startled the household awake. Mow Bowli and Jadelin quickly dressed and ran to the main hall where Shanli, Chongli, and their wives gathered with Wu, their senior tea master. What could infuriate the eldest Mow brother, the paragon of control? Within minutes their trusted supervisors ran panting into the hall.

"In the middle of the night. Eight men. Their families, their tools, all gone," Wu roared. A husky man bronzed by the drying and processing of tea, his family had worked with the Mows for five generations. His eight tea masters, linked by bloodlines and marriages, had proven themselves through the labor-intensive fires of tea production. They were distinguished by faces stained from roasting tea leaves, lungs filled with the scent of smoke, and leather-like hands thickened and stained by hand-rolling leaves into specialized shapes from gunpowder pellets to perfect pearls. These prized tea masters, choosing a lull between harvests when they would be least missed, had stripped their homes with no intention of returning. "My supervisors were busy all day cleaning out the tea sheds to be sure they were ready for the next harvest. At the end of the day, we noticed no cooking fires from the ridge where our tea masters live. We went to see what could be the problem." He thundered, "What evil could have made them disappear?"

Bowli rubbed his pensive brow. For a number of days he sensed restlessness and anxiety creep into the normally convivial conversations in the teahouses and disturb the rhythms that usually dominated their peaceful agrarian villages. Could it be that the further the British, French, Russians, Dutch, and Americans intruded into China the more they disturbed the ch'i of the land and people? He worried that soon China would be on its knees, helpless, and at the mercy of the Westerners. How could the stranger from the north convince their loyal men to leave the work they had done their entire lives? The answer had to be strings of cash and golden promises.

Chongli bowed his head and rubbed his furrowed brow. He felt especially responsible because he had trained the tea masters who left. Their departure was his fault, because of something he had done or not done.

Shanli reassured Chongli that they could train others. They had succeeded for a thousand years and would survive for a thousand more. No, Chongli and Wu were determined to get their tea masters back; they possessed the Mow family's tea secrets. They would leave immediately.

"Stay with the children. I must see what I can do," Bowli whispered to his wife.

"No, there's nothing you can do to change things," Jadelin pleaded. "Money has more influence than tradition, loyalty, and honesty." But she saw sadness and resolve in the depth of his eyes. She grabbed his hands and felt his smooth calluses as she pressed them to her cheeks. He enveloped her fingers in his.

"We need those men. They have our tea and our secrets in their blood. At least I can try, my dearest. I will appeal to their honor." He cupped her face in his hands. "Don't cry, my love. You are my life and heart, my soul and spirit. I carry the teaching of Grand Master Ping with me. I shall be safe."

Jadelin put her fingers on his beating heart. Her eyes never left his. "I will always be here," she promised. Then she placed his hands on the swell of her belly. "We wait for your return."

His laugh was low. "I was wondering when you'd finally tell me." He lifted her tunic to kiss the roundness he had felt a week before. But he hadn't said a word because he knew how superstitious women were about showing too much happiness. There were too many legends about gods who would, in a fit of jealousy, take away the source of a person's joy.

After Bowli left with Shanli and Wu in a thunder of horse hooves, Jadelin lit a lantern and walked out into their courtyard. She looked up at the moon, an almost-full orb set in an ebony sky. She closed her eyes and remembered one evening when Bowli, his arms around her shoulders, recited a poem of how the moon lit her face with the stars of heaven. She remembered his warm musky scent, how smooth his body felt against hers. Then she sensed a movement. She whirled around.

Mow Chow Ching strode towards her from the children's bedrooms and raised his hand in greeting.

She bowed. "Father-in-law." She wondered when he had arrived.

He held a finger to his lips. "I saw my grandchildren. They are sleeping well." He looked fit and trim for a stout brick of a man. He was wearing the simple tunic of a sage and carried only his staff with the core of iron. His voice resonated strong and serious. "Jadelin, these are bad times. I came to tell you to be strong for your children's sake."

What could be worse than what had already happened? The house of Mow had lost their tea masters and three good men had gone after them.

"Mow Chow Ching, tell me. Tell me what I must be prepared for."

She felt his hard hands when he grasped her shoulders. His breath brushed her neck when he leaned towards her, his head bowed. "Jadelin, I do not know the future. But if and when you need us, you know where you can find me and your grandfather."

"I doubt I shall ever need to run to you. I have the finest husband in Mow Bowli. He gives me everything my heart needs. I am more than content. But I thank you for your concern." She saw the glow of starlight radiate from his eyes.

He nodded sagely. "My heart rests."

"Mow Chow Ching," Jadelin shouted as he turned and walked away. "Where are you going?" Her candle didn't even flicker when he dissolved into the ether.

NINGPO

Sing Hoo's recruits each carried a bundle of new clothes when they sauntered onto the junk to meet up with Fortune. Their families, who would accompany them to Ningpo where they would bid farewell, were the only ones allowed to carry their precious tea making tools. They felt this was an honor for these golden sons would regularly send home mountains of cash to compensate for their absence. Yes, Sing Hoo had promised that their extraordinary talents were needed and their pay would reflect how much they were appreciated. It was a small sacrifice to make because their families would be rich with more than enough rice for all. In no time, the tea masters would return home with so much gold they would never need to work again. Sing Hoo had promised.

Shanli and Bowli's ship was so fast they were tied up before Sing Hoo's junk arrived at Ningpo. The brothers had discussed what each would say to the eight tea masters. They would appeal to their honor, loyalty, and trust. They promised no recrimination or shame; it was natural that they would consider the financial welfare of their families over their own sacrifice of working in a distant land. The three waited.

As soon as Sing Hoo disembarked to fetch Fortune, they boarded the junk.

The errant tea masters cried when they saw Shanli, Bowli, and Wu. They begged forgiveness for they now saw the mistake of their decision. Shanli promised passage for them and their families back to West Lake on his junk; there was room for all. "Quick, follow me. To save face, we will depart before Sing Hoo returns and asks for an explanation. He will not be pleased."

The tea masters thanked the Mows for their forgiveness and quickly herded their families towards the gangway.

But Sing Hoo and Fortune returned too soon.

"Who are you?" Sing Hoo demanded. He stood arms akimbo in his yellow livery, his big feet planted far apart, blocking their passage.

A frown creased Mow Bowli's brow. He remembered Fortune from their meeting years ago in Shanghai. He thought the Scot looked jittery and anxious. He addressed him directly in a calm voice. "I am Mow Bowli, Jadelin's husband. These eight tea masters and their ancestors have worked for my family for many generations. They thank you for your offer, but they have changed their mind. My brother Shanli and senior tea master Wu have come to take them home." He gestured to his brother and Wu.

"Never," shouted Sing Hoo. "I am Sing Hoo. I have worked for a mandarin and for Sing Wa who travels from beyond the Great Wall." He whipped out his yellow flag and waved it in their faces. "These are my men now."

Fortune looked from Sing Hoo to Mow Bowli. "Sing Hoo, what did you promise these men? They gave their consent, didn't they?" He remembered how Sing Hoo had deceived the porters and coolies in Wuyi.

Sing Hoo nodded, "Of course, they did."

"I'm sorry, Sing Hoo. We must leave now. Goodbye, Mr. Fortune." Mow Bowli turned and gestured to those who wished to follow him.

Sing Hoo's face turned crimson and puffy. He noticed how powerfully Mow Bowli moved, that his chest was broad, and his arms and legs were long and muscled. He was a superior adversary, and Sing Hoo could not hope to win against him. He whipped out one of Fortune's guns that he had taken for its visual power. "I'll shoot anyone who leaves." He waved it wildly.

Fortune turned to his man. "Shoot! One shot in the air. That will frighten him," he ordered. Time was short. Landers was waiting and ready to sail on the tide.

Mow Bowli held out his hands in peace. Calmly, he said. "Please, put down the gun. We do not wish anyone to get hurt." He turned to his men. "Anyone who wishes to follow me may do so. I keep my promise to you. You know the honor of the house of Mow. I understand if any of you wish to go with Mr. Fortune." He approached to pass Fortune and Sing Hoo.

Sing Hoo felt the weight of the gun in his hand. He had never fired such a weapon, but Fortune had shown him how it worked, and he had seen the barbarian drop birds from the sky. He waved it again and grasped it with two hands to fire a warning shot. The kick threw him off balance, and he dropped his hands.

∾

*F*or the rest of his life, the tea thief would see the bloody nightmare replay over and over again. Mow Bowli, handsome and strong, approached him with steady eyes and a resolute jaw. The next minute, his broad torso was covered with a red blot that grew so large it covered his body. The air was filled with the smell of death.

There was so much blood.

Rivers of blood covered the deck.

Fortune closed his eyes to blot out the sight of so much red.

Shanli and Wu shoved Fortune and Sing Hoo aside. Tenderly, they carried Mow Bowli off the ship with remonstrations for him to stay in this world.

The tea masters and their families screamed and wailed. The air reverberated with their shrieks. Sing Hoo raised the gun again. It felt hot and powerful, like anger and victory. The eight tea masters and their families cowered against the far side of the junk, as far from him as they could shrink. But they did not stop their deafening howls.

Fortune bellowed, "Sing Hoo!" What had he done? No, it was Sing Hoo's fault. Sing Hoo was guilty. Terrified, the Scot ran. His bloody footprints glistened in the sun.

The tea masters and their families clung to each other and cried as if they were being dragged to hell. Grandparents, wives, and children begged their men not to go. Their goodbyes were taking so long that finally Sing Hoo, who had not said a word until now, gave a command and his crew, who had boarded to see what caused their delay, tore the new recruits from their families' embrace.

∾

*M*ow Bowli lay in Dr. Chang's surgery at his home in Ningpo. Although Dr. Chang rarely used the room in retirement, he had kept it fully equipped. The good doctor traced his patient's strong jaw, the smooth skin of a very handsome face. The young man looked like he was sleeping, unperturbed and calm, at peace with himself and the world. But his wound was massive, the blood loss great.

"We should have run faster! We could have saved him." Shanli wept and tore at his clothes and hair.

"No, you did the best you could. He died instantly. The coward shot him at close range; the damage is enormous." Dr. Chang patted the two men on the shoulder and asked his daughters to take them out to a quiet spot where they could grieve. He would prepare the body for its return home. Jadelin should not see her husband torn apart like this. He thought of her saucy smile, how the faint tinkle of bells on her hem announced her movements. She didn't deserve to see such violence, such hate.

Overcome by sorrow, Dr. Chang lowered his head and wept. He had always felt that the human body was one of the most beautiful creations, one filled with majesty and mystery. During the Opium War he had seen how English guns could rip apart such perfection, and he had learned to steel his soul against the horror. But not Jadelin. She would never understand how any man could destroy her lover, the father of her children, her husband. He would put Mow Bowli together and dress him in the finest silk robes before he sent him home to his wife.

Thirty-Seven

BOWLI'S FAREWELL

LONGJING MOUNTAINS

*M*ow Bowli! Jadelin suddenly awoke and, feeling his presence, reached out for him in the darkness. Was he home so soon, she wondered? Her hand touched his pillow. It was cool. She tossed aside her quilt, slid open her chamber door, and followed the full moon out to the garden. She lifted her head and listened to the tall bamboo groves moaning and rustling as it bent to the night wind.

"Mow Bowli, my darling, you've returned." Outlined by the light of the full moon, her husband entered the garden lit by a canopy of stars. She ran laughing to him with open arms. The garden stones were cold on her bare feet but her heart was glad and warm.

"Jadelin, my love, my life." His voice was comforting and sad. He wrapped his arms around her and clasped her to his heart. They bodies rocked back in forth, in harmony and emotion.

His passionate kisses made her gasp for breath.

He held her tight. "I'm sorry. I can't stay."

"But you're here. Don't scare me, Bowli. You said you'd love me forever." She nestled her face into her favorite spot between his neck and the curve of his shoulder. She ran her hands down his broad chest, feeling his heat. "Come to bed, my darling." She longed for him, the closeness of his body and the intensity of their love. They would be wrapped in each other's arms like this for the rest of their lives. Together they'd grow old and bent, wrinkled and white-haired, but young in heart with an undying passion.

"Jadelin, listen to me. I will always love you." He lifted her face to his. "You must be strong for both of us. Tell the children I love them."

She saw his eyes, how they twinkled and glowed. His whole body shone, but it wasn't with the heat of his body. Then she knew. "No," she whimpered. "No!" She screamed as his radiance faded in her arms.

"I will love you forever Jadelin, my wife, my heart, my love." His words lingered in the starlight.

"Come back," she wailed. "Come back to me, Bowli." She opened her arms to the moon as if she could catch him. The bamboo grove roared in the wind. She turned around and around looking for him, hoping it was just a trick of the eye. She screamed and screamed until she could breathe no more. Then she ran.

She ran barefoot to the stables and leapt on the back of her Mongolian horse. "Hai," she shouted. "Let's go!" She laid her face against its hot neck. "Faster! Faster," she sobbed. She felt the icy mist close in against her body and relished the pain. She rode long into the night until she arrived at the Dragon Well. "Here, my Mongolian princess, we stop here," she panted.

She slid off her mount and bent over the water. "Bowli, my husband, my love," she sobbed. She gasped for breath as rivers of tears pooled on the water's surface. Her tears, lighter than the dense well water, awakened the dragon that swirled and rose from the depths towards the full moon reflected in the water. The reflected moon glowed like the Pearl of Wisdom the dragon chases for insight and knowledge. She watched, mesmerized. She needed the special powers of this Chinese dragon who could fly through air and swim seas. "Bowli," she moaned, "You promised to return with me to see the dragon chase the Pearl of Wisdom."

She grasped the well's wall when the pain came. "No," she moaned. "No, not now." She bent her head to contain the pressure in her belly.

She gasped when the hotness gushed between her legs. She wailed when she saw the helpless form that would have been her baby in the spreading pool of blood. So impossibly tiny. Already dead.

Everything was wrong. The ch'i of her country, her family, her body, everything was out of balance. This could not be happening to her.

Her Mongolian horse reared back when she caught the scent of blood. The mare flung her hooves in the air, nostrils flaring, eyes wide.

Jadelin reached out a hand. "Go home! Get help," she gasped. The horse snorted and danced nervously, then turned and ran off into the night as if chased by demons, leaving her sobbing, wretchedly alone.

ॐ

"*J*adelin, Jadelin!"

She waved away her sisters-in-laws and turned away from the light.

"Your brothers are here to see you," the voices gently cajoled. She heard them whisper, "She has been wild and inconsolable. We're taking care of the children, giving her time to grieve. She was like a ghost during the funeral. Mow Bowli looked so handsome, as if he was sleeping. She sat by his side during the entire vigil but then, she hasn't been sleeping. It is as if her anger keeps her awake. She sits here in her shuttered room or paces the garden."

With great effort and indifference, Jadelin turned towards the sounds. She peered through the tangles of hair that took too much effort to comb and saw the look of disbelief on giant Benjamin's face. He cleared his throat and harrumphed a few times, unable to speak. She had turned into a shadow, a pale, wasted woman wrapped in an old quilt, the same quilt she and Mow Bowli had cuddled under while sipping tea that first winter in Soochow.

John rushed forward and put his hands on her shoulders as if to confirm it was really her. "Jadelin, what can we do?" His voice shook with worry and tenderness. He wiped the tears from her streaked face with his fingertips. "This is not who you are. This is not Mow Bowli's Jadelin."

"Bowli," she whispered. "Bowli is gone." She crumpled into her brothers' arms. All the fear and anger and sadness welled out of her soul in heartbreaking sobs. She felt Benjamin's huge arms lift her from her chair.

Benjamin cradled her on his lap and rocked her as if she were one of his own children. "How about your dragon babies, Jadelin? They need you, too," he asked, his voice low and sad.

She buried her head in his chest, calmed by the rumble of his sonorous voice. "I lost one. I didn't deserve to keep it. The dragon took it back." She cried until she ran out of breath. Her whole body shivered as she gasped for air.

John stroked her face and hair. "No one can bring Bowli or your baby back. But you have your other children to think of."

She let him untangle the knots in her hair. She had been so wrapped in grief, she couldn't see past her pain.

Benjamin lifted her chin and searched her blood-shot eyes to be sure she understood what he was about to tell her. "Grand Master Ping requests you come to Soochow. It is a place of healing. Mow Chow Ching is there, also. Both need you."

Jadelin, a wasteland of emotions, huddled in his arms. "I don't know what to do anymore. Tell me," she whimpered. Her skinny arms shivered.

Benjamin's voice cracked but he was decisive. "We will take you to Grand Master Ping's." He then asked her sisters-in-law to prepare the children Blossom and Danli and pack their things. He and John would ask Shanli for permission even though he was sure the Mows would agree.

Thirty-Eight

JADELIN RETREATS

SOOCHOW

Grand Master Ping marveled how the full moon had transformed the night into an enchanted landscape of silvered rooftops and trees. How delicate the bridges looked. Even the waterways had turned to jewels. He touched his heart with his right hand and thought of Jadelin. She had arrived broken in spirit, a wisp of energy clutching two frightened children. Her husband's family might have insisted she remain with them, and her natal family in Shanghai could also have asked for her return. She was where she needed to be right now.

He glided silently to his tearoom. The doors had been flung open. On his veranda, where he used to find Jadelin and Mow Bowli, he heard his granddaughter gasp and cry as she tried to practice the art she had once mastered. "Granddaughter," he called softly, "you should rest."

Her whole body shivered when she answered, "No. When I close my eyes, I see Bowli. A red flame is coming out of his chest. I cannot put out the fire, Gung Gung. It burns in my chest now." She wrapped her arms around her chest as if to keep it from shattering.

"You cannot change the past. Only yourself." Widowed at twenty with two young children, she could not control her emotions.

"No, Gung Gung, I like the heat," she answered. Her eyes blazed like meteors.

Ping placed his fingers at the base of her throat as if he held a cup there. He closed his eyes and furrowed his brow until all her negative ch'i glowed in the palm of his hand like a ball of fire. He held it up so she could see it burn. "Now, you will sleep."

∾

Benjamin and John guided their junk towards the dock where Grand Master Ping's students in their blue silks stood ready to grab their lines and tie them off. Wrapped in a dark blue cloak, Mei stood at the bow searching each face. She gasped happily when she saw her father, ageless and vibrant. His black cape billowed behind him like eagle wings as he descended the steps of his compound to greet them. His hands were firm when they grasped his daughter's. "I'm glad you came."

"John and Benjamin must return since there's only the four of them to run the hong, but Flora and the children came to keep Jadelin company."

"I'm not sure she wants company."

"Is she that inconsolable?" She clasped a fist to her chest as if she could feel her daughter's pain within her own heart.

With a gesture, Ping sent his students to help Flora and her children disembark.

Just then three figures flew down the steps to the dock, Jadelin with a child in each arm, and all were in fighting silks.

"What is this?" Benjamin asked. He pinched a flushed cheek that had been sunken and sallow just months before.

"I can sleep now," she said.

"You've returned from the land of shadows."

"I couldn't find my way back. I was so far away."

Mei heard the toughness in her daughter's voice and noticed how her body moved with a new confidence and determination. "Do you remember me?" she asked her grandchildren. She had attended their births in West Lake and prepared all the proper foods for the recuperating new mother, which normally the husband's mother would do. But Bowli's mother had died long ago in a virulent flu epidemic that claimed only seemingly healthy young men and women. Mow Chow Ching, who could have cared for the young mother himself, had asked Mei to take his deceased wife's role for the few months her daughter needed her. After that, Jadelin's place had been in Longjing mountains of West Lake with the Mows just as Mei's was with the Poes in Shanghai.

"Come," said Grand Master Ping. "We will dine properly before your brothers depart. I'm sure you have questions for them."

∾

"*W*ords could not describe my world," said Jadelin. She looked around the tearoom, responding to the faces of her family. Mow Chow Ching had brewed a special tea with recuperative powers, and Jadelin knew better than to ask him where or how he obtained it. He insisted on pouring out the tea himself. As he served he paused to look deep in the eyes of each person as if he were searching their future. When he came to Jadelin, she saw Bowli in his eyes. Then his expression hardened as if to say that now she must, too. She nodded her gratitude and took a deep drink. She continued, "After Bowli said goodbye, only my children kept my mind and soul on this earth. My husband's brothers have lost a brother and eight tea masters, so they struggle to do the task themselves. Mow Shanli allowed me and my children to leave with his blessings. The women cried and begged me to stay. But West Lake, once far from the reach of the barbarians and the Emperor, is not the haven it once was.

"Although I do not have the strength, skill, and philosophical training of Mow Bowli, my husband's spirit inspires me. In my dreams, I repeatedly break my Buddhist vows of charity and nonviolence. My heart thirsts for vengeance against the man who stole our tea shrubs and their secrets that China guarded for over five thousand years." She bowed to Ping. "I'm sorry, grandfather." She lifted her eyes to her brothers. "One day, tea, the heart of our culture, will no longer be ours. China's ch'i is irrevocably and irreversibly shattered. But I will return and take my husband's place."

"You will handle the books and accounts?" asked John. Mow Bowli had kept detailed ledgers of all that went on, a mind-boggling job.

"The Mow brothers taught me every aspect of running the tea farm," she explained. Work overlapped in a small family business like theirs. She was ready to return to West Lake with her children, with the intention of spending their winters, the quiet time on the tea farms, here in Soochow as Mow Bowli used to do.

⟳

"*I* don't know if I should stay or return with you," Flora whispered to John that night. She tucked their little ones into quilts on the floor next to them and returned to his side.

"What do you want to do?" he asked. He parted her robe and ran his hands down her sides.

"Bowli's murder made me realize I could lose you in an eyeblink." She snuggled closer and closed her eyes, inhaling his crisp, wild scent that reminded her of bamboo forests.

"Life is transitory. Nothing is forever." He pressed their naked bodies together and sighed with the pleasure of her silkiness.

She breathed softer as his hands probed her body. "I will stay by your side until my last breath is forced from my body."

John was lost in her now, in the tangle of her ebony hair that blanketed the pillow, the curve of her limbs, and the floral seductiveness of her kisses.

⟳

*J*adelin and Mei watched the Poes's junk skim away across the water, Benjamin at the helm, John at the mast, and Flora sadly waving farewell. Each felt great sadness, but for Jadelin and Mei, much work lay ahead.

Every morning before dawn, Mei and her daughter meditated with all the students in the Great Hall, led by Grand Master Ping and Mow

Chow Ching. As the rays of sunlight touched their shoulders through the open windows, they joined in the dining hall for a communal meal, then chores and studies. Endless drills and practice followed. By the end of the day when the sun turned into an orange orb that touched the horizon, Jadelin was ready for sleep.

Her grandfathers had found an amah for her children, a former student who had been a formidable force in her day. Besides their daily lessons with Ping's students, Butterfly and Danli were tutored in both Chinese and English. As the youngest at the school, they flourished with the attention.

"I have grown soft," Mei admitted to her father. "Taking care of my husband is easier than taking care of my daughter." She carried a tray of hot water and tea into the tearoom. Jadelin and her children were napping. The other students were practicing calligraphy, which strengthened and refined wrist control, in the Great Hall. She took down her teapot and one shaped like a dragon for him. She picked up a teapot in the shape of a crab for Mow Chow Ching, and then looked around, puzzled. "Where's Mow Chow Ching? I saw him sitting next to you when I entered." She narrowed her eyes. "Baba, did he just disappear?"

Grand Master Ping held a fat brush of goat hair chiseled to a fine point, laden with black ink. He put down his brush and nodded. "He had to go." He cleaned his brush and motioned her to sit. "You need to align your ch'i. You are too consumed with domestic matters."

"Baba, my husband needs my care." She deftly poured hot water over the tea.

"Rest and daily training has restored Jadelin's warrior spirit and rebalanced her ch'i. She is developing into a formidable force, on par with her father and husband. She possesses an inner vision that drives her energy."

"Greater than me?" She sat next to him, nestling the steaming tea in her hands. Pleased, she closed her eyes and inhaled the fragrance. All parents hope their children fulfill their potential, exceeding their parents' accomplishments.

"My daughter, tragedy has lit an unquenchable fire within her which drives her now."

Mei shuddered. "I would not wish for that tragedy."

Her father shook his head. "It is her fate. Benjamin advised me of the situation in Shanghai. It is time for you and your husband to leave business matters to your capable sons." He drank his tea and pondered all that Benjamin and John had told him.

"Tell me, Baba. You know what will happen."

"You need to ask Mow Chow Ching."

Thirty-Nine

THE UNSEASONABLE STORM

Sing Hoo nervously paced the deck of Landers' ship. He wasn't alone; it seemed as if the entire ship was morose and anxious. Fortune, who no longer talked to him, had locked himself in Landers' cabin for the entire trip to Hong Kong except to check on his plants eight times a day. The eight tea masters, who got seasick as soon as they headed out to sea, avoided Sing Hoo and Fortune as if they were marked by the plague.

Captain Landers, who relished the foulest weather as much as he delighted in a fair wind, did not like this passage to Hong Kong. It had started badly when his helmsman broke out with red pustules that oozed green pus the day before they were set to sail.

As soon as his sick crewman was carried off the ship another junk, captained by a friend who had raced Landers up and down China's coast for decades, limped into port. A freak storm had overpowered their sails and snapped his wooden mast. His helmsman had masterfully brought the ship to port where it would remain at least a month for repairs.

Quickly, Landers hired away his friend's helmsman, a squat, squarely built man who looked neither young nor old, but carried with him the air of a sage. The captain thought it curious that his new helmsman always wore a set of small daggers strapped to his thigh.

"Bah," Landers grumbled when he sighted their course the first day out. "The seas shouldn't be this rough. We should be sailing a smooth passage." But the wind wasn't blowing from the proper direction for this time of the year and monsoon-type rains and rogue waves swamped their decks. Fortune and the sea-hardened crew were all seasick. Fortunately, Landers' new helmsman, who had an unnerving habit of checking each blade of his daggers for sharpness before he came on duty, was unruffled by the unseasonable winds and treacherous waves. He braced himself with his thick legs far apart, shoulders back, and fists firmly on the wheel.

"This is a bad omen," declared Sing Hoo as he paced the deck. He wore his distinctive yellow livery as if it could protect him from the evil spirits that tossed their ship. Even his yellow flag wouldn't help them now. He felt uneasy, as if someone, something, was watching him. Grasping any solid surface, he'd turn suddenly, convinced that Mow Bowli stood just beyond his sight. He was glad to have someone to talk to, even it was only the one-eyed Landers. He wasn't comfortable with the helmsman. Whenever the man looked at him, Sing Hoo felt those small dark eyes pull out all his secrets and examine his soul.

Landers lit his pipe and puffed furiously to draw smoke. "You heathens are too superstitious. We've just hit a bad spot. But I'll be damned if I understand where this storm is coming from. This must be one of those weather cycles."

"No, it's not a cycle. I've never seen a tormented wind like this in all the years I've traveled through China," said Sing Hoo. He couldn't wait to leave Fortune's employ. As soon as they landed in Hong Kong, even before they had unloaded, he demanded his pay. He watched Fortune count out the cash, then quickly ran down the gangway to find a ship home.

As soon as Sing Hoo's feet touched the dock, his knees buckled and he fell flat on his face. He howled with agony when they rolled him over. Blood poured out from where his knees should have been. Blood spurted from his open wounds and pooled under him. No one could explain how it happened that both his kneecaps had been sliced off right through his precious yellow livery.

It must have been a razor sharp knife, the police concurred, so sharp he didn't feel the cuts. Either an unknown assailant or an accident. He would never walk again.

Meanwhile, Captain McFarlane and *The Island Queen* waited for Fortune's shipment.

On the morning of Feb 16, 1851, Robert Fortune, 23,892 young tea shrubs, and eight Chinese tea masters sailed to India.

Forty

10 YEARS LATER

*J*ohn Poe picked up a teapot on the old desk in his study. It sat cold and empty. He spread his hands over the desk's polished surface to feel the patina of generations before him. He had tried to maintain the semblance of normalcy, tried to maintain control through the deprivations of one of the bloodiest civil wars, which had claimed twenty to thirty million people. They had survived despite the Taiping Rebellion led by a Chinese Methodist who declared himself to be the younger brother of Jesus Christ. The civil war and chaos opened the doors to the military intervention of Britain and France. The frontier lands to the north were falling to the Russians. Yunnan and Turkestan had fallen to the Muslims.

He picked up the optical microscope that Robert Fortune had given his father decades ago. How much beauty it had revealed: the delicate patterns of petals, the symmetry of living things. His 'old friend' had lived a lie. The Scot had stolen 40,000 of the finest tea shrubs and eight experienced tea masters to establish tea in India. There was no beauty in what he had done. On his first two trips they had thwarted Robert Fortune's path with harrowing adventures and great misfortunes. John shuddered to remember, then laughed to himself. How clever they had been. Those tales would liven a long, chill winter.

Thanks to Paul's friendship with Tu in Alistair Mackenzie's household, they learned that after the tea thief had established tea plantations in India, he had taken advantage of the lawlessness that wracked China and returned once more to collect plants in areas forbidden to foreigners. He never wrote to the Poes to tell them he had returned.

But the Poes knew.

With the East India Company's success with China's plants and tea masters in British India, China's tea industry collapsed. Cheap tea flooded India and the Western world. China alone could not drink all the tea it grew. Many tea hongs collapsed to dust along with China's economy. Disharmony brought further misery.

He cocked his ear when he heard light steps approach with the quickness that belonged to only one person, someone he wasn't expecting, someone who was not supposed to be in Shanghai. He leapt to his feet.

"Brother, what happened to your guards? Thieves might think the house of Poe is still filled with jade and gold." Dressed in dusty leggings and a cloak, one could mistake Jadelin for a trader who spent his days on the road. Her voice was rough and parched from her journey.

He stepped quickly towards her. His voice shook with both anger and love. "Jadelin, how did you get here? The ruthless Taiping army controls most of the area between West Lake and Shanghai."

"I saw. Bodies pepper the land." She had wondered why so many rafts clogged Shanghai's canals until she saw that they were swollen corpses jumbled like logs. She shook off the disturbing sight. "Between India stealing our tea market, the plagues, famines, and the Taiping army, what is left of China? But where are our guards? No one answered, and I found the front gate unguarded." Fearing the worst, she had sneaked through the main rooms ready to attack. She was relieved to find her sisters-in-law and the servants huddled in the kitchen. "I found Wen, who used to supervise the courtyard gardeners. He's to keep the gate bolted at all times and open it only for family."

John nodded his assent. "Wen and his wife have replanted our flower beds with vegetables. They have one hundred ways of preparing the same squash and beans so we think we're eating something different every day. As for our guards, Han and Huang valiantly fought off the Taiping rebels who tried to force their way through the front gate during New Year's. They took down a dozen, but a rebel's sword pierced Han's belly. We could not save him. Huang now splits his time guarding both the house and the hong. We've let all our workers go at the warehouse, Jadelin. Why did leave your quiet tea farm? It's safer there."

She shook her head. There was no peace there. "Neither the Mows nor the Poes can afford to lose a single case of tea now. Since we haven't been able to send messages to you with any reliability, nor have your letters reached us in almost a year, I hired armed mercenaries to escort me here with the last of our tea."

"The Taiping Army is on its way right now to attack Shanghai! Adam sends word from Beijing that the British are joining with the Emperor's forces to repel them. It is perilous for him, even with all his Imperial protection. This is not a safe place for you."

At that point Mei entered with a tea service and Big Amah bearing a pot of hot water. When she saw her Jadelin, Big Amah's tears coursed down her slack-skinned, wrinkled face. Bones protruded from her husky shoulders when she held out her arms to greet her.

Mei wrapped her arms around her daughter. She felt the sinewy muscles of her daughter's arms tighten. Still beautiful, although lines furrowed her brow, she lifted Jadelin's chin to lovingly study her face. "Where are Danli and Blossom?" she asked.

"Mow Chow Ching and Grand Master Ping have taken over their education. They are personally passing on all their knowledge to my darlings. By living with their grandfathers full-time, Danli and Blossom will develop their full potential. I miss them, Mama, but I had to come now. Baba is dying."

"How did you know?" Mei's voice trembled as a tear trailed down her pale cheek.

"He came to me in a dream." One night, the bamboo grove outside her room swayed so loudly it woke her up. The silk curtain of her bedroom parted and when her father entered, her room shone with a gentle glow. She had leapt out of bed and run to him. She felt his cheeks, cool and smooth against hers. She looked into his eyes and saw how they shimmered in the night. She knew what this visit meant and wasn't afraid. Yet she trembled, sad and grief-stricken. She leaned her head against his chest. He wrapped his arms around her shoulders as if to protect her.

"I cannot wait much longer," he told her.

She felt his voice rumble into her heart, warm and safe. She clutched him harder and kissed his cheeks. When she awoke, she was still crying.

"I'm glad he called you home." Mei dabbed at her eyes with a square of cotton clutched in her fingers. She had held her breath during Jadelin's tale, and now she took a sad breath. For Mandarin Poe, family was most important. He would understand that Shanghai was too dangerous for little Danli and Blossom, but his daughter could handle herself in any situation.

Pulling her control from within, Jadelin prepared and served tea to the others. "They say millions of people have died in the famines and plagues. Millions more have been killed by the rebels of the Taiping Army who rove unimpeded across so many provinces. With such civil unrest, both tea farms and hongs suffer. I was not prepared to see so many bodies in the canals and fields."

Big Amah paled. "That was not a proper sight for a lady," she har-rumphed. She huffed angrily, "What is the Emperor doing?" Then she burst into tears and, in a reversal of roles, Mei comforted her.

"It was a terrible sight, Big Amah, but I endured because Baba is waiting." Jadelin put down her teacup. When she looked up her eyes were glassy with tears.

Mei stood up and held out her fingers for her daughter's hand. "The doctors say they are amazed he has not yet departed for the Seven Bridges of Heaven. He is determined to see you all before he goes."

Mei and Jadelin, followed by Big Amah, hurried to the spacious bedroom in the central part of the Poe estate which commanded views of all the wings. Jadelin's eyes widened to see the empty halls stripped of the large porcelain vases, Tientsin carpets, and jade carvings. After the first burglary, the most valuable possessions were stored in their underground vault. They were sold as times grew lean. Thieves thought the Poe's estate was still filled with jade and gold so the men took turns patrolling at night, always ready to sound the alarm if anything was amiss.

Mandarin Poe lay in a fitful sleep; his lips were pursed, his jaw gripped, and a frown creased the brow above his closed eyes. His silk coverlet rose and fell with each shallow breath.

Jadelin put her arms around his shoulders and lay her cheek next to his. "Baba, I am here now." She felt his fingers grip hers. He opened his mouth but no words came. "Baba, thank you for the gift of life. I shall do all I can to bring honor to you." His fingers squeezed hers. Her heart cracked apart, just as when she learned Mow Bowli had died. The patriarch of the family, their level-headed leader, was on his way to the next life.

Jadelin nodded to the wives of Benjamin and Daniel, and her brothers' sons and their families who greeted her with tears and clasped hands. Flora hugged Jadelin's shoulders to thank her for coming. Otherwise, the room was as peaceful as the garden outside where a three hundred year old bonsai, only four feet high, stood in timeless grace. Big Amah moved a chair close to Poe's right hand so Jadelin could sit.

For the first time in her life, she realized her father had grown old. In her mind's eye he was always robust and energetic, with a voice that matched his larger than life persona. She had seen him spar with her brothers and had heard stories that in his prime, men feared to fight Mandarin Poe not only because he was powerful and quick, but because he could find his opponents' weaknesses within seconds. She motioned for water. Flora brought a piece of silk dipped in fresh water. She put one end between his lips so he could sip the moisture. Jadelin dabbed his dry lips with the wet silk. "Baba, I love you."

He opened his eyes. "Jadelin," he sighed. She felt the pressure of his grip in hers. "My little girl." Tears coursed from the corners of his eyes and pooled upon the sheets.

Jadelin couldn't contain her grief. "Oh, Baba," she wept. "Don't go yet."

"Your brother Edward was just here. He said he was waiting for me to come."

"Oh no, not so soon," she wept. Benjamin, Daniel, Paul, and John knelt down next to her so their father could see all their faces.

"My sons. My precious sons. Do not worry. First mother and Auntie will take care of me. See all our ancestors who have come to escort me?" He feebly gestured to the opposite wall where he saw generations of Poes waiting for his spirit to join them. "I bless you all. I will watch over you from the other side."

"Baba," gasped Jadelin. Her brothers grabbed her father's other hand and they all bowed their heads. One by one they kissed his sunken cheeks.

As if he had been waiting for this moment, Mandarin Poe gazed upon Mei with a final farewell. Then he exhaled.

The room was hushed with an unearthly stillness. Reverently, Mei placed two pearls beneath his tongue to be his eyes to guide him to the Seven Bridges of Heaven.

∾

The undertakers cleaned and prepared his body as if they were arranging the fine funeral procession Mandarin Poe deserved. But with the Taiping Army closing in on Shanghai and the Emperor's army and the European officers training and preparing for war, the family held a dignified burial at the family tomb without the scores of wailing mourners and conspicuous procession with cymbal clanging bands. Keeping to tradition, they scattered money behind them as they accompanied Mandarin Poe to his final resting place so the evil spirits would not follow.

Still dressed as a man, Jadelin accompanied her brothers to work in the days that followed. "I've never seen it so bare," she said to Benjamin as they stood in his aerie looking down at their vast space. The crates of tea she had delivered stood out among the cavernous emptiness.

"Thousands of tea farmers have died of plague and starvation. It's perilous for those who have survived to get their tea here." Benjamin shook his head. "Just as well. The East India Company has tea plantations in India that cover hundreds of acres, much larger than our family-owned tea farms. They pay Indians pennies per day, then sell them the tea they have harvested and produced."

"It isn't fair. Robert Fortune stole our tea plants and our knowledge."

"If the Emperor had acted earlier, the outcome might have been different."

"I wish I could do something. But I am just one person, and a woman. The Emperor didn't even listen to the men who give him good advice, like you and Baba and Adam."

"Was my advice any good?" asked John. He had leapt up the steps to join them after helping Paul to store Jadelin's tea in a secure storage and check the figures with Daniel. Paul and Daniel followed a minute later.

"You weigh each decision with great thought," she answered diplomatically. "How is Flora handling the uncertainty?" Although she liked the wives of Benjamin, Edward, and Daniel, they acted more like older aunts and especially disapproved of her male attire. She had stopped wearing the cork shoes after Mow Bowli's death. There was no need to act like a lady after that.

"I've asked her to return to her family in Soochow now that Baba is gone. Even though it's wise to leave Shanghai, she said she would worry too much not knowing if I were safe."

Benjamin warned, "The Taiping Army could arrive any day. The combined army of Western officers and the Emperor's Imperial forces will put up a strong defense."

"Flora needs to leave immediately," Paul insisted. "The British, Americans, and French sent their wives and children home on the first ships. Any available ship is now booked, and their holds are stuffed with as much Chinese furniture, porcelains, and jades they could crate up. Their Chinese servants, who they once treated like family, begged to go with them but they say there's no room. They're even abandoning their Chinese mistresses, wives, and children."

"That's heartless," said Jadelin angrily. "They'll be the first ones the Taipings will slaughter."

"How about Alastair Mackenzie's wife and the children he adored?" John asked Paul.

"Even with his consul connections he couldn't get them out of Shanghai, so he gave her all the money he had with promises to send more until he could come back for them. Then he sailed for England with the rest of the expats to avoid the bloodbath that is marching into Shanghai."

Benjamin's voice was deep and commanding. "You must leave immediately, Jadelin."

"Where to? Go back to West Lake to grow vegetables with the memory of my murdered husband haunting me?" she asked bitterly.

John put his arms on her shoulders. He felt her hardened muscles and the anger pent up within. "Go to Soochow, to Grand Master Ping. He will balance your ch'i." Jadelin lifted her chin in defiance. He knew she was thinking of the one person who fueled the fire of her anger.

∾

*J*adelin kicked at the dust motes swirling lazily in the empty warehouse. The tea she had brought with her had been quickly sold and was headed for Europe and America. No more coolies trudged here over inland mountains bearing precious cases of tea on their backs. The doors were now bolted against the chaos of fighting in the streets. She looked up to see Benjamin banging around in his aerie, packing up anything of value. He sounded like he was in a grumpy mood.

She poked her head into Daniel's office. He pushed his spectacles up his nose when she walked in. "Paul said it is better to burn our archives so they don't fall into enemy hands," he sighed. Stacks of scrolls and ledger books he had sorted through were piled at his feet. "I'm keeping the most important historical documents to store in the vault for future generations. It's so hard to choose what to let go. This was our history."

Jadelin knelt and unrolled a scroll describing the quality teas purchased over the decades from the Mow's of the Longjing mountain area of Hangchow, southwest of West Lake. She touched the elegant calligraphy that documented the various harvests and the number of cases their porters had carried thousands of miles over narrow paths. "This is a great legacy," she agreed with nostalgia and sadness. The stack of ledgers and scrolls seemed to multiply as Daniel pulled them from his shelves. "Can I help?" she asked.

"I should personally go through these." His forlorn look swept his bare walls and emptying shelves.

"You can help me," Paul huffed. He rushed in uncharacteristically covered with dust. He handed her an armload of scrolls from the pile Daniel had set aside and grabbed an armload himself. "I'm loading them into a wagon for transport home. Benjamin is having a tough time separating himself from his office." He nodded up at the curses coming from the aerie. "But we only have enough manpower to protect one location, home." He hadn't lost his good humor, though. His smile gave her a jolt of hope. "I'm glad you stayed. It's like having another brother. We need all the help since it's just us now." The two packed everything they could into cases that had once held tea, then loaded them onto a wagon already half-full with similar boxes. They returned many more times, with encouragements to Daniel to hurry up.

"It's painful closing the hong." Jadelin panted to compete with Paul's long strides. When she wasn't needed at the hong she helped Flora with the housekeeping and laundry between her shifts as guard. She kept watch from the estate towers and patrolled the perimeter to check all doors and gates were secure. She stopped her brother before they headed back for the last load. They could hear Daniel muttering, reading some of his favorite documents to himself. "Paul," she whispered. "Now that we're closing, John is taking his family to Soochow. Mama is returning with him to join Grand Master Ping. I should leave, too. We can't grow enough vegetables to feed us all."

"I go wherever you go, Jadelin. There's no business to cultivate."

"No. Stay here, Paul. You have powerful friends who can take care of you. You don't know where I'm going."

"Yes, I do," he said. "I can open doors in ways you cannot believe."

∽

*B*enjamin, Daniel, Mei, and Flora didn't believe Jadelin and Paul. "Mama, you're leaving with John for Soochow," Jadelin reminded her mother. "Benjamin and Daniel have their sons and their sons' families in Shanghai to care for them."

"A family must stay together," thundered Benjamin. "Together we are strong."

Daniel, the analytical one, nodded. "But Jadelin has always gone her own way. She's stubborn and headstrong like you. Who else could we trust to join her on her adventures? Paul," he said affectionately, "knows people. He knows what people want and gains their trust. He trained at Grand Master Ping's, as we all did, and can protect her."

"I need no protection," retorted Jadelin. She saw sincere concern in the faces of those who loved her. "But a backup helps."

"My daughter," protested Mei. "You can't just leave and not tell us where you're headed."

Paul diplomatically assured them, "It's probably best no one knows. The most powerful Taipan has arranged for us to travel to Hong Kong on his last ship in port, which leaves tomorrow. No one dares to question Jardine of Hong Kong. We speak English fluently and know the ways of foreigners."

∾

*M*ei couldn't sleep that night. She kept her hand on Jadelin's shoulder as they hugged each other to sleep for the last time.

In the morning, Jadelin and Paul, fitted in the latest British style tailored for them by one of Paul's friends, slipped out the front gate with one leather satchel apiece. All the Poes had lined up for their last farewells.

"The House of Poe will continue, maybe not in China," muttered Benjamin. "Go on, little sister. Cause trouble somewhere else." He wiped away a tear when he hugged her. She had to pry herself out of his beefy arms.

"You have the ability to move through many worlds of people," Mei said tenderly to Paul. "I'm glad you are the one Jadelin trusts on this quest."

Daniel whispered to Paul, "You have the documents?"

"I'm carrying them on me." His brother patted his vest. "Passage to Hong Kong for the son and daughter of Jardine's favorite Shanghai mistress." He reached into a trouser pocket. "Documents from the British Embassy for a missionary and his wife to London." He touched a side pocket. "I'm a Chinese diplomat with papers from the American Embassy for passage for myself and my sister to New York."

Paul doffed his top hat. Then he and his sister climbed into a waiting rickshaw.

ॐ

The wind whistled through the fretwork of the Poe estate and ghosted from the gardens to the sitting rooms to the deserted bedrooms. A gust lifted the tasseled silk hangings as if to smell the lingering scent of the mandarin's First and Second Wives. Too late. They had joined their ancestors long ago.

Masters and servants were in the same dire straits now. At night, they huddled together around one cooking fire and shared the duties of protection and nurture.

John had hoped to track Robert Fortune down in London someday, to give him a taste of what havoc he had wrought. But there was no time for vengeance; he had to keep alive what was left of the family. Quickly, he washed his finest brush of exquisitely soft wolf hair. He pulled out a sheet of rice paper and wrote in his strong, eloquent hand.

To be recorded in the Poe Ancestral Hall
From Sixth Brother John Poe

A crazed gang of twenty Taiping rebels attacked Third Wife Mei on her way back from the temple where she had gone to pray for our family's safety. She broke the limbs of five attackers.

With the blessings of my brothers, my mother and I will join Mow Chow Ching and the Dragons of the Mist to resist the barbarian incursions. My children and dearest Flora will accompany us to Soochow. She and our children will be safer behind the walls of her mother's family home.

Eldest brother Adam reports from the West Empress Dowager Tz'u-Hsi's court in Peking that the situation is dire. The French Army, driven by lust for revenge and destruction, marches closer. At his signal, the Dragons of the Mist will rise from their lair.

Warlords scour our lands. There is talk of storming the Forbidden City and overthrowing the Empress.

Second brother Benjamin runs what is left of our tea trade with Daniel and their sons. Our wives and children dug out our courtyard gardens to grow vegetables; food is more important than beauty. There is no time for contemplation, meditation, and poetry. We apologize that to feed our families and anyone who came to us for help, we sold many family heirlooms including the jades that my father held for his grandsons. Yet there is never enough.

We are more vulnerable than before. England floods the world market with tea made with the expertise Robert Fortune stole from us. Our Nanking cotton industry was destroyed by cheap English imports and the secrets of our silk trade are ours no longer.

Farewell, my dear brothers, sisters-in-law, nephews, and nieces. We leave all that we have to you and your families so you may stay alive as long as possible. Seek not for us, for we go disguised into the countryside and cities. You will not find us anywhere except in your hearts. Your faces are etched in our souls forever. We are nowhere and everywhere, in the mountains and valleys, on the coast and inland. China as we knew it is no more.

May you find prosperity, health, and peace.
John Poe

Epilogue

On the tree-lined Kensington street, a figure ducked under the fog-shrouded sign which read, 'Chinese Antiques, Robert Fortune, Proprietor,' and jiggled the brass doorknob, an ornate lion's head. Locked. A powerful twist and the lock surrendered. Once inside, the figure turned the key in the door until it bolted like the fall of an axe.

The air smelled of old lacquer and older porcelain, of fine Chinese silk and carved figurines well-oiled by decades of collectors' caresses. An ornate mantle clock, Chinese-made but gilded for the European market, chimed. Round-back Chinese armchairs, Coromandel lacquer cabinets, and elegant two hundred years old altar tables of polished huanghuangli wood were arranged to appeal to a discriminating clientele. Fine Ming porcelains and oversized cloisonné vases created to impress gleamed from every corner and shelf.

Robert Fortune didn't notice the intruder. As the afternoon light fingered his jade landscapes of China's craggy Wuyi Shan Mountains, those gleaming carvings took on the dark green of tea bushes when their buds sent their scent to heaven. Within this shop, as cozy as an over-stuffed parlor, Fortune's memories could return to those inland mountains when the pure wind swept through the precious tea-growing areas of China forbidden to foreigners, like him.

For now, he rested because tonight the powerful Jardine of Hong Kong had invited the cream of society to a ball in honor of his son and daughter, who had grown up in war-torn China. He heard the two brought an exotic touch to this year's season. Fortune was eager to meet them, to surprise them by speaking in their native Chinese. He heard that the son, so handsome and charismatic, had created a sensation among the men and ladies. But everyone raved about his slender sister who had the most charming Scottish accent.

"Sing Wa," his visitor called in a low, throaty voice. Although dressed in the style of a British gentleman, the scent of sandalwood, of China, emanated from the folds of a finely woven wool cloak.

From his desk at the back of his shop Fortune craned his neck forward in the waning light and squinted over the top of his wire-rimmed spectacles. "Who are you? What do you want?" he barked. Behind him, on a cast-iron stove, a tea kettle puffed quiet clouds of steam.

The stranger stepped under the glow of a sconce. "Sing Wa, don't you recognize me?" The caller lifted a stylish top hat. A shiny black braid slinked down the erect back.

"I haven't heard that name in years," the antique dealer rasped. Now he recognized the strong dark eyes, arched eyebrows, and brow. He stumbled backwards in his chair. "How did you find me?" He covered his face with his hands, overcome with emotion.

"Sing Wa," his visitor crowed triumphantly and, removing worn leather gloves, placed them on the top hat. "In China you were always easy to recognize: a towering, wild-haired blond with mutton chops. Your skin has lost its robust glow, but your eyes are still alarmingly pale." His caller pulled up a carved chair of honey-hued huanghuangli wood and sat facing the old merchant. "Sing Wa, share a cup of tea with me." The voice was inviting, seductive. "Which one?"

"White Jasmine Pearls are in the double gourd," the Scot answered without hesitation and tipped his head towards the cabinet behind the desk. In each partition was an exquisitely decorated canister that held an exceptional tea.

"Your tastes are still Chinese, Sing Wa." His guest picked up a pewter canister shaped like a double gourd, a symbol of prosperity, and swirled the compact pearls of tea to release their aroma. Very fresh. The jasmines had been plucked at dawn, blended with first flush leaves until the blossoms popped open in the evening, then removed. The scenting had been repeated at least five times to obtain the intense fragrance and flavor. "What a surprise. You're offering me expensive tea."

"If you were a client, I would have chosen Longjing, Dragon Well," Fortune boasted.

His caller shut the almond eyes that had always enchanted the adventurer with their glistening depths. "Dragon Well, first flush, no doubt, picked from Longjing, the very essence of the spring winds blowing above the temple and teahouse near the natural spring, home of the munificent Dragon. Where you found China's premier tea masters."

The veins of Fortune's face flushed through his papery skin. His mouth quivered and he pursed his lips. "I paid them handsomely for their expertise. It was my job."

"You did well." His visitor poured a stream of cool water from a fine eighteenth century celadon pitcher into the little pot and placed it on the cast iron stove where a puffing kettle had been humidifying the air to keep the antique lacquers and veneers from peeling. "Your government sought the black tea and green tea plants. We kept you confused for years. By now you know all tea comes from the same plant, *Camellia sinensis*."

Fortune wiped his rheumy eyes as he followed his visitor's every move. His lips parted with pleasure to watch his guest prepare tea in the classic Chinese style following the eighth century Tang dynasty scholar Lu Yu's treatise Ch'a Ching, or *The Classic of Tea*. He nodded appreciatively when his caller selected two teacups of palest green which would bring out the color of the tea, then covered their bottoms with a layer of fragrant tea pearls. When the layer of bubbles that covered the bottom of the pot looked like tiny fish eyes with a hint of sound, the water had reached the optimum temperature. After steeping, Fortune's bony fingers grasped the offered cup with possessive delight.

His guest settled in a stiff chair opposite him. "Long ago China alone knew the secrets of tea. Our legends tell us that when Bodhidharma meditated, he was so angry when he fell asleep that he ripped out his eyelids so he would never sleep again. His eyelids became tea plants, his gift to us. He knew its ability to keep sleep at bay. For five thousand years we guarded our tea plants and the secrets that produced our many teas. We alone knew how to add the fragrance of flowers such as jasmine and lychee and chrysanthemum to tea. Until you, Sing Wa, came to China."

The Scot's bushy eyebrows rose like mountain peaks. His thinning white hair and papery skin clung to his skull. But he still possessed rigidity and characteristic long silences. The afternoon light waned quickly this time of the year. Soon they would be sitting in shadows. But neither moved to light more candles.

Fortune's words flew with his spittle. "Chinese were healthy because they drank tea. Pestilence and disease were rampant in India, but natives could not afford to pay four to six schillings a pound for Chinese tea. They had to grow their own and produce it cheaply."

His visitor took a sip and smiled to ease the Scot's mind, to deceive him. "Sing Wa, you enabled England to satisfy its lust for cheap tea by growing your own in India. Now India exceeds China as the largest producer of tea in the world."

"You cannot blame me."

His guest looked around the antique shop and recognized many treasures. "They say that the East India Company makes more money on tea than on all its India trade."

Fortune gripped the arms of his chair. "I have the greatest admiration for the Chinese people. But the days of China's highest achievements were long past. Your government and culture were decaying, not advancing. Surely, you saw that." Fortune's mission had been for God and Queen, for the Honorable East India Company, and for the British Empire.

"You betrayed my family's trust, destroyed the tea trade that twenty-seven generations protected and nurtured. You stole my family's secrets and the finest tea masters."

"No!" Fortune flung his arms to beat back the damning words, to dismiss any dishonor. He justified his actions with the glory and might of his country. Clenching his fists to his head, he admitted he had despised China at first, railed against what he perceived as stupidity and arrogance. Then, disguised as a 'Chinese from beyond the Great Wall,' for the first time in his life he felt sophisticated and cultured with refined taste and manners as if he had been born to that ancient civilization. He was sorry he hurt them, sorry for their losses.

His caller placed the teacup on Fortune's desk. The tea was of such fine quality it would be good for three or four more infusions. Alas, there was no time. The sun set. Sudden darkness left them in the shadows of night. His visitor leaned forward so Fortune could look deep into those eyes he once sought and spoke so each word would resonate in his heart. "You murdered my husband. You betrayed us! You!"

Fortune jerked back. "No!" He stood up, hands shaking in front of him. "It wasn't my fault!"

His visitor stood up and coiled her hair under the top hat so she once again resembled a proper Englishman in the evening light. She swung her right hand back and shot forward. Once. Twice. The years of rigorous training had taught her how to defend, how to disable.

Fortune's torso caved in. The antique dealer crumpled, his eyes open and jaw slack. Drool dribbled from his lips. He struggled to speak.

His attacker washed her teacup in the small basin, dried it with the cotton towel folded by the stove, and replaced it in its precise spot in the cabinet. "Sing Wa," she continued in Chinese, "I can't kill you, for Buddhists believe all life is sacred. But you will find it harder to get your breath. As your paralyzed body screams for air, devils will come for the Christian soul you claimed made you superior to us heathen Chinese. For this, I may be reincarnated as a mosquito, but I have done you a favor by sending you to your judgment sooner. You will lose control of your functions and pride. You will suffer."

Fortune's jaw jiggled, but the only sound he could make was a choked rattle. The contents of his bladder dripped onto the antique Tianjian carpet. He tried to raise his hands, to plead that he was not responsible for the outcome of time and politics. Too late!

"The first time I met you, Sing Wa, I was so frightened by your pale eyes, I thought I was looking through your head to the sky. I fear nothing now." His caller leaned close so Fortune could feel the breath of each word. His assailant leapt to the ceiling and shattered the towering Ming vases with a single kick. Another thrust crushed the true antique porcelains to shards and dust. A swift fist shattered the desk and tea chest. Dozens of tea caddies spilt open releasing the luxurious scents of jasmine pearls, swallow tongue greens, crinkled oolongs, and compressed blacks.

His eyes wobbled, pleaded with her for understanding as his body collapsed.

She glared down on him. "Before I leave England, I'll tell a constable you need help. If he does not get here in time, he will think you've had a heart attack and flailed in despair. The best of your collection, like China, is destroyed. I leave you to contemplate how you misused your friendships and stole China's treasures for England's glory. Farewell, Sing Wa."

As she slipped on her gloves, her eye caught a glitter on the floor. She plucked the fine crystal snuff bottle from the shards of a zitan treasure box. The artist had used the brush of a single hair to paint pink peonies, Mei's favorite flower, in its interior. She had seen her mother hand it to the Scot. Now it rested cool and heavy in her palm. She tightened her fingers around its gleaming surface.

Lowering the brim of her top hat, she nodded goodbye and shut the door firmly behind her. Then the night closed in, ominous and murky as she disappeared in the fog.

Acknowledgements

Thank you to Robert Fortune, who was sent by the Royal Horticultural Society to collect plants in China after the Treaty of Nanking in 1842, the unequal treaty that marked the end of the First Opium War. Only 30 years old and untrained as a plant collector, he returned to write three books, *Wanderings in China*, *A Residence Among the Chinese Inland on the Coast and at Sea*, and *A Journey to the Tea Countries of China* about his experiences.

Thank you to my dearest friend, Dr. Barbara Bundy, for her insightful editing and steadfast support. She has critiqued numerous revised drafts, transcending the bonds of friendship.

Sincere thanks to Elizabeth Pomada, Michael Larsen, Mari Campbell, Christy Cannon, Myrna Chase, Patti Itano, Mary Hammond, and Don Porteous for their encouragement and critique. They are the best readers any writer could wish for.

Thanks to all the librarians and professors whose brains I picked over the past ten years researching China, Britain, and the tea trade during the one hundred years of unequal treaties in China.

My fondest Mahalo to my husband, Fred J. Joyce III.

Thank you to my son, Ryan C. Leong, and his wife, Erzsebet, for widening my horizons and opening new vistas into the world.

About Pam Chun

*P*am Chun was born and raised in Hawaii in a family of storytellers THE MONEY DRAGON, Pam's first novel, named one of 2002's Best Books in Hawaii, topped the best seller charts for months, and received a 2003 Kapalapala Po'okela Award for excellence in literature. Her second novel, WHEN STRANGE GODS CALL, received the 2005 Ka Palapala Po'okela Award for excellence in literature. Her third book, THE SEAGULL'S GARDENER, is a resource and memoir of distance care-giving for her father who passed away in Hawaii at age 97.

Pam has been featured on National Public Radio, at the Smithsonian Institute in Washington D.C., at the National Archives and Records Administration's Conference on Asian Americans and Pacific Islanders, and in the documentary, *Hawaii's Chinatown,* which premiered on Hawaii PBS.

Pam has been a speaker at Alameda's first Literary Festival for readers, San Francisco's first Litquake, the San Francisco Writer's Conference, the Bamboo Ridge Writer's Workshop, and many universities. She volunteers as a storyteller at the Asian Art Museum of San Francisco.

Pam lives in the San Francisco Bay Area with her husband, where her tropical flowers bloom despite fog, drought, and icy winters. She has one son, a U.S. diplomat stationed overseas with his family.

Thank you for reading THE PERFECT TEA THIEF.
If you enjoyed it, won't you please take a moment to leave me a review at your favorite retailer?

I look forward to hearing from you.

Visit me on the web at http://www.pamchun.com

Email me at pamchun@cal.berkeley.edu

THE MONEY DRAGON

2003 KAPALAPALA PO'OKELA AWARD-

HONORABLE MENTION

"Fast-paced and utterly addictive"
--Kirkus Review

"carefully researched and atmospherically evocative...."
--Publisher's Weekly

"Money Dragon roars with intricate, juicy drama....A TV producer should buy the rights, NOW."
--Honolulu Star-Bulletin

"...the American version of Raise the Red Lantern, a family saga on the triumph and fall of L. Ah Leong, the Money Dragon, and his family caught between his deeply rooted Chinese values and those of the New World...explores the delicate human relationship in this fascinating and powerful story. It is a jewel in American Chinese literature."
--Peter Xinping Zhou, University of California, Berkeley, Director of the East Asian Library

"THE MONEY DRAGON is a meticulously rendered chronicle of the rise and fall of a legendary Chinese-Hawaiian family. A cautionary tale

about one man's boundless ambition and appetite-for wealth, sex, and power."
-Aimee Liu, author of <u>Solitaire</u>, <u>Face</u>, and <u>Cloud Mountain</u>

"Pam Chun's family reminds me of my own in its eccentricities, ambitions, back-stabbing, and romance. THE MONEY DRAGON is a wonderful and entertaining contribution to the world of Asian-American stories."
-Lisa See, author of <u>On Gold Mountain</u>

WHEN STRANGE GODS CALL

2005 KAPALAPALA PO'OKELA

AWARD-WINNER

"Pam Chun writes lovingly of Hawai'i—a land of beauty and tradition, where the scent of plumeria fills each page and a love once lost can be found again."
--Gail Tsukiyama, author of <u>Women of the Silk</u>, <u>The Samurai's Garden</u>, <u>Night of Many Dreams</u>, <u>The Language of Threads</u>, and <u>Dreaming Water</u>

"Vividly evokes the lush, sensual land and effectively dramatizes the conflict between old traditions and fast-pasted modernity."
-- Booklist

"Enjoy a curl-up-in-bed-with-a-good-book read."
--Francesca De Grandis, author of <u>The Modern Goddess' Guide to Life</u>

"...this is one for a quiet weekend, a box of chocolates, and the couch."
--<u>Honolulu Advertiser</u>

"Good family epic enlivened with a nice locale and a stiff dose of history."
--Kirkus Reviews

Bonus Preview: The Seagull's Gardener

by Pam Chun

Introduction

The last time I saw my father alive he asked me to write him 'a good book.' So frail then, he fixed me with eyes glossed with such sadness I was afraid to ask what he meant. Did he mean a book about his life? Or his obituary?

Two weeks later he was gone.

Throughout his six month slide from robust independence at home to his passing in a Kane'ohe hospice, he faced death by refusing to accept it. He did not go gently into the night as expected of a soft-spoken gentleman. His last two months he was fed through a tube in his side. On his worst days, he fought for air, even while on oxygen. Although he was over ninety-seven when he got his pacemaker, he fretted about outliving his batteries. He swam against the current, fought the outgoing tide, and struggled to dig his toes into the shore of life until his eyes closed for the last time.

I was thousands of miles away in one of the oldest cities in China when my eldest brother left a message. Dad had died. He scheduled the funeral for next week, two days before I could return. My brother would not wait for me.

The lines failed repeatedly each time I called home. I stared up at the hazy sky, such an odd shade, unlike the clear blue of Honolulu. Before me stretched the vast flood plain of central China here at the eastern terminus of the Silk Road, so far from home. So far from my father.

When I was a child, every school day I waited for him to walk home from the 5:10 bus from downtown Honolulu. The crisp smell of his air conditioned office, conjuring images of files and stacks of paper forms, wafted in when he opened the door. After he changed out of his ironed shirt and tie, placed his natty felt hat on the top closet shelf, and positioned his polished leather shoes on the shoe tree, I'd kneel with him in the garden to dig weeds and work the earth before Mom called us for dinner. With hands deep in the soil, earthworms wiggling through our fingers, we plucked weeds and brown leaves under bowers of orchids, plumeria, pikake and Tahitian gardenias. Mynah birds cackled at us and doves cooed in the evening trades.

My father and I had a special bond that time, space, and death could not diminish. But I could not start his 'good book.' So he appeared in my dreams, each time to teach me one more lesson, to reveal one more truth he felt I needed to know.

Three months after his death I dreamt I had entered an outdoor promenade filled with shoppers wearing bright Hawaiian prints. The shops were colorful, clean, and bright in the sunlight as if only goodness and happiness were allowed here. The trees were lush and green. Flowers bloomed everywhere. My father wore one of his favorite Hawaiian shirts, large flowers on a subtle background of muted florals. He turned from where he chatted happily with his friends, all equally tanned and in bright Hawaiian prints. He looked directly up at me and asked, "Did you get my letter?" His face shone with a healthy glow. With his eyes twinkling upwards in a smile, he stood and clasped me in a hug.

'Oh!' I gasped. I felt the press of his firm chest and the crisp cotton of his shirt against my cheek. He smelled like a fresh breeze, like clouds and angels.

He laughed at my surprise.

I woke up laughing. I hugged my shoulders and remembered the feel of his body against mine. His new scent, which had enveloped me when he held me close in my dream, still clung to my arms and cheeks. Never, I told myself, will I forget that fragrance. In his own way, he was immortal.

I knew he was trying to tell me it was time.

In my father's last few years I flew home more and more often. Although he lived independently in the house in which he had raised us, a modest home painted white to reflect the tropical sun, the perfect backdrop for a profusion of plumeria, bougainvillea, birds of paradise, orchids and anthuriums, he grew to depend on my return. He greeted me at the airport with lists of house repairs, doctor appointments, and errands. He wanted my company to explore newly opened developments, beaches, and stores. He liked to go to festivals and parades and examine the haunts of his past. I plotted out our visits in detail. But as I flew back and forth between California and Hawai'i and my letters and phone calls increased, I realized I wasn't the only one coping with this routine.

Conversations with neighbors, friends, and co-workers always touched on how we were caring for our parents, some who lived in other states, other countries. We weren't alone. According to the Pew Research Center, seven to ten million adults care for their aging parents from afar. And by the year 2030, according to the US Census Bureau, the number of Americans 65 or older will double to over 70 million. We conferred on our parents' ailments, discussed symptoms and medications, and compared living arrangements and outside help. We felt guilty for not living closer to our parents. We felt frustrated that they did not want to live with us or move closer.

I learned that Death changes family dynamics, changes people, changes their desires. Death reveals the soft underbelly of their soul, their weakness. I kept that painful part of my life cloaked, close to my heart.

I write from my own experience, aware that there are many sides to every story. There is no absolute truth. There are as many variations of the truth as there are unshared conversations and decisions. I changed some names to protect my family's privacy. If there are errors, the fault is entirely mine.

Hawai'i is a meld of cultures, Asian and Western, mystical and spiritual. For many, one's passing means a journey onward. For some it is truly the end of the story. My reality may not be yours. Your truth may not be mine.

But I believe the love we hold for each other, a love which rises above all other emotions, sustains us for many lifetimes.

AGAINST THE WAVE

*W*oody tracked the waves breaking in even sets, one large followed by a second and third that diminished in a pattern, gentle and rhythmic. The waves curled at the toes of his two boys at water's edge, then pulled back stranding dozens of jellyfish, the glassine Portuguese-man-of-war that blew to shore eight days after the full moon. The sky was azure blue and a twenty knot offshore wind eased the heat on the sun-glazed sand.

For whatever reason, a change in harmonics or a storm thousands of miles across the Pacific, the wave pattern changed. The rogue wave swelled suddenly, engorged with the power of the sea. It towered so high it blotted out the sun.

His younger son looked up and scrambled up the beach kicking sand in his haste. His older brother dreamily watched the wave crest. It broke over his head and carried him out to sea.

Woody instantly dove into the retreating swell. He grabbed his first-born with one arm and paddled with the other. The two rode the glass-like crest of the wave like fish floats. The next wave carried them towards shore. My father dug in his toes to plant his feet as soon as the wave crashed. A lull, a moment of hope. But the sea sucked the duo back out.

Two Hawaiians, no more than sixteen but experienced in the ways of the sea, their broad backs muscled and sinewy from swimming this beach most of their lives, waved their arms and shouted to my father. The fourth wave in the set was the weakest; they would pull him in then.

My father and brother slid down the curl of the third wave, swallowed water, and gasped for breath. Dad wasn't a strong swimmer; he got seasick just watching the waves. His only hope was reaching shore before he ran out of luck. He bent his head down again as the wave swept them back in. Intent and calm, he felt his son's heart race like a baby bird's. The vast ocean stretched endlessly behind him, dwarfing him with its power. He wailed when it pulled them out for the third time.

The Hawaiians lunged for my father. But the wave was quicker and yanked its hostages from their fingers. Father and son were mere dots on the face of the wave now. All voices hushed on the beach.

The two rode the crest of the fourth wave. As predicted, it curled in huge and sweet. The Hawaiians had already slipped into the surf. When the wall of water crashed over their heads, they grabbed the two and hung on.

My father lay on his stomach under the shade of a wide-leafed tree. He breathed heavily, deeply, as if all his emotions and heart were gasping for air from that deep space inside him. Water beaded on the knotted muscles of his back and arms. A moan rumbled in his chest. And with each breath he released the terror of the sea until his muscles relaxed and he fell asleep.

I sat by his side watching the beads of water drip from his smooth skin onto the straw mat. I was five years old and he was my world. I wanted to touch him, to ask if he was all right, to assure myself that he was safe. I had screamed when he dove after my brother and fought for their lives. I never doubted he would return. I leaned close and inhaled the comforting scent of his ocean-washed skin.

Only when I heard fear and terror escape in little cries as he lay in the shade did I realize that possibly, my father might be mortal.

In my callow teens, I went to Honolulu Airport to say goodbye to friends from California my father had met only once before. My friends missed their plane so we returned to their hosts' house in Wai'alae Kāhala to wait for the morning flight. By then it was midnight and, knowing my parents would be asleep, in a serious lapse of judgment I decided I needn't bother them. Over our animated collegiate chatter, at five a.m. a strong voice from the dark called my name. When I saw my father standing in the driveway, I cringed. My father said that he had waited up for me. When I didn't return he got in his car. How did he know where I was? I had mentioned Wai'alae Kāhala and a certain street sign so he drove, guided by an inner sense, through an area of over a thousand exclusive homes and pulled up in exactly the right driveway.

∾

*I*n my most frightening dreams I race from evil through dark alleys, across jungle valleys, over ragged mountains and endless seas in the nightmare maze of dreams. I flee from plumes of molten lava threatening my jungle village, paddle through shrouded rivers overhung with vines, and race inland from tsunamis. Always, I awaken frozen with fear, heart racing.

In the worst of these, my father plucks me from disaster. He appears as if summoned by an inner sense that I need him. He drives up in a rugged military vehicle or nondescript white sedan, all diametrically opposite of what he drove in real life—a blue vinyl-topped El Dorado and a 1952 Plymouth Cambridge the color of lapis lazuli. I run to him yelling "Dad," energized with relief at the sight of his face. His cavalier shrug tells me he's doing what he's done a thousand times before when he picked me up from school or piano or ballet lessons.

Then I wake up. How did my father know I needed him?

My life took me three thousand miles across the Pacific to the fast-paced world of Northern California, so different from the tropical ambiance of Honolulu. Here, I prided myself on my self-sufficiency, my independence. Yet, my father had the power to bring sense and order and security by his presence, even in dreams.

Purchase THE SEAGULL'S GARDENER at your favorite online retailer.

14523987R00228

Made in the USA
San Bernardino, CA
28 August 2014

War Comes
to Willy Freeman

YEARLING BOOKS are designed especially to entertain and enlighten young people. Patricia Reilly Giff, consultant to this series, received her bachelor's degree from Marymount College and a master's degree in history from St. John's University. She holds a Professional Diploma in Reading and a Doctorate of Humane Letters from Hofstra University. She was a teacher and reading consultant for many years, and is the author of numerous books for young readers.

War Comes
to Willy Freeman

James Lincoln Collier • Christopher Collier

A Y E A R L I N G   B O O K

Visit us on the Web! www.randomhouse.com/kids

Educators and librarians, for a variety of teaching tools, visit us at
www.randomhouse.com/teachers

ISBN: 0-440-49504-0

Reprinted by arrangement with Delacorte Press

Printed in the United States of America

February 1987

31 30

OPM

for
Catherine Bromberger

War Comes
to Willy Freeman

1

WHAT I REMEMBERED most was the way the sun flashed and flashed on the bayonets. The British soldiers marched past our cabin in their red jackets, raising dust from the road, and the bayonets flashed and flashed, now this one, now the next one, as they turned just so in the morning sun. Oh, it scared me something awful, knowing that before too long they would march up to Fort Griswold and try to run them bayonets through a lot of our people, and maybe Pa, too, if they hadn't caught him already.

"Ma, I'm scared for Pa," I said.

"Hush now, my honey," she said. "Your Pa'll be all right."

She was just saying that. Ma, she didn't like for me to be unhappy, and she was just saying that so's I wouldn't worry. We stood side by side in front of our little wooden cabin, the September sun still warm on our skin, smelling the dust raised up by the marching men dry in our noses. Their feet went clap clap clap on the ground, and the drums rolled, and the bayonets flashed. Sometimes a soldier would give us a quick look as we stood there, but mostly they just marched on, staring straight ahead in the dusty sunlight.

"I wish Pa was here," I said.

"Just as good he ain't," Ma said. "He's bound and determined to fight. I'd rather he was out there on the water fishing than chasing up to Fort Griswold to get himself stuck with one of them bayonets."

"Will he really fight?" I said. But I knew he would. He was mighty brave. I'd seen him go out on Long Island Sound in the jolly boat when it was storming so fierce you could hardly stand up. There was nothing Pa was afraid of.

"Oh, he'll fight all right," Ma said. "He'll fight. I told him until my jaws ached that there wasn't no use in us niggers fighting, we wasn't going to get anything out of it no matter who wins. But he says no, we're free now, and it's our country, too."

She looked mighty grim and bitter, like there wasn't nothing fair in anything. Pa'd got his freedom from Colonel Ledyard by joining up in the militia. That was the law—if a black slave was going to join up to fight the British, he had to be set free first. So Pa joined up, and then Colonel Ledyard gave me and Ma our freedom, too. Pa took the name of Freeman, so he was

Jordan Freeman, and Ma was Lucy Freeman, and I was Wilhelmina Freeman. It was kind of a funny feeling having a last name all of a sudden, after nine years of not having one. But now I was thirteen and I'd got used to it. Besides, nobody called me nothing but Willy, anyway.

So the soldiers went marching past, raising up the dust, and I watched, wondering if one of those bayonets would go into Pa. Finally Ma said, "Willy, war or no war, the cow ain't going to milk herself. You go along now."

The cow was Ma's. Mrs. Ledyard had given it to her once when she'd nursed the Ledyards' little girl through the fever, when nobody thought she would live. Ma was mighty careful about that cow. We had a horse, too, down in the salt marsh, but it belonged to Colonel Ledyard.

We lived out on a little spit of land that bordered on the Thames River, where it ran into Long Island Sound. There was a salt marsh on the water side. On the inland side the land rose up into hills, with oaks and pines on them. Further up the Thames was the village of Groton, where Fort Griswold was. On the other side of the Thames was New London. It was a mighty big place, with docks sticking into the river, and hundreds of houses and six church steeples you could count if you went up into the hills.

I went into the house, got the wooden milk bucket, and came out again. Ma took a look at me. "Put on them milking britches, Willy," she said. "I ain't having no child of mine sitting on a milking stool with her skirt pulled up, and all them soldiers marching by."

That was Ma—she didn't hold with anybody seeing a girl's legs. I didn't care one way or another, I just hated changing my clothes all the time, because I'd have to change back into my dress soon as the milking was done—naturally, Ma didn't hold with a girl going around dressed up like a boy, neither. "Ma—" I started to argue.

She gave me a look. "You do like I say, Willy."

I might have argued, too, but I was feeling terrible scared by the British, and I didn't have much mind for arguing like mostly I would. So I went into the cabin and put on the milking britches, and then I went down to the salt marsh behind the cabin and started to milk the cow, while the horse stood near and watched.

I'd just got started when there was a great boom from somewhere behind me. I jumped. Then there was a tearing sound overhead, and I knew they'd begun to fire cannon from Fort Griswold out onto the British ships.

That cannon ball tearing out to sea scared me even more, because Pa was out there somewhere in the jolly boat. If a ball struck the boat, it would smash it to smithereens and drown Pa for sure. Oh, how I wished he was back home with us, never mind what Ma said.

Mostly Pa worked for Colonel Ledyard, chopping wood, hoeing corn, and running and fetching. But early in the mornings he went out fishing, so as to make a little money to improve himself. I thought

4

about him out there amongst the British fleet and I wondered if he was scared. Then I began to think about if he would really fight, the way Ma said, and what that would be like. What would it be like to get stabbed by a bayonet?

Thinking about that scared me so much I had to squinch my eyes closed and think about milking the cow. By and by I was finished, and I left the cow on her tether and carried the milk bucket up to the cabin. There was cannons rolling past now, and the dust was worse than ever. Just as I got to the door there came another boom and the tearing noise overhead. I jumped inside and shut the door, even though I knew if a ball hit, it would go clean through the cabin, door and all. 'Course, there wasn't much to our cabin—just a rope bed with a corn shuck mattress for Ma and Pa and a pallet for me, and a pine table and a cupboard and the fireplace and such.

Ma was fixing some cold pork and biscuits for breakfast. I said, "How am I going to get the milk up to Colonel Ledyard's, Ma?" We sold our extra milk to Colonel Ledyard, and most mornings I rode up there on the horse with it. I'd done it for years. I could ride pretty good. I wasn't supposed to race the horse, but sometimes I did anyway, when nobody was looking.

Ma went to the window and looked out at the troops marching through the hazy sunshine. "Colonel Ledyard will have to wait for his milk," she said. "I reckon he's got other things on his mind this morning."

But the troops was making just an awful noise. The

cannon wheels was rumbling, the axles squeaking, and the drums rat-tat-tatting; still we didn't have no trouble hearing the cannons up at Fort Griswold booming and the balls whistling overhead. I stood by the window, staring out, scared and wondering how our militia could ever stand up to them men and cannons going by.

Ma put the piece of cold pork and a plate of biscuits on the table. "No reason for us not to eat breakfast," she said. "You got to feed yourself, war or no war." I sat down. I didn't much feel like eating, but I chewed some biscuit anyway, because I knew I'd better keep my strength up for whatever happened that day. And just about the time I was washing the biscuit down with a swallow of beer, the rumbling and squeaking of the cannon began to die down, and the drums to fade off. I jumped up and went to the door.

The air was still filled with the brown dust drifting up everywhere and a few men was straggling through it. As I stood there a horseman galloped up and sped by; and then they was all disappearing through the dust down the road toward Fort Griswold.

"They're gone, Ma," I said.

"Not far," she said. "Not far enough."

I turned away from the door and looked at her. I'd never seen her so terrible grim before, her eyes hard as steel, her lips clenched tight. She was pretty, Ma was, with chocolate-colored skin and hair cut short like mine, and I hoped I'd be as pretty as her when I was grown. But she didn't look pretty right then.

"Maybe the militia won't fight, Ma," I said. "Maybe they'll just give up when they see all them British."

"They'll fight," she said. "There'll be plenty dead before night."

Then a shrill, high scream cut like a knife through the air. We jumped up. "The cow," Ma cried.

We dashed out of the cabin into the sunlight hazy with dust. There were two soldiers down in the salt marsh. The cow was collapsed down on her side, kicking her legs and trying to stand up. The soldiers stabbed with their bayonets. The cow shrieked again, and tried to roll up onto her feet.

"Stop, for the love of God, stop," Ma cried. She began to run, and I ran after her.

The soldiers turned, and I saw a funny thing: they was black. They watched us run up.

"Stop, please stop," Ma cried.

We came up to them. The cow was gasping for breath and there was foamy blood all over her mouth and nose and I knew she was dying. She rolled her eyes up to look at us, like she couldn't understand what was happening to her.

"For God's sake, why are you doing this?" Ma shouted.

The two soldiers looked uneasy. "If we'd known you was niggers, we'd have left the cow alone," one of them said. "We ain't supposed to bother the black folk."

Ma dropped down on her knees by the cow. Now I saw a big cut in her side where they'd run her through.

7

"You've killed her," Ma said. Her voice was flat and her eyes hard as steel again, like she wasn't going to let nothing bother her, no matter what. She stood up and looked at the soldiers with that flat, steely look. "You've killed her. She was mine. She was the only thing I ever owned."

"If we'd known you was—"

"The cabin ain't mine, the boat ain't mine, the clothes on my back ain't mine, but Mrs. Ledyard, she said, 'Lucy, take the cow, it's yours, a woman ought to have something that's her own.'" Then Ma did something I never heard her do before. She cursed. "God damn you to hell," she said. "You killed her, now take her."

She turned around and walked off across the salt marsh to the cabin, and I followed after her. We got inside. She stood by the window, staring out at the haze, but I knew she wasn't seeing it, she was seeing something inside her head. I didn't know what, but she was so grim-looking I didn't dare speak. Then suddenly she got soft again. She came away from the window, knelt down in front of me, and put her arms around me. "Oh, my honey," she said, "I shouldn't talk like that. Your Pa, he's a good man. He's always done right by us and don't drink and carry on like some. But there ain't much a woman can have for herself, and it hurts mighty awful to lose what little you got."

But I was thinking about something else. "Ma, was them soldiers right when they said they wasn't suppose to bother black folks?"

8

She sighed and stood up. "I reckon so," she said. "The British generals figure if they don't treat us too hard we'll come onto their side. Some black folks say there ain't much sense in fighting for the Americans when most likely they'll keep black folks slaves if they win."

"Pa don't feel that way."

"No, your Pa, he's made his mind up he's an American by law and right and he's going to fight for it. Why do you think he's up drilling with Colonel Ledyard's militia all the time? There's your uncle Jack, too, gone off to fight with General Washington years ago. Your aunt Betsy, she hardly sees him from one year to the next."

"But then he'll be free."

"If he ain't killed," Ma said. "And it won't do Betsy much good, nor your cousin Daniel, neither, because they'll still be slaves, no matter what."

"But you said that Uncle Jack will buy them free."

"If he lives and gets his soldier's pay, and they don't get sold off to the West Indies first."

I knew all about that. After Colonel Ledyard set us free, Ma took a trip down the coast to Stratford to visit Aunt Betsy and Uncle Jack and my little cousin Dan. They was slaves of Captain Ivers. When she came back, she told us about Uncle Jack going off to fight. If he saved up his pay, Ma said, he'd maybe have enough money to buy Aunt Betsy and Cousin Dan free, too. But like Ma said, it wouldn't be no use if he got killed first.

And I was thinking it wouldn't be no use for Pa to be free if he got himself killed, neither, when suddenly there was a knock on the cabin door. Ma went and opened it a little, cautious. It was the two black soldiers. I noticed their uniforms was different; they had no leggins, short jackets, and no white straps across their chests. One of them was carrying a haunch of the cow, and the other had a bucket. "Here," he said. "If we'd known you was black we wouldn't have touched the cow."

Ma gave him that cold look. "I don't want it. You killed her, take it."

I knew I should be quiet and not get into trouble, but I was curious and couldn't help myself. "I didn't know niggers was British," I said.

"We ain't British. We're from New Jersey. The Third New Jersey Volunteers."

"Why are you fighting for the British?" I said.

"Why are you rebels?" the soldier said. "What's the use in fighting for the Americans when they're just going to keep you slaves?"

"We're not slaves," I said. "We're free."

"Keep your mouth shut, Willy," Ma said.

"You know what you ought to do, missus," the soldier said to Ma. "You ought to take the boy down to the boats and go back to New York with us." I forgot I looked like a boy in the britches.

Ma cocked her head. "We hear a lot of black folks that joined up with the British got sold off to the West Indies."

10

"That's just stories," the soldier said.

"Maybe," Ma said.

"I'm giving you good advice. Go off with us. There won't be much left around here anyways when we get finished today."

That made me go cold, for Pa would have to fight, if he wasn't dead already. "What are you coming up here to make trouble for?" I said.

"Hush up, my honey," Ma said.

She shouldn't have said it. The soldier leaned forward and looked hard into my face. "Are you a boy or a girl?" he asked.

I began to blush. "Can't you tell?"

"He's a boy," Ma said.

The soldier went on staring into my face. "I don't believe it," he said. Suddenly he reached his hand out to my shirt and felt for my breasts. "I figured you was a girl," he said. It gave me a queer, dirty feeling to have him mess with my body like that.

And just then Pa stepped up behind them. He had a log in his hands. My heart jumped. "Take your hands off that child," he said calmly, "or I'm going to kill you."

2

THE SOLDIER WHO WAS touching me swiveled around to look at Pa, but he didn't take his hand away.

"I told you to take your hand off that child," he said again.

The soldier let go of me and laughed. I kind of jumped back into the cabin door. The soldier raised up his musket and poked the bayonet toward Pa. "You're going to do what?" he said.

"If you touch her again, I'll tear your head off," Pa said, still in that calm way.

He stared at the soldier and the soldier stared back, and for a minute they stood like that. Nobody moved. Finally the soldier said, "If you was white, I'd run you through."

Pa didn't say anything. He just went on staring,

holding the log with both hands over his shoulder. Then the other soldier said, "Never mind this. Let's get the water." The first soldier didn't move, but went on staring at Pa. "Come on," the other one said. "We're going to catch it from the lieutenant if we don't get back soon with some water." He grabbed the first soldier's arm and shook it.

The first soldier spit into the dirt in front of the cabin. "You're lucky," he said to Pa. "If you'd been white, I'd run you through." He turned and strode off, the other one coming after him, the bucket handle creaking in its sockets.

We watched them go off for a minute. Then Pa said, "Is the horse all right?"

"Yes," Ma said. "They got the cow, but they never saw the horse."

"Good," he said. Suddenly we heard a fast pop-pop-pop from across the river. They were fighting in New London already. "I've got to get up to Fort Griswold."

"Jordan—" Ma started. Her eyes looked hurt and sad.

"Get me something to eat, Lucy," Pa said.

"Jordan, please, you have a child."

He pushed past her into the cabin. "Don't be arguing with me, Lucy," he said. Pa didn't like no arguing. Sometimes I'd just open my mouth and he'd tell me not to be argumentative. "Get me something to eat."

Ma went into the cabin behind him and I came after her. Pa sat down at the plank table, and Ma got out

14

the pork and biscuits and put it on a plate in front of him. She wanted to argue with him, but she didn't dare. He was the man, and she had to do what he told her to do. She was hurting inside, I could see that pretty clear.

I figured Pa knew it, too, but he sat there like he didn't know. While he ate, he told us what had happened. He'd gone out as usual to get the jolly boat and go fishing, but the minute he got down to the beach where he kept the boat pulled up on the sand he'd seen the British fleet standing offshore about three miles. They were beating back and forth, and from the distance he hadn't been able to tell whether they were coming into New London or not. He knew right away he ought to find out, so's to warn people if the ships were headed for us. So he'd pushed the jolly into the water, jumped in, hoisted sail, and went on out. It was a risky thing to do, because it would be pretty clear to the British that a lone fishing boat sailing around them was spying on them. But that was the way Pa was—he wasn't afraid of anything.

He had the wind at his back, and it didn't take him more than fifteen or twenty minutes to get close enough to see that the fleet was driving for New London. He came about to head back and raise the alarm, but now he had the wind against him. Just about then the British spotted him. They began shooting at him with muskets, but he was too far away, and them muskets wasn't very good at that range. So they let go at him with a cannon. Tacking back and forth across the wind the way he had to, he was going to be in cannon range a long time, so he turned and started east up the coast. On a reach across the wind like that he could make pretty good time. The British kept flinging cannonballs after him, trying to smash the boat, or at least tear out the sail. They came mighty close to doing it, too. A couple of times he saw the balls skip off the water right alongside the boat. But they never got him, and by and by he was out of range and they gave up.

But now he was way up the coast, six or seven miles from home, near a place called Long Point. He angled into shore, came about, and headed back, keeping as close to shore as he could, so's the sail would blend in with the white sand of the beach. But he didn't dare come all the way in. He turned into Baker's Cove a couple of miles to the east of Groton Point. He tied the boat up there to a tree where nobody was likely to see it. Then he crept up into the woods and waited there until the British got finished marching past. As he was coming back down he saw the two soldiers talking to us, and he picked up the log: he figured they were up to no good and he wanted to be ready. It was pretty foolish, just a log against a couple of men with guns and bayonets, but that was the way Pa was. If that soldier hadn't taken his hand off me, Pa would have whacked him one with the log, that was for sure.

The muskets kept popping away in New London

across the river, and there was sounds of firing from Fort Griswold now, too. Out the window we could see smoke rising up from someplace and drifting around in the air. There were faint, distant shouts, too.

Pa jumped up. "I've got to go," he said. "I've got to get to the fort before the British get up there."

Suddenly I realized that Ma was standing in the doorway. Her two hands were clenched together and she wasn't moving. She stared at Pa. "Jordan, please—"

"Lucy, get out of my way," he said.

Then she dropped down on her knees. "I'm begging you, Jordan." Her eyes were hurt and sick, and I knew how much she hated begging him. But she went on kneeling there. "Please, Jordan."

He looked away to me. "Willy, I want you to ride up there with me to bring the horse back."

"Not the child," Ma cried. "You'll get her killed."

"I ain't going to get her killed," he said in his calm voice.

She jumped up. "Don't go, Willy," she cried.

"She'll do what she's told," Pa said.

"She's just a child, Jordan."

"No, she ain't. She's thirteen."

"She's a girl, she's not a man."

That stopped him for a minute. He stood looking at me. Then he said, "Willy, get one of my cockade hats out of the cupboard. With them britches on, you look like a boy, anyway."

So I got his cockade hat—it was brown, with a

yellow ribbon—and put it on. Pa looked me over. Then he pushed past Ma through the door and I went with him. I didn't dare go against him.

He brought the horse around the cabin and I climbed up behind him. There wasn't any going against him; he was the man. I sort of wanted to go, anyway. I wanted to see what it was like. But I was mighty scared, too. As we rode away up the road I turned to look back at Ma. She was standing in the doorway with her hands over her face, all bent over. I waved, but the way she had her face covered she couldn't see me.

We went on up the road a ways. All along there was people running, carrying stuff in their arms or slung over their backs—taking boxes and bags and chairs or pictures into the fields and woods to hide them from the British. Crazy old Granny Hyde was leading a piglet along on a string.

Fort Griswold was up ahead on a steep slope off the road. There was plenty of popping coming from up there, and sometimes the big boom of a cannon. We went on until we was about a mile or so from the fort, and then Pa turned the horse off into woods, so's we could circle around and come up to the fort from behind. The woods rose up and when we got a little higher I could see New London across the Thames. There was smoke drifting up out of it now, and there was flames and black smoke boiling up on the dock. The British was going to burn the town down, I knew that. They'd done it to plenty of other towns, like

Danbury, over in the western part of Connecticut, and New Haven and Fairfield and Norwalk right along Long Island Sound. I wondered if they'd burn Groton down, too.

Now we began to circle back toward the fort. The firing kept getting louder and louder. Each time a musket cracked I jumped and closed my eyes. The gunsmoke was drifting through the trees like thin ghosts. I was scared pretty good by now, and I wished Pa would change his mind and turn around and go home. Or maybe we'd get up there and find the fort surrounded by the British and no way to get in. But he just kept pushing forward.

Then ahead the woods began to thin out and the smoke got thicker. My heart began to race and my legs felt weak and wobbly. We climbed down off the horse, and Pa tied her to a tree. We crept forward on our hands and knees to the edge of the woods.

Fort Griswold was dead ahead of us. It was made of stone, maybe nine feet high. They'd piled dirt partway up the stone. On top of the stone walls was a plank fence, sticking out at an angle to make it hard to climb over. A couple of cannon stuck out through gaps in the boards. I could see the heads of men and muskets and bayonets.

The British were off to the left on the downslope, lying behind rocks and little ridges in the ground, firing up at the fort. Some of the New Jersey soldiers with bare legs were pushing cannons up the slope. I looked at Pa, lying beside me. He was looking at the

British and then over to the fort and back to the British again, calculating. Then he turned to me. "Willy, I'm going to make a run for it round the north side. There's no one shooting from there yet, and once I'm up against the walls the British won't be able to get a clean shot at me, anyway."

"How are you going to get over them walls, Pa?"

"Somebody up top is bound to see me," he said. "They'll give me a hand up." He took another look down the slope to the British. Then he turned back to me. "Now, you wait here until you see me safe into the fort, just in case I can't make it. Once I'm up in there, you get on the horse and run on home to your Ma. Understand?"

"Yes, Pa," I said.

He put his arm around my shoulders to give me a quick hug and kissed me on the forehead. "You be a brave girl now, and help your Ma all you can."

"Yes, Pa," I said. A shiver passed through me, because I knew he was likely to be killed up there in the fort.

Then he jumped up onto his feet and, crouching low, began to run across the open space to the fort. I looked down at the British. They spotted him right away. They swiveled around and let go at him. My heart was pounding. "Oh, run, Pa," I said aloud. He went running crouched over and in a moment he was up against the wall of the fort, looking up, hollering and waving. He wasn't there more than five seconds before they let down a rope. He grabbed onto it and they pulled him up headfirst over the wall. I wondered if those legs disappearing over the wall was the last I'd ever see of him.

Now I turned and crawled back through the woods to where the horse was tied to a tree. She was prancing around and snapping her head up and down, and I knew she was as scared as I was of the noise and the smoke ghosts drifting through the woods. I patted her a couple of times to calm her down a little. Then I untied her and climbed up on her, and that was when I saw a whole bunch of red jackets come through the woods smack toward me.

I jerked on the reins to swing the horse around so as to circle past them in the woods, but they saw me. "Spy, spy," I heard one of them shout, and then I heard a bang just behind me again. I kicked the horse, and the next thing I knew I was charging out of the woods into the open space toward the fort. I hunched down on the horse's back, hanging on to her neck, trying to push myself right down into her skin. My eyes was closed and all I could think was that any second a musket ball could catch me in the back.

3

I FELT WEAK AND COLD and my heart was pounding so hard I could hear it racing in my head over the noise of the fighting. It seemed like I was galloping across the clearing for hours. I opened my eyes. The fort was dead ahead, twenty-five yards away. I kicked the horse again, and we came up to the wall. Just as I slid off her back, she shrieked and rose up on her hind legs, and I knew she'd taken a musket ball somewhere. I reached out to pat her, but she broke and ran, and then I felt something hit my shoulder. It was a rope. I grabbed it and looked up. There was Pa, looking down over the wall, and then I began to rise up, keeping my head turned away toward the wall, so's at least I wouldn't catch a ball in my face. Something snapped against the stones of the wall, flinging tiny bits of rock into my face. The bits of rock stung, and some got into my mouth. I spit, and then Pa was pulling me over the wooden palisades into the fort and I was safe.

I was up on a kind of wood platform that ran all the way around the inside of the fort about four feet below the top of the palisades. There were men crouched all along here, firing out at the British. There was cannons at the corners, with three or four men on each. Down in the center of the fort there was a well and a low wooden shed that I figured was a barracks for the soldiers to be in when they wasn't fighting. Underneath the platform there was a little room where they stored the gun powder and balls and such.

In the middle of the fort, next to the well, there was four men stretched out. I stared at them. One of them was moving his legs slowly back and forth and holding his side. He was pale and breathing hard. I didn't know if he was dying or not, but he was suffering something awful. The other three wasn't moving at all. They just lay on their backs and stared up at the sky.

All at once the shooting began to die off, and in a minute it stopped altogether. The silence was queer. The men began to talk and look over the wall, and Pa and I looked over the wall, too. We saw three British officers walking slowly up the slope to the fort, carrying a white flag. On a platform across the fort from us I saw Colonel Ledyard, with some men clustered around him. Suddenly one of the men raised his musket and fired. I looked out. The three British officers had stopped walking and were standing in the dusty ground, still holding the white flag. Then three of the men who had been with Colonel Ledyard climbed down from the platform, went out the door to the fort, and down the slope to talk to the British. In a couple of minutes they came back and climbed back up onto the platform to report to Colonel Ledyard.

"I'm going to find out what's happening," Pa said. He worked his way along the platform, stopping to talk with the men here and there, and in a moment he came back. "The British want us to surrender," he said. "We ain't going to. We're going to fight." He looked pretty serious. "They threaten to massacre us if we don't surrender."

"Will they, Pa?"

"No," he said. "It's just threats." He looked out over the palisade. "I wish you wasn't in here to see this, Willy." He went on looking around outside the fort. "I wish you could make a run for it, but it's too risky. They're moving around behind the fort now. The woods is full of them. There ain't any good way to get out."

"I'll be all right, Pa," I said. But I wasn't so sure I would. I couldn't keep my eyes off those men lying out there in the dirt—one of them still moving his legs slowly back and forth, and the others so still. There were flies on their faces now. My mouth was dry and my stomach began to turn over. I wished they would move, but they never did. I wondered if I would be able to stand it if I saw somebody get killed.

"Willy, go down into the powder magazine. You'll

be safer down there, and you can help them make cartridges."

I was glad enough to get away where I wouldn't see too much. I was curious, but I didn't know how much of it I could watch. Here and there was ladders going down from the platform. I climbed down one and trotted across the fort to the powder magazine, steering around the bodies with the flies on them. The magazine was just a little room. It was pretty dark in there, and they'd left the door open so's to get some light. There was boxes of balls and barrels of powder; you couldn't have any kind of lantern down there with all that powder around.

There was a white boy down there about my age. I knew who he was, too—William Latham. His Pa was Captain William Latham, and they lived in Groton. I went in. "My Pa says I'm to help," I said.

He gave me a funny look. He knew he knew me, but dressed up like a boy the way I was he couldn't figure me out. I was going to tell him, but then suddenly it came to me that if I told him I was a girl he'd start giving me orders and maybe wouldn't let me help with the cartridges. Of course me being black and him white he was likely to give me orders anyway, but not so much as if I was a girl. So I didn't say anything about who I was. "Are you making cartridges?"

He showed me how to do it. First he tore off a little square of some paper that was lying near him and wrapped it around a stick to make a tube. He twisted the bottom of the tube closed and took it off the stick.

26

Then he dropped in some powder and a ball, twisted the other end of the tube closed, and put the cartridge in a basket. All a soldier had to do was pour the powder down the barrel of his musket, drop the cartridge in and tap it home with the ramrod to make sure it was all the way down the barrel. Then he'd spill a bit of powder on the pan and fire. It saved an awful lot of time for the soldiers to have a pile of cartridges ready.

So I set to work, feeling mighty scared, and just about then the firing took up again. From down there in the magazine I could hear the cannonballs thudding against the wooden palisades, and men cursing and shouting and running along the platform overhead. Every few minutes the cannon would go off, shaking the whole fort. The sharp smell of gunsmoke drifted around everywhere. Oh, I was scared, just as scared as I could be, feeling cold and pale and trembly. I knelt next to William Latham, making cartridges and putting them in the basket.

"Do you think they'll break in?" I said.

He shook his head. His eyes was wide and he was as pale as I was. "They said they'd kill us all if we wouldn't surrender."

"Pa said that was just bluster."

He gave me a look. "Who's your Pa?"

"You don't know him," I said. "We're from over to New London."

He gave me another look, like he knew I was lying, but just then a soldier swung his head into the door and shouted, "Get some cartridges up there, quick."

I looked at William and he looked at me. "I'll go," he said. "You can go next time."

He picked up the basket and went out the door. I went on kneeling there, making cartridges, feeling sort of numb from the noise and shouts and the uproar. Out in the yard now there was a half dozen more men lying there, some of them just wounded and shaking and moaning, and some of them lying still. It kept worrying me that one of them might be Pa, but kneeling down that way I couldn't see them very well. I wondered if I ought to go out there and help the ones that was wounded, especially if one of them was Pa. They might need water, or to have their wounds tied up. But I reckoned it was more important to go on making cartridges.

Suddenly William dropped down from the platform in front of the door and jumped inside.

"What's happening?" I asked.

"Oh, it's mighty bad," he said. "The British are all around the fort, right up by the walls. They're trying to climb up, and there's a bunch of them at the door, hammering at it."

"Did you see my Pa?" I'd forgotten that he wasn't supposed to know who we was.

He gave me another funny look. "There's two or three niggers up there," he said. "I didn't see any dead ones."

"There's a lot of dead?"

"Lots," he said. "Leastwise there's a lot down. The

British are climbing up the palisades and we're fighting them with pikes."

Now it was all roaring and shouting and banging. I could hear hard thumping on the fort door, and the splintering of wood and shouts and shrieks. "Are they breaking down the palisades?"

"It's your turn to go up with the cartridges," he said.

Oh, how I wished I hadn't decided to be a boy. If he'd known I was a girl, he'd have never sent me up there. But I wasn't going to go back on it now. I wasn't going to let him see me be a coward. Pa would hate that if he knew. So I picked up the basket, ducked out the magazine door, and started up the nearest ladder to the platform. As soon as I got halfway up I could see a big gap in the wooden palisades where the British had ripped out a couple of planks.

There was two or three British in the gap, hanging on with one hand and jabbing around with their bayonets. And there was three or four Americans jabbing back at them with pikes. Pa was with them, and I climbed on up and dropped down the basket. I saw Pa ram his spear right into the stomach of a British soldier. The soldier grabbed at it with both hands. Just then there was a great splintering crash.

The main door to the fort was busted open, and the British flooded in. They poured into the fort, roaring and shouting, and flashing those shiny bayonets around. My heart was racing and I didn't hardly even

29

know what I was doing. I got into a corner of the palisades and crouched there. Down below, the Americans was running back across the fort to get away from the British, and the British was swirling among them with their bayonets, jabbing and jabbing. They was going to kill us all, just like they said.

I looked over at Pa. A stream of British were climbing through the gap in the palisades. Pa and the others was backing away down the platform, poking at the British with their pikes, but there was about ten British for the three of them, and I knew they couldn't last. I just crouched there, sick and shaking and so scared I couldn't move.

Then I saw Colonel Ledyard in the middle of the fort. There was a British officer there. Colonel Ledyard jumped up to him, holding his sword sideways with a hand at each end and waving it up and down. He was going to surrender, and I thanked God for it, so the awfulness would stop.

"Who commands here?" the British officer shouted.

"I did," Colonel Ledyard said, handing his sword forward. "But you do now, sir."

The British officer took the sword and then, without waiting one second, jabbed it into Colonel Ledyard's side so that it went all the way through him and came out the other side. Colonel Ledyard never even made a noise, but fell down into the dirt.

And suddenly there was some Americans there, and Pa was among them. Somebody rammed a pike through the British officer. I couldn't see who done it, whether it was Pa or somebody else, but the next thing I knew there was British soldiers all around him, and I saw a bayonet go through his back and he flung his arms out like so, and fell off the bayonet to the ground. I began to shriek. The shouting and the killing went on and on, and I crouched there on the platform with my eyes closed, crying and moaning and waiting to be killed.

4

I DON'T KNOW HOW long I crouched there with my eyes closed and tears running down, and sort of gasping; it seemed like forever. Then I felt the platform rattle next to me. I opened my eyes. A British soldier was standing over me, his musket pulled back with a bloody bayonet pointing right at me. I shrieked and flung myself up against the palisades and put my hands out in front to ward off the bayonet. His eyes were blue and his hair was blond, and he seemed young even to me. It was queer that this man who was going to kill me was an actual person, not some kind of devil or madman. And I guess it was realizing that he was a human being like me that let me open my mouth and say, "Please don't kill me. I'm not a boy, I'm a girl."

He had his musket half drawn back. He stopped and stared into my face for a moment. "Why, so you are," he said, looking surprised. "What are you doing in this?"

"I came up with my Pa." I started sobbing. "He's already dead."

He grabbed me by the shoulder, spun me around, and took hold of the collar of my shirt. "Out of here now." He sort of shoved me off the platform onto the ground, jumped down beside me, and grabbed my collar again. Then he began shoving me through the terrible place toward the door. There were bodies everywhere, and the blood so thick in places it made the ground slippery. Soldiers was lying on the ground writhing while the British rammed bayonets into them, so's some of them must have got killed a dozen times. I wanted to close my eyes, but I couldn't. And then I was out of the fort and running across the battlefield toward the woods as fast as I could go, sobbing so much that the tears flew off my face behind me as I ran.

There were soldiers all around on the hillside, some of the British regulars with white leggins and some of the New Jersey ones with bare legs, who we'd seen pushing the cannons up the rocky slope. They'd got a couple of the cannon up now, but there wasn't anybody left for them to kill.

As I ducked into the woods I could still hear shouts from up at the fort, and muskets banging away. But it had slowed down a lot, and I knew that they'd killed most of the American militia and didn't have anybody to shoot anymore. There was the smell of wood and molasses burning from New London across the river. I wondered if they was going to burn Groton, too. I thought about that, and what we'd do if they burned our cabin. I tried to think about the molasses burning so's not to think about Pa being stabbed by those bayonets.

The thing I wanted the most was to get home to Ma. I wanted to be with her so bad I could hardly stand it. I waited a few more minutes, and then I decided I was going home, British or no British.

I slipped down the hillside through the woods until I came to where the ground leveled out by the river. There was a little road here running along the shore. Smoke was boiling up from New London. It covered the river, but through it I could see boats being rowed hither and yon, and ships at the wharf burned to the waterline and another big ship afire drifting down the river. There was a few people going up the road to get away from Groton, women mostly, carrying bags and furniture and such, all looking mighty scared. Nobody paid any attention to me, so I began trotting along.

I was feeling odd, the queerest I'd ever felt in my life. My head was numb and I couldn't think straight about anything: ideas just came and went with no order nor reason. Down inside me was an awful pain. Try as I might not to, I kept seeing Pa with that bayonet going into his back and his arms flung out so. And all I knew was that I wanted my Ma in the worst way.

I trotted along, dazed, the only one going toward the beach; all the others were running north, trying to get away from the British. Once I passed a wagon with some men lying in the back of it all bloody, and I knew the British was bringing the wounded out of the fort. I wondered if Pa was still up there, and I hurried along to get home to Ma to tell her what had happened.

As I got along down toward our cabin, I could see out in the ocean the British fleet, standing at anchor, as calm as you please. Finally our cabin came in sight. It was sitting there in the afternoon sun just the way it had been in the morning when I'd left with Pa. It was just the same, but everything else was changed, and nothing would ever be the same again.

When I got to within a little ways of it, I began to run. I just wanted to throw my arms around Ma and hug her and have her hold me tight. I ran up to the door. It was open. I looked in. Nobody was there. Where was she? Why wasn't she waiting for me? "Ma?" I called out. "Ma, where are you?"

I looked around. Her bonnet and her cloak was hanging on the hook by the door where they always was. I went back outside and walked around the cabin, looking off in the distance for her and shouting "Ma, Ma" over and over; but I didn't get nothing back. Tears began to run down my cheeks again. I went back into the cabin to see if there was any signs of where she'd gone. I figured maybe she'd hidden some stuff out in the woods like the rest, and was out there collecting it back. Oh, there were a lot of places she could have gone. She could even have gone up to the fort looking for me and Pa.

I sat on the ground by the roadside with my back up against the cabin wall so I'd see Ma when she was heading home. I sat there for a long time, trying not to cry, but gasping sometimes and wiping tears away. The sun was way out to the west, dropping down behind New London lighthouse, and the woods was filled with shadows. A little evening breeze came up off the water. With the sun going down it was getting chilly. I shivered. Where was Ma? Had the British got her? Had they done something to her and flung her away someplace?

So I went on sitting there, watching the night come up and wondering what I ought to do. And just when I was thinking that maybe I should go up to Groton and look for her, I saw somebody coming down the road toward me. I waited and watched, praying that it would be Ma. But it wasn't; it was the old darkie named Granny Hyde. She lived alone in a little hut in the village and was always talking to herself, sort of crazy-like. She still had her pig tugging on a line be-hind her. She came up to me and stopped and stared at me. Then she said, "We thought you was dead, Willy. We thought you was dead for sure."

"Pa's dead," I said. "I saw it happen. They ran him

through with their bayonets. They killed most near everybody."

"I know," she said. "We thought you was dead, too, Willy."

"Where's Ma?"

She shook her head. "Gone."

"Gone?"

"Gone," she said. "The British took her. They took three or four niggers, heaved them into their boats and took them off to New York with them." She shook her head. "We won't see none of them ever again."

I couldn't believe it. I didn't want to believe it. What would I do with Pa dead and Ma captured? It gave me such a hopeless feeling, like all the air just went out of my stomach. The tears were running down my cheeks in rivers, it seemed like, and run into my mouth all salty. Try as I might to stop, I was sobbing again. Granny Hyde put her arm around my shoulders. "You go get your things, Willy," she said. "You come stay with me. I've got to go along now. You come soon." She went off with her pig along behind.

I didn't know what to do. I couldn't believe that Ma was really gone. I went back into the cabin. I was dead tired and I didn't feel like eating nothing, but I was thirsty and I drank a pot of beer. Then I took Ma's cloak down, lay on the bed with it wrapped around me, so's I could smell her smell. I just lay there sobbing and heaving and after a while I must have just fallen asleep.

When I woke up, the morning sky was getting gray

and the birds was chirping. It took me a minute to come to myself and remember what had happened. I sat up and said "Ma?" and looked around the cabin. She wasn't there. I busted out crying again. Where was she? Finally I realized that I couldn't go on crying forever, I had to do something, so I wiped my face on my sleeve, got up off the bed, and ate the rest of the biscuits that was there. Then I went out of the cabin and had a look around. It was gray dawn, but the sky was clear and it was going to be another sunny day. There was still smoke in the air drifting over from New London, with that burned molasses smell to it.

I didn't know if the British was gone or not. I knew I would be able to see out into the water from the hill that rose up toward Groton, so I walked up there through the woods, smelling the oaks and hemlocks. When I was far enough up, I looked out to sea. The British fleet was there, more ships than I'd ever seen in my life. There was a lot of transports, and among them great three-masted frigates with rows and rows of cannons along their sides and the British flag hanging limp in the light breeze. They was so close I could see the sailors scurrying around the decks. Oh, my, it scared me all over again to see those ships. They was like death itself.

I looked in the other direction, toward New London. It was mostly just ashes and chimneys, with columns of smoke coming up here and there. The wharves was all burned right down to the water, and there was a lot of hulls drifting around the harbor, burned down to the waterline, too. It was surprising to see a town just gone like that—there one morning and gone the next. It was like seeing half a person—just a pair of legs walking around with nothing above its belt.

All that really mattered to me, though, was that Pa was dead and Ma was gone. I was so numb from that that I could hardly think about anything else. But I had to get hold of myself and figure out what to do next. One thing I knew was that I wasn't going to go live with crazy old Granny Hyde.

I went back down to the cabin and sat at the plank table and thought about it. The question that come to me was how was I going to live. Colonel Ledyard, he was dead, so there wasn't any hope of working for him. Of course, Mrs. Ledyard, she might need help and maybe would take me on. But that wouldn't be no different from going back into slavery again. Mrs. Ledyard, she was going to be poor now and wouldn't be able to pay me nothing, just room and keep. The only way I'd ever get out of that would be to get married. But there wasn't hardly any black men left around, and none that I wanted to marry, anyway.

What I wanted most of all was to have Ma back. I missed her so, I felt all hollow in my stomach, and sometimes I missed her so much I just sort of gasped for breath.

But she was gone, and what could I do? Who was there for me? What relatives did I have? Only Aunt Betsy and Uncle Jack Arabus, and Cousin Dan, and

I'd never met any of them. Would they take me in? Ma always said how much she and Aunt Betsy loved each other. She was bound to take me in. I was kin. And right then I resolved that's what I'd do—I'd go down to Stratford to Aunt Betsy. She'd take me in.

Just thinking about it made me feel a whole lot better. I wasn't exactly happy, but I stopped gasping for breath, and such.

But how would I get there? It was fifty miles to Stratford. I could walk it in three days probably. But there was Pa's jolly boat. He'd moored it up on Baker's Cove, he said. It might still be there. The British might have found it, or somebody might have come along and just plain stole it. But it was worth a chance.

So I searched around in the cupboard for something to eat. There was a few apples and some cornbread. I wrapped them in Ma's kerchief and then I left the cabin and set off for Baker's Cove. Soon I came to the beach. The British ships was raising their sails and getting ready to head back to New York. Judging by the sun it was about halfway between sunrise and noon. I didn't want to go sailing down amongst the British ships, but I figured they'd be gone pretty soon. The tide was up and the air was fresh and salty. I walked along the beach for a ways. Sure enough, tied up under a willow tree, so that the branches hung down over it, was the jolly boat. It was sixteen foot long, and pretty wide, so's to have room inside for plenty of fish if you got a good catch. It was lateen rigged, which means the sail hung down from a yard about two thirds the way up the mast. Pa had painted a yellow band around it just below the gunnels for decoration.

I untied the boat, climbed in, and pushed off the bank with an oar. Then I hoisted the sail and swung out into the ocean. It was around thirty-five miles to New Haven, and maybe fifteen more to Newfield in Stratford, where Aunt Betsy lived with Captain Ivers. Ma had told me about the place lots of times. Captain Ivers had a wharf by the shore in the New-field part of Stratford, and a warehouse, and a black brig. I figured I'd recognize it.

I could see the British fleet clear now. Their sails was full and they was moving down past the river into the Sound where the ocean was cut off by Long Island. The wind was from the southwest, so's I couldn't run straight down but had to tack back and forth, staying in close to shore as much as I could in case something went wrong.

I sailed all day that way, feeling lonely and sad, but determined to get there. When the sun was overhead, I pulled into a little creek to look for fresh water. I dipped the bread in the water to soften it, and ate it and the apples.

As I sat there eating, it came to me: What if Aunt Betsy wouldn't take me in? What if they didn't have no place for me? Or what if Captain Ivers, her master, didn't want no more niggers around?

42

I decided not to let myself think of that. I took a big drink of water out of the creek to store up, and set off again.

For a long time I could see the British fleet ahead of me, pushing toward New York. They was going faster than me, but it took them hours to pull away. Oh, I hated seeing them. Finally the ships dwindled down to sails, and then, by the middle of the afternoon, the sails was gone, too.

I sailed on. I went past New Haven, which looked even bigger than New London, with two long wharves sticking out into the water and behind them a great patchwork of roofs with three or four church steeples sticking up out of them. I couldn't see but one sloop in the harbor; I guess the rest had got sunk in the war.

I went on sailing, watching the sun set, and the light fade out in the sky, and by and by I came to the mouth of a big river opening out into the Sound. I figured it was the Housatonic. I'd heard Pa talk about it. I knew that Newfield wasn't much further along; and sure enough, in fifteen minutes, here came a wharf with a black brig tied up to it, and on shore a warehouse facing out to sea.

I headed the jolly boat in and beached it on the sand alongside the wharf, and climbed out. I was feeling mighty cramped from sitting in the jolly boat all day, but oh so glad I'd soon be with somebody. I had a good stretch, twisting and squirming with my arms over my head, and then I walked up the beach to the warehouse and found a little path there. Back across a field I could see lights. I walked along the path until I could make out a brown shingled house in the dark.

Then I stopped, and began to worry all over again. Suppose they didn't want me after all? Suppose Aunt Betsy didn't love Ma so much as Ma thought? Besides, she'd never met me and didn't know me from a goat. Suppose they didn't need no extra mouths to feed? But I was lonely and tired and I wanted to be with somebody as bad as could be. So I slipped around behind the house. There was a barn there. Somebody was moving around in it with a lantern. I crept up to the barn door and took a peek inside. There was a little black boy there in the lantern light, pitching hay into a stall where a cow was tied up. I figured he must be my cousin Dan.

I stepped into the barn. He sort of jumped around and looked at me. "You're Dan, ain't you?"

"Yes, sir," he said.

It kind of surprised me to be called sir. Nobody had ever called me that before. But he was only seven and I guess I looked like a grown-up to him. "I'm your cousin Willy from Groton," I said.

His eyes went wide. "Cousin Willy?"

"Where's your Ma?" I said.

"She's in the kitchen fixing supper for the Iverses, sir."

For the first time in a while I felt like smiling. "You don't have to call me sir," I said. "I ain't a boy. I'm a girl."

44

"Oh," he said. He looked kind of doubtful. "I'll tell Ma you're out here." He dropped the pitchfork and ran past me out of the barn and through the back door into the house. And in about five seconds Aunt Betsy came running out, wiping her hands on her skirt.

I went out towards her. For a moment we stood there in the dark, with only the light from the lantern making shadows on our faces, just looking at each other. Then she said, "Willy?"

"Yes, ma'am," I said. "It's me."

"I would have known, anyway," she said. "You're the spittin' image of your Ma." Then we came together and hugged. It felt mighty good to be hugged again.

She pulled back. "We heard about Fort Griswold. Did your Ma send you down here?"

"No, ma'am," I said. "I came by myself. The British took Ma down to New York."

She put her hands over her face. "Oh, no," she said. "I was scared it would be like that. We heard terrible stories, but we didn't know what to believe."

"Pa's dead," I said. "They killed him. I saw it. They stabbed him in the back and—" I started to choke and quit talking. Aunt Betsy put her arms around me again and held me like I was a baby. I wished I was a baby, too, and had somebody to look after me and didn't know about all the terrible things that had happened.

"What are you going to do now, Willy?"

I lifted up my head and looked at her face, all yellow in the lantern light. "I figured on staying with you," I said. "I'll work hard."

She looked sad and shook her head. "I don't know, Willy," she said. "I don't know what Captain Ivers'll say about that. I wouldn't want to trust him none."

Just then there came around the corner of the house a big black man wearing white army trousers and an old shirt. I knew it must be Uncle Jack.

"It's Willy, Jack," Aunt Betsy said. "Jordan got killed at Fort Griswold and the British took Lucy down to New York."

He didn't say nothing, but looked at me, and then he put his arms around me and gave me a big hug. "You poor child," he said. I was mighty glad I'd come there.

5

It was just luck that Uncle Jack Arabus was home when I got there. He was in the American army—the Fifth Company of the Third Regiment of the Connecticut Line, under Captain Bradley. There was seven or eight black men in the company, he said. There was lots of black men in George Washington's army. The rule was that they got themselves free if they would join up.

Uncle Jack had been staying way over in New York up along the Hudson near some place called Cold Spring. They'd furloughed the men home to get fresh clothes and new shoes. Uncle Jack, he'd already fought at Trenton and Stony Point, and some other places, too. They were fixing to fight again. Uncle Jack didn't know where, but he figured they might attack New

47

York to drive the British out. But there was no way of being sure.

They took me into the kitchen. There was a big brick fireplace, with a fire going, a rough wooden table where the Arabus family ate, big pans hanging up along the walls, and cupboards with pewter mugs and plates inside. It was nice to be with them, all warm and cozy, instead of all alone by myself on the water. Aunt Betsy fed me some corn bread and salt pork and I sat there and ate, kind of sniffling and putting out a little sob every once in a while. I told them the whole story: about seeing the British land and the battle and then Ma disappearing. And I'd just about got to where I was sailing off in the jolly boat, when a thin white woman, with a pointed nose, came into the kitchen. I figured she must be Captain Ivers's wife. She looked at me. "Who's this?" she snapped out.

"She's my sister's child," Aunt Betsy said. "Her name's Wilhelmina."

I got up and started to give a little curtsy, the way Ma had taught me, but in the middle of doing it I realized I couldn't because I didn't have no skirt on; so I bowed instead.

"Why's she dressed like a boy?" Mrs. Ivers sort of spit when she talked.

"She just came down from New London, ma'am," Uncle Jack said. "She was in the fighting. Her Pa got killed and her Ma taken off by the British."

Mrs. Ivers went on staring at me as if I was lower than dirt and she was afraid she'd soil herself just by looking at me. It made me mighty uneasy, that stare. "Well, she can't stay here," she said. "I'm not going to feed another lazy nigger. I've got enough of them as it is."

"She hasn't got anyplace to go, ma'am," Uncle Jack said, kind of quiet.

"I can't help that," Mrs. Ivers said. "I can't be responsible for any stray who happens up."

"Please, ma'am," Aunt Betsy said. "She ain't a stray. She's my sister's only child."

"Let your sister look after her, then," Mrs. Ivers said.

"But, ma'am," Aunt Betsy started to say, when Captain Ivers himself came into the kitchen. He was thin like Mrs. Ivers, but taller. His hair was silver, and his nose was pointed, too. "Someone left a lantern burning in the barn," he snarled. "Arabus, you go take care of that." Then he noticed me. "Whose nigger boy is this?" he said.

"She isn't a boy, she's a girl," Mrs. Ivers said.

"She's kin, sir," Uncle Jack said. "Her Pa was killed yesterday at Fort Griswold fighting the British." Then he went out the door.

Now it was Captain Ivers's turn to stare at me in that way his wife had. He stared for a while, thinking, his face dead still, like a frozen pond. Then he said, "Whose nigger are you?"

"Nobody's, sir." I said. "We're free niggers."

The captain thought about that for a minute with that frozen look. Then he said, "You sure you didn't run away when you had a chance during the fighting?"

"No, sir," I said. "Colonel Ledyard, he set us all free four years ago so Pa could join up with the army."

"It'll be easy enough to check that with Ledyard," he said.

"Colonel Ledyard, he's dead," I said. "Some British officer killed him with his own sword. I saw it."

He stared at me some more, thinking. It was amazing he could hold his face so still. Talking to him was like splashing eggs off ice; they didn't leave no mark. Finally he said, "How'd you get down here, anyway?"

"I came down in Pa's jolly boat, sir."

"By yourself?"

"Yes, sir."

"She can't stay here," Mrs. Ivers put in.

"Be quiet, Mother," Captain Ivers said. "Don't trouble yourself with making decisions." He looked up at the ceiling and rubbed his neck, which was the most expression he'd shown so far. Then he said, "The colonel left a widow, I suppose?"

"Mrs. Ledyard?"

"What sort of idiot are you?" he snapped. He snatched at my ear and gave it a twist. It hurt mighty good, but I knew better than to cry out. "Who did you think I was talking about?"

"She's alive, sir," I said. "Unless she got killed."

He let go of my ear. "She's from New London?"

"No, sir," I said. My ear smarted and I wanted to rub it, but I didn't dare. "The Ledyards are from Groton, across the river from New London."

50

"I know where Groton is," he said. "Don't advise me."

"No, sir," I said. Oh, he was making me mad and I felt like arguing back, but there wasn't nothing I could do about it.

Suddenly Mrs. Ivers got her courage up and said, "I don't want her in my house," which would have been all right by me.

"She's staying," Captain Ivers said. "Until I decide what to do with her." He gave Mrs. Ivers a look. She looked mighty cross, but she didn't dare go against him.

"Very well, Father," she said. "If she's staying, she's going to work for her supper, I promise you that." Captain Ivers didn't pay any attention to her, but went away. She turned to Aunt Betsy. "She can start by scrubbing the floors. And put her in a dress. This is a God-fearing home and I won't have anybody under my roof dressed unnatural." Then she stomped out of the kitchen.

We sat there quiet for a moment, Aunt Betsy and Dan and me. Then Aunt Betsy said, "I don't like it none, Willy. He's got something in mind for you."

I didn't have to ask what it was. Captain Ivers was trying to figure a way to put me back into slavery. I didn't know what he'd do with me once he'd done it—sell me off to the West Indies most likely. The trouble was, I didn't have no freedom papers. I knew I was free, but that didn't prove it. Pa had papers hid

51

up in the cabin somewhere, but that wasn't no use to me now. And even if I had them, I couldn't read them, so I wouldn't know what they said. "What can I do?" I said.

Aunt Betsy shook her head. "I don't know what you can do, Willy. All I can say is, it's going to be mighty risky for you to stay around here."

I thought about the jolly boat, tied up at the wharf. "Maybe I could go down to New York and find Ma."

She shook her head again. "You couldn't hardly do that, Willy. The British have it. There's thousands of troops there. They set the town alight twice and half burned it down. There's hardly anything to eat, either, even for the British. You'd never find her, and the chances are you'd starve, too."

"I might find her, though."

"You'd never get through. There's skirmishing and such going on all around the city. If you asked too many questions, you might get hanged for a spy. We know about it. Your uncle Jack, he has a friend down there, Black Sam Fraunces. He owns about the biggest tavern in New York. The British let him go in and out of the city so's he can search out food for the tavern. A lot of the officers eat there. He came up to where your uncle Jack was stationed with General Washington and told Jack about it."

"Maybe Mr. Fraunces would help me find Ma," I said. "Maybe he'd know where she was."

"It's rough down there, Willy," Aunt Betsy said. "It ain't no place for a girl to be wandering around in."

I knew I shouldn't argue with her—she was a grown-up, and I was just a child. But there was this picture in my head of me coming along some street in New York and suddenly here comes Ma, and we run up and hug each other. Just thinking about it gave me a lovely feeling. I wanted to be with her so much I could hardly stand it.

Another reason for leaving there was that the whole Arabus family slept down in the Iverses' cellar on heaps of straw. It was a mean, damp place down there and bound to be cold in the winter. I wasn't used to it; I was used to having a cabin of our own, and a real straw mattress. I was worried I'd take sick living down in a cellar like that.

The next day Mrs. Ivers put me to work scrubbing floors. I hated it. If it had been Ma who made me scrub floors, I wouldn't have minded so much, because it would have been for a good reason; and if I was getting paid for it, it would have been all right, too. Being ordered around by Mrs. Ivers like I was a slave again made me mad, and it was all I could do to keep from shouting at her. But I knew if I did that she'd twist my ear and maybe beat me, too, so I made myself keep quiet.

Captain Ivers, he was down at his warehouse all morning. He came back at lunchtime and into the parlor where I was scrubbing. "Stand up," he said.

"Yes, sir," I said.

There wasn't no skirt for me so I was still wearing my milking britches. He looked me up and down like I was some kind of livestock for sale. Then he stared at me with that cold face. "Colonel Ledyard's dead, you say."

"Yes, sir," I said. "I seen it. They ran him right through side to side, and he dropped—"

"A simple 'Yes, sir' is enough." He stared at me some more, his mouth curved down tight. "And he promised your father his freedom."

"He didn't promise," I said. "He set us—"

He reached out and cuffed me on the side of the head. "A simple yes or no." He stared some more. "I suppose you have papers," he said.

"Oh, yes, sir," I said. I wanted to go on about it, but I didn't want to get hit no more.

"Where are they?"

"In our cabin, sir," I said.

He nodded, and then he turned and walked away. I dropped back down to the floor and started scrubbing, and I knew I'd just better get out of there as fast as ever I could. It seemed likely to me that Captain Ivers would take over Pa's jolly boat as soon as he could figure out a way to make a claim for it.

But Uncle Jack and Aunt Betsy were against me going down to New York. Uncle Jack had to go off back to camp, so I had to find a chance to talk to him quick. The first time I was with him alone I brought it up. "I figure I could make it in the jolly boat," I told him.

"It's too risky, Willy," he said. "You'd best forget

about it. We'll think of something else. Where would you stay in New York?"

"Aunt Betsy said you're friends with Black Sam Fraunces."

"Yes, but Sam, he's got a tavern to run. He ain't going to have time for no runaway. I want you to forget about it, Willy."

But I wasn't going to forget about it. I kept getting that picture in my head of going along a street and seeing Ma coming toward me. I was resolved to go: but even with Uncle Jack gone, I would still have to slip away from Aunt Betsy and the Iverses.

It was hard to make a run for it. Captain Ivers was down at the warehouse all day long, early morning until near dusk, where he could see anyone on the beach. And Mrs. Ivers, she hardly ever left the house. So two or three days went by and I got more and more worried—scared that he'd find a way to take the jolly, scared he'd find a way to sell me off.

Then, around the fourth day, Captain Ivers came up to the house toward suppertime. The sun was setting. Aunt Betsy was cooking stew over the fire in the kitchen. Dan was out in the barn feeding the cow, and Mrs. Ivers was in her bedroom reading her Bible. Then Captain Ivers came in the back door. "Where's Dan?" he said. "I want him to take a message for me."

I saw my chance. "He's in the barn, sir," I said. "I'll take it."

He gave me a suspicious look. He wasn't used to nobody offering to do anything, and he didn't trust it. But he said did I know where Dr. Beach's house was, and I said I did, which was a lie. So he went into the front room and wrote out a note, and then he folded it over and gave it to me, and told me to be quick about it.

There was an old coat hanging by the kitchen door that Aunt Betsy used when she was outside in the cold weather. I hated taking it from her, because she needed it, but I knew I'd like to freeze to death out there on the Sound without it. So I put it on.

"Hurry back so's you can help with supper," Aunt Betsy said.

"I will," I said. I wanted to hug her good-bye, but of course I couldn't do that. So instead I took a good look at her face, to memorize it so I could remember what she looked like. Then I went outside. The barn door was open and I could see Dan in there with the pitchfork, throwing hay in to the cow. I wanted to hug him, too, but I couldn't do that, either. So I just gave him a wave and he waved back, and I trotted down the path toward the beach, my heart beating fast.

In a couple of minutes I was on the beach. The jolly boat was still where I had left it. For a minute I stood there looking around. There was nobody in sight. The sun was just going down and a light night breeze was springing up. Captain Ivers's brig rocked in the waves lapping around the wharf. I'd have a fair wind for sailing.

I tossed Captain Ivers's note onto the beach and ground it down into the sand with my foot. Then I climbed into the jolly, hoisted the sail, and I was off.

The wind was coming out of the south and I could make pretty good time on a reach. I angled out until I was about a half mile from shore—far enough so's nobody on shore could tell who I was or where I'd come from. Then I pointed her west down the Sound toward New York. I reckoned I'd only been gone fifteen minutes. They'd begin to miss me pretty soon, but they wouldn't miss me yet.

I was mighty sorry to be alone and cold again. I began to miss Aunt Betsy and Dan almost as much as I missed Ma. But I missed her the most, and even if I was alone and cold, I was headed toward her.

The sun had got down now. The sky was all streaks of red and pink, mighty pretty, too. But the darkness was rising up behind me fast, the wind was chilly, and I knew it wasn't going to be no fun. There was lights here and there along the shore. I slid past a couple of little villages. It got darker, and behind me to the east a few stars was out. Pretty soon it'd be too dark to sail—there was too big a chance of hitting something in the water that'd punch a hole in the boat. I'd have to pull into an inlet and hide until morning came. And I was looking along the shore, through the dark, trying to spot a good place, when I heard oars creaking.

I stood up in the jolly with my hand on the tiller and looked around. The sound was coming from somewheres toward the shore ahead of me, off the starboard bow. I stared through the dark, and then I began to see the shape of sails, just gray patches in the starlight. They was coming out from shore and they was traveling mighty fast, with sails and oars going all at once. There was five or six boats, and they wasn't no little dories, either, but whaleboats thirty feet long. I swung into the wind and let the sail luff to stop me from running up to them. On they came, lickety-split. Now I could see the outlines of them against the sky. There was maybe thirty men in each of them, with eight or ten on a side at the oars. Right then I realized what it was: a big raiding party of Americans crossing the Sound to hit the British on Long Island.

Then I heard a low shout, and the next thing I knew the whaleboats had turned and was heading right toward me.

6

I CAME ABOUT TO make a run for it back up the Sound the way I'd come, but I didn't have no chance. The next thing I knew they was all around me, speaking in low voices. They shipped oars, grabbed hold of the sides of the jolly boat, hauled me out and dumped me on the bottom of one of the whaleboats.

I lay there on my back, staring up at the sky. I could see the top of the mast of the jolly boat slipping away out of sight and I knew I'd never see it again. The first thing I thought was that Pa would like to kill me when he found out; and then it hit me that he was dead himself and wouldn't never find out. Just then one of the men hunkered down beside me, his face so close to mine I could hear him breathe and see the whites of his eyes shine in the starlight.

"Where you coming from, boy?" he said in a low, scary voice.

I didn't want to tell them I was a runaway—there was no guessing what they'd do then. But I didn't have much of an idea where I was, so it was hard to make up a good lie. "I was trying to find my friends, sir, but I got lost in the dark."

"What friends? Where do they live?" still keeping his voice low.

I decided to come as close to the truth as I could. "Stratford, sir."

"You're a long way from Stratford, boy. What're you doing way down here?"

"Like I said, sir, I must have slid past it in the dark. I was just putting into shore to ask somebody."

"He's a spy," a low voice in the dark said. "The niggers are all for the British. Throw him in the water and be done with it."

"Honest, I ain't a spy," I said.

"Hold up a minute, Ned," the man hunkered beside me said. "What were you going down to Stratford for?"

I knew I'd better convince them I was on the American side. "My Pa, he got killed at Fort Griswold and my Ma got taken away by the British. I was going to Stratford to find my aunt."

Nobody said anything for a minute and I knew they was thinking if they should believe it. Finally the man beside me said in that low voice, "That's the truth?"

"I saw it happen, sir," I said. "They stabbed him in the back and he flung his arms out, just so, and died."

The man beside me turned his head away. "Were there any niggers killed at Griswold, Ned?"

"There was some. Two or three, I think."

"All right, son. What time did the British get up there?"

"It was just around noon, I reckon, sir," I said. "They busted down the door and came pouring in, and when Colonel Ledyard tried to surrender, they ran him through with his own sword."

Nobody said anything for a minute. Then the one called Ned said, "That sounds right to me. I heard about it."

The man next to me rose up. "All right, son. You just lie there. Don't be moving around and don't make any noise. We'll decide what to do with you when we get back."

It was a raiding party, all right. They'd land somewheres on Long Island, bust something up, capture some British officers if they could, and run back across the Sound. I was going to find myself in the middle of a fight again.

And, of course, the chances was they'd take me back to Connecticut after the fight. There was no way of telling what would happen then. Maybe they'd find out I'd run off from Captain Ivers and send me back to him. Or maybe one of them would take me for a slave himself. Or I didn't know what all else. And then how

61

would I get down to New York to find Ma? I had to escape; somehow, while I was over on Long Island with the raiders, I had to escape.

But there wasn't anything I could do about that right then. So I just lay on my back staring up at the stars and trying not to think about Pa. Oh, the stars were bright and beautiful and there was a sliver of silver moon coming up in the east. When the whaleboat rocked down on that side the silver sliver would suddenly rise up, like a slice in the sky; and then the whaleboat would rock back and it would disappear again. By and by it got high enough so's it was in view all the time and I lay there watching it and feeling the whaleboat rock in the waves; and after a while I dozed off.

I woke up to the crunching of pebbly sand under the keel. I opened my eyes and stared at the sky again. In the starlight I could see the shapes of men shipping their oars and jumping out of the boat onto the beach, talking in whispers and moving as quiet as they could. I took a chance and sat up. We was in an inlet. There was high bushes along the edge of the beach and woods beyond. I could hear more crunching, and I knew they was pulling the boats up across the sand and tucking them in under the bushes to hide them as best they could.

Somebody grabbed me by the shoulder. "Out of there now, boy." I stood up and climbed over the side of the boat and some men grabbed it and pulled it up into the bushes. Then they began to disappear silently off into the darkness. I wondered if they was going to just leave me behind, but then I noticed about twenty men standing by the boats, which they'd left for guards.

What should I do? Could I try to slip away in the dark? Or break and run for it in hopes they wouldn't want to shoot at me for the noise, and I'd get lost in the dark. Once I escaped I knew I could find New York just by heading west; I'd know which direction that was as soon as the morning sun started to come up.

The men wasn't paying much attention to me. They'd sent four of themselves off to stand guard out in the woods. The rest of them sat on the gunnels of the whaleboats or on the beach and talked together low. Some of them lay down in the bottom of the whaleboats and went to sleep. I'd had a rest and didn't feel too sleepy, so I sat on the gunnels of a boat, feeling the cool night breeze blowing across my skin and hearing the slap-slap-slap of waves on the shore. I began to wonder what was going to happen to me and what the war was about, anyway.

Who was it good for? Not me, I figured. I'd lost my Pa, killed, and my Ma gone somewheres, I didn't know where. On top of it, it looked like I'd been turned back into a slave. Although when I came to think about it, when you was a woman you was half a slave, anyway. You had to get married, otherwise you couldn't hardly support yourself, and after that your husband, he was the boss and you had to do what he said. That was so even for white women: Mrs. Ivers couldn't go against Captain Ivers no more than Ma could go against Pa. And of course, if you was black, you was down at the bottom, anyway.

When I looked at it like that, it seemed that it was the white men who was going to come out of it on top, the way they always did. The black men, leastwise the ones who fought and got their freedom, would come out second best, and the women wouldn't be no better off than they always was. I mean, if Uncle Jack got his freedom by fighting for the Americans and bought free Aunt Betsy and Dan, Mrs. Ivers wouldn't have nobody to be boss over no more. Not that I was likely to feel sorry for her: she was too hard and cruel for that. But still, she didn't have much to gain out of the war.

Why was they fighting, then? Well, I guess it was like children growing up: after a while, they won't do what their folks tell them to do no more. The way it looked to me, the Americans—leastwise the white men—figured they was grown up and shouldn't have to do what the British told them; and the British figured the Americans wasn't grown up and ought to obey. That was what the war was about. But no matter who won, it wouldn't leave the slaves no better off, nor the women, neither. It was a funny thing to me how people wanted to be free. If you was scrubbing a floor for your own self in your own cabin, why, that was all right; it didn't hardly seem like work. But if you was scrubbing somebody else's floor, it was just awful. Maybe somebody else wouldn't feel that way, but I did.

But thinking about being free wasn't getting me free. If I went back to Connecticut with the raiders, the chances was good that I'd end up with the Iverses again. I had to get out of there someways.

I looked around. The men wasn't paying any attention to me. They was just lounging around talking amongst themselves. The moon was down now and they was just shapes in the dark. If I could creep off a ways down the beach, they wouldn't be able to see me, and then I could slip into the woods and disappear. But creeping off wasn't going to be so easy.

Then I had an idea. I got up off the gunnel and strolled across the beach to the water's edge, like I wasn't going anywhere in particular. A couple of them glanced at me, and then went on with their quiet talk. At the water I crouched down, like I was going to wash my hands. Then I fumbled around in the sand until I got hold of three or four small rocks. I collected them up in my hands and strolled back to the boat where I'd been sitting and squatted down beside it.

I was pretty well out of sight of the men, except for the top of my head. Quickly I flung one of the pebbles off into the woods. It smacked off a tree and rattled down through the brush. The men stopped talking and froze. "What's that?" one of them hissed.

I flung another stone. It rattled through the brush like the other one. The men was on their feet now, their muskets up, staring off into the woods. "Who's there?" one of them said in a gruff voice.

I flung another stone off into the woods and listened to it click-click through the trees. "Somebody's out there," one of the men said. "Let's spread out." They formed a line, about ten feet apart, and the next thing I knew they was pushing off into the woods. Crouching low, I began to slip off down the beach. When I'd gone fifty feet, I turned and looked back. All I could see was the dim shape of the boats. I stood up and ran down the beach, tripping and stumbling and banging my toes on rocks and driftwood; and then, when I was hot and panting and sweaty, I stopped running, ducked into the woods, and pushed on into them.

With my hands out to feel for trees, I moved along as quick as I could, bumping into things and catching my clothes on twigs and branches. And by and by the woods ended and I was standing at the edge of a field. I looked out across. It was lighter than it had been down at the beach. There was a patch of gray sky in the east. Dawn was coming. I didn't like going out into the open, but I didn't have no choice.

So I started across the field as fast as I could go, and in a bit I came to the fence at the other end. Over the other side of the fence there was a little dirt road. I jumped over the fence and started down the road toward the west, moving at a pretty good pace, and a half hour later I came to a bigger road. There was signs here, but being as I couldn't read, I didn't know what they said. So I kept on going as near to a westerly direction as I could, and after I'd gone a little farther I realized I'd got clear of the raiders. I was free. Oh, my, that felt good, even if I was out somewheres all by myself.

I walked all day to the west, and slept in a barn that night, and walked all the next day. I didn't know how far I had to go; I just kept going west knowing that sooner or later I'd bump into Manhattan Island, where New York was.

I went through three or four little villages. There wasn't much to them—just a few clapboard houses and a little store and tavern and not much else. There was a lot of British soldiers around, too, lounging in the streets or going in and out of the taverns. Once I passed a detachment of them sitting in a field smoking pipes. Nobody paid me no mind. I just sort of slouched on through the villages like somebody sent me on an errand and I wasn't in no hurry to get back. Nobody bothered me. Mostly, though, there wasn't any people, just farms and fields and sometimes woodlots.

Once I got a ride with an old darky who was driving a wagonload of potatoes. When he let me down, he gave me a half dozen potatoes. I took them into another piece of woods and borrowed a light from a pile of smoldering cornhusks and made a little fire and roasted them. I ate two, and saved the other four down in my shirt. Oh, they tasted mighty good, them hot roasted potatoes.

Finally, toward the end of the afternoon, I began to

smell the salty, fishy smell of ocean water. I kept on going down the road I was on and after a bit I could see blue water ahead. The road carried me right there.

I was on a low bluff, looking down into a bay in a river. Across the river, about a mile away, was a long island, stretching out in front of me. Most of it was low hills, with farms and woods. But dead across from me was New York. It was the biggest place I'd ever seen. There was hundreds of houses and a dozen church steeples as far as I could count, and a lot of great stone buildings, some of them five stories high. There was docks sticking out into the river, with every kind of ship tied up to them.

On my side of the river there wasn't so much to see—just marshy beach, a little dock, and a few small boats out on the river. And anchored in the bay was some extra big ships. I knew right away what they was—prison ships.

They was loaded down with American prisoners. We'd been hearing about them prison ships all through the war—how the men was crowded in so close they couldn't hardly sleep, and eating rotten bread and spoiled pork. The windows was tiny so's nobody could escape, and in the summer the men was like to boil to death down there. It was too bad they couldn't save any of that heat for the winter, because then they half froze. There was always sickness in them prison ships, a half dozen men dead every morning and carted away to be buried in the riverbanks and their families never knowing what happened to them.

Of course, it came to me right away that Ma might be on one of them. Maybe the British had captured her back at Groton and brought her down and slung her into a prison ship. There wasn't any way to know for sure. Oh, the idea of her being on a prison ship, all crowded in, no clean air to breathe and eating rotten bread, was terrible. It made me feel so bad for her.

Still, there was no telling if she was on a prison ship. Maybe she was and maybe she wasn't, and the only way I could find out was to go and see for myself.

7

It was late afternoon and the sun was behind New York. Across the river it slanted off the roofs and windows so's the whole city sparkled like fire; and it shone off the ripples in the river, too, like sparks. It was a mighty fine sight, all magical and exciting, and I wished it didn't belong to the British, but was ours again. It wasn't right, them owning it, when it had been the people here who'd made it in the first place.

And then I began to wonder: Why was I on the Americans' side, anyway? What had the Americans ever done for me, except keep me at the bottom of the pile? I took one of the potatoes out from under my shirt and began to eat, thinking. There was Captain Ivers trying to put me back in slavery again, and nobody teaching me how to read or do sums, so's I couldn't even tell what town I was in without asking. And knowing I would have to take orders so long as I lived. Maybe in heaven black folks gave orders to white folks and women gave orders to men.

On the other side of it, Colonel Ledyard had freed us. That was mainly so Pa could join the army and get himself killed. Of course, the colonel didn't have to free me and Ma; he did that just to be fair. And it wasn't the Americans but the British who'd taken Ma off and maybe slung her into a prison ship.

When I thought about it that way it didn't seem to me that there was much difference between the British and Americans; and it wouldn't matter which of them won. But the truth of it was, I *felt* like an American. I didn't know why I felt that way, but I did. Maybe it was because Pa swore he was an American. I don't know. But I felt like an American and I wanted the Americans to win, and it made me angry that the British should have that sparkling city and not us, who made it.

Was Ma in a prison ship? The only way to find out was to go down there and ask. I didn't want to do it. I was mighty scared of going near the British—there was no telling what they might do to me. But I didn't have no choice. I wanted to see Ma so bad I was willing to look anywheres for her.

Down at the bottom of the bluff a rowboat had been tied up at the little dock and some British soldiers under an officer were loading boxes on it. I figured it was supplies for one of the prison ships. There was a road leading down the bluff to the dock. I went on down it and up to the British officer who was lounging there, watching the soldiers load the boxes. "Sir," I said, "do you know if there's any black women on any of them ships?"

"Black women?" he said. The soldiers was curious and they stopped working to listen.

"I'm looking for my Ma, sir."

"Your Ma?" the officer said. "Well, we don't keep women on prison ships. We British aren't animals, you know."

But I wasn't sure if he was telling me the truth. "None at all, sir?"

"Are you deaf, boy?" he snapped. "Didn't you hear what I said?"

"Oh, yes, sir," I said. "I heard."

"When I say something, I don't expect to be questioned on it."

"Yes, sir," I said. There wasn't going to be any arguing with him, I could see that. "Well, thank you, sir," I said. I started to turn to go back up the road, when he grabbed me by the arm.

"Where are you from, boy?"

I sure didn't want to say I was from Connecticut, which was rebel country. I didn't want to say I'd got carried over on a raiding party, neither. But I didn't know the names of any of the towns on Long Island.

So I just sort of waved my hand behind me and said, "Back there, sir."

"Back there?" he said. "What kind of an answer is that?"

"It ain't much of a place, sir," I said. "You wouldn't never have heard of it."

"Let's try and see."

"It's called Long Point," I said, which was the name of a place back home in Connecticut.

"Long Point?" the officer shouted. "I never heard of it. Where is it?"

"Back there a ways," I said. My lies wasn't going very well and I knew it.

"Come, come," he shouted in that way he had. "It's on Long Island, isn't it? The north shore or the south shore?"

I gave that a quick think. "More in the middle," I said.

"A point? In the middle of the island? You're lying. You came out spying. Guard, take hold of this boy," he shouted. "I think we might give you a taste of prison for a few days to see if we can't get a better story out of you." He gestured to the soldiers. "Take him out with you when you go," he snapped. Then he started to walk off up the road. One of the soldiers grabbed me by the arm and started to pull me toward the rowboat. The potatoes under my shirt started to slip and I grabbed at them through my shirt.

"Wait, sir," I cried. "I ain't a boy, I'm a girl."

The officer whipped around and the soldier let go of

my arm. The officer peered at me, looking me over. Finally he said, "By George, you are a girl."

I blushed. "Yes, sir," I said.

He shook his head, looking mighty annoyed. "Get out of here," he shouted. "Get out of here before I put you in prison anyway." He turned and strode off up the road, and I turned and started to follow after. But I hadn't gone more than a couple of paces when I felt something clutch my arm. I spun around. It was one of the soldiers.

He stared into my face. "So you're a girl?" he said.

I looked up the road. The officer was pretty far away already, striding along at a strong clip. I looked back down at the other soldiers. They was standing at the end of the dock, watching. I didn't say anything.

The soldier pushed his face close to mine. "So you're really a girl."

"Charlie, better leave her alone," another soldier said. "You'll get in trouble."

"I'm just trying to find out if she's a girl," the one called Charlie said. He'd now got his face so close I could smell the sweat and rum and pipe tobacco.

"Please," I said.

Suddenly he grabbed for my shirt at the waist and started to pull it off over my head. I wrapped my arms around my chest so's he couldn't get it off. "Please," I cried. "That was a lie. I ain't a girl, I'm a boy."

He reached his big hand up and touched me on the chest. "The hell you ain't a girl," he said. He grabbed my arms to unwrap them from my chest.

The other soldiers gathered around. "You better leave her alone, Charlie," one of them said. "You'll get in trouble."

Charlie turned to the other soldiers. "I ain't going to get in trouble. I'm just going to take her shirt off to see if she's lying." Quick while he was turned away I got one hand free and reached under my shirt and whipped out one of the roasted potatoes. I held it up. "See?" I said. "I ain't a girl. Look."

Charlie let go of me and grabbed the potato out of my hand. He scowled and the other soldiers busted out laughing. "Charlie, you're a blame fool," one of them said.

Charlie gave me a scowl, and then he turned and flung the potato way off into the water. I skipped out of there as fast as I could, leaving all the soldiers laughing and hollering at Charlie.

8

I RAN ALONG FOR a mile or so, until I figured I was well away from the soldiers, and then I stopped and caught my breath. It was pretty clear that I'd better go on being a boy for a while, and in general try to lie as low as I could and not attract attention. I'd got this far, and I didn't want to mess it up.

But what was I to do next? The best thing would be to get on across to New York and see what information I could pick up there. The officer had said that there wasn't no women on the prison ships. That might be right and it might not; but the best thing would be to get over to New York and see what people was saying.

How was I to get across? I didn't know. There must be a ferry so I decided I'd go find it and see if maybe I could work my way over or something. So I took up walking again, and by and by I came to a little village called Brooklyn. Leastwise, I found out later it was called Brooklyn. There was a fair number of houses and some taverns, and down at the end of the main street there was a ferry tied up at the dock. But it was coming on night and I reckoned there wouldn't be no ferries going over to New York until morning. So I slipped out behind one of the taverns and found a barn where they stabled horses. I borrowed a light from a lantern and made a little fire to heat my last two potatoes. It took a good long time for them to get hot, and after I ate, I was ready to sleep. I went up into the loft, and slept in the hay. I woke up at dawn and slid out of there before anybody could see me. I started on down the main street toward the ferry, and I'd only got a little ways when along came a wagon loaded with cordwood driven by a black boy. He was about my age, and mighty tall and skinny, so's he looked more like a length of rope than any human being.

I shouted up to him. "How much is the ferry?"

"Tuppence," he said. "I'm going down. Hop up and I'll give you a ride."

I climbed up. "Well, I ain't got tuppence," I said. "The fact is, I ain't got nothing at all. I didn't even have no breakfast."

He gave me a look and right away I knew he was suspicious of me. Most darkies, they wouldn't turn you in if they thought you was a runaway; most of them would help you if they could. But some would turn you in, and it was best to be cautious.

"How'd you reckon to get across if you didn't have no money?" he said.

"Well," I said. "I *did* have some money, but somebody stole it."

"How'd that come about?" he asked.

"I fell asleep along the road and somebody nipped it out of my pocket."

He had a way of twisting around and wrapping and unwrapping himself when he talked. He gave me another look. "Where'd you say you was from?"

"New York," I said.

He was still mighty suspicious. "Who's your master?"

That was a hard one. I didn't know nobody in New York at all, and I started to say I belonged to Mr. Brown, because there was bound to be somebody named Brown in New York, when I remembered Uncle Jack's friend, Black Sam Fraunces. "Mr. Fraunces," I said.

"Mr. Sam Fraunces?" He bent and twisted away from me and back again.

"That's him," I said.

He kind of scratched his forehead and looked at me some more. "I heard that Fraunces don't keep slaves."

"Oh, well, that's true," I said. "I ain't exactly his slave. I just work there."

He shook his head. "Well, you're about the worst liar I ever seen. I work for Mr. Sam Fraunces. That's where I'm going with this load of wood. You ain't never been within miles of the place."

It made me blush to be caught in a lie. But how was I to know he worked for Sam Fraunces? I put my hand on the edge of the wagon, getting ready to jump and run for it. "I ain't no runaway," I said. "I'm a free nigger."

"I don't believe that neither," he said, twisting away from me. "But I ain't going to tell on you. Where are you really from?"

I still didn't know whether to trust him or not. He sounded like he was safe enough, but there wasn't no point in taking a chance on it. For one thing, being as he was from New York, he might be a loyalist on the side of the British. It sure wouldn't do to tell him about Pa fighting at Fort Griswold. So I said, "I come from New London. My Ma got carried off by the British to New York, and I'm going down to look for her."

He gave me one of his twisty looks. "Where's your Pa?"

"He's dead." I didn't say how.

"New London is a mighty long ways from here," he said.

"I know that for sure," I said. "I came down as far as—well, I don't know where—in my jolly boat and some raiders caught me and carried me across to Long Island."

He unwrapped himself and laughed and slapped himself on the chest. "Well, you are the worst liar I ever heard in all my born days. Some raiders caught you, did they? Now I don't blame you for lying, if I was a runaway, I'd lie myself. But I can tell you ain't had much practice in lying, for you don't know anything about it."

He was making me feel mighty argumentative, but I could see there wasn't no use in telling the truth. So I said, "All right, if you're so blamed good about telling lies, make up a story for me."

He shook his head sort of solemn. "Now, the first thing about a lie is, it's got to be ordinary. You don't want to tell people you got caught by no raiders. You tell them that you came across with a load of hogs. There's nothing more ordinary than hogs. Besides, going with hogs lowers you some. That's another thing about lying. You always want to lower yourself. Don't tell people your money was stolen. You tell them that you got drunk and went to sleep in a ditch and when you woke up your money was gone. People will always believe anything like that."

"That's not so ordinary," I said.

"Around New York it's more ordinary than you think, especially with all them soldiers around and refugees and loyalists flooding in to be under the British, and nothing for none of them to do *but* get drunk and fall down and lose such money as they have. Besides, if it lowers you enough, it don't have to

81

be ordinary, people will believe it, anyway. Just so your lie lowers you, that's the main thing." He twisted around to look at me again. "Now tell me where you're really from."

There wasn't no hope in getting him to believe the truth. Still, I wasn't going to tell nobody I was a slave. "Well, if you really want to know, my Pa, he beats me most every time I turn around and finally I couldn't stand it no more so I ran off."

"Well, that's ordinary enough," he said. "Where'd you live at?"

I still didn't know the names of any places on Long Island, but he was from New York and didn't figure to know much about Long Island, either, so I said, "Long Point." This time I had enough sense not to put it in the middle of dry land. "Up on the Sound."

"What's your Pa do back there?"

I looked down at my lap, like I was ashamed of myself. "We was pig scrapers for a tanner."

He twisted away from me to watch the horse, looking satisfied. "Well, that's more believable," he said.

We had got down to the end of the main street, about a hundred yards from the ferry. It was a flat barge with an oar out each side, and a small sail, in case the wind was right. A couple of wagons was rolling onto it. "Well, I got to get down and figure out some way of earning tuppence."

He twisted around to look at me. "Look, if you get down in the middle of the wood, nobody'll see you and I'll carry you across. So long as you don't sneeze or do something foolish."

"That's mighty kind of you," I said.

He put out his hand. "My name's Horace," he said.

"Mine's Willy." We shook hands, and then I kind of hollowed out a little hole in the middle of the cordwood and crept down there, and sat listening while the wagon creaked onto the flatboat. Then I heard the chain rattle as the ferry cut loose from the dock; and then oars creaking and little waves slapping on the hull; and then after a little while the chains rattling again, and the wagon creaked off the ferry and I was in New York at last.

We rode along a little ways, until we turned a corner. Then Horace told me to come out, and I climbed out and sat up on the seat beside him again, and we went along to Black Sam Fraunces' tavern.

It was a big building, bigger than anything in New London for sure. It was brick, four stories high, and four or five chimneys sticking out of the roof. There was big windows everywhere and a fancy door with windows over it, too. Horace read the sign out front. It said THE QUEEN'S HEAD, which was to suit the British while they was occupying New York.

We swung around back. There was a barn here for the horses and some sheds and a well, and such. I was beginning to feel nervous, and wondered what to do. What I ought to do, I knew, was get introduced to Mr.

Fraunces, and ask him about Ma. He was a big man in New York and would know how to find out if there was a black woman captured by the British somewhere. Besides, Uncle Jack knew him—leastwise he said he did—and Mr. Fraunces was likely to help me on account of that.

But it was pretty bold for somebody low as me to go marching up to somebody as high up as Mr. Fraunces and ask for help. Most probably he'd tell me he never heard of Jack Arabus, go away and stop bothering me. But even so, I knew I had to try it and it made me scared to think about it.

I helped Horace unload the cordwood and stack it alongside one of the sheds. Then he said, "You still ain't had nothing to eat."

"I'm pretty hungry," I said.

"Well, all right," he said. "You come on into the kitchen and I'll get you something."

"Will Mr. Fraunces mind?" I said.

"Mind? Mr. Fraunces? Why, I don't have to ask Mr. Fraunces about nothing like that. We're this close. He always says, 'Horace, you just go ahead and do what you think best.' He trusts me that much."

Well, I wondered about it: the story didn't seem to lower Horace none. But I didn't say anything.

We went into the kitchen. It was a big room, with a huge fireplace at one end and big pots hanging there steaming away. A couple of cooks was slicing apples at a big table. There was barrels of sugar and flour and molasses and such around, too, but I noticed they was pretty empty. "It was different before the war," Horace said. "Then we'd have a whole side of beef on a spit over the fire and apple pies and puddings and spice cakes and everything. But food's scarce now."

He grabbed up a couple of wooden plates from off a shelf and went down to the fireplace where the stew pots was, with me following along, getting hungrier by the minute from the smells. I hadn't had a proper meal for nearly four days. Just staring down at that stew bubbling away made me swallow hard. Horace grabbed up a ladle that was hooked over the edge of one of the stew pots.

Just then one of the cooks jumped over to us and snatched the ladle out of his hand. "Here, you boy, what do you think you're doing?"

"Hey," Horace shouted. "Mr. Fraunces says I was to help myself when I wanted."

Then a voice from behind us said, "Mr. Fraunces says you're to do what, Horace?"

We spun around. Standing at the door was a tall black man dressed in a blue suit with a silver buckle at his belt and ruffles on his chest. I knew right away it must be Mr. Fraunces, and my heart jumped.

I looked at Horace and back at Mr. Fraunces and then at Horace again.

Horace was wrapping his long self up and unwrapping himself a mile a minute. "Well, sir—well—I—sir," he said, and stopped there.

Mr. Fraunces looked at me. "Who's this?" he asked.

"He helped me unload the wood," Horace said. "He's hungry."

"I see," Mr. Fraunces said. "But we can't be feeding the entire populace, Horace. Food's scarce."

I was feeling mighty nervous, like I'd done something wrong, and I didn't know whether I ought to speak up about Uncle Jack or just scoot on out of there. I knew I shouldn't ought to miss my chance, but I was scared.

Mr. Fraunces didn't give me no time to think about it, for he walked over, took a look at me, and said, "When was the last time you had a meal, son?"

"I ain't had nothing much but a couple of roast potatoes the past two days."

"I see," he said. "Where are you from?"

It was now or never. "Sir, my uncle says he knows you. He's a soldier with General Washington. His name is Jack Arabus."

"Jack Arabus?" he said. "Why, I know Jack. Where is he now?"

"In camp. Up on the Hudson Highlands somewhere."

"And you're his nephew?"

It still took me by surprise when people called me a nephew instead of a niece, and I knew I'd better get used to it. "Yes, sir," I said.

I didn't know what to tell him. Was he on the American side or the British? Here he was running a tavern right in the middle of New York, which was owned by the British. On the other side of it, Uncle Jack would sure have told me if he was for the British. Unless maybe he'd changed over to the British side and Uncle Jack didn't know. A lot of people did that during the war—changed sides.

I decided to be cautious. So I said, "Well, I been staying with Uncle Jack up at Newfield in Stratford. My Ma, she was taken off by the British. Well, maybe she ran off with them, but I don't know. I figure she's down here in New York somewheres and I came down to find her."

"Your Ma went off with the British? How did that happen?"

I was getting into it more than I wanted, and I began to sweat a little. I figured I'd better be careful about telling lies: Mr. Fraunces was likely to be smarter about it than Horace. "We had some skirmishing up around where I'm from and I went and hid out and when I came back she was gone, and they said she went off with the British."

"Where was that?"

"Groton," I said.

He nodded his head. "That was a very sad business up there," he said.

"Yes, sir," I said. "I know it was. I saw some of it."

"I suppose you did," he said. He didn't say nothing for a moment. Then he said, "What's your name?"

"Willy." Then I said, "Willy Freeman," so's he knows I wasn't no slave.

"Horace, give Willy something to eat. Then send him around to my office."

Well, I felt like crying. For four days I'd been pushed around and chased, and swore at and shot at, too; and slept in boats and barns; and nothing to eat but potatoes and apples, and all of a sudden here I was in the fanciest tavern in New York, about to be fed on good hot stew. I could feel the tears come stinging up behind my eyeballs, and I had to rub my eyes, pretending I'd got some smoke in them.

So we sat down at a little table there in the kitchen and fed up on stew. Horace, he ate as much as I did, too, which was hard to believe. Him being so skinny and all, you wouldn't have thought he'd have enough stomach for it. I felt a lot better, just sitting there feeling warm and comfortable full for a change; then tiredness crept over me and I put my face down on the table and fell sound asleep.

By and by Horace woke me up. At first I didn't know where I was, and then I remembered, and sat there rubbing my eyes. "Mr. Fraunces wants to see you," Horace said. He led me out of the kitchen and down a back corridor to the end. There was a door there. He knocked on it and Mr. Fraunces said to come in and I did.

"Shut the door," he said.

It was a small room but pretty fancy, with a carpet on the floor and a polished desk, and a safe and bookshelves with glass doors on them and pewter sconces on the walls. There was a window that looked out on the barn and sheds in the back so's Mr. Fraunces could keep an eye on things. I could see Horace come out there and start hauling water out of the well.

Mr. Fraunces sat behind his polished desk, with his hands behind his head, looking at me. He didn't say nothing for a minute. Then he said, "Your Ma—she's Jack's sister?"

"No, sir," I said. "She's my aunt Betsy's sister."

"Ah," he said. "Jack's sister-in-law." Now that I got a good look at him in the light I began to notice something curious about him. His skin was dark, all right, but he didn't exactly look like a nigger. It was hard to tell: it seemed more like he must be part something else, too—Spanish or Portuguese, or Indian, maybe. But, like I say, it was hard to tell.

"You know, Willy," he said, "a lot of black people favor the British. They believe that the British will free them if they fight for them. Did you think you'd be better off with the British here in New York?"

Seeing as he'd asked me point blank, I was stuck. There wasn't no way out of it. I remembered what Horace said about lying—to make it ordinary, and lower myself. But I didn't know what kind of lie to tell and I decided I might as well tell the truth. "Sir, my Pa got killed by the British at Fort Griswold. I saw it myself. They stabbed him with their bayonets, and he flung his arms back like so—" I started to cry again and couldn't finish and stood there sobbing away like a fool. He didn't say anything and finally I got ahold of myself and stopped crying and wiped my face off with my sleeve.

"What was a young boy like you doing up there?"

"I ain't even a boy, sir," I blurted out. "I'm a girl."

He gave a kind of a jump. "A girl?"

"Yes, sir."

He stared into my face. "Why, I suppose you are," he said. "How on earth did you land in that battle?"

So I told him the whole story, about the British coming and me going to the fort to bring the horse back and the fighting and going down to Stratford and the rest of it. He just sat there listening. When I got done he didn't say anything for a minute, but thought about it all. Then he said, "Well, I guess you've had enough trouble for a while, Willy. We'll manage to put you up for a bit, until you can get settled."

"Thank you, sir," I said. "I'll work hard, I promise."

"I'm sure you will," he said.

"The main thing is, I got to find Ma." Once more I got the image of her coming along the street and us seeing each other and hugging.

He shook his head. "You don't even know she's in New York."

It was true. I looked at him, feeling discouraged. I guess it showed on my face, for he said, "Well, there are a couple of places you could try. And, Willy," he said, "I think it best that you stay a boy for a while."

9

I WAS TO STAY OUT in the barn with Horace. He said it wasn't bad. There was horse blankets around that you could roll up in, and the horses kept the place pretty warm, even in the worst weather. There was cows in the barn, too, and chickens and ducks. I was to help out with the livestock and cleaning, and anything else there was to do. I'd get my room and board and maybe a few pennies, too, Mr. Fraunces said, if I did my work well. I wasn't a slave, he said; I was free and ought to get wages for my services, even if it wasn't very much. I knew I wasn't expected to stay forever, but Mr. Fraunces didn't seem in no rush to push me off.

So I moved in. It worried me some, being up in the barn loft with Horace. How was I to keep him from finding out I was a girl, unless I slept in my clothes? And then, my shirt might slip up or something. It wasn't going to be easy.

Another thing I was worried about was getting a letter off to Aunt Betsy to tell her I was safe. Pa, he could write and cipher some, too, and was always intending to teach me, but never got to it. Horace claimed Mr. Fraunces had sent him to school and he could write. I figured I could get him to write me a letter.

So I settled in. I made up a story to tell folks, that I came from Long Island, my Pa beat me all the time and finally he died of the pox and I ran off to New York so's I wouldn't be put into slavery. I just had to be careful when I washed, or changed my clothes, that nobody was around. Horace was the main problem. He'd come up into the hayloft to go to sleep and strip off his clothes just as casual, and I'd have to fuss with my blankets so as not to see him naked. But he never noticed nothing. He wasn't much of a noticer.

I'd found out from Mr. Fraunces all the places that my Ma might be. He said he didn't think there was much chance she was on a prison ship, or one of the other prisons they had around the city. He said she *might* be there, but it wasn't likely. The British didn't usually put women into prison with men.

If she'd really come to New York, he reckoned, the most likely place for her to be was Canvas Town, over to the west side of the city. Just around the time the British were driving the Americans out of New York, there'd been a terrible fire. Nobody knew how it started. The British blamed the Americans and the Americans blamed the British. Mr. Fraunces, he figured it got started by accident. The wind caught it wrong, and it spread all around and five hundred houses burned down before they could stop it. That made houses in mighty short supply. Of course when the British came in, a lot of rebels ran off, leaving their houses empty. But in came the British troops and a lot of loyalists from other states, to be under British protection. A lot of plain drunkards, prostitutes, and roustabouts came in, too. There wasn't near enough housing for everybody, and people went over to the burned-out area and stretched canvas sailcloth over the chimneys and walls that was left standing to make places to live in.

There was a lot of black folk living in Canvas Town, Mr. Fraunces said. Black workmen made no more than a shilling and a half a day, where the whites made four shillings, and a lot more if they were blacksmiths or sawyers or skilled in some ways. So the blacks, being poorer, was likely to live in Canvas Town. And maybe my Ma was there, too. I resolved to go there as soon as I could, but the tavern was a mighty busy place.

Along about this time we got the news that Cornwallis had surrendered his army to General Washington at Yorktown. When that happened, everybody knew that the British wouldn't fight much more. Still, we knew that it would be a while before they actually settled the thing and declared peace. In the meantime the British didn't have nothing to do but sit around, and they was always at the tavern drinking punch and playing cards, and making us jump. So for a while I wasn't able to get away to go look for my Ma.

But then there came a day when there was to be a big ball at some other tavern. It would be pretty quiet for us, and Mr. Fraunces said Horace and I could have some time off in the afternoon, if we got our work done. It was my chance to go to Canvas Town.

I was pretty uneasy about going over alone. It was rough there, with drunkards and thieves and such. I told Horace what I was planning to do, figuring he'd be curious, and wouldn't want to be left out of an adventure. He said he'd go, and as soon as we got finished bringing in the wood and water, we left.

It was the middle of October. The sky was overcast with clouds, and looked like rain, but it wasn't too cold. We walked up Broad Street and over Beaver Street. It was the first chance I'd had to get a look at New York. I'd ridden into it under a pile of wood and hadn't gone anywhere since. A lot of buildings were three and four and even five stories high, mostly wood or stone, but there was new brick ones mixed in, too. The streets was narrow and dirty and there was hogs and dogs and even cows running loose in them. It was crowded—people going along carrying things, and carts and wagons in the streets and drovers coming along with cattle or sheep.

Horace, he knew all about everything we saw as we walked along. That man was old such-and-such; he was a known smuggler and had killed six men. That apothecary shop was no ordinary apothecary shop; it was a place where they ground up dead bodies and such to make potions that you could slip into some- body's drink and make them go crazy and die in a frenzy. He just rambled on like that the whole way along, and by and by we came to Canvas Town.

It was a pretty mean-looking place, and scary, too. It was a forest of chimneys, with here and there part of a brick or stone wall standing. There wasn't no wood in sight at all. There was an awful shortage of firewood in New York, because of the war, and the people who lived in Canvas Town had burned up any wood left over from the fire long before. Everywhere you looked you could see sailcloth stretched from walls and chimneys to make little shelters. The streets was just a field of mud. You could hardly push a cart through, it was so deep and thick. Over the whole place was a smell of charcoal and old garbage and rotten stuff. You wouldn't think anybody could stand living in a place like that, but they did. There was people everywhere, skirting around through the mud or standing around talking. I figured they was outside because it was gloomy under those tents, and they wouldn't go inside unless they had to. It was better to stay outside, even on a gloomy day like that one. They were smoking pipes, a lot of them, even the women, and some of them were drinking from bottles of rum.

We stood there at the edge of the place, staring around. Some people looked at us, but they didn't pay us no mind. We were just a couple of black boys, and wasn't worth more than a glance.

"I ain't much interested in walking around in all that mud," Horace said. "There's no telling what you might step on—a dead body, probably."

"Horace," I said, "there ain't so many dead bodies in all the world as you've provided today."

"Willy, you don't know nothing about it. This here place is filled with dead bodies. When they die, they just push them down into the mud. You could walk on dead bodies from one side of Canvas Town to the other."

Well, I didn't believe it. Still, hearing him talk like that scared me some. But if my Ma was there, I wanted to find her. "I'm going in, anyway," I said. I started along the street, trying to keep close to the burned-out walls, where there'd been less traffic and it wasn't so muddy. I figured Horace would follow me: he wouldn't want to be left out of anything. After a bit I looked over my shoulder, and sure enough, he was coming along after me, and in a minute he caught up.

We went on a ways, passing people perched up on broken walls, or picking their way through the mud the way we was doing. Finally I came to a big black man sitting on a broken brick wall, smoking a pipe and admiring the view. He had a scar on his chin, his nose was busted over and half his teeth was missing. He looked mighty rough.

Stretched back from the wall was one of them tent shelters. Right next to where his feet dangled down there was a hole in the wall where there'd been a window once, to make a kind of door for the tent.

" 'Scuse me sir," I said. "I'm looking for a pretty nigger woman. She's about thirty—"

He began to chuckle without taking the pipe out of his mouth, puffing and blowing smoke with his chuckles, until some of it got sucked down the wrong way and choked him. He took the pipe out of his mouth, coughing and choking, and waved it at us. "Damn you," he shouted between coughs. Then he twisted down and shouted into the window hole, "Rum."

In a moment the head and shoulders of a woman popped out through the hole. She handed out a flask. The man snatched it away and took a long drink, which didn't seem to do him any good, for it made him choke some more.

The woman stayed there in the window, looking at us. She was pretty young—younger than Ma, I reckoned—but her face was bruised and swollen and her hair didn't look like it had been combed for days. Her dress hadn't been washed for a long time, neither, for it was splotched with food and mud. "What're you two doing here?" she said.

"I'm looking for my Ma," I said.

The man on the wall stopped choking. "She ain't

here," he said. "There ain't no mothers in Canvas Town." He put the stopper back in the flask and handed it to the woman. "Don't touch it, you slut," he said.

She took the bottle, turned away a little so's he couldn't see her, and licked the bottle around the top where a little rum had dribbled down. Then she said, "Don't pay him no mind. Who's your Ma?"

The man took the pipe out of his mouth and glared at us, looking mighty fierce. "I said there wasn't no mothers in Canvas Town." He put the pipe back in and sucked at it to make it go.

The woman lowered her voice. She had a bad fever, I could tell that. "Who is she?"

"Lucy Freeman is her name," I said. "She's from Groton, Connecticut. She's pretty, too, kind of chocolate-colored skin."

"She won't be pretty if she's down here long," she said.

The man sucked hard on his pipe, making it squeak. No smoke came out. "Damn," he said. He twisted down toward the woman again. "Give me a coal for my pipe."

"Fire's out," she said.

"You slut," he shouted. "Why's the fire out?"

"No wood," she said.

He slid off the wall into the muddy road and tromped off, looking for a coal to light his pipe with. The minute he had his back to us, the woman leaned farther out of the hole and grabbed my arm. "Now listen," she said. "I seen your Ma," she said, kind of excited. "She was around just the other day. I'm sure it was her. A pretty woman from Connecticut."

"That's right," I said. I wasn't sure I ought to believe her, but I couldn't help feeling excited.

"Now you listen," she said, clenching my arm tight and staring at me. "You come back tonight, and bring me a few coppers for my medicine. I'll scout around and see what I can find. You understand?" She gave my arm a squeeze. "A few coppers for my medicine, understand?" She looked down the road. "He's coming back," she whispered. "But he won't be here tonight, he'll be off looking for rum. So you come back after dark. And bring me a few coppers."

"Yes," I said.

She let go of my arm. "Now run, before he catches you."

We turned and trotted back through the mud the way we'd come. We were both mighty anxious to get out of there, and we hustled straight on back to Mr. Fraunces' tavern.

I didn't know what to believe. At suppertime Horace and me helped the cook in the kitchen serve out the food. We wasn't allowed to go out into the dining room. They had waiters, dressed up in red jackets, that carried the food back and forth. But I'd snuck out there a few times when there wasn't nobody around. I tell you, it was a mighty fine room. There was glass chandeliers filled with candles hanging down from the ceilings, polished walnut wall panels with designs carved into them, and tables where the officers and rich folk sat to eat. Horace, he said that someday he was going to be a waiter, too, and wear one of them red jackets. Mr. Fraunces had promised, he said. But I knew I'd never be one, unless I wanted to stay dressed up like a boy the rest of my life. Women wasn't allowed to be waiters.

So we worked in the kitchen and I thought about the woman in Canvas Town, and between times I went over it with Horace. "Do you think she's lying, Horace?"

"Well, that's hard to say," he said. "Maybe she was, and then again maybe she wasn't."

"That ain't no help, Horace," I said.

"Well, I *know* it *ain't*," he said. "That's the idea of it. You shouldn't be too helpful to people—you should let them think things out for themselves. Otherwise you're to blame if it don't work out in the end. Now, you take somebody like me, Willy, who's spent all of his life in New York and knows how things is done and where the pitfalls lie, why, I'd know just how to decide a thing like that. But you ain't had the experience. So my advice to you is to think it through real careful, and then decide."

That wasn't no more use than the other, but I knew better than to say so, for if I did, he'd carry on in the same way until my head ached. So I did what he said. I thought it through careful, and in the end I decided I didn't have no choice—I had to go back down there and find out. For if that woman really did know where Ma was, it'd be just terrible to miss her.

So after we'd finished up with the suppers and got the dishes cleaned and the kitchen scrubbed out, we helped ourselves to some stew and sat there at the little table in the kitchen, talking in low voices. "I'm determined to go, Horace."

He frowned down into his stew, and thought about it awhile, and then he said, "Well now, Willy, I just knew that was the decision you'd come up with. I knew it. I knew you'd work it through and come out the wrong way. I knew it all along and I let you go ahead and do it, because I knew there ain't no way you can talk sense into nobody until they've worked their way through it theirself. Then you can come in and set them straight."

He didn't fool me none. He wished now that he'd discouraged me from going down there right off, because it was coming to him that if I went he'd have to go along with me and lend the coppers, besides. He didn't want to go down there at night any more than I did—less, because he didn't have nothing to gain out of it, and a good deal to lose. So I said, "What's wrong with going down there?"

He frowned over his stew, folded himself up, and unfolded himself again. Then he said, "There's a lot of things wrong with it. There's a good chance we might get killed. That's what's wrong with it."

"Oh, nobody's going to bother with a couple of nigger boys. There wouldn't be no point in it—we ain't got anything worth stealing."

"You don't know them people down there like I do. They'd kill you just to see the blood flow."

It kind of made me shiver to hear that, because I knew it was partly true. I figured there was bound to be some of them down there that would kill for nothing, especially when they was drunk—oh, maybe not mean to kill you, but push you around just to scare you and push you too hard. But I was determined to go, and I wanted him to go with me, because I was mighty frightened about going down there alone. So I said, "You're just scared of it, Horace."

He unfolded himself so's he could look me in the eye. "You bet I'm scared," he said. "And if you had any sense, you'd be scared, too."

"Well, I'm going," I said. "And you're going, too."

"Maybe we ought to think it over for a few days."

"No," I said. "We maybe would never find that woman again. We're going tonight."

He folded himself back over his stew, looking pretty gloomy. "I reckon you'll want to borrow some coppers, Willy."

"That's mighty good of you to think of it, Horace," I said. "I wouldn't have thought of it myself."

He got the sourest look on his face and I nearly busted out laughing. But I knew better than to do that, for fear of getting him mad at me, so I didn't say nothing. He went off to the hayloft to get some coppers out of a handkerchief he'd got them tied up in and hid down in the hay, and I took from the kitchen a couple of candle ends and a little lantern with dozens of tiny holes poked through the tin, and we set off.

It was still overcast, and there wasn't no moon at all, nor no stars, either. A little fog was drifting in from the river, like floating spirits. There was oil lights along the streets every fifty feet and the thin fog made them shine like small white balls. There was pigs sleeping here and there in the streets, and dogs that stood in cellarways and barked at us, and a few people hurrying along silent with their cloaks pulled up over their faces against the fog and looking around for fear of robbers. And about every two minutes I'd have a feeling for turning around and going back. But I'd made Horace go out with me, and I didn't dare back down.

Horace kept twisting himself around on the lookout for robbers, until I thought he would wind himself up like a spring. He wasn't watching the ground and he stumbled and cursed, which was a thing he wouldn't have done if he'd known I was a girl. Then he'd whisper that we was a pair of fools and ought to be put in the lunatic house for it. And I would say there wasn't nothing lunatic about looking for your mother, and we'd go on.

Finally we came to where Canvas Town began. Here and there they'd put up pitch pine torches that snapped and flickered amongst the forest of chimneys, making the shadows of them waver on the walls. The fog drifted in wisps among them, pale white. Oh, it was terrifying. My heart was beating real fast and I wondered if Horace was right, that we hadn't ought to have come.

But there wasn't no way to turn back, so I started along the muddy street toward the place where the sick woman lived, holding the little lantern so I could see the broken walls as I went. Horace came along close behind me. Lights shone through the canvas of some of the tents, so's we knew they'd got fires going inside, or at least candles. There was voices coming out of them, too, laughing or shouting or arguing. There wasn't many people in the muddy streets—just two or three that jumped out of the dark at us and went on by.

All the tents looked the same and it was hard to tell which one was the sick woman's. A couple of times we came to places where there was a hole in the wall, and we'd think it was hers; but when we held the lantern inside, they was empty, just some straw in there and a couple of empty bottles glistening in the light.

Finally we hit one that seemed like it must be it. "I think this is the one," I said.

"I surely hope so," Horace said.

I bent down and reached in with the lantern. I could see somebody in there, sleeping, but pretty indistinct. "I think it's her," I said. "I'm going in. Hold the lantern and pass it down when I get in." I handed Horace the lantern. Then I swung my legs into the hole and dropped down inside. "Give me the lantern."

104

I reached out for it and he handed it to me, the little specks of light darting around as I pulled it down inside under the sailcloth roof. The light shone through the cloth and anybody who came by would know somebody was moving around in there.

I shone the light on the sleeping person. It was her, all right, lying facedown. I kneeled over her and shook her by the shoulder. She didn't wake up; she just sort of rattled there. I figured she was drunk, which worried me, in case she was too drunk to remember about Ma. So I gave her cheek a little pat, like a soft slap, and as soon as I did I realized that her face was cold. My stomach jumped. I held the lantern down closer to her face. It was turned pretty far down, so's I couldn't see much of it, but I could see one eye shining in the light. It didn't move or wink in the light. I didn't want to touch her no more, but I had to, just in case she was still alive and maybe could be saved. So I laid my hand on her face again. She was stone cold dead. I jumped for the window hole. The candle in the lantern tipped over and went out. I spun around and tumbled out of the hole into the mud. "She's dead, Horace," I whispered, and we ran for it.

10

Now I WAS STUCK. I didn't know if Ma was down in Canvas Town, or had ever been there, or if the sick woman had made the whole story up just to get the money. I was having the hardest time about the whole thing. Ma might be anywhere: a prison ship, a prison, Canvas Town, or somewheres altogether different.

There was one other thing, too: She might be dead. I'd been trying not to think of that, but after seeing the dead woman it came to me that in war a lot of awful things happened to people. Ma could have been killed back there in Groton, somehow, and got buried in a common grave along with Pa. Or she could have got put in a prison ship and took sick and died even before I left Newfield to look for her. Or she could have got to Canvas Town and got murdered there. I just didn't have any idea where to look for her anymore. I was plain stuck.

There wasn't nothing I could do except to feel lucky that I'd got regular meals and a warm place to sleep, which so many around New York didn't have. The city was in bad shape. It'd been occupied by the British for six years, since 1776, when I was a little girl. Food was short, firewood was short, water was short, too. They'd started washing their clothes in Freshwater Pond, and garbage had got into it, drifting in from the swamps where they'd dumped it. But at the tavern we generally had enough to eat, enough firewood, and good water from our own wells.

That was because it was the best tavern in New York, and the British officers saw to it that Mr. Fraunces got what he needed to keep it going. They still didn't have much to do but drill the troops every once in a while. They was bargaining for the end of the war, but everybody said it was going to take a long time, months maybe, to get it settled. Meanwhile the British sat in New York.

Like I said, Mr. Fraunces was a mystery. I couldn't tell for sure if he was black like me, or something else, and I couldn't tell for sure whose side he was on, the British or ours. Uncle Jack had said that he was on the American side. But he was polite to the British, and when they was around, he said things like the rebels was scoundrels and ought to be hanged and such. But maybe he was just saying them things so's the British wouldn't take away his tavern.

One thing that I found mighty instructive was being a boy for a change. If Horace had known I was a girl he'd have always been pushing me around—Willy, do this, do that, fetch me my dinner, see if them chickens have enough water. That was the way Pa treated my Ma. It was his right. He loved her, but he had a duty to command her, too, and she had a duty to obey. It would have been the same with Horace. We wasn't married or anything, and he didn't have no real rights over me, but he'd have taken them, just the same. It was a reason for not letting on to Horace I was a girl. Oh, I didn't want to stay a boy all the rest of my life. I didn't feel like a boy, I felt like a girl. But I was going to be kind of sorry to go back to being a girl and get pushed around by boys again.

I still had in my mind to get Horace to write me a letter to Aunt Betsy, if it was really true that he was such a prince at writing as he said he was. To hear him tell it, he could do the hardest kind of sums in his head like lightning. And spell: why, according to Horace he could spell out the longest words and never make a mistake once. He just amazed his teachers, he said. There wasn't nothing more they could teach him, they told Mr. Fraunces, which was why he didn't go to school anymore.

But the question was how to get the letter up there. So when I got a chance I went around to Mr. Fraunces' office and knocked on his door. He told me to come in and I stood in front of his polished desk amongst the glass bookshelves and polished sconces.

"Sir, I'd like to get word to my aunt Betsy that I ain't dead or anything."

"She's in Stratford?" he said.

"In Newfield, sir. It's part of Stratford."

He thought about it for a minute. "You can't write, can you, Willy?"

"No, sir, but Horace, he said he'd do it. He said he was a prince at spelling."

Mr. Fraunces smiled, which gave me some idea of it. "Well, he'll manage somehow, I expect." He thought some more. Finally said, "There is a young Connecticut man named Elizur Goodrich in Greenwich arranging for an exchange of some prisoners with the British. Greenwich is just a few miles up the North River. I think you might find them at Richmond Hill. I'm sure he'd be willing to take a letter out and leave it nearby when he gets home. Horace is going up Manhattan soon after a load of hay. He can go through Greenwich and if you ride up with him, you could see if somebody will take your letter for you."

So it was settled, and that night, after we finished our suppers, Horace sneaked a piece of paper that they used for writing out bills on, borrowed a quill from the accounts keeper, and we sat at the little table in the kitchen and worked it out.

I said, "Say, 'Dear Aunt Betsy, I'm living down in—' "

"Hold it, not so blamed fast," Horace said. He'd got himself folded so far over, his nose was nearly touching the paper, and I was afraid he'd stab himself in the eyeball with the quill. He was working out the letters like a man scratching on glass.

"I thought you was a prince at writing, Horace."

"I am," he said. "The only thing is, I sprained my wrist this afternoon combing the horse and I have to go slow on account of it."

"That explains it, then," I said. So I slowed down and gave him the rest, and this is what it came to:

> Der Ant Besty
> Im living don her in N.Y. with Mr. Frawnses. Im al rit & in good helth. I hev loked for ma but dont find hir nowere. If you noe where she is rit Mr. Froansuz.

There was a whole lot more I wanted to say, but it took near a half an hour to get this far. Horace was complaining that his wrist hurt something awful and he'd better quit before he did it permanent damage. So he signed it "Love Wily" and we folded it up and waxed it, and then of course Horace had to struggle with the address, complaining the whole way. But finally it was done.

A couple of days later we set out. We followed Greenwich Road along the North River. It was a beautiful sunshiny Indian summer morning, with the birds peeping, the low rustle of the river against the shore, the clumping of the horse's hooves and the wagon complaining. There wasn't much of a breeze, and it was going to be hot when the sun got high.

111

We passed through some farmland, and after a couple of miles we came to Greenwich—some small houses here and there, and amongst them a few grand ones. We didn't have no trouble finding Richmond Hill. It was the grandest house of them all, with a fence around it and a great long drive going up to it. We parked the wagon and I walked up around to the back and asked for Mr. Goodrich. By and by a black man came out. He said he was Mr. Goodrich's servant and that Mr. Goodrich was too busy to bother with an ignorant nigger boy. So to soften his heart I explained about Pa getting killed at Fort Griswold and Ma going off, and finally he said he would find Mr. Goodrich.

I waited around for a while, and then out came a white man. He was real young, in his twenties, and dressed up mighty fine in a ruffled shirt and silver buckles at his knees. "You're the boy who was at Fort Griswold?" he said.

I could see that he thought I'd been in the fighting, and I decided there wasn't no harm in letting him think that. "Yes, sir," I said.

He gave me a sharp look. "You must have been pretty young to be fighting."

"I wasn't supposed to be there," I said. "I went up with my Pa to take the horse back and I got stuck."

He thought about that for a minute. Then he said, "Who's your Pa?"

"Jordan Freeman, sir."

"Ah, yes," he said. "I remember the name. He was killed, wasn't he?"

"Yes, sir," I said. "I saw it happen."

He nodded and pursed his lips and I could tell he was sorry for me. "Well, all right, then," he said. "Give me the letter. I'll take it back to Connecticut with me and leave it off."

"Thank you, sir," I said. "That's mighty good of you." I handed him the letter.

He took a quick look at it to see where it was going. "Arabus? Jack Arabus?"

"Yes, sir," I said. "He's my uncle."

"I know Jack," he said. "He sails with Captain Ivers —or he used to. They take me from Norwalk to New Haven and back on the *Junius Brutus* on my way to and from Yale. Is he still in the army?"

"I reckon so, sir," I said. "Unless he got killed."

He nodded again. "You have a very patriotic family, I see. Yes, I'll take the letter for you." He went back into the house and I skipped on out of there.

Then we clumped on out to the farm where we was to get the hay. It was across a little river called Turtle Creek. It was a mighty pretty sight, that river running through meadows, and a line of trees along the banks. We got off the wagon, and I pushed and Horace pulled at the horses to get them across. There wasn't no clouds at all, and it was hot work. Then we got out to the farm and loaded up the hay. That was even hotter work. We finished around noon. The farmer gave us some biscuits and cider and then we turned around and started back. Soon we came to Turtle Creek again, running along through the meadows.

"I'd sure like to have a swim and cool down," Horace said.

I wasn't too pleased by that idea. "We ain't supposed to fool around, Horace. We're supposed to head right back."

He frowned. "I reckon so," he said.

So we got down off the wagon and pulled and heaved it across. Of course it was loaded down with a ton of hay now. It took us a good fifteen minutes to get it across, and we was pretty well sweated up when we got finished.

Horace stood on the bank, looking down at the cool, running water, hearing it gurgle. "Well, I *am* going to have a swim," he said. "Mr. Fraunces, he'd say so himself. He'd say, 'Boys, it's a mighty hot day, just climb in the water and cool yourself down.'"

I was worried. I could see that he was determined to do it. "Mr. Fraunces wouldn't say no such thing, Horace. He'd say for us to get on back to the tavern as quick as we could clump it."

"How's he going to know, unless you plan to tell him, Willy?"

"Well, no, I wouldn't do that."

"I'm going to do it," he said.

I was pretty anxious. "You'll like to freeze to death going home in wet britches," I said.

He gave me a look. "I ain't going to swim in my clothes, you idiot."

"Oh," I said. "Well, I don't feel much like swimming. Maybe I'll just go out in that field and see if the

114

blueberries is ripe. You just go ahead and have your swim."

"Blueberries?" he said. "Why, what's the matter with you, Willy? Blueberries is long gone."

"Grapes is what I meant to say." I could feel myself getting hot and blushy.

He knew something was wrong and he gave me another funny look. "Come on," he said. "Come on swimming with me."

"I think I'm coming down with a cold," I said.

"You ain't got no cold, Willy," he said.

"All right," I said, "I'll admit it. I don't know how to swim." That was a lie. I could swim as good as anybody. My Pa taught me when I was little.

"Oh, there ain't nothing to swimming," Horace said. "I'll teach you. I'm a wonderful swimmer. Whenever somebody got out too far in the bay, or their boat went over and it looked bad for them, they'd say, 'Quick, send for Horace at Fraunces Tavern. He'll save them if anyone can.' Oh, I was known for it."

I gave him a squint. "How come they ain't sent for you since I been around?"

"Oh, I pulled a muscle in my shoulder a while back, so's I couldn't swim but with one hand. I *could* swim with one hand, too, but that didn't leave no arm to pull the victim along with, so's I had to give it up, temporary. But the one who took over, he's white. Naturally he doesn't want to be beat out by no nigger, so's he won't let them send for me no more."

"Well, Horace," I said, "you're just too good for me.

115

You go have your swim and I'll see about them grapes."

"Come on, Willy," he said.

He looked hurt, but he'd have looked a whole lot worse if he'd seen me with my clothes off. "No, Horace, it'll just make my cold worse." So I walked out into the field pretending I was looking for grapes. After a few minutes I stood still and listened. Sure enough, I could hear him splashing away down there. The grapes was just come ripe, and I collected up a pretty good bunch in my hat. The sun was warm on my back and the grapes smelled so sweet I couldn't keep from eating some, even though I knew I ought to share them with Horace. Then I realized quite a bit of time had gone along, and we was likely to be late getting back.

I raised up my head and shouted, "Horace, ain't you never coming out?" He didn't answer, and I figured he couldn't hear me at the distance splashing around in the water. I folded the hat over so's the grapes wouldn't fall out, and then I trotted back across the field, and slipped up behind the wagon, where I wouldn't see him. "Horace, it's getting late," I hollered.

There was no answer, and I didn't hear no splashing, neither. Suddenly I began to wonder if he'd drowned or something. I raised up my head from behind the wagon a little. I could see some of the stream, but no Horace. I raised up a little more, and here came Horace up the creek bank stark naked.

I squeezed my eyes shut, dropped the hatful of grapes onto the ground, and ran back out toward the field.

"Hey, Willy," he shouted. "Where're you running to?"

I didn't turn around, but kept on running. "I lost something out in the field," I shouted.

"I'll help you find it," he shouted, and started running after me. With those long skinny legs of his I wasn't no match for him. I kept on running, trying to think of what to do, and the next thing I knew he was right there beside me.

There wasn't no point in running no more, so I stopped and faced him, sort of gazing off up into the sky, like I was watching for birds. "You just go back and get dressed, Horace," I said. "I'll find it myself."

"I ain't dried off yet," he said. He dropped down into the grass and sat there, and I went on looking for birds. "What'd you lose, Willy?"

"A pin out of my hat," I said.

"You'll never find it out in this here field, Willy."

"I aim to try," I said. I turned and walked away from him, keeping my eyes stuck to the ground. I figured he'd dry off pretty soon, and I'd just keep looking for the pin until he did.

Then I heard him shout. "Hey, Willy, look what I found."

I sort of half turned, like I was looking at him, but really wasn't. "What is it, Horace?"

117

"Come and see," he shouted.

"I can't," I shouted back. "I'm looking for my hat-pin."

"You ain't going to find that pin in this whole field," he said. "Come and see what I found."

"In a minute," I said. "Why don't you get dressed while you're waiting."

Then he was trotting over straight toward me. There wasn't any way to get out of it now. "Willy," he said, "what's the matter with you today? You're acting mighty strange. You don't want to go swimming, you don't want to do nothing with me."

I was looking up at the birds again. "Horace, I can't do none of them things with you unless you put your clothes on. I ain't a boy, I'm a girl."

I snuck a look down from the birds at him. His whole face seemed to go in six directions at once, with his chin heading south, one eye going east and the other north and his nose sliding around among them trying to make up its mind.

"Willy, you're a girl?"

"I sure am," I said. "I've been one all along." And the next thing I knew he was racing back across the field to the wagon. I gave him a couple of minutes to get dressed and then I walked slowly over there. We stood by the wagon, looking at each other, then we looked away, then we looked at each other again. Finally I said, "I'm sorry I fooled you all this time, Horace, but Mr. Fraunces, he said it was better if nobody knew."

"You could have told *me* at least." He was pretty down about it.

"Well, I reckon I should have," I said. "I told you now, anyway."

"That's something, anyways," he said. He was pretty gloomy about it, and angry, too.

"What's so terrible about me being a girl?" I said. "It ain't that awful."

He climbed up onto the seat of the wagon. "It's a mighty big surprise," he said. "It'll take some getting used to."

We didn't say much on the way home. I felt kind of ashamed I'd fooled him so long, but I'd made up my mind there wasn't no reason to be ashamed I was a girl.

11

Winter came, mighty hard for everybody. Food was short and firewood was short and about everything else was short, too. I worked at the tavern and hunted around town for Ma. The British had so many American soldiers in prison they had to use churches for them, and sugar houses, too, which was empty because there wasn't any sugar coming in from the West Indies. I went around to the prisons and asked the guards if there was any black women inside. But there never was; leastwise they said there wasn't.

But I kept getting that picture in my mind of coming across Ma, just like that, and so when I had the chance, I walked in the streets, looking. I even went back to Canvas Town a couple of times to look.

Meanwhile I'd made it up with Horace for turning

out to be a girl. The first thing he did was to say that I couldn't stay in the barn loft with him anymore. It wasn't right, he said, for a boy and a girl that was nearly growed to sleep together like that. But I didn't like being shoved off like that; it made me mad. I told him lots of times grown men and women who wasn't married had to sleep in the same bed, when there wasn't beds enough to go around, and if he didn't like it, *he* could find some other place to sleep.

But to tell the truth, it made me feel a little funny. We was just friends, and all, but still. So I tried to be careful about how I dressed and undressed. Of course, I didn't have to wear the milking britches no more; one of the cooks got hold of a dress for me. Usually I woke up in the morning before Horace did, and quietly slipped into my clothes. But one morning I happened to glance over at him when I was putting on my dress, and I saw one of his eyes was open. That night I took a horse blanket and slung it over one of the beams in the loft, so's it hung down to the hay. "What's that for, Willy?" Horace said.

"I saw you peeking this morning."

"I wasn't," he said. "I never did." But I noticed that he was blushing red as a baked apple and twisting himself up like a snake, and it gave me the idea that he'd been doing a fair amount of peeking all along.

But finally Horace got used to me being a girl. He left off cursing in front of me and was more polite, but every now and then, if he dropped a board on his foot, or mashed his finger in a door, he'd forget and rip off a string of curses that'd singe the hair off a cowhide. Then he'd remember and look at me sheepish and say he was sorry. I'd tell him there wasn't no point in being sorry, he'd been talking like that in front of me for months. But he'd still look sheepish.

So the winter went along, with everything short. Seventeen eighty-two rolled around. In March the story came that Lord North, the Prime Minister of England who'd been in favor of the war, was out, and the new one coming in would settle the thing and take the British troops back home. In April they began having meetings in Paris between the British, the Americans, and the French, who'd helped the Americans in the war, to work out a peace treaty. Spring was coming, too, and everybody was cheered up a good deal. But it turned out to be a hot, dry summer, and water was shorter than ever. Our wells at the tavern held up, but we had to be careful with it. We was all so impatient for the British to leave, so they'd let the prisoners out. But the whole thing went slow as molasses. Even though they'd been meeting in Paris for months, they didn't get down to real negotiations until September, and it wasn't until November that they signed the first articles of peace.

But aside from still missing Ma, I was pretty content. I liked working at the tavern. It was a lot more interesting than milking Ma's cow or scrubbing Mrs. Ivers's floors. And I liked the people. Mr. Fraunces, he was good to his help so long as they did their work, and I got on with the cooks. So far as Horace was concerned, that was a bit of a puzzle. I didn't exactly know what I felt about him. I wasn't thirteen anymore, I was going on for fifteen. He liked me, I knew that, because if he was in the barn and he saw me come out of the kitchen to pump water, sure enough, about two minutes later he'd come sauntering out, trying to look as if he had a lot of important things on his mind, but wasn't in no rush to decide them, and start giving me orders. It wasn't anything very much, just little things. Like he'd say, "Willy, I've got to go somewheres for Mr. Fraunces, you see to the water for the cook." Or he'd say, "Willy, I ain't got time to mess with them chickens today, you'll have to do it."

He wouldn't have said none of those things before. It might have worked out the same, but he'd have more likely said, "Willy, I've got to go somewheres for Mr. Fraunces. If you do the water today, I'll do it tomorrow." Something more fair and even. But now it was like his time was more important than mine. He couldn't fritter time away, but it didn't so much matter if I did. I don't mean that he tried to lord it over me all the time: he knew better than that. It was mostly little things. Oh, it made me mighty argumentative when he gave me orders like that, and I'd answer him right back, "You ain't my boss, Horace." I liked him, but sometimes he made me mad.

Winter came. In February the British finally proclaimed the end of the fighting, and after that there wasn't no more skirmishing. But still the British troops didn't go. Oh, I was impatient. I didn't know for sure that Ma was in prison somewhere, but it was the like-liest thing. The truth was, though, it had been so long since I'd seen her I couldn't hardly remember what she looked like. I still kept getting this picture in my head of her coming along the street and us hugging and all that, but the picture wasn't so clear anymore. It had been coming up to two years since the fighting at Fort Griswold. Living back there in Groton seemed like another life, and the old me was another person. I missed Ma and sometimes when I remembered Pa and saw that bayonet slide in and him fling his arms out like that I'd get low and would want to go off by myself and not to talk to anybody. But mostly I didn't think about them things. My life now was the tavern and Horace and Mr. Fraunces and the cooks and the rest of them I'd got to know.

I'd saved up a little money. Mr. Fraunces, he wasn't one for throwing his money around casual, but he al-lowed that me and Horace wasn't slaves and we ought to get wages. So he gave us each a shilling a week, which was twelve pence and would buy a quart of molasses or a half pound of cheese. Horace, he was very near with his money. He wouldn't spend it short of his life depending on it. He'd been saving for years, and he'd got over eight pounds put away. He was going to get his own tavern someday. He'd be a waiter first and learn all about the tavern business, then he'd start his own. Mr. Fraunces told him that he had the smartest head for business he'd ever seen, he said. I didn't dispute that. Horace had his ways, but he wasn't no idiot.

I'd saved some, too, but only about a pound. The trouble with me was I had a sweet tooth. Even though New York was occupied, there was sweet things you could buy. In particular Mr. Joseph Corre's shop was dangerous for me. He always had custards there and Jordan almonds and sugar candies and macaroons. Sometimes the cooks would send me over there to fetch tarts or cakes for the tavern. Of course I'd have to stand around and wait while they did up the parcel, with all of them things smelling just so tempting. I'd promise myself I wouldn't buy nothing, and I'd tell myself to go outside and wait while they made the parcel ready. But I never could do it, and in the end I'd spend sixpence on macaroons or some such. They was expensive, too, being as everything was short and prices up. But I couldn't help myself. Then I'd feel bad about wasting the money and give one of the macaroons to Horace. So he came out a winner no matter what.

March came, and the rumors got stronger and stronger that they was going to end the war once and for all and let the prisoners out. Of course most of the people in the city was loyalists and they was feeling mighty bad. Here they'd gone and stuck up for the British and the king and fought for them and suffered, and now the British had given the whole thing up. The loyalists, they didn't know what they was going to do.

Some of them had the idea of going to England and starting over there, but most of them figured they'd go up to Canada, if they could get the British Parliament to give them land up there. Oh, there wasn't too much jollity in the tavern anymore. The loyalists and the British officers, too, who came in were low as could be. There was a lot of stories going around that some of the loyalists had shot themselves, or hanged themselves, or flung themselves in the river and drowned.

And then one day, early in April, the rumor swept around like a bullet that it *was* over and the prisoners would all be out in a day or two. I was so excited I could hardly stand it. I kept waking up at night with my heart racing, and I wasn't no use at all around the kitchen, because I kept seeing Ma coming along, and couldn't remember what I was doing. I don't know how long I could have stood it, but two or three days later in the middle of the morning Mr. Fraunces came into the kitchen with a big smile on his face and said, "It's over. They've signed it."

Well, we flung up our arms and let out a cheer. We'd won at last. I guess even the loyalists was glad to have it done with, even if they'd lost. And a lot of people, they'd never cared one way or another whether we was ruled by British or Americans, just so long as they could hold on to their property and live their own lives.

Then Mr. Fraunces looked at me. "Willy, they're bringing the prisoners in from the prison ships. Go on down there and see if you can find her."

I didn't wait. I flung on my hat and raced out of there over Dock Street and Water Street to the wharf on the East River. The streets was full of people rushing here and there, some of them looking happy and cheering, some of them mighty worried.

Finally I reached the dock. There was already a lot of prisoners there. They was standing there hugging each other, or so weak they couldn't walk and was lying down, or crawling because their feet was ruined. Out in the water there was boats coming in with more of them. There was British officers there shouting for them to move along. They wasn't doing nothing for them. They was just pushing them off the dock so's they could unload another batch. Oh, it was a terrible sight. They was all so thin from starvation and their clothes all torn and a lot of them sick with sores on their faces, or flushed with fever, or quivering so hard from the ague it seemed they'd shake apart.

After a bit they began to spread off away from the dock. The ones with frostbitten feet couldn't stand at all. I heard later that some of them crawled on their hands and knees all the way to Virginia, where their homes was.

I began running up and down the dock, looking everywhere. I was scared that Ma'd come off the boat and walk away before I could see her. I went up and down the dock twice and didn't see her. So I went to the end of the wharf where the prisoners was landing, and stood there, and waited. I stood there all morning, watching boatload after boatload come in. But she wasn't on any of them.

So I began asking; I went from this one to the next one: did they know of any black woman who was on the prison ships? No, they said, they'd heard a story that there was some women on one of the prison ships, but they'd never seen any themselves. The boatloads kept coming in and I kept asking and all I heard was the same thing: Nobody'd ever seen any women on the prison ships.

It got toward nightfall, with the sun going down over the town and the dark coming up in the rivers. The shadows of the buildings fell across me. The boats kept coming and going and I kept on watching and then I noticed that the boats wasn't going back to the prison ships after they unloaded; they was staying tied up at the dock. Finally there was just one more boat coming in. It tied up, and unloaded the prisoners. I didn't see Ma anywheres among them. The prisoners come onto the dock and went slowly off to town; and then the British officers went off, and finally I was standing there on the dock all alone, with the night coming down around me, and I put my hands over my face and I began to cry, with my shoulders shaking and the tears leaking out through my fingers. I'd waited two years for the war to be over so I could find her. Wasn't I ever going to see my Ma?

Finally I got myself to stop crying and walked back to the tavern. Horace and the cooks, they saw how I looked and didn't say much, but left me alone, and I went into the barn loft. I couldn't fall asleep. I lay there on my back, staring up through the dark, trying to remember what Ma looked like. But I couldn't—I couldn't get a picture of her. All I remembered was that she had chocolate-colored skin and was pretty. And I knew the only thing I could do was forget about her. I wouldn't never see her again. She was gone— dead, or taken back to England, or sold off to the West Indies. Dead, most likely, I figured, for so many of them had died on those prison ships; but whatever had happened to her, I knew I wouldn't never see her no more, so the best thing I could do was forget about her. I was on my own now. It didn't matter how old I was—I was a grown-up now, and had to look out for myself.

Time went on, and still the British didn't leave. Summer came. Loyalists began to go off to Nova Scotia, Canada—a whole fleet of them in April, and more in August, and more in September. The fall came and still the British was there. Finally, around the middle of November, the stories went around that the British was going to leave soon. We waited, just hop- ing and praying, and then one frosty morning we heard drums beating in the street. We raced out of the kitchen, all of us—me, Horace, the cooks, and every- body—and there out on the street we saw the British redcoats marching down toward the harbor, drums beating, flags waving, looking straight ahead and solemn.

We began to cheer, and in about two minutes the street was full of people cheering the redcoats away. I was standing there, cheering and waving my arms. They marched on and on, and finally they were gone, and there was only the sound of the drums, getting fainter and fainter as they reached the Battery, where they loaded up in ships and sailed away. The terrible war was over.

We went back to the tavern, and I grabbed a bucket and went out into the yard to pump water for washing the breakfast dishes. And I was doing this when a man dressed up in a green suit with silver buckles came out of the kitchen. "I'm looking for Willy Freeman," he said.

He looked familiar to me. "I'm Willy, sir," I said.

He stared at me for a moment. "I thought Willy Freeman was a boy," he said.

I blushed, and suddenly I realized who he was—Mr. Goodrich from Connecticut, who'd taken my letter up to Aunt Betsy. "I *used* to be a boy," I said. "I mean Mr. Fraunces said it would be better if I dressed like a boy."

He thought about that for a minute. "Yes, I see," he said finally. "I have some news for you. I'm afraid it isn't very good news."

"News, sir?"

"I've seen your mother."

"Ma?" Suddenly I felt dizzy. It was like the world had spun around. I'd got things fixed one way in my head, and now they was different. "Ma?"

"Yes," he said. "She's up at the Ivers place in New-field. I'm afraid she's very ill."

"Ma's sick, sir?"

"I'm afraid it's serious," he said.

12

Mr. Goodrich, he went back into the tavern, and I stood there by the pump, dumbstruck. It was the queerest thing; here I'd suddenly got Ma back, and in the next breath I was going to lose her again, for I knew what Mr. Goodrich meant when he said it was serious. It meant that they figured she was going to die.

Oh, I wanted to go up there and save her. I wanted to go up there to give her medicines and feed her right and see that she was warm and comfortable and help her to get better. I couldn't stand her to be dying like that, without me there to look after her.

But if I went up there, Captain Ivers was sure to clap me back into slavery. There wasn't no doubt about that. He'd claim that I was his, and it wouldn't make no difference what I said to anybody because I was just a nigger girl and nobody would pay any attention to me. Oh, how I wished I'd had sense enough to get Pa's papers out of the cupboard in the shack and tote them along with me wherever I went. Oh, how I wished I'd done that.

But it was too late for that. And what was I going to do? Was I going to let Ma die up there and not try to help her, and never see her before she died? Or was I going to go up there and help her, and get myself clapped into slavery?

There wasn't any two ways about it. I had to take the chance and go. So I went back into the tavern, and down to Mr. Fraunces' office, and there was Mr. Goodrich standing by the door, talking with Mr. Fraunces. They looked at me coming along. "Sir—" I said.

"I've heard about it, Willy," Mr. Fraunces said.

"I have to go back there," I said.

"I wish you wouldn't," Mr. Fraunces said. "It's a risk. We may never get you back again."

"I know that, sir," I said. "I know Captain Ivers will try to put me back into slavery. But I have to do it."

Mr. Goodrich gave me a sharp look. "You're free, then?"

"Yes, sir," I said. "When Pa joined up, Colonel Ledyard set Ma and me free, too."

"Do you have papers?"

"No, sir. I didn't think to take them from our cabin."

"That's too bad," Mr. Goodrich said. He took hold of his chin and thought for a minute, and then he said, "I know about Ivers. He'll do it if he can. If you have any trouble along those lines, you come and see me."

"Yes, sir, thank you," I said. "I'll surely do that."

Then Mr. Goodrich said he knew of a ship leaving for Black Rock in two or three days that would let me work my passage that far. I could walk the rest of the way to Newfield pretty easy. So I thanked him for that, too, and it was settled.

I spent the next three days all of a twitch, hardly able to sit still, nor eat anything, nor get on with my work. I was just scared as I could be that Ma would die before I could save her. But then word came that the ship was going to leave in a couple of hours, and I went around to Mr. Fraunces' office to say good-bye.

"I just wanted to thank you for everything you done for me, sir."

He was sitting at his desk, amongst the books and the pewter sconces on the wall. "I've been glad to have you, Willy," he said. "I was hoping you'd be staying with us."

"I wished I was, too," I said. "But I don't know what Ma'll want to do."

"Yes, I understand that," he said. "Just remember, you'll be welcome back anytime."

So he hugged me a little and then he gave me a Spanish dollar and said he hoped I'd saved my wages, and I lied and didn't tell him I'd spent most of it on macaroons. Then I went out into the yard, where Horace was hauling water up from the well.

"I guess I have to say good-bye, Horace," I said. "I'm going directly."

He set down the bucket and looked at me. "Well, good-bye, Willy," he said. "I hope you come back."

"You didn't mind that I turned out to be a girl?"

"I'll admit, it startled me some," he said.

"But you got used to it."

"Yes," he said. "I sort of did."

"It wasn't too bad, was it?"

He thought about it for a minute. "You know, the truth is, Willy, there was times when I was glad you was a girl."

He blushed when he said that, and I blushed and felt like crying a little. So I reached up and put my arms around his neck and hugged him. Then I went after him to kiss him on the lips. He squirmed around but I caught him and gave him a good kiss. "Horace, you ain't much of a kisser," I said.

"I ain't used to being kissed by no boy," he said.

I laughed. "You ain't used to being kissed by no girl, neither," I said.

"Oh, Willy, you'd be amazed by the number of girls that want to kiss me," he said. "I wouldn't never let them. The next thing you know, they want to marry you."

"You got to get married someday, Horace," I said.

"I ain't in no rush," he said. He picked up the water bucket. "Well, maybe you'll come back."

"Maybe I will," I said.

I went to the dock and got on board the ship. They set me to polishing brass, and after a bit we set off out of New York harbor. I went out on deck and took a look at the city slipping away behind me. I felt mighty sad and lonely. I missed the tavern already, and Horace and Mr. Fraunces and the cooks and the rest of them. Groton wasn't my home no more, nor Captain Ivers's place, even if Ma was there. The tavern was my home now. But even so, I wanted to see Ma about as bad as anything I'd ever wanted, and it scared me that she might die before I got there to save her, if I could.

We sailed all afternoon, and just as dark was coming we pulled into Black Rock harbor and up to one of the wharves that jutted into the water. There was ships there now that the war was over, and the houses was lit up, looking cheerful. But I'd lived in New York for two years, and Black Rock didn't look like much of a place. I got off the ship, asked my way to Newfield, and started off walking, first up the street from the harbor and then into the country along dirt roads. The dark come up full, the sky was clouded over, and there wasn't no stars. Every once in a while I'd stop at a farmhouse and ask if I was going right for Newfield. Pretty soon I was in Stratfield, the next village to Newfield. There I had to rouse the ferryman to take me across the Pequonnock River. And I had to give him twelve coppers to do it.

Even then he grumbled and said it was against the law to carry niggers unless they had a pass, and I'd better be telling the truth, because he'd check with Captain Ivers, sure enough. But he finally took me, anyway.

Once on the other side, I found the little path going back to the house and walked around to the kitchen yard between the house and the barn. But I didn't dare go in until I found out how things was. So I slipped up to the kitchen window and took a look in. The Arabus family was sitting at the table eating stew. Uncle Jack, Aunt Betsy, and Dan. I was surprised at how big Dan was. He'd grown considerable. It was late to be eating dinner, and I knew that Captain Ivers had kept them working a long day. But why was Uncle Jack sitting there with them? The war was over, and he was supposed to be free, and could eat dinner whenever he wanted.

There was no sign of the Iverses, so I rapped on the glass a couple of times with my knuckles. Their heads snapped around. I pressed my face to the window so's they could see me, and in a minute they came boiling out the back door into the kitchen yard. Aunt Betsy hugged me, and Uncle Jack hugged me, and Dan, he sort of circled round and round me, all of us whispering and trying not to make any noise. Aunt Betsy said how I'd grown, and I said how Cousin Dan had grown, and then I said, "How's Ma?"

Uncle Jack looked serious. "She's pretty bad, Willy."

"I got to see her," I said.

"It's risky," Uncle Jack said. "Ivers has been telling

people for two years you ran away from him. He claims he bought you from Colonel Ledyard just before he was killed."

"It's not true," I said. I was getting angry.

"You'd best not be caught, anyway," Uncle Jack said. "He's a bad one."

Aunt Betsy touched my arm. "He's trying to put Jack back into slavery. He says he never promised Jack his freedom."

"But the law says Uncle Jack is free," I said, too loud. My trouble was I'd got use to being free.

"Keep your voice down, Willy," Aunt Betsy said.

"Ivers, he ain't much interested in what the law says," Uncle Jack said. "He's going to keep me in slavery if he can. Now, I know you want to see your Ma, but it ain't safe here for you."

"I got to see her," I said.

"Let her, Jack," Aunt Betsy said. "She's got to see her Ma at least once."

That had a terrible sound to it, but I didn't say anything. We slipped into the kitchen.

Ma was down in the cellar, where the Iverses made the Arabuses sleep. I went on down the cellar stairs. Being as it was November, it was cold and damp down there—cold and damp most of the year, anyway. They'd set up a candle on a board. Ma was lying on a straw pallet with a blanket over her. The light flickered across her face. It was thin and pale and wrinkled, and her hair was thin, too, and gone gray.

She wasn't pretty anymore. If I hadn't have known who it was, I would never have recognized her. It hurt awful for me to see her look like that.

She heard me come down and turned to me. "Who's that?" she said in a whispery voice.

"It's me, Ma."

"Willy? It's you, Willy?" She looked like she couldn't hardly believe it.

I went over and crouched beside her. "It's me, Ma." Close up she looked just awful. There was sweat on her face and her eyes were blank, like whoever it was supposed to be behind them had gone away. She seemed like a stranger to me, an old woman who didn't have nothing to do with my Ma. "I'm here now, Ma. I'm going to take care of you."

"You mustn't stay, Willy," she said. "Captain Ivers will catch you. He's trying to catch Jack already."

"Don't worry about me, Ma," I said. "I'm going to take care of you." Strange as she looked, I didn't want to touch her. But I put my hand on her forehead. She was awful hot. "Ma, I'm going to get you a doctor."

She shook her head slowly. "Captain Ivers, he won't allow it," she said in her whispery voice. She closed her eyes. "I'd best just die."

It troubled me that she'd give up so. "No, Ma," I said. "I ain't going to let you die."

She didn't answer, but lay still. I watched. She seemed to be asleep, so I went on upstairs. They were waiting for me. "She's mighty bad," I said. "I've got to get her a doctor."

Uncle Jack shook his head. "Captain Ivers, he won't allow it."

"I can pay for it," I said. "I have my own money." I had the Spanish dollar Mr. Fraunces had given me, and over a pound I'd saved from my wages. Now I wished I'd saved more, but it was too late for that.

"It won't matter," Uncle Jack said. "He says she's going to infect the whole household. He wants us to take her out of here." He stood up. "Now look, Willy, you can't let Ivers catch you here. You best go out and stay in the barn."

So I did that, and Uncle Jack came out with me with a lantern so's it would look like he was seeing to the cow in case the Iverses noticed the light. He got me a horse blanket and a piece of sailcloth to sleep under. Then he sat with me for a minute and told the whole story.

The British had kept Ma on a ship for two years to wash clothes for the officers. After a while she'd got sick with the fever. She was sick for weeks before she got better. But she never really got over it—sometimes better, sometimes worse. Finally, when the peace was signed, the British had to put her off, because they wasn't allowed to take any American slaves away with them. They put her off on Long Island. She got word over to Uncle Jack where she was, and Uncle Jack, he borrowed a sailboat and come and got her. "She was mighty sick, and I didn't know as she'd make the trip across," he said.

Then he told me about the trouble with Captain

Ivers. Uncle Jack *was* free; he had his discharge papers and his soldier's notes that was supposed to be good as money, that they'd paid him for fighting for seven years. But Captain Ivers said no, he wasn't free. And Uncle Jack didn't dare run off because he was afraid Ivers would sell Aunt Betsy and Dan down to the West Indies. "I got to figure out a way to get some money to buy them free," he said. "I got to get a fishing boat and earn some cash money."

"Ain't your soldier's notes enough?"

"It ain't certain what they're worth. The Congress don't have no way to raise money to pay them off. All they are now is just paper. I could get maybe a few pounds for them. Not enough to do any good. All I can do now is wait."

Well, it was a terrible thing. It seemed like the black folks was bound to lose, no matter what happened. But I was too tired and worried about Ma to think about it, so I crawled up into the barn loft, snuggled down in the hay under the horse blanket and the sailcloth, and went to sleep.

I woke up at daybreak, and sat there in the barn loft until Dan came out to look after the cow. He climbed up the ladder into the loft and gave me some biscuits, some cheese, and an apple. I was mighty glad to get them. "Ma says to tell you that the Iverses are going off toward suppertime," he said. "You'll get a chance to come in and see your Ma."

I was glad of that. I was bound and determined to get the doctor for her. So I waited, feeling pretty scared and worried, but I worked hard all day to keep my mind off it. Then in the late afternoon I heard Uncle Jack come into the barn and take out the horse; and then I heard voices; and finally I heard the horse go off; and Uncle Jack climbed up the ladder and told me to come down, the Iverses would be gone for a couple of hours. So I climbed down and went into the house and into the cellar.

Ma was lying there with those blank eyes staring up at the ceiling the way she was before, her face pale and sweaty. But she was breathing very hard now, in a sort of raspy way, and I knew she'd got worse in the night.

"Ma," I said.

She moved her head around to look at me, but she didn't say anything. "Ma, don't just look at me, say something."

She shook her head. "Willy," she said in a low raspy voice. Then she began to cough and turned away from me again. When she stopped coughing she went back to staring at the ceiling again and breathing hard.

"Ma, I'm going to get the doctor." She didn't say anything, but shook her head.

"I'm going to get him, Ma."

Now she slowly turned her head to look at me, as if she wasn't sure it was worth the trouble. "It ain't no use, Willy," she whispered.

I jumped up. She was going to die for sure if I didn't get some medicine. "Ma, I'm going for the doctor."

143

She reached out to touch me, but I dashed for the stairs and raced up. I didn't know how much it would cost, but I figured I had enough. Uncle Jack and Aunt Betsy and Dan was in the kitchen, waiting for me.

"I got to get the doctor for Ma," I cried.

Uncle Jack shook his head. "Captain Ivers don't want no doctoring for her. He says it's a waste of money."

"I got my own money," I said. "I've been saving my wages."

"The doctor ain't going to come unless Captain Ivers sends for him."

"I got to get him. I got my own money."

"We sent for him a week ago," Uncle Jack said. "He says he can't come if Ivers don't want him."

"He has to come."

I saw what it was: They'd given up on Ma. They figured she couldn't live and there wasn't no sense in causing trouble over it. "I'm going to save her," I said.

"No, you ain't," Uncle Jack said. "Nobody—" Aunt Betsy give him a look. "You just stay right here, Willy," he said.

I never felt so argumentative before in my life, but this time I wasn't going to argue. "Uncle Jack, I'm going. You aren't going to tell me to let my Ma die."

Uncle Jack let his breath out in a long sigh. "Well, I reckon you got a right to try to save her if you want."

So they told me where the doctor was, who was Dr. Beach, and off I went as fast as I could through the

144

dark. I followed along the way they said and by and by I saw a light, and then the house loomed up out of the dark. I rang the bell. Dr. Beach's wife came to the door.

"My Ma is real sick," I said. "She needs the doctor."

She shook her head. "He's busy. He can't come now."

"He's got to come," I cried out. "She's going to die."

She thought about it for a minute. Then she said, "Well, come in. I'll see."

I came into a little hall where there was a bench and a rack for coats and a door and nothing else. His wife opened the door. I could see the doctor talking to somebody. She said something to him and then she came out and shut the door. "He'll come out as soon as he can," she said. Then she went away.

So I sat there and waited, feeling scared and sick inside, like I was slowly breaking to pieces in there. The doctor didn't come and I went on waiting and trying to think of prayers, and still he didn't come. Time just went on. The Iverses would be home soon. I sat there for what seemed like hours.

Finally he came out. There was another man with him, and they chatted and then the other man went off and the doctor said to me, "Yes?"

"I'm from Captain Ivers's house, sir. My Ma's there, and she's dying. You got to come, sir." My heart was beating fast.

He looked at me for a minute. Then he shook his head. "I'm afraid I can't."

"Can't come?" I stared at him, confused. "I can pay," I said. "I have my own money."

"It isn't that," he said. "Captain Ivers doesn't want me."

"But she ain't his Ma," I shouted. "She's mine."

"It's his house," he said. "I can't go into a man's house if he doesn't want me there."

I dropped down on my knees in front of him and the tears began to run down my face. "Please, sir," I said.

He winced like he was hit. Then he said, "I'll give you some medicine. It might help."

"Oh, thank you, sir," I said.

He went into his office and in a minute he came out again with a little vial of powders. "Mix this with rum and give it to her," he said.

I took the vial and reached into my pocket and drew out the Spanish dollar. "I don't want any money," he said.

"Thank you, sir," I said. I tore out of there and ran all the way back to the house. The Iverses were still away. I went around to the kitchen door. "I've got to have some rum," I said.

Aunt Betsy got out a bottle of rum, put some in a cup, and I mixed the powders in. Then I went down into the cellar with it, going as quick as I could without spilling. Aunt Betsy came down behind me. Ma was lying on her back, breathing with that hard, raspy sound. She was just staring at the ceiling, waiting to die.

146

"Ma," I screamed. "Don't do that." I knelt down beside her. "Ma, I have the medicine."

She turned her head to look at me and give me a little smile. "Willy," she said in a soft voice. She reached out her arm to touch me, but just then she had a fit of coughing and put her hand over her mouth.

"Ma, take the medicine."

She looked at me for a little bit as if she was trying to remember something, and then she turned and went back to staring at the ceiling. I put my arm under her head, lifted it up a little, and tried to pour some medicine into her mouth. It just went in and then she turned her head a little, coughed, and the medicine sprayed out.

I jumped up and ran upstairs for more rum. Uncle Jack came rushing up behind me. "Willy, stop," he shouted. Captain Ivers was standing in the kitchen. I jerked back when I saw him.

"You," he said in that cold voice.

"Captain Ivers, we got to have the doctor," I shouted. "I can pay for it. I've got my own money."

"You," he said. "You back here?"

I jumped over to him and grabbed him by his jacket. "Oh, God, she's dying, she's dying."

He slapped my hand away from his jacket. I looked at Uncle Jack. His fists was clenched and he was shaking. "Willy," he said in a low voice, "you go back down to your Ma."

I swung around to Captain Ivers again. "She's dying," I hollered. "You're killing her."

147

He didn't answer. Uncle Jack grabbed me by the shoulders and shook me. "Get ahold of yourself, Willy," he said. "Go down to your Ma."

There was tears streaming all down my face and I could hardly see to get down to the cellar. Aunt Betsy was kneeling over Ma, praying. Ma was kind of shaking and rattling and Aunt Betsy had lifted her up and was holding her there.

"Ma," I shouted.

She turned her eyes to me again, looking kind of confused, like she didn't know who I was anymore. "Ma, it's me," I shouted.

"Willy?" she murmured. She tried to reach out her hand to touch me, and then she gave a rattle and died, with her hand stuck out toward me like that.

What I did then I've never been sure. The next thing I remember is being up in the kitchen pounding away at Captain Ivers with my fist. I must have clawed his face, too, because he had big scratches running down his cheeks. I remember seeing the blood oozing out of the scratches and then I felt a bang and heard a crash, and I was lying on the floor and he was standing over me with his whip, just looming up over me, and the whip rising up and starting down. I closed my eyes and the whip ripped across my face, making me cry out.

Then I heard a smack. The captain shouted and Mrs. Ivers began to scream. I opened my eyes. The captain was slumped against the kitchen wall and Uncle Jack was standing over him, his fist clenched.

148

Captain Ivers was spitting blood out of his mouth and blood was still oozing out of the scratches I'd made on his face.

"Arabus," Captain Ivers said in a hoarse voice, "I'll have you jailed for that."

Uncle Jack had saved me. Captain Ivers would have whipped me half to death. Then Uncle Jack turned, ran out the door, and disappeared into the dark. The next thing I knew Captain Ivers was racing out into the dark after him, with the biggest pistol I ever saw in one hand. Aunt Betsy came dashing up from the cellar. We heard a shout and running feet and suddenly the gun went off as loud as a cannon shot. Aunt Betsy sort of gasped and put her hands over her mouth.

Mrs. Ivers had stopped screaming. "I wouldn't be Jack Arabus for anything," she said. "The captain's going to kill him now for sure, if he ain't dead already." She whirled around and stamped out of the kitchen, and we heard her locking herself into her bedroom.

Aunt Betsy looked at me. I felt just terrible. If it hadn't been for me losing my head and going for Captain Ivers, Uncle Jack wouldn't have done it, no matter what Captain Ivers did. I could see Aunt Betsy was thinking the same thing, too, and I turned my head down.

"I got to do for your Ma," Aunt Betsy said. She went back down the cellar.

Oh, I felt so bad. Ma was dead and Uncle Jack was

in bad trouble for hitting a white man. Maybe he was wounded or worse. I wanted to do for Ma myself. But I knew, no matter what, I'd better get myself away from there. Ivers, he was sure to catch me now. There wasn't anybody left to testify that I was free, except maybe Mrs. Ledyard; and she was up in Groton and no use to me.

Dan was standing there, looking mighty confused and worried. I gave him a hug and said, "Tell your Ma I'm sorry for all the trouble I made. I'm going to try to get back down to New York." He said he would, and I hugged him again because I figured it would be a long time before I got to hug anybody again. Then I darted out the kitchen door.

It was starless overhead, and cold, and it looked like it might snow. I stood in the backyard, looking around. Out behind the barn was a field and beyond that a woodlot. I didn't know what was behind the woodlot, but it seemed like the safest place, so I began to run, skirting around the barn and then across a field, until I came to the woods. The leaves was off the trees, which didn't make it too good of a hiding place, but I figured once I was pretty far in they wouldn't be able to see me from the house, anyway. So I went on in, pushing through the brush until I could just barely see the barn and the house through the trees, and then I stopped and crouched down to think. As I did so, something fluttered cold on my cheek. It was starting to snow.

I'd sure made a mess of things. I'd got Uncle Jack in

a lot of trouble, and myself as well. I felt awful that Ma was lying down there in that cold, damp cellar, and I wasn't there to do for her. It hurt me to think of that. But what could I do?

Suddenly I remembered Mr. Goodrich. Hadn't he said he'd help me if I needed it? Yes, he'd said it. But would he?

I was thinking about that, when I heard something from somewhere down by the house. My heart started to beat fast. I wondered if I ought to run off through the woods. I watched the house, and in a minute I saw Captain Ivers, looking small in the distance, come running out of the house and into the barn. I went on watching and a couple of minutes later he came riding out on his horse and galloped away.

What did that mean? Had Uncle Jack got away? I stood there, not knowing what to do. After a minute it came to me that maybe, if Captain Ivers stayed away for a while, I could take a chance on slipping back to the house and see Ma buried proper. But suppose Captain Ivers came back and caught me there? I'd end up in the West Indies for sure.

And suppose I went into New Haven looking for Mr. Goodrich and Ivers caught me *there*. I'd end up in the West Indies, too. There wasn't no doubt about it, the best thing would be to clear out as fast as I could. If I could steal a boat somewhere, I could sail back down to New York. That was going to be risky, but trying to walk down through woods and fields would be riskier, because of being spotted by farmers and such. In a boat I could cross over to the Long Island side of the Sound and go along there.

But where was I going to find a boat? Then a thought came to me. Captain Ivers had a dory down by his dock. Maybe nobody was watching the dory.

So I crept back into the woods a bit, and then began to scramble off through the brush and branches toward the east, figuring on circling around to the water, and then coming up to the dock from the opposite direction. Of course, I didn't know what I'd run into—fields, or more woods, or a road, or what—but there was only one way to find out. It was snowing heavier now and I was fearful cold.

I pushed on through and after a while the woods ended and I came to a field. I crouched down there and studied it. There was a barn in the middle of the field. I'd have to make a dash for it. I figured I'd be all right, because the falling snow would make me hard to see.

And then all at once it came to me that Aunt Betsy and Dan was going to have to go out into that snow all by themselves and bury Ma. She was my Ma, and I'd left somebody else to do for her. And on top of it, I'd got Uncle Jack into a heap of trouble, and here I was just running off and leaving them all to get out of it as best as they could. It was wrong, and I knew it.

But if I went back to Iverses' they'd sure as anything tie me up or send for the constable to keep me till the captain could sell me off. I couldn't save Ma. I couldn't do nothing for Uncle Jack—or could I? If Mr. Goodrich could help me, maybe he could help Uncle Jack. At least I should tell Aunt Betsy about Mr. Goodrich.

I felt so ashamed of myself I could hardly stand it. So I turned and scrambled back through the brush and the branches the way I came, and in a few minutes I was back at the edge of the field looking toward the Ivers house and the barn. The snow was coming down steady now, and I knew we was in for a good storm.

I ran out of the woods and across the field through the falling snow to the house. When I got to the kitchen, I crouched down by the window and peered in. There wasn't nobody there. I figured Aunt Betsy was down in the cellar with Ma. I slipped into the kitchen and opened the cellar door. There was a little light coming up from below. I went on down. Aunt Betsy and Dan was there in the chill damp, kneeling beside Ma and praying. The candlelight flickered across their faces, cutting them up into orange and brown patches, and flickered on Ma's face, gray and thin and blank. I knelt down beside them to pray myself, but the tears began to leak out of my eyes and I couldn't think of no words except please God, please God, please God. Upstairs overhead I could hear Mrs. Ivers tromping around the keeping room, but I knew she wouldn't dare come down to the cellar where there was a dead body; she was too scared.

Then Aunt Betsy started in singing "Old Hundred" in a low voice and Dan and I joined in. After we was finished we said the Lord's Prayer, and that was the best we could do for Ma. Aunt Betsy pulled the blanket over her face, and I knew it was the last time I'd see her. "We got to bury her right away," Aunt Betsy said. "Before the ground freezes any deeper."

"It's snowing," I said.

"It figured to snow," Aunt Betsy said. "What are you aiming to do now, Willy? You can't stay here."

"What's going to happen to Uncle Jack if they catch him?" I said. We were talking in low voices so's Mrs. Ivers wouldn't hear.

She looked at me, mighty somber, the orange and brown patches sliding around her face as the candle flickered. "He'll sell him off now," she said. "He'll steal his soldier's notes and sell him off to the West Indies."

"But he's got his discharge papers."

"He ain't got them with him," she said. "They're right down here, hidden." She looked grim. "Well, they ain't caught him yet, so far as we know. We'd best get your Ma buried before the snow gets too deep."

We wrapped her up in the blanket, and Aunt Betsy sent Dan up for a needle and thread and we sewed the blanket up around her. Dan stayed at the top of the cellar stairs to watch for Mrs. Ivers, and Aunt Betsy and I carried Ma up. She didn't weigh hardly anything; I could have carried her myself. I felt so sorry for her, to be so little. We left Dan in the kitchen, so's to come running to warn us if Captain Ivers came back. Aunt Betsy collected a pick and a shovel from the barn. She gave them to me and she picked up Ma, sewed up in that blanket, and carried her like a baby out to the woodlot. We didn't want to bury her in the field where they would be plowing in the spring, even though they wasn't likely to plow so deep as to disturb a body. We found a place that was partly cleared, and began to dig.

The snow was coming down steady now, like a flurry of cream. We went on digging. Aunt Betsy swung the pick to chop the dirt loose and I shoveled it out; and then we switched around. And all the time Ma lay there sewed up in the blanket, with the snow gradually covering over her. It gave me a queer feeling to think of her lying there, cold and stiff—not a person anymore, just nothing at all. I tried not to think about it, but went on digging.

It took us an hour to get down three feet. We knew we ought to go down six feet, but we wasn't likely to. "Another foot'll be enough," Aunt Betsy said. And we'd got a good deal of that done when suddenly we heard footsteps and saw Dan come running across the field. He came into the woods, breathing hard. "They caught Pa," he said.

We stopped digging. "They caught him?"

"Some man just come running up and told Mrs. Ivers that they'd caught Pa and the captain wouldn't be home tonight, but would be staying in New Haven to sell him off. They got him locked up in jail."

Aunt Betsy looked like death. She leaned her arm against a tree. "We got to get his discharge papers to him. It's the only thing that'll save him."

"I'll take them to him."

She looked at me. "You daren't, Willy. Soon as Ivers sees you he'll lock you up and sell you off, too."

I thought for a minute. Then I remembered. "Mr. Goodrich, he'll do it. He's a lawyer, he'll know what to do."

She stared out across the woods to the house. "It's a mighty big risk, Willy."

I knew that, but I had to take the chance. Uncle Jack had got himself in all this trouble saving me from a flogging. I wouldn't have to go nowheres near Captain Ivers. All I had to do was give Mr. Goodrich the papers. He'd know what to do. "I'll do it anyway," I said.

She left off gazing across the field. "It's our only chance," she said. She sent Dan back to the house to get the papers from where they was hidden in the cellar, and we went back to digging. Just about the time Dan came back with the papers we'd got the grave deep enough. We picked up Ma and set her down in the grave. We pushed the dirt back in, and tamped it down, and then we piled up some rocks on top so no animals could dig down, and we'd know where the grave was. After we was all finished, we knelt down and said the Lord's Prayer again. Then Aunt Betsy told me how to get to New Haven—across the woodlot to the Milford Highway, and along to the Housatonic River and across that, and through Milford on the other side into New Haven. The hard part was going to be getting across the river; most ferrymen wouldn't be so lax as the last one. The law was they couldn't carry no black folks without a pass, but I figured I'd work out a way. Aunt Betsy gave me a heavy cloak; I remembered how I'd taken her old one. I put the papers in my shirt and hugged Aunt Betsy and hugged Dan, and set off through the trees.

The snow was coming down hard now, blowing cold into my face. I was just as glad of it, because anybody who came along wouldn't be able to see me very well. I figured if I kept moving pretty brisk I'd stay warm enough. I pushed on through the woodlot, and then across the field beyond, through the orchard beyond that, and onto the Milford Highway. Then I put my head down and just plowed along, as fast as I could go. The snow was flinging itself at me and sometimes the wind would gust up and toss a great patch of flakes in my face, so's I'd have to stop and turn away. The snow was making a whooshing noise and muffling other sounds, and I knew I wouldn't be able to hear anybody coming along until they was near on top of me. That worried me, and I tried to keep looking around. Looking behind wasn't so bad, but it wasn't easy looking straight forward, with the snow blowing direct into my face. There wasn't nothing to do but push along, and by and by I came to the Housatonic River.

The snow was whipping around the ferryman's house, but I could see a light on inside. There was a wharf sticking into the river with three or four rowboats of different sizes tied up to it. I went to the ferryman's house and knocked. In a minute the door opened and an old man came out, holding a pot of mulled cider. He hadn't shaved for a while and his face was covered with white hairs.

"Yes?" he said.

The steam coming up from the mulled cider smelled so warm and sweet I could hardly stand it, I was so cold and wet. Just looking at him I knew he wasn't going out in a snow storm for no nigger. "Sir, did Captain Ivers come along here a while ago?"

"What business is it of yours?"

"I got this paper I got to give to him," I said. "He sent for it. That big nigger of his is locked up in New Haven and Captain Ivers needs the paper."

He squinted at me. He didn't fancy going out in that storm at all. "You telling the truth?"

"Oh, yes, sir." I reached into my shirt and pulled out the paper. "He needs it right away."

He took a swallow of the mulled cider. The steam came off it into my nose and I could almost taste it going down. "I expect somebody's going to pay for this?" He never even looked at the papers. I reckoned he couldn't read any more'n I could.

"Oh, yes, sir," I said. I reached into my pocket and took out a shilling. He looked at it, like he didn't trust it. Then he put it into his pocket, and we went down to the wharf and he rowed me across.

After that there wasn't nothing to do but keep on walking. It was coming up to dusk, which made me harder to spot. I plowed on, the snow whipping into my face and getting down under my shirt. My feet was soaked, and my clothes was soaked through, too, and I was scared I'd catch the ague, and scared somebody'd catch me, too. But there wasn't nothing to do about that, so I plowed ahead, and by and by the houses began to get closer and closer and soon I was near the center of town.

The streets was mud, but it was frozen and covered with snow and pretty slippery going. I went along between the houses. Some of them was shut up and dark, but in others there was a light going and a red glow from the fire. It looked so cozy and safe in them houses—I wanted to be someplace like that.

Finally I came to a tavern. I went in and asked where Mr. Goodrich lived. They said he lived with a family just a little ways from there.

In a few minutes I was there, and knocking on his door. In a minute a woman opened it. I figured it was his landlady. "I have to see Mr. Goodrich, ma'am."

She looked me up and down. I was so covered with snow and damp you could hardly tell if I was black or white. "It must be mighty important to come out on a night like this."

159

"Yes, ma'am, it is."

"Well, Mr. Goodrich is very busy. I don't know as I ought to disturb him."

"I walked all the way from Stratford, ma'am."

"Glory," she said. "That's a good ways. You brush yourself off good, now, before you come in. I don't want no water dripping on my floors. I'll go see if he's busy."

"Yes, ma'am," I said. I brushed myself off with my hands and came in. There was a little fire in the fireplace and the room was so warm and cozy I liked to cry. I went over to the fire and stood there dripping on the hearthstone. I wished I could take my clothes off and dry out.

I waited, and then Mr. Goodrich came down, wearing that same green suit he had on before. I guessed, being as he was just starting in as a lawyer, he hadn't made enough money yet to spend on clothes.

He looked at me, puzzled. "Why, it's Willy Freeman," he said. "I didn't expect to see you again so soon."

"Nor me either, sir. But we've got bad trouble." So I told him the whole story, about me coming up from New York, and Ma dying and Captain Ivers flogging me, and Uncle Jack hitting Captain Ivers and getting put in jail. At the end I showed him the paper.

He studied the paper for a minute. Then he looked up at me. "You mean Ivers intends to sell Jack off South?"

"That's what we reckon, sir. He never agreed that

Uncle Jack was free. He always wanted to keep him a slave."

Mr. Goodrich shook his head. "He can't do that. That's contrary to the law." He took out his watch and looked at it. "I'm going down to the jailhouse to see your uncle. Want to come?"

"I daren't," I said. "Captain Ivers might be there. He means to stay in New Haven tonight."

"You'll be safe with me. I can just as easily claim you're my slave as he can."

"Still, if you don't mind, sir, I'd rather not take the chance."

He shrugged. "As you like." He put on his hat and his cloak and went out, and as soon as he done that I lay down in front of the fire and fell asleep, even though my clothes was wet and awful uncomfortable.

13

___

WHEN I WOKE UP, the sun was shining through the small windows of the boardinghouse, bright as could be. I could hear the tink tink of melting snow dripping from the eaves. I raised my head and looked around, trying to make out where I was. Then I remembered.

I stood up. My clothes was pretty well dried, and I felt a lot better than before, but hungry. I could smell biscuits cooking somewhere. And I was thinking about food when Mr. Goodrich came into the room, still wearing that same green suit. I felt kind of sorry for him, that he wasn't rich yet, the way a lawyer was meant to be.

"I saw your uncle last night, Willy," he said. "I'm going to court now to petition for a writ of habeas

corpus. I'm going to try to get a hearing on it immediately."

"Habeas corpus?"

"It means that they have to show some good reason
for keeping your uncle in jail. I don't think they have
any. The only thing that worries me is the possibility
of an assault charge. He admits to hitting Ivers."

"That was only for saving me from a beating."

"It'll depend on what the court believes," he said.
Then he put on his cloak and hat and went out.

The smell of biscuits was still coming from somewhere, and there was bacon added onto it, too, now. I
put my nose up and sniffed, and in a moment I judged
the smell was coming from the back of the house. I
found my way back, and sure enough, there was a
kitchen. The woman who'd let me in the day before
had got a pan of meat over the fire, and she was just
taking a load of biscuits from the brick oven in the
fireplace.

I swallowed hard. "Ma'am," I said, "I'd be glad to
work out a couple of them biscuits."

She cocked her head at me.

"You missed your dinner last night, didn't you?"

"I missed pretty near everything yesterday."

"You poor thing," she said. "Well, you set down and
eat, and after I get finished feeding my boarders you
can help me clean up." So I ate, and then I helped her
serve the boarders, which was mostly students at Yale
College, and then I started to wash the dishes in a big

wooden tub she had. And I was doing this when Mr. Goodrich came into the kitchen.

"Dry your hands off, Willy," he said. "We've got to get back to court in five minutes."

"Sir, I don't dare. Captain Ivers is sure—"

"Don't worry about that," he said. "I may need you to testify. I think it would be helpful all around if you came along."

I didn't feel like arguing with Mr. Goodrich, but I sure didn't want to get into a courtroom with Captain Ivers. It flashed through my mind that I could just run off again like I had before. But that wouldn't help Uncle Jack none, and besides, Mr. Goodrich kind of left it up to me. I decided that I had to forget whatever Captain Ivers might do to me and do my best to help Uncle Jack. I'd go along with Mr. Goodrich and take a chance that he'd save me from Captain Ivers. So we set off at a good pace down the street and across a big green with three churches in it and hundreds of little elms and buttonwoods they'd just planted. Next we came to a row of brick buildings, which was Yale College. Across the green was the courthouse with wide steps going up, columns along the front, and great big windows.

We went up the steps and inside, and down a long corridor and into the courtroom itself. It was mighty fancy, a great high room with tall windows around most of it, a high bench for the judge, and rows of pews for anybody that was watching. There wasn't too

165

many people there, but one of them was Uncle Jack, sitting in a pew, with manacles on his wrists and a guard on either side of him. And a little farther down the pew was Captain Ivers. There was a man sitting next to him done up in a fancy suit. I figured he was Captain Ivers's lawyer.

One look at Captain Ivers and all I wanted to do was skedaddle out of there, but Mr. Goodrich marched right to the front and plunked himself down about two feet from Captain Ivers. There wasn't nothing I could do but march along behind him and plunk myself down there, too. Then the judge came in and we all stood up; and that was when Captain Ivers spotted me. "Well," he said. "Look who's turned up." A little smile twisted his lips.

The judge told us to sit down. He looked to be in his fifties. His name was James Wadsworth, Mr. Goodrich said. The judge wore spectacles and had a great shock of hair, like a lion.

So they started up. Captain Ivers stood to one side with his lawyer, whose name was Mr. Chauncy, and Uncle Jack stood to the other side with Mr. Goodrich.

Captain Ivers had a bill of sale for when he'd bought Jack years before. His lawyer read it out, and then the judge asked for it and read it over to himself, peering through his spectacles.

Mr. Goodrich stepped forward. He had some papers that he read off about all the battles Uncle Jack was in and the names of his officers. He read that out, and then the judge asked for the papers and sat at his desk reading them over and frowning.

"Under the law," Mr. Goodrich said, "no slaves were permitted to enlist, Your Honor. Captain Ivers consented to my client's enlistment. Indeed Ivers sent Arabus as his substitute in the first place. It is therefore implicit that Captain Ivers manumitted my client at that time. I would point out further that Captain Ivers kept the state bounty afforded to a slave owner who frees a slave in order to allow him to enlist."

The judge took off his spectacles and leaned forward. "How do you respond to that, Mr. Chauncy?"

Mr. Chauncy stood up. "Your honor, there's a question of assault. Arabus deliberately attacked Captain Ivers with no provocation."

Mr. Goodrich got up, too. "Your honor, I have another client here besides Jack Arabus. Her name is Wilhelmina Freeman and she wishes to lodge an assault charge against Captain Thomas Ivers."

"What nonsense is that?" Captain Ivers shouted. "I've a right to beat my niggers."

"Your honor, my client is a free black and as such a citizen of the state of Connecticut, and under the protection of our laws. Yesterday morning Captain Ivers lashed her with no provocation."

"No provocation?" Captain Ivers shouted. "No provocation? She attacked me." The judge held up his hand. He looked at Captain Ivers, and then at me, and back to Captain Ivers. Then he said, "This girl at-

167

tacked you, Captain? Why, she's half your size." He waved to me. "Come here, Wilhelmina, and let's hear your side of it."

So I told the whole story: about Captain Ivers not letting Ma have any doctoring, and her dying, and Captain Ivers lashing me, and I didn't leave none of it out, even the part about me losing control of myself and scratching his face. And when I was finished, the judge said, "Captain Ivers, did you really take a lash to this girl here while her mother was dying?"

Captain Ivers stood there staring at the judge with that cold face still as a frozen pond, but he didn't say anything. Then Mr. Goodrich said, "Unless Captain Ivers can produce a bill of sale for Willy, she's free." He stared at Captain Ivers, and Captain Ivers stared back. Then Mr. Goodrich said in a soft voice, "Her father was killed fighting for his country and her mother was imprisoned by the British and died from it. And this man, Jack Arabus, spent seven years fighting to protect his country, too. And all the while you sat at home and did business in order to enrich yourself."

Captain Ivers turned to Mr. Goodrich. "Goodrich, you damned little pipsqueak, what do you know about it? Do you take a nigger's word against mine?" He started to go on, but Mr. Chauncy grabbed his arm.

"Your honor," Mr. Chauncy said to the judge, "the statutes are not clear. Arabus has no certificate of manumission. This little pickaninny's word is certainly not to be trusted. My client is a respectable Christian white man. Surely you will return his legal property to him."

"Mr. Chauncy, the only documents I see tell me that Ivers sent Arabus to fight for the nation's freedom— and by law he couldn't do that without freeing him first. Clearly Arabus is a free man. As for the girl—" Captain Ivers stomped his foot and banged his fist on the bench.

"Damn the whole lot of you!" Ivers said, and turned around and stomped out. Nobody said a thing for a minute. Then Mr. Wadsworth leaned over the bench and said, "Mr. Chauncy, it looks like you've lost a client. Mr. Goodrich, I see no reason to hold the girl. You prepare a certificate for me to sign. She's paid a heavy price for her freedom. Let's see that she doesn't lose it again."

I nearly busted out crying again, but Uncle Jack had such a big smile across his face that I just started laughing instead.

14

So that's what happened. Uncle Jack and me went off to Mr. Goodrich's house and had a little celebration. Then Uncle Jack went back to Stratford. It was his plan to get a little dory and set himself up in the fishing business and try to save enough money to buy Aunt Betsy and Dan free. It wasn't going to be easy, though; it would take a good while to collect up that much money. But he was bound to do it, and I figured he would.

But of course I sure didn't want to go back to Stratford. There was only one place I wanted to be: That was back down at Fraunces Tavern in New York.

It had something to do with the argumentative way I was sometimes. I'd got it figured out that being argumentative was the same as being free. I mean, if somebody could boss you around, you wasn't free, and that's why I was argumentative, because there was always somebody trying to boss me around. I hated having somebody over me, and I don't guess I was any different from anybody else. I mean the whole war, that had got my Ma and Pa killed, was just to keep the British from being over the Americans. And I could see that people had a mighty strong feeling for being free, if they was willing to risk being shot for it. So that was why I wanted to go down to New York. There was more of a chance of doing what I wanted to do there.

Of course, some people was going to be more free than others. There wasn't no way around that. Slaves wasn't going to be no freer under the Americans than they was under the British, and women was still going to have to keep to their place. I was black, and I was a woman, and I knew there was limits. But I could see that nobody was free all the way. There wasn't nobody who could do anything he wanted—not even Captain Ivers, nor Mr. Goodrich, nor Mr. Fraunces, nor anybody. Captain Ivers couldn't keep me and Uncle Jack in slavery; and Mr. Fraunces, he had to do what his customers wanted; and Mr. Goodrich took his orders from the judge; and the judge—well, I didn't know what his limit was, but I reckoned he had one. They was all stuck one way or another. It was just that some people was way down at the bottom of the heap and a lot more stuck than others. And if I went to New York and learned about taverns and such, maybe

172

someday I could have a tavern of my own. Oh, there was a chance that I couldn't, neither. But it was worth trying.

So Mr. Goodrich fixed it with a friend of his for me to work my way down to the city, and I went. They put me to work scrubbing the deck; but as the sloop pulled out of the New Haven harbor I stood up and watched the houses sink down as we sailed away. For I knew I wasn't just saying good-bye to Connecticut. A whole part of my life was over now. I was grown-up; and it was all going to be new.

How Much of This Book Is True?

THE STORY OF JACK ARABUS, as we have told it in this book, is basically a true one. We have invented the details, of course, but Jack Arabus did exist and did fight with Washington's troops as we have told in the story. Upon his discharge, his former owner, Captain Thomas Ivers, attempted to return him to slavery. He ran away and was jailed, but successfully sued for his freedom, about as we have described it. The case is known as *Arabus* v. *Ivers*, and you can read the official account of it in the *Connecticut Reports* of trials. That one case guaranteed the freedom of about three hundred Connecticut Negroes who fought in the American Revolution.

The story of Black Sam Fraunces and his famous tavern is also essentially true. During the British occupation of New York, the tavern was renamed The Queen's Head and was a favorite inn for British officers. It got its old name back after the war, and has existed under that name more or less continuously until today. The tavern burned down twice, and we are not sure what the original building looked like. However, the present building on the original spot is a good replica of the sort of building that was used for taverns in those days. There is a museum there, as well as a restaurant, and you can visit it sometime if you are in New York City.

Black Sam Fraunces was a somewhat mysterious character. He was born in the West Indies, went to New York, and became a respected businessman there. Even though he was called Black Sam, we are not sure whether he was in fact black. On the New York census report of 1790 he is listed as white. It is our best guess that he was at least part black. But we cannot be sure of this.

We are not exactly sure what role he played in the war, either. He was certainly allowed by the British to continue to operate his tavern. But also during the war he was victualler for American troops, supplying food to encampments outside New York City. After the war President Washington hired him as steward of his household. He must certainly have been sympathetic to the rebel cause, and perhaps was spying for Washington.

The general background as we have given it here is also as accurate as we could make it. Whaleboat raids on Long Island Sound of the kind we have Willy caught up in were common. Canvas Town was a real place and was as we have described it. In particular, the story of the massacre at Fort Griswold is taken from eye-witness accounts of the time. In fact, the inhumanity there was much worse than we describe it here. We found the events inside the Fort so gruesome that we could not describe them in print. There is a replica of Fort Griswold in Groton, which you can see if you are ever in that part of Connecticut.

Uncle Jack Arabus, Captain Ivers, Sam Fraunces, Mr. Goodrich, Mr. Chauncy, and Judge Wadsworth and Willy's Pa, Jordan Freeman, were real people. But the other main characters in this story are made up. Willy, Horace, Willy's Ma, Aunt Betsy, and Daniel and the rest are fictional. We have tried to make them as much like people of that day were, but it is always difficult for even the most careful historians to know exactly how things were in another time.

The language used in this book is a case in point. It is almost certainly not how people spoke at that time, for the reason that nobody knows how they spoke. We know how they wrote, because we have their diaries and letters, but of course the spoken language perishes with the times. We have therefore tried to give something of the flavor of how an uneducated black person might have spoken then. In truth, Willy's way of expressing herself is much too modern for the times, but once again we cannot be sure. We are more sure about the attitudes that Willy and others around her had—the idea that women were inferior to men, blacks to whites, children to adults. Almost all historians agree that such ideas were held by nearly all Americans of the Revolutionary era.

In particular, we had to consider very carefully our use of the word *nigger*. This term is offensive to modern readers, and we certainly do not intend to be insulting. But it was commonly used in America right into the twentieth century, and it would have been a distortion of history to avoid its use entirely.

In sum, what we have tried to do in this book is give you something of the feeling of how life was lived in those days, and how it felt to be somebody like Willy or Horace, or Jack Arabus. And if you want to know if Jack was ever able to buy the freedom of Aunt Betsy and little Dan, you can read another book we wrote, *Jump Ship to Freedom*.

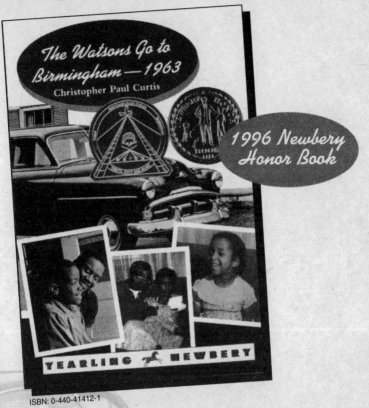